QUE Bee

From Doubts to Distinction

Your ICSE 2026 Exams Partner

GIST OF THE TEXTBOOK
Crisp & Complete Theory - No need to go back to bulky textbooks!

ALL TYPES OF LATEST PATTERN QUESTIONS
MCQs | Case-based | Assertion-Reason; All in one place!

KEYWORDS HIGHLIGHTED
Important points and key words are neatly highlighted; Never miss what matters

COUNCIL-STYLE ANSWERS
Write responses like an examiner expects

SAMPLE PAPER
Practice in real-exam mode. Perfect your timing, strategy and confidence.

arihant
SUCCESS AND NOTHING LESS

ARIHANT PRAKASHAN
(School Division Series)

卐 **ADMINISTRATIVE & PRODUCTION OFFICES**
Regd. Office
'Ramchhaya' 4577/15, Agarwal Road, Darya Ganj, New Delhi -110002
Tele: 011- 47630600, 43518550; Fax: 011- 23280316

卐 **Head Office**
Kalindi, TP Nagar, Meerut (UP) - 250002, Tel: 0121-7156203, 7156204

卐 **SALES & SUPPORT OFFICES**
Agra, Ahmedabad, Bengaluru, Bareilly, Chennai, Delhi, Guwahati, Hyderabad, Jaipur, Jhansi, Kolkata, Lucknow, Nagpur & Pune.

PO No : TXT-XX-XXXXXXX-X-XX

Published By Arihant Publications (India) Ltd.

For further information about the books published by Arihant, log on to www.arihantbooks.com or e-mail at info@arihantbooks.com
Follow us on

卐 **PRICE** ₹ 225.00

PRODUCTION TEAM

Publishing Manager
Keshav Mohan

Project Head
Pooja Verma

Cover Designer
Bilal Hashmi

Inner Designer
Ankit Tyagi

Page Layouting
Sachin

Proof Reader
Nidhi, Prashant

QUE Bee

ICSE
BIOLOGY
Class 9

Types of Questions & their Respective Number

Types of Questions	Total Number
Multiple Choice Questions (MCQs)	216
Matching Type Questions	28
Assertion-Reason (A-R)	76
Very Short Answer Questions (VSA)	266
Short Answer Type Questions (2 Marks)	149
Short Answer Type Questions (3 Marks)	108
Structured Based Questions	54
TOTAL NO. OF QUESTIONS	**897**

Created by

Meenakshi Walia
B.Sc. Hons. (DU) M.Sc. (Eco-Physiology), B.Ed.
PGT-Biology

Contributors
Himanshi, Manvi, Anushree

From Learner to Leader

Step-Into the Spotlight

QUE Bee is more than just a book - it's a platform for young achievers like you to guide future toppers. If you've cracked the code to smart study or have insights that can make learning easier for others, this is your moment to shine!

What Can You Share?

- Your study techniques, time management tips, or motivation hacks
- Feedback or suggestions to make QUE Bee even better
- Real experiences that can guide other students through the exam maze

What's in It for You?

- Your name will be featured in our exclusive Student Panel in the next edition
- Win exciting & surprise rewards for impactful suggestions
- **Get published** - your photo, Ideas-or even interviews can be featured in the book
- **Become a student icon** - recognized and followed by peers across schools

Let your learning become someone else's ladder.
Be remembered. Be featured. Be the guide.

SCAN TO SHARE YOUR IDEA

QUE Bee

Index

Latest Course Structure

There will be one paper of **two hours** duration of 80 Marks and Internal Assessment of Practical Work carrying 20 Marks.

Basic Biology

(i) The cell, a unit of life, protoplasm, basic difference between prokaryotic and eukaryotic cell; differences between an animal and a plant cell.

- A basic understanding of the cell theory, structure of plant and animal cell with functions of various cell organelles. (Protoplasm, Cytoplasm, Cell Wall, Cell Membrane, Nucleus, Nucleolus, Mitochondria, Endoplasmic Reticulum, Ribosome, Golgi bodies, Plastids, Lysosomes, Centrosome and Vacuole).
- Major differences between a prokaryotic and eukaryotic cell.
- Differences between a plant cell and an animal cell should be mainly discussed with respect to cell wall, centrosome, vacuoles and plastids.

(ii) Tissues : Types of plant and animal tissues.

- A brief understanding of their location, basic structure and functions with examples.
- A brief understanding of their role in different physiological processes in plants and animals.

Flowering Plants

(i) Flower : Structure of a bisexual flower, functions of various parts.

- A brief introduction to complete and incomplete flowers.
- Essential and non-essential whorls of a bisexual flower; their various parts and functions.
- Inflorescence and placentation (meaning only) (Charts or actual specimens may be used to help enhance clarity of concepts.)

(ii) Pollination : Self and cross-pollination.

- Explanation, advantages and disadvantages of self and cross-pollination.
- Agents of pollination and the characteristic features of flowers pollinated by various agents such as insects, wind and water.
- A brief idea as to how nature favours cross-pollination.

(iii) Fertilisation

- Events taking place between pollination and fertilisation leading to the formation of zygote in the embryo sac.
- A brief explanation of the terms double fertilization and triple fusion.
- Fruit and seed - definition and significance.

Plant Physiology

(i) Structure of dicot and monocot seeds, Germination of seeds, types and conditions for seed germination.

- Structure and germination of Bean seed and Maize grain.
- Differences between monocot and dicot seeds.
- Differences between hypogeal and epigeal germination.
- Conditions for seed germination - To be explained and supported by experiments.

(ii) Respiration in plants : Outline of the process, gaseous exchange.

- A brief outline of the process mentioning the terms Glycolysis, Krebs' cycle and their significance.
- A reference to be made to aerobic and anaerobic respiration with chemical equations in each case.
- Experiments on gaseous exchange and on heat production.

Diversity in Living Organisms

(i) A brief outline of the five kingdom classification.

- Main characteristics of each kingdom with suitable examples:

- Monera, Protista, Fungi.
- Plantae - Thallophyta, Bryophyta, Pteridophyta and Spermatophyta.
- Animalia - non-chordates from Porifera to Echinodermata and Chordates - all five Classes.

(ii) Economic importance of Bacteria.

(a) Useful role of bacteria:
- Medicine: antibiotics, serums and vaccines.
- Agriculture: nitrogen cycle (role of nitrogen fixing, nitrifying and denitrifying bacteria)
- Industry -curing of tea, tanning of leather.

(b) Harmful role of bacteria - spoilage of food, diseases in plants and animals, bio-weapons.

(iii) Economic importance of Fungi.

A brief idea of the useful role of Fungi in breweries, bakeries, cheese processing and mushroom cultivation (Processes of manufacture are not required).

Human Anatomy and Physiology

(i) Nutrition

(a) Classes of food; balanced diet. Malnutrition and deficiency diseases.
- *Functions of carbohydrates, fats, proteins, mineral salts (calcium, iodine, iron and sodium), vitamins and water in proper functioning of the body.*
- *Sources of vitamins, their functions and deficiency diseases.*
- *Meaning and importance of a 'Balanced Diet'.*
- *Role of cellulose in our diet.*
- *Causes, symptoms and prevention of Kwashiorkor and Marasmus.*

(b) The structure of a tooth, different types of teeth.
- *Structure of a tooth to be discussed with the help of a diagram.*
- *Functions of different types of teeth.*
- *Dental formula of an adult.*

(c) Digestive System: Organs, digestive glands and their functions (including enzymes and their functions in digestion, absorption and assimilation of digested food).
- *Organs and glands of the digestive system and their functions with reference to digestion, absorption and assimilation.*
- *Brief idea of peristalsis.*

(ii) Skeleton - Movement and Locomotion
- Functions of human skeleton.
- Axial and Appendicular Skeleton.
- Types of joints with reference to their location:
  - *immovable joints*
  - *slightly movable joints*
  - *freely movable (hinge joint, ball and socket joint, gliding joint, pivot joint).*

(iii) Structure and functions of skin.
- *Various parts of the skin and their functions.*
- *Special derivatives of the skin with reference to sweat glands, sebaceous glands, hair, nails and mammary glands.*
- *Heat regulation - vasodilation and vasoconstriction.*

(iv) Respiratory System: Organs; mechanism of breathing; tissue respiration, heat production.
- *Structures of the respiratory system.*
- *Differences between anaerobic respiration in plants and in man.*
- *Role of diaphragm and intercostal muscles in breathing to provide a clear idea of the breathing process.*
- *Brief idea of gaseous transport and tissue respiration.*
- *Brief understanding of respiratory volumes.*
- *Effect of altitude on breathing; asphyxiation and hypoxia.*

Health and Hygiene

(i) A brief introduction to maintaining good health.

General idea of personal hygiene, public hygiene and sanitation.

(ii) A brief introduction to communicable, non – communicable, endemic, epidemic, pandemic and sporadic diseases; modes of transmission.

- *Meaning of each of the above with examples.*
- *Modes of transmission: air borne, water borne; vectors (housefly, mosquito, cockroach).*

(iii) Bacterial, Viral, Protozoan, Helminthic diseases:

- *Bacterial: Cholera, typhoid, tuberculosis.*
- *Viral: AIDS, Chicken pox, Hepatitis.*
- *Protozoan: Malaria, Amoebic dysentery, Sleeping sickness.*
- *Helminthic: Ascariasis, Taeniasis, Filiariasis. (symptoms and measures to control the above diseases.) (Scientific names of causative agents not required).*

(iv) Aids to Health: Active and passive immunity.

- *Meaning of Active and passive immunity.*
- *An understanding of the use and action of the following – vaccination, immunization, antitoxin, serum, antiseptics, disinfectants, antibiotics.*
- *An idea of the local defence system and its merits, difference between antiseptics and disinfectants.*

(v) Health Organisations: Red Cross, WHO.

Major activities of the Red Cross and WHO.

Waste Generation and Management

(i) Sources of waste - domestic, industrial, agricultural, commercial and other establishments.

- *Domestic waste: paper, glass, plastic, rags, kitchen waste, etc.*
- *Industrial: mining operations, cement factories, oil refineries, construction units.*
- *Agricultural: plant remains, animal waste, processing waste.*
- *Municipal sewage: Sewage, degradable and non-degradable waste from offices, etc.*
- *e-waste: brief idea about e-waste.*

(ii) Methods of safe disposal of waste.

- *Segregation, dumping, composting, drainage, treatment of effluents before discharge, incineration, use of scrubbers and electrostatic precipitators.*
- *Segregation of domestic waste into biodegradable and non-biodegradable by households: garden waste to be converted to compost; sewage treatment plants.*

01

CELL : THE UNIT OF LIFE

- Cell is the basic structural and functional unit of all living organisms. It is the smallest component of an organism's body that can exist independently and carry out vital life processes, including growth and reproduction.
- Discovery of cell became possible after the invention of microscope. **Robert Hooke** (1665) examined a thin slice of cork under his microscope and observed small box-like compartments. He named these compartments as **"cells"**.
- The first **living cell** was described by **Antonie van Leeuwenhoek** in **1674**.

Cell Theory

- Cell theory was proposed by two biologists, **Matthias Schleiden** (1838) and **Theodor Schwann** (1839)', which states that
  - All living organisms are composed of one or more cells.
  - The cell is the basic unit of structure and function in living organisms.
- This theory was later modified by **Rudolf Virchow** (1858), who gave the concept of *Omnis cellula-e-cellula*, which means that new cells arise from the pre-existing cells.

Shape and Size of the Cell

- The shape of the cells is variable and depends upon the specific functions they perform. Some cells have a fixed shape (e.g. plant and animal cells), while others, such as White Blood Cells (WBCs) and *Amoeba*, keeps changing their shape.
- Examples of fixed shaped cells includes
  - WBC (amoeboid)
  - RBC (circular and biconcave)
  - Guard cells of stomata (bean-shaped)
  - Smooth muscle cells (spindle-shaped)
- The size of the cell varies significantly from the smallest cell of *Mycoplasma* (0.1 to 0.3 μm) to the very large egg cell of an ostrich (approx. 15 cm in diameter).
- The longest cell of human body is the **nerve cell** (neuron), which can reach up to 1 metre in length.

Types of Cells

Based on the structural organisation, cells can be of following two types

Prokaryotic Cells	Eukaryotic Cells
These are always unicellular such as bacteria.	These may be unicellular or multicellular.
No well-defined nucleus is present due to the absence of the nuclear membrane, hence the region is called nucleoid.	Well-defined nucleus is present.
Membrane-bound organelles, such as mitochondria are absent.	Membrane-bound organelles, such as mitochondria, ER, chloroplasts are present.
Single, circular chromosome is found.	Multiple chromosomes are found.
Ribosomes are small (70S).	Ribosomes are large (80S).
Cell division takes place by binary fission. Reproduction is by asexual methods only.	Cell division takes place by mitosis or meiosis. Reproduction is asexual or sexual.

- Eukaryotic cells are further divided into two types based on the presence or absence of a cell wall; **plant cell** and **animal cell**.

Features	Plant Cell	Animal Cell
Cell wall	Present (made of cellulose)	Absent
Plastids	Present (e.g. chloroplasts for photosynthesis)	Absent
Vacuoles	Large central vacuole (prominent and permanent)	Small or absent (temporary if present)
Centrosome	Absent (no centrioles: spindle fibres form differently)	Present (contains centrioles)

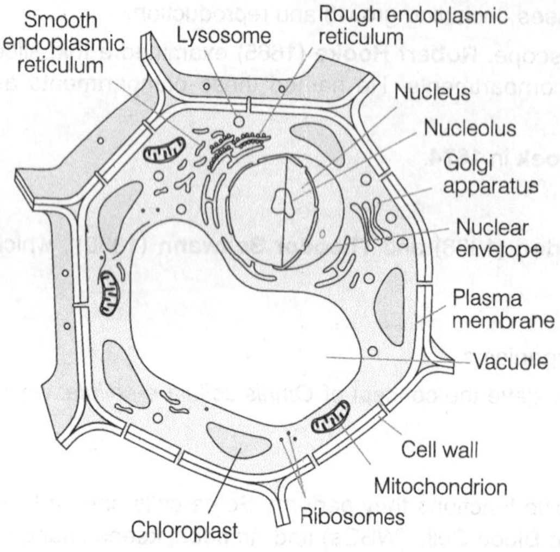

Plant cell

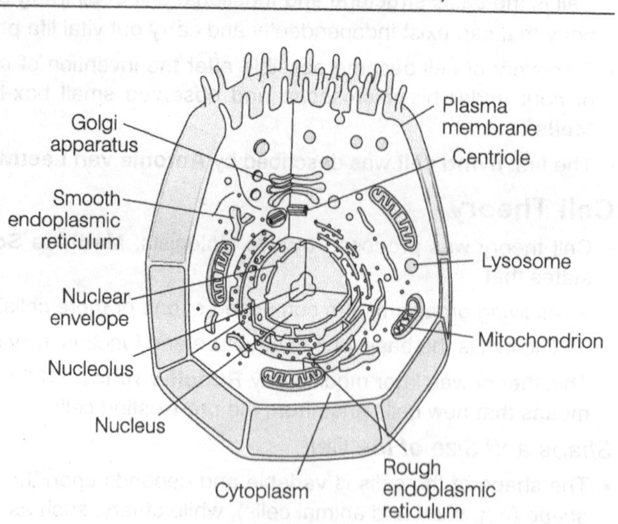

Animal cell

Structural Organisation of a Cell

- All the components of a cell are found in a jelly-like substance known as **protoplasm. Huxley** referred it as the "physical basis of life."
- Protoplasm can be distinguished into two parts – **cytoplasm** (extracellular protoplasm) and **nucleoplasm** (protoplasm in the nucleus). Together, these components form the foundation of the cell.
- Cell can be broadly categorised into three main parts; **the outer coverings** (i.e. cell wall and cell membrane), **a nucleus** and **cytoplasm**.

Cell Membrane/ Plasma Membrane

- Plasma membrane is thin, living and delicate outermost layer of an animal cell that separates cellular contents from its external environment.
- It is also called **selectively permeable membrane** because it controls the entry and exit of materials.
- Protein and lipids are the main components of the cell membrane.
- It helps to provide shape and support to the cell.
- Plasma membrane acts as a protective covering for the internal contents of the cell.

Cell Wall

- The cell wall is the non-living covering that lies outside the plasma membrane in a plant cell, bacterial cell and fungal cell and made up of cellulose, a complex carbohydrate.
- It provides structural strength and rigidity to plant cells.
- When compared to cell membrane, it **is freely permeable** in nature.
- It serves as a protective barrier, safeguarding the cell against pathogens and injury caused by bacteria and fungi.

Nucleus

- It is the largest organelle of the animal cell popularly called the '**brain of the cell**'.
- Double-layered covering called **nuclear membrane** surrounds the nucleus, with **nuclear pores** for material exchange between the nucleus and cytoplasm.
- **Nucleoplasm** is present inside the nucleus, which contains
  - **Nucleolus** involved in ribosome production.
  - **Chromatin**, a tangled network of thread-like structures that condenses to form **chromosomes** during cell division.
- Chromosomes carry **DNA** (Deoxyribonucleic Acid), which contains genetic information for inheritance.
- Nucleus control all metabolic activities of cell and also plays an important role in cell division.

Cytoplasm

- The space inside the cell between the cell membrane and the nuclear membrane is filled with a jelly-like substance which is known as **cytoplasm**.
- It stores essential molecules like amino acids, glucose, vitamins and minerals.
- It contain all the cell organelles, hence it is the site where many chemical reactions occur.
- All metabolic biological reactions take place in the cytoplasm.

Cell Organelles

- They carry out many crucial functions of the cell.
- Detailed account of these organelles is given below

Cell Organelles	Structures	Functions
Endoplasmic Reticulum 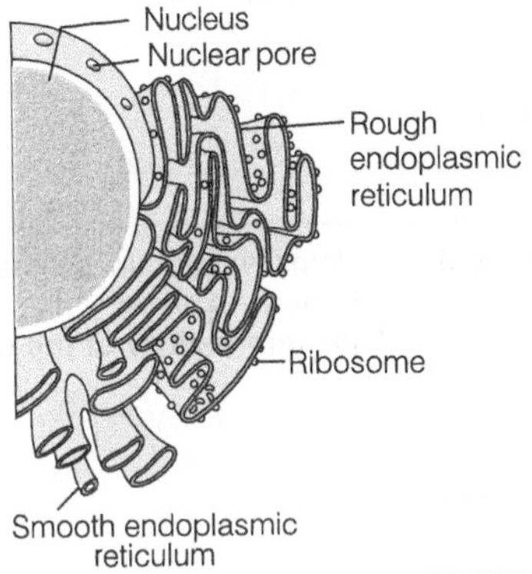 	• Irregular network membrane bound tubules and sacs, continuous with nuclear membrane. • It is of two types; Smooth Endoplasmic Reticulum (SER) and Rough Endoplasmic Reticulum (RER).	• RER helps in protein synthesis. • SER helps in lipid synthesis.
Golgi Body 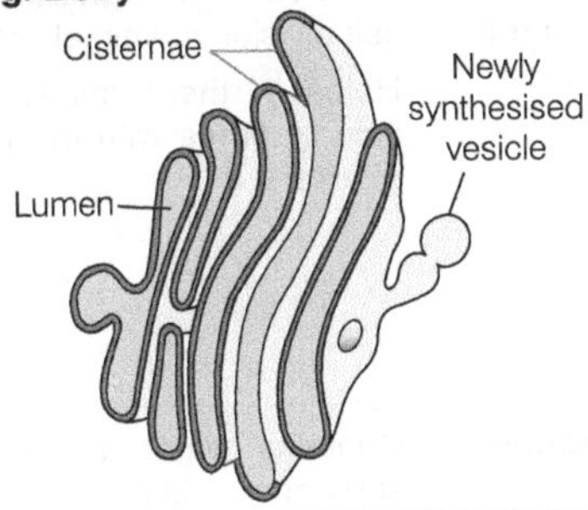 	• It consists of tubules (cisternae) vesicles and vacuoles. • It is located near the Endoplasmic Reticulum (ER). • In plants, these are known as **dictyosomes**.	• It stores, modifies and packages products in vesicles. • Formation of cell wall and acrosome of sperm.

Cell Organelles	Structures	Functions
Lysosomes 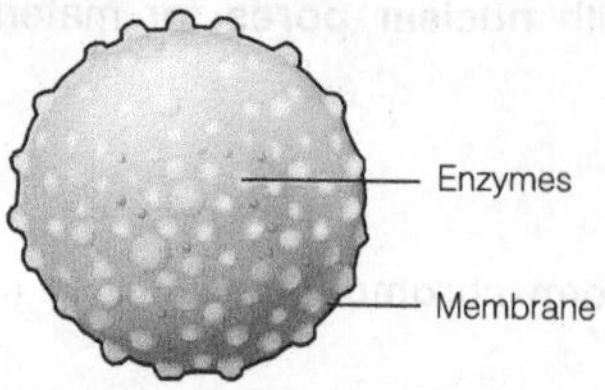 	• They are single membrane -bound organelles, containing digestive enzymes. • Also called **suicidal bag of a cell.**	• Lysosomes breakdown waste and cellular debris. • They digest old cell parts and foreign substances entering the cell. • Destroy the cell organelle when a cell is injured.
Mitochondria 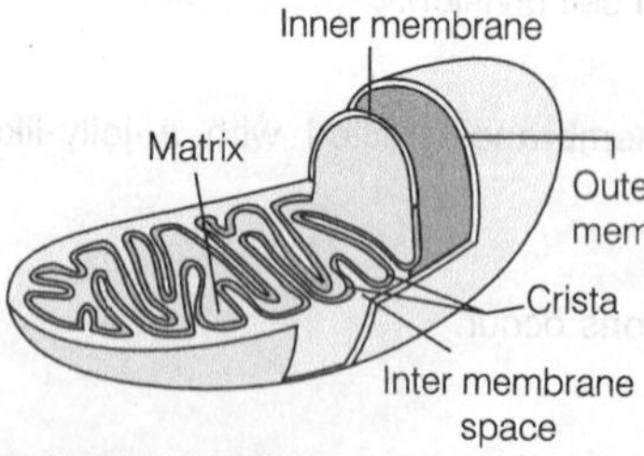 	• A sausage-shaped structure. • Double membrane bound cell organelle. The outer membrane is porous and freely permeable while, the inner wall is folded (cristae). • Contain its own DNA and ribosomes. • Also called **powerhouse of the cell.**	• Its main function is to produce and store energy in the form of ATP or Adenosine Triphosphate, **energy currency of the cell.** • Mitochondrial matrix is the site of respiration (Krebs' cycle).
Plastids 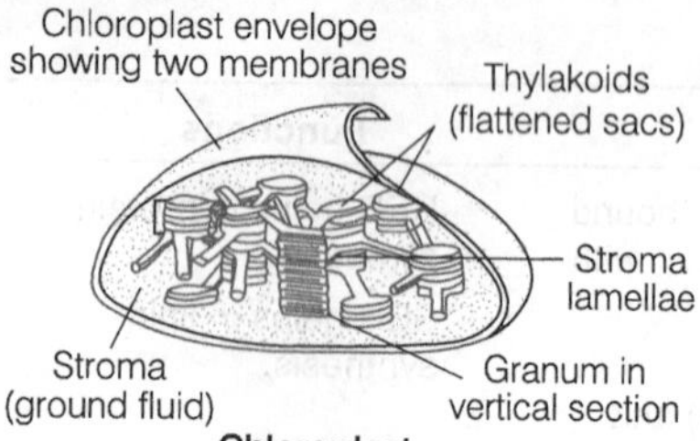 **Chloroplast**	• They are large cytoplasmic organelle present only in the cells of plant and algae. • Divided into three types; chromoplasts, leucoplasts and chloroplasts. • **Chloroplast** is a double membrane structure which has its own DNA. • Chloroplast contains disc like structures known as **thylakoid** and a proteinaceous matrix of fluid called **stroma.**	• It gives colour to fruits and flowers (chromoplasts). • Helps to store starch (leucocytes). • Helps in photosynthesis (chloroplasts).
Ribosomes 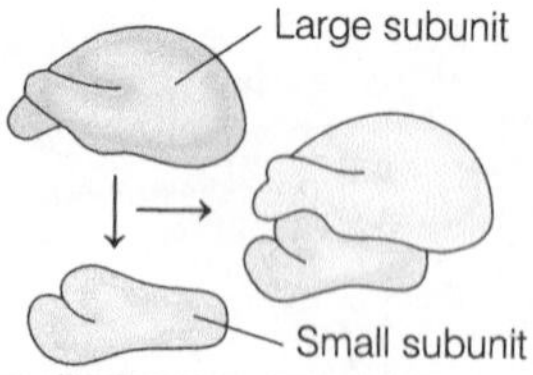 	• Ribosomes are small, spherical organelles made of RNA and proteins. • Not bounded by any membrane. • Found either scattered freely in the cytoplasm or attached to ER. • They consist of two subunits: a large subunit and a small subunit.	• Helps in protein synthesis, hence known as the **protein factory of the cell.**
Centrosomes 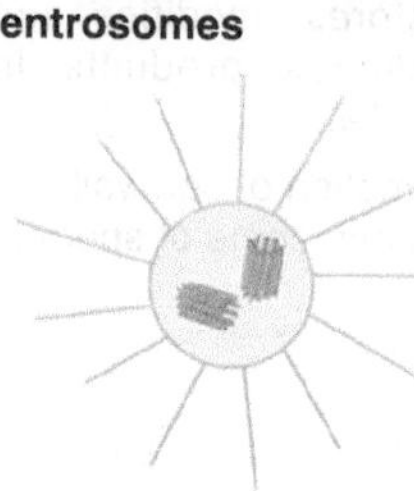	• Centrosomes are made up of two centrioles that are placed at right angles to each other. • Found in animal cells.	• Initiates and regulates in cell division in animal cell. • Helps in the formation of spindle fibres with the help of asters.
Vacuoles	• Vacuoles are membrane-bound structures in the cytoplasm. • Surrounded by a membrane called the **tonoplast.**	• Contains water and other substances like food and waste products. • Helps to maintain turgidity. • Contains pigments like anthocyanin.

EXAM ORIENTED QUESTIONS

TYPE - 1   01 Mark

Multiple Choice Questions

Q.1 The cell theory proposed by Schleiden and Schwann, states that
(a) All cells have a nucleus
(b) All living organisms are composed of one or more cells
(c) Cells arise spontaneously from non-living matter
(d) Cells contain their own DNA and ribosomes

Ans. (b)

Q.2 A biology teacher asked her students to give examples of a largest and a longest living cell.
Raj said: Ostrich egg and nerve cell, respectively
Neha said: Nerve cell and mycoplasma, respectively
Riva said: Mycoplasma and nerve cell, respectively
Rohan said: Nerve cell and ostrich egg, respectively
Who is correct?
(a) Rohan (b) Neha
(c) Raj (d) Both Rohan and Raj

Ans. (c)

Q.3 Which part of a plant cell is made up of dead cells?
(a) Plasma membrane (b) Plastids
(c) Cell wall (d) All of these

Ans. (c)

Q.4 Well-defined nucleus is absent in
(a) plant cell (b) animal cell
(c) eukaryotic cell (d) prokaryotic cell

Ans. (d)

Q.5 An undefined nuclear region in prokaryotic cell is known as
(a) nucleus (b) nucleolus
(c) nucleic acid (d) nucleoid

Ans. (d) Nucleoid is an irregularly shaped region within the prokaryotic cell that contains most of the genetic material.

Q.6 The nuclei of both plant and animal cells contain one or more dense bodies known as nucleoli. Which one of the following correctly describes the function of nucleoli?
(a) The formation of new DNA molecules
(b) The organisation of the spindle during nuclear division
(c) The replication of mitochondria following nuclear division
(d) The formation of ribosomes

Ans. (d)

Q.7 Which of the following cell structure contains the highest concentration of RNA?
(a) Centriole (b) Chromosome
(c) Lysosome (d) Nucleolus

Ans. (d)

Q.8 Cells without nucleoli die because they do not possess
(a) centrioles and are unable to undergo cell division
(b) lysosomes and are unable to destroy worn out organelles
(c) mitochondria and are unable to obtain energy
(d) ribosomes and are unable to manufacture proteins

Ans. (d) If there would be no nucleoli then there would be no ribosome synthesis and therefore no protein synthesis which would make it difficult for a cell to survive for very long.

Q.9 The outer membrane of mitochondria is very ...*P*... while, the inner membrane is deeply folded into ...*Q*... .

	P	*Q*
(a)	porous	cristae
(b)	light	cisternae
(c)	non-porous	vesicle
(d)	selective permeable	cristae

Ans. (a)

Q.10 The table below describes some of the organelles visible in a cell under microscope. Identify the type of living organism to which cell belongs.

Cell Organelles	Descriptions
Cell wall	Present
Vacuole	Large
Centriole	Not visible
Nucleus	Present

(a) It is the cell of an animal
(b) It is the cell of a plant
(c) It is the cell of a bacterium
(d) It is the cell of the virus

Ans. (b) The given description proves that it is the plant cell because cell wall is present and vacuole is large in size.

Q.11

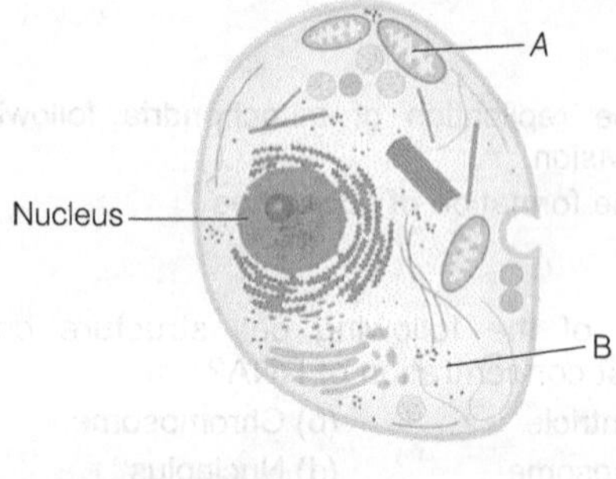

Given is a diagrammatic representation of an animal cell. Identify the correct functions of the organelles marked as *A* and *B*.

	A	B
(a)	Provides support to the cell.	Protein synthesis
(b)	ATP production	Photosynthesis
(c)	ATP production	Protein synthesis
(d)	Lipid synthesis	Formation of acrosome of sperm.

Ans. (c)

Q.12 Which of the following is not present in plant cells?

(a) Cellulosic cell wall (b) Plastids
(c) Centrioles (d) All of these

Ans. (c)

Q.13 Match the following cell organelles with their respective function in a plant cell.

Cell Organelles	Functions
P	Storage of starch, oil or proteins.
Q	Responsible for colours in flowers.

(a) *P* - Chloroplast, *Q*- Vacuole
(b) *P* - Vacuole, *Q*- Chromoplast
(c) *P* - Leucoplasts, *Q*- Chromoplast
(d) *P* - Leucoplasts, *Q*- Vacuole

Ans. (c) In a plant cell, leucoplasts (*P*) are responsible for storage of starch, oil or proteins and chromoplasts (*Q*) are responsible for colour in flowers.

Q.14 The unique feature of plant cell is the absence of .....*P*..... and presence of .....*Q*..... .

(a) *P* -chromosome, *Q*-mitochondria
(b) *P* -centrosomes, *Q*-chloroplast
(c) *P* -mitochondria, *Q*-plastids
(d) *P* -centromere, *Q*-centrosome

Ans. (b)

Q.15 Some cellular organelles are bound by a single membrane, while other organelles have two membranes (envelopes) around them. Which one of the following is correct?

	Single Membranes	Two Membranes
(a)	Tonoplast, Lysosome	Nucleus, Chloroplast
(b)	Chloroplast, Lysosome	Nucleus, Tonoplast
(c)	Nucleus, Chloroplast	Lysosome, Tonoplast
(d)	Nucleus, Lysosome	Chloroplast, Tonoplast

Ans. (a)

TYPE - 2

01 Mark

Matching Type Questions

Q.1 In the table given below shows different cell organelles in a plant cell. Match the organelles with their correct functions.

Cell Organelles	Functions
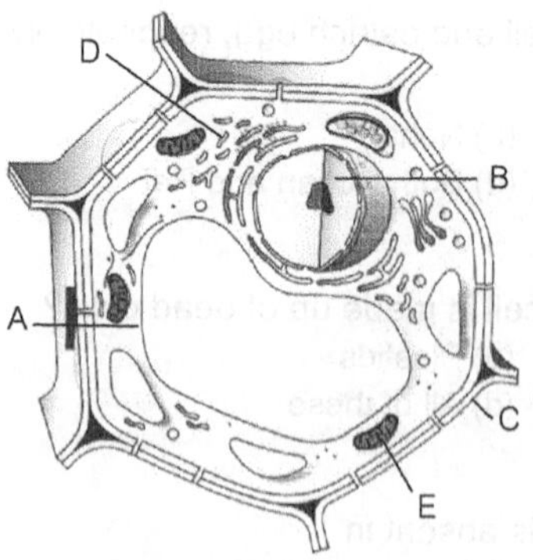	I. Controls cell activities and stores genetic material.
	II. Provides structural support and protection to the cell.
	III. Maintains cell turgidity and stores nutrients and waste.
	IV. Synthesises proteins and lipids; transports materials within the cell.
	V. Produce energy (ATP) through cellular respiration.

Ans. A-III, B-I, C-II, D-IV, E-V

Q.2 Match the following columns.

Column I	Column II
A. Vacuoles	I. Intracellular digestion
B. Nucleolus	II. Respiratory enzymes
C. Lysosomes	III. Covered by tonoplast
D. Plastids	IV. Chloroplast
E. Cristae	V. Forms ribosomes

Ans. A-III, B-V, C-I, D-IV, E-II

TYPE - 3   01 Mark

Assertion-Reason Type Questions

Direction (Q. Nos. 1-5) In the following questions statements are given as Assertion (A) and Reason (R).

(a) A is true, but R is false.
(b) A is false, but R is true.
(c) Both A and R are true.
(d) Both A and R are false.

Q.1 Assertion (A) The cell is the fundamental, structural, and functional unit of all living organisms.

Reason (R) Robert Hooke discovered cells in 1669 by observing a thin slice of cork under a microscope.

Ans. (a) A is true, but R is false. R can be corrected as Robert Hooke discovered cells in 1665 by observing a thin slice of cork under a microscope.

Q.2 Assertion (A) Cells exhibit a wide variety of shapes and sizes depending on their function.

Reason (R) Some cells, such as WBCs and *Amoeba*, can change their shape.

Ans. (c)

Q.3 Assertion (A) Ribosomes are the site of protein synthesis in cells.

Reason (R) Ribosomes are made up of RNA and proteins and they are found only attached to the endoplasmic reticulum.

Ans. (a) A is true, but R is false. R can be corrected as Ribosomes are made up of RNA and proteins and they are found either free in the cytoplasm or attached to the endoplasmic reticulum.

Q.4 Assertion (A) Vacuoles are non-living cell organelle.

Reason (R) Vacuoles are surrounded by the tonoplast.

Ans. (c)

Q.5 Assertion (A) Granules are found only in plant cells.

Reason (R) Granules in plant cells are responsible for storing starch, proteins or lipids.

Ans. (b) A is false, but R is true. A can be corrected as Granules are found in both plant and animal cells. In plants, they store starch or other substances, while in animal cells, granules may store proteins or lipids.

TYPE - 4   01 Mark

Very Short Answer Type Questions

Q.1 Name the single cell which is visible from the naked eye.

Ans. An ostrich egg, it is the largest single cell and is visible from the naked eye.

Q.2 Give two examples of cell which have the ability to change their shape.

Ans. WBCs and *Amoeba*.

Q.3 *X* is a cell in which nuclear envelope is absent and DNA is circular. Identify the *X*.

Ans. Prokaryotic cell

Q.4 Name the organism in which only one cell performs all the necessary functions.

Ans. *Amoeba* and *Paramecium*.

Q.5 What is protoplasm?

Ans. Protoplasm is a jelly-like substance in which all the components of a cell are found.

Q.6 Name the two components which are responsible for the formation of cell membrane.

Ans. Lipids and proteins are the two components which are responsible for the formation of cell membrane.

Q.7 Name the hereditary unit of an organism.

Ans. Genes

Q.8 Which organelle is responsible for lipid production in the cell?

Ans. Endoplasmic reticulum.

Q.9 Name the organelle which helps in the formation of acrosome of sperm.

Ans. Golgi body

Q.10 Which organelle contains hydrolytic enzymes?

Ans. Lysosomes.

Q.11 Name the organelle known as the factory of ribosomes.

Ans. Nucleolus.

Q.12 Name the cell organelle which is made up of RNA and proteins.

Ans. Ribosomes

Q.13 How permeable are the cell wall and cell membrane in a plant cell?

Ans. The cellulosic cell wall in plant cell is a permeable membrane while, the cell membrane is a selectively or partially permeable membrane.

Q.14 The diagram show a generalised animal cell. Which structure replicates during mitosis and generates the spindle?

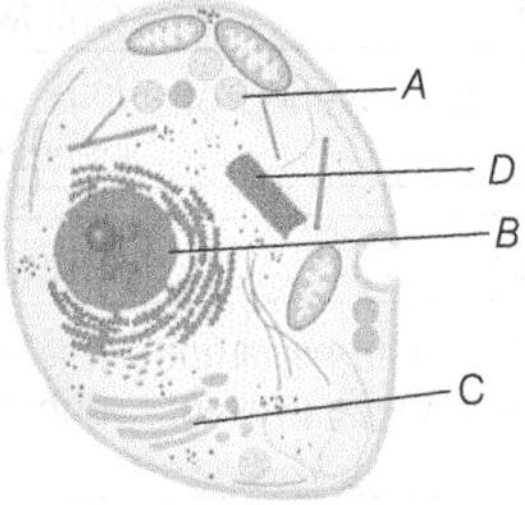

Ans. *D* represents centrosome, which helps to generate spindle fibres and replicates during mitosis.

Q.15 Give biological reasons for the following. **(1 Mark each)**

(i) The shape of the cell usually affects its functions.

(ii) Plasma membrane is called selectively permeable membrane.

(iii) Mitochondria are known as powerhouse of the cell.

(iv) Lysosomes are known as the suicidal bag of the cell.

(v) Mitochondria and chloroplasts are the semi-autonomous organelles.

Ans. (i) The shape of a cell plays an important role in the functions performed by it. For example, white blood cells do not have any fixed shape. Thus, they can easily squeeze out from thick blood vessels by changing the shape and come to the body fluid to kill the invading pathogen.

Similarly, RBCs have concave shape and lacks cell organelles, so that they can carry maximum oxygen.

(ii) Plasma membrane selectively allows the entry and exit of some materials in and out of the cell. Therefore, it is called selectively permeable membrane.

(iii) Mitochondria are known as powerhouse of the cell because these are associated with cellular respiration and energy generation of the cell.

(iv) Lysosomes are called the suicidal bag of the cell because when a cell gets damaged beyond repair or its metabolism is disturbed, the lysosome bursts and digest the cell.

(v) Mitochondria and chloroplasts possess their own DNA, RNA and ribosomes. So, they are capable of replication and synthesise proteins. Hence, considered as semi-autonomous organelles.

Q.16 Differentiate between the following pairs on the basis of what is given in bracket. **(1 Mark each)**

(i) Cell wall and Cell membrane (location)

(ii) Cytoplasm and Protoplasm (structure)

(iii) Chloroplast and Chromoplast (function)

(iv) Prokaryotic cell and Eukaryotic cell (nature of DNA)

Ans. (i)

Cell Wall	Cell Membrane
It is the outer covering of plant cell.	It is the outer covering of animal cell.

(ii)

Cytoplasm	Protoplasm
A viscous semi-transparent jelly-like substance present in the cell.	It is a translucent living substance of a cell.

(iii)

Chloroplast	Chromoplast
It helps in photosynthesis.	It gives colour to fruits and flowers and helps in pollination.

(iv)

Prokaryotic Cell	Eukaryotic Cell
Circular, free in cytoplasm.	Linear, inside nucleus.

Q.17 Given below are sets of five terms each. Rewrite the terms in correct order of logical sequence. **(1 Mark each)**

(i) Cell membrane, Cytoplasm, Cell wall, Nuclear membrane, Nucleolus

(ii) Nuclear membrane, Nucleolus, Chromosome, Nucleoplasm

Ans. (i) Cell wall, Cell membrane, Cytoplasm, Nuclear membrane, Nucleolus

(ii) Nuclear membrane, Nucleoplasm, Nucleolus, Chromosomes.

Q.18 Name the following. **(1 Mark each)**

(i) The scientist who discovered nucleus.

(ii) A cell with primitive nucleus.

(iii) The non-living structure present only in plant cell.

(iv) The area of cellular activities in plant and animal cells.

(v) The cells of human body that do not contain nucleus at maturity.

Ans. (i) Robert Brown (ii) Prokaryotic cell (iii) Cell wall (iv) Cytoplasm (v) Red blood corpuscles

Q.19 Correct and rewrite the following statements by changing the underlined words. **(1 Mark each)**

(i) <u>Purkinje</u> discovered the cell.

(ii) The three components of a cell include cell membrane, nucleus and <u>Golgi bodies</u>.

(iii) <u>Centrosome</u> is known as the factory of ribosomes.

(iv) The functional segments of DNA are called <u>chromatin</u>.

(v) <u>Leucoplasts</u> are the green-coloured plastids found in plants.

Ans. (i) Robert Hooke discovered the cell.

(ii) The three components of a cell include cell membrane, nucleus and cytoplasm.

(iii) Nucleolus is known as the factory of ribosomes.

(iv) The functional segments of DNA are called genes.

(v) Chloroplasts are the green-coloured plastids found in plants.

Q.20 Choose the odd one out from the following terms given below and name the category to which other three belong. **(1 Mark each)**

(i) *Amoeba, Paramecium, Euglena, Hydra*

(ii) Yeast, Mycoplasma, Bacteria, Mushroom

(iii) Chloroplast, Chromoplast, Leucoplast, Protoplasm

(iv) Nucleus, Mitochondria, Chloroplast, Golgi apparatus

(v) Nuclear membrane, Nucleolus, DNA, Cytoplasm

Ans. (i) Odd term is *Hydra* as it is a multicellular organism, while *Amoeba*, *Paramecium* and *Euglena* are unicellular organisms.

(ii) Odd term is mushroom as it is a multicellular organism, while yeast, mycoplasma and bacteria are unicellular organisms.

(iii) Odd term is protoplasm as it is a not a cell organelle, while chloroplast, chromoplast and leucoplast are type of plastids in plant cell.

(iv) Odd term is Golgi apparatus as it bound by a single membrane, while nucleus, mitochondria and chloroplast are double membrane bound organelles.

(v) Odd term is cytoplasm as it is not a part of nucleus, while nuclear membrane, nucleolus and DNA are related with structure of nucleus.

Q.21 Give appropriate biological/technical terms for the following. **(1 Mark each)**

(i) The controlling centre of a cell.

(ii) Powerhouse of a cell.

(iii) Colourless plastids.

(iv) Suicidal bag of a cell.

(v) Protein factories of the cell.

Ans. (i) Nucleus (ii) Mitochondria (iii) Leucoplasts (iv) Lysosomes (v) Ribosome

Q.22 The diagram given below represents a cell and its organelles. Observe the diagram given below and fill the blank spaces correctly. **(1 Mark each)**

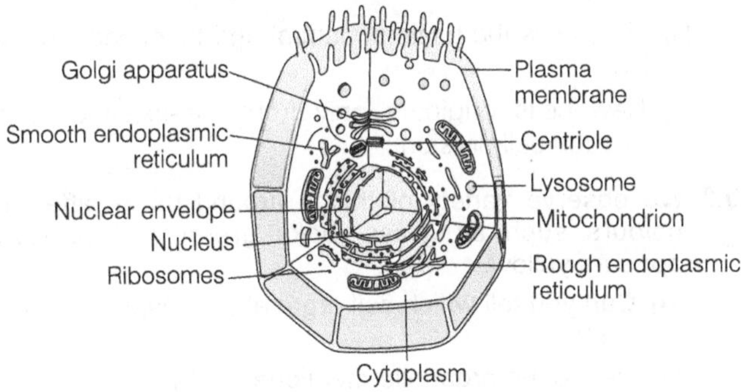

An ....(i)........ is a type of eukaryotic cell. Due to the presence of ....(ii)........, these cells permit the movement of substances selectively. ....(iii)........ is the double membrane-bound organelle found in all eukaryotes and helps in cellular respiration. It contains its own ....(iv)........ and ....(v)........ .

Ans. (i) animal cell (ii) plasma membrane (iii) Mitochondria (iv) DNA (v) ribosomes

TYPE - 5   02 Marks

Short Answer Type Questions

Q.1 Why are the cells called the structural and functional unit of life?

Ans. Cells are called the structural and functional units of life because they form the basic building blocks of all organisms and perform essential life processes like growth, reproduction and metabolism.

Q.2 Answer the following questions.

(i) Who proposed cell theory?

(ii) Name some common features of both plant and animal cells.

Ans. (i) Theodor Schwann and Matthias Jakob Schleiden.

(ii) Some common features of plant and animal cells are as follows

(a) Both animal and plant cells are eukaryotic cell.

(b) Both animal and plant cells contain nucleus and mitochondria.

Q.3 Why does plant cell possess large-sized vacuole?

Ans. Plant cell possess large sized vacuole because

(i) It stores salt, sugar, amino acid, organic acid and some proteins.

(ii) The vacuole contains cell sap that helps in maintaining turgidity of the cell.

Q.4 Write any two differences between prokaryotic and eukaryotic cells.

Ans. The differences between prokaryotic and eukaryotic cells are as follows

Prokaryotic Cells	Eukaryotic Cells
These are always unicellular such as bacteria.	They may be unicellular or multicellular.
No definite nucleus because the nuclear membrane is absent.	The definite nucleus is present with the nuclear membrane.

Q.5 Draw a labelled diagram of a plant cell.

Ans.

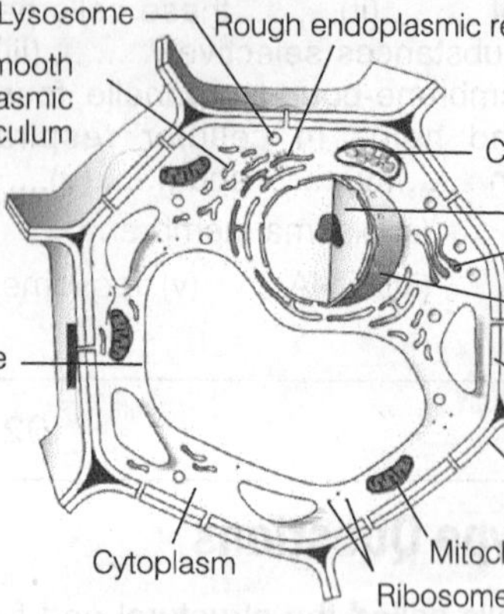

Q.6 Explain the following terms.

(i) Protoplasm

(ii) Cytoplasm

Ans. (i) Protoplasm is a jelly-like substance in which all the components of a cell are found.

(ii) Cytoplasm is a substance present between the cell membrane and the nuclear membrane.

Q.7 Write any two characteristic features of cytoplasm.

Ans. Two characteristic features of cytoplasm are as follows

(i) Stores essential molecules like amino acids, glucose, vitamins and minerals.

(ii) It contain all the cell organelles, hence it is the site where many chemical reactions occur.

Q.8 Which organelle is represented by the given diagram and state its main function.

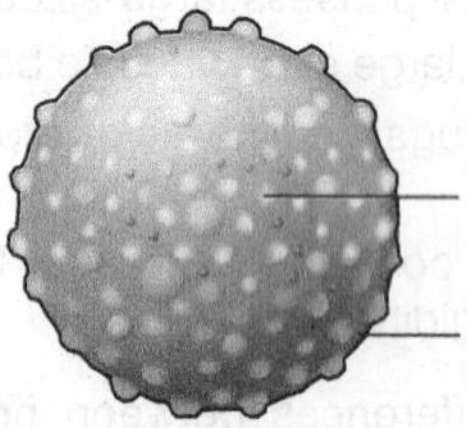

Ans. The above diagram represents lysosomes. Lysosomes are responsible for intracellular digestion, breaking down of waste materials, cellular debris and foreign substances.

Q.9 Expand the following biological abbreviations.

(i) DNA (ii) RNA

(iii) ATP (iv) RER

Ans. (i) Deoxyribonucleic Acid

(ii) Ribonucleic Acid

(iii) Adenosine Triphosphate

(iv) Rough Endoplasmic Reticulum

Q.10 Which is the main component of cell wall and write the function of cell wall?

Ans. The cell wall is made up of cellulose. It provides structural strength and rigidity to the plant cell.

Q.11 Draw a labelled diagram of nucleus.

Ans.

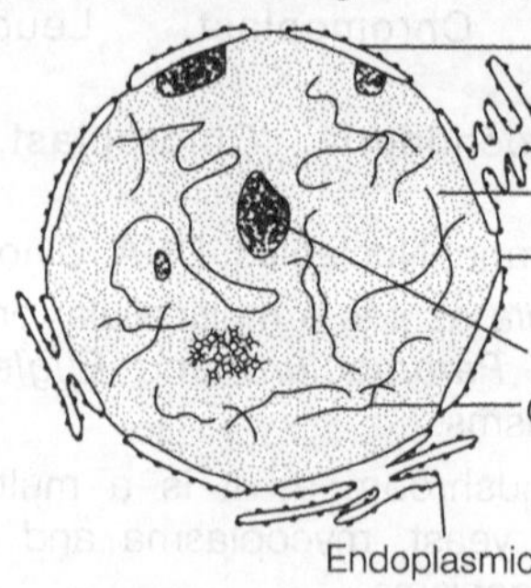

Q.12 Draw a labelled diagram of centrosomes.

Ans.

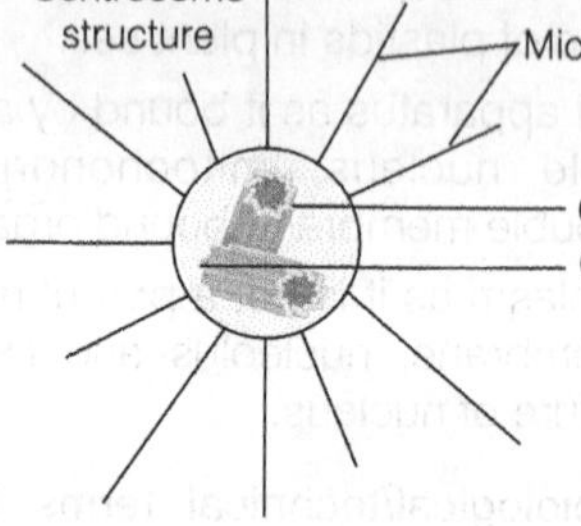

TYPE - 6 03 Marks

Q.1 Who modified the cell theory? Also explain the cell theory.

Ans. Rudolf Virchow modified the cell theory by saying that all cells arise from pre-existing cells (*Omnis cellula-e cellula*).

Cell theory states the following.

(i) All living organisms are composed of one or more cells.

(ii) The cell is the basic structural and functional unit of life.

(iii) New cells originate only from pre-existing cells through cell division.

Q.2 We observe variety of things around us in different colours such as grass looks green and papaya appears yellow.

(i) Can you tell which cell organelle is responsible for this?

(ii) Define the organelle mentioned in (i).

Ans. (i) The colour of grass as green and papaya as yellow appears due to the presence of a plastid.

(ii) Plastids are the cell organelles found in plant cells only. On the basis of the pigments present in plastids they are divided as chromoplasts, leucoplasts and chloroplasts.

Q.3 Write the exact location of cell membrane. State any two functions of it.

Ans. Cell membrane is the outer most covering of an animal cell.

Functions of cell membrane are as follows

(i) It acts as a protective covering for the cell.

(ii) It is called selectively permeable membrane because it controls the entry and exit of materials.

Q.4 How are organisms divided based on cellular composition? Explain the types.

Ans. On the basis of cellular composition organisms can be classified into two types, which are as follows

(i) **Unicellular Organisms** These organisms consist of only one cell, which carries out all the necessary functions, e.g. *Amoeba, Paramecium*, bacteria.

(ii) **Multicellular Organisms** These organisms are made up of many cells that work together to perform different functions and form various body parts, e.g. fungi, plants, animals.

Q.5 Explain the types of endoplasmic reticulum and state their functions.

Ans. Smooth Endoplasmic Reticulum (SER) and Rough Endoplasmic Reticulum (RER) are the types of endoplasmic reticulum.

Functions of SER and RER are as follows

(i) SER helps in lipid synthesis.

(ii) RER helps in protein synthesis.

Q.6 What would happen to the life of a cell, if there were no Golgi apparatus?

Ans. If Golgi apparatus is absent in a cell, then following activities will not take place

(i) Storage, modification and packaging of different materials.

(ii) Synthesis and secretion of enzymes, hormones, etc.

(iii) Formation of cell plate during cell division.

(iv) Formation of lysosomes, acrosome and peroxisomes.

TYPE - 7 — 03 Marks

Structured Based Questions

Q.1 Observe the diagram along side, shows a person with a cut on their index finger, which results in bleeding.

Answer the following questions.

(i) Which cells are present in his blood?

(ii) Which cells are responsible for the red colour of blood?

(iii) Write the shape of RBC.

Ans. (i) Blood cells (platelets, RBCs, WBCs and blood plasma) are present in his blood.

(ii) RBCs are responsible for the red colour of blood.

(iii) The shape of RBC is discoidal (biconcave).

Q.2 Given along side is the diagram of a cell. Study the same and answer the questions that follows

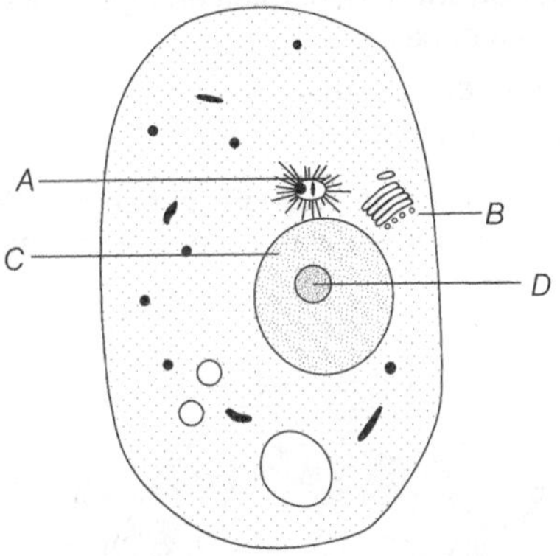

(i) Name the parts *A, B, C* and *D* indicated in the diagram.

(ii) State the functions of parts *B* and *C*.

(iii) State the function of *A*.

Ans. (i) The parts *A, B, C* and *D* indicated by the guidelines are

A– Centrosome, *B*– Golgi body

C– Nucleus, *D*– Nucleolus

(ii) *B*– Golgi body helps in storage, modification and packaging of material in vesicles.

C– It is nucleus which controls cell activities and contains hereditary material.

(iii) *A*– It is centrosome which helps in division of animal cell.

Q.3 The diagram shows some of the structures present in an animal cell.

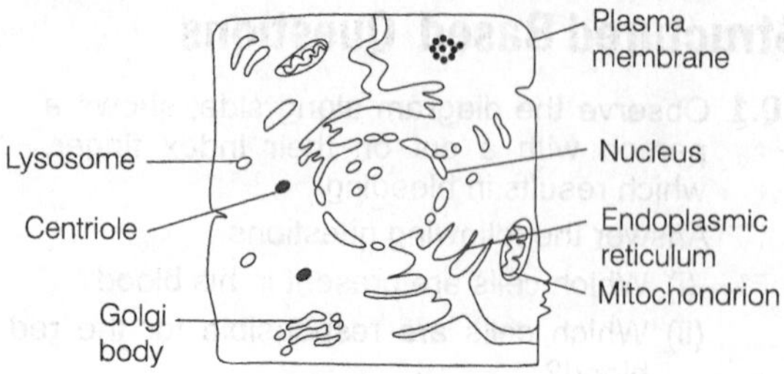

Which of these structures are responsible for

(i) manufacture of lipids and steroids?

(ii) release of energy?

(iii) manufacture of hormones and digestive enzymes?

Ans. (i) **Smooth endoplasmic reticulum** is responsible for the manufacture of lipids and steroids.

(ii) **Mitochondrion** generates energy (ATP) for various activities of cell.

(iii) **Lysosomes** are responsible for the production of hormones and digestive enzymes.

Q.4 A plant is grown in a bright sunshine. The diagram shows what is seen when the leaf is placed under a microscope.

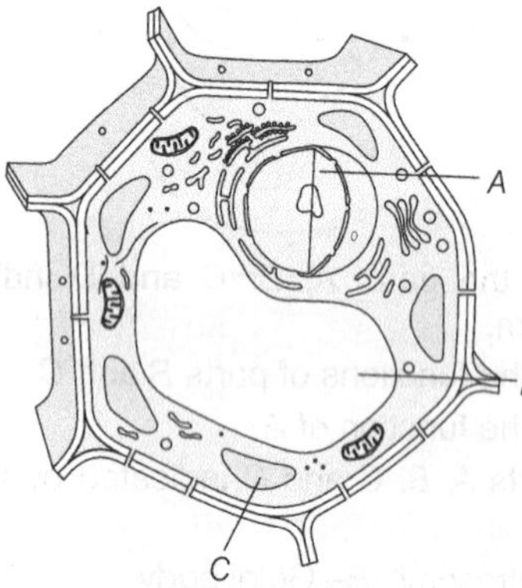

(i) Identify the structure that contains a pigment chlorophyll from *A*, *B* or *C*.

(ii) Which structures are found in plant cells that make them different from animal cells?

(iii) Why chloroplast is called 'kitchen of the cell'?

Ans. (i) Structure *C* in the diagram is called chloroplast which contains a pigment chlorophyll.

(ii) Plant cells have chloroplasts and a cellulosic cell wall which are absent in animal cell.

(iii) Chloroplast is called kitchen of the cell because it help in the synthesis of organic food in a plant cell through photosynthesis.

Q.5 Given below are the four different structures related to a cell. Study the same and answer the questions given below.

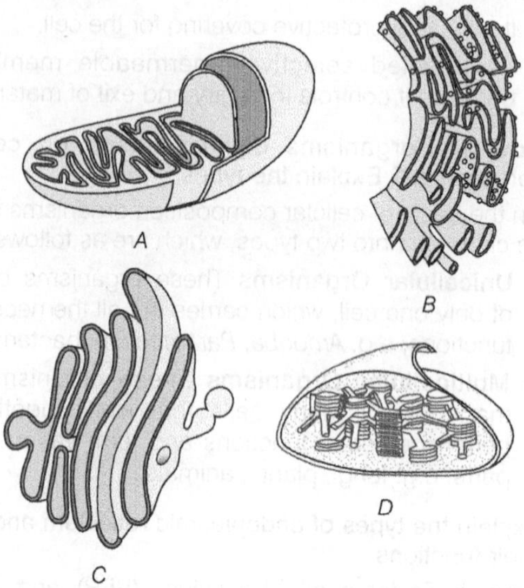

(i) Name the structures labelled as *A-D*.

(ii) Which cell organelle is formed from the structure *C*?

(iii) What role does the structure *D* perform in a cell?

Ans. (i) *A*- Mitochondria

B- Rough endoplasmic reticulum

C- Golgi apparatus

D- Chloroplast

(ii) Lysosomes are formed from the structure *C* (i.e. Golgi apparatus).

(iii) Structure *D* (or chloroplast) prepares organic food in plant cells with the help of inorganic substances by using solar energy.

02

TISSUES

- All living organisms are made up of cells.
- A group of cells possessing a similar structure and performing specific functions together are called **tissues**.
- On the basis of different structure and organisation, they can be categorised as plant tissues or animal tissues.

Plant Tissues

On the basis of the dividing capacity, plant tissues are mainly divided into two types, i.e. meristematic tissue and permanent tissue.

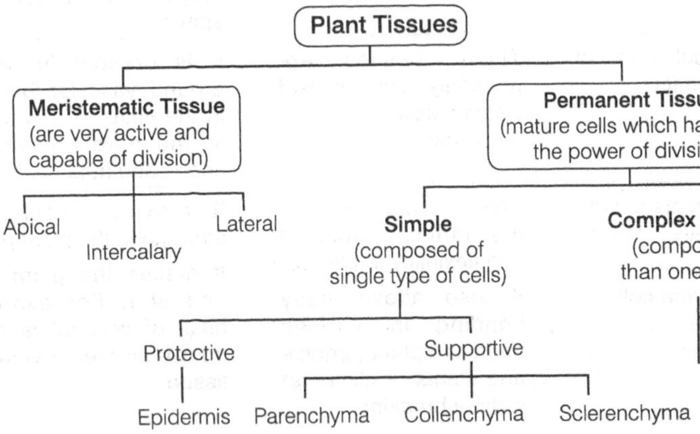

1. Meristematic Tissue

- The tissues in which cells always keep on dividing and give rise to new cells are called **meristematic tissues**.
- Plants grows only in those regions where meristematic tissues are present and active, i.e. root and shoot tip. Thus, known as **growth tissues**.
- Cells of meristematic tissue are usually cubical, small and thin with large nuclei.
- Cells are tightly packed with almost no intercellular spaces and vacuoles.
- On the basis of the region where they are present in plant, meristematic tissues are classified into three main types. These are
  - **Apical** (terminal) **Meristems** Present at the growing tips of stems and roots and on the tips of axillary buds. These help to increase the length of stems and roots.
  - **Intercalary Meristems** These are present at the base of leaves or internodes of stem. Important for the longitudinal growth of plants by adding primary tissues.
  - **Lateral Meristem** These are present on the lateral sides of the stems and roots. They help to increase the thickness (girth) of stems and roots.

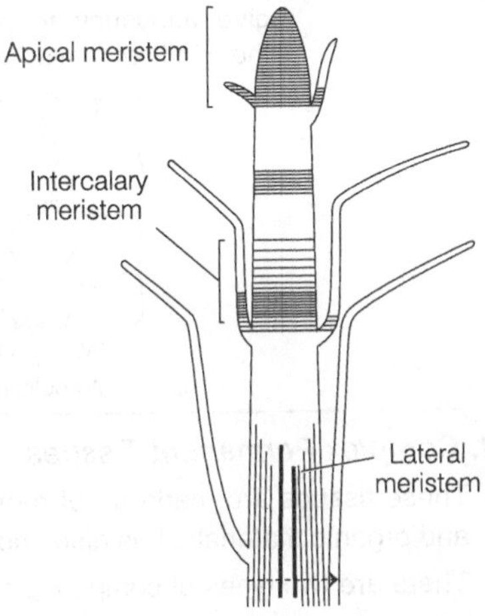

Meristematic tissue in plant body

2. Permanent Tissues

- The structurally and functionally specialised meristems which have lost the ability to divide.
- These tissues consist of non-dividing cells with a specific shape, size and function. They are formed from the meristematic tissue when they lose the ability to divide.
- These tissues may be dead or living and have definite shape, size, thickness and function.
- On the basis of structure, permanent tissues are classified into simple permanent tissue, complex permanent tissues and specialised permanent tissue.

I. Simple Permanent Tissues

They are made up of only one type of cells. It can be further divide into three types; parenchyma, collenchyma and sclerenchyma.

Features	Parenchyma	Collenchyma	Sclerenchyma
Structure	• It is the most abundant tissue in plants. • It consists of simple living cells with little or no specialisation, thin cell walls and a single large vacuole. • The cells are usually loosely packed with large spaces between them (intercellular spaces).	• Cells of this tissue are living, elongated and irregularly thickened at the corners. • These have very little intercellular spaces.	• The cells of this tissue are dead, long and narrow in appearance. • Cell walls are thickened due to **lignin** deposition. • There is no intercellular space.
Location	• These are present in the soft parts of the plant like leaves, roots, fruits and flowers, etc.	• These tissues are generally found in leaf stalks below the epidermis.	• It is present in stems, around vascular bundles, in the veins of leaves and in the hard covering of seeds and nuts.
Functions	• Parenchyma of stems and roots serves as a food (nutrients) and water storage tissue. • In some situations, parenchyma cell contains chlorophyll (i.e. **chlorenchyma**) and performs photosynthesis. • In aquatic plants, large air cavities are present in parenchyma cells in order to give buoyancy to plants, which help them to float (called **aerenchyma**).	• Collenchyma provides mechanical support and flexibility to plants. • It also allows easy bending in various parts of a plant (tendrils and stems of climbers) without breaking.	• It provides mechanical strength to the plant parts. • It makes the plant hard and stiff. For example, husk of coconut is made up of sclerenchymatous tissue.

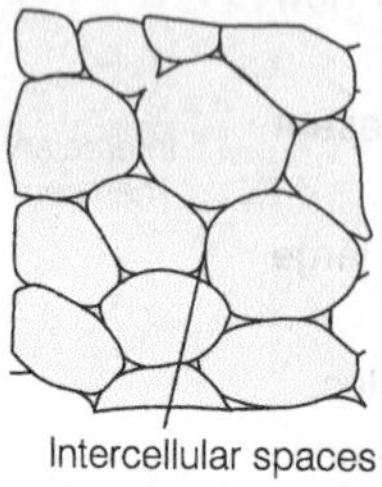

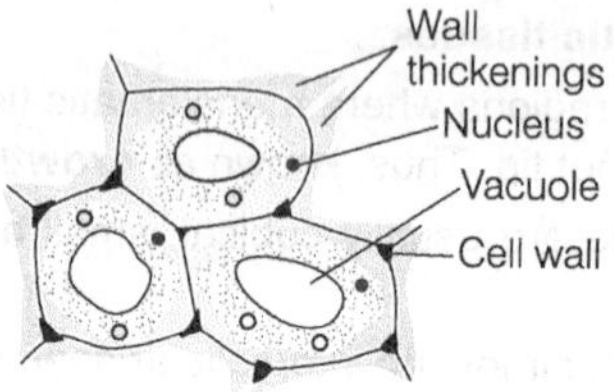

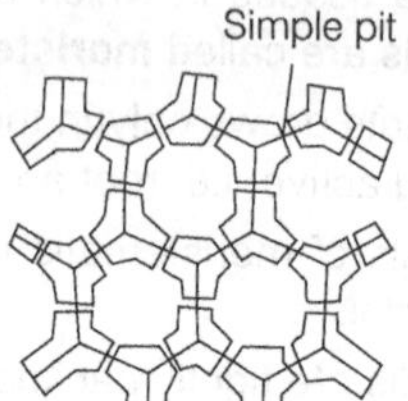

II. Complex Permanent Tissues

- These tissues are made up of more than one type of cells which works together for transport of water, minerals and organic materials. It is also known as **vascular tissue** or **conducting tissues**.
- There are two types of complex premanent tissues, i.e. xylem and phloem.

  (i) **Xylem** It is a type of conducting tissue responsible for the transport of water and minerals from roots to other parts of the plant.

  Xylem consists of four different types of elements, which are as follows

  - **Tracheids** These are dead, long, tubular structures with tapering ends. They transport water and minerals vertically.

- **Vessels** These are also dead, long and tube-like structures that helps in the vertical conduction of water.
- **Xylem Parenchyma** These are the only living cells of xylem with thin cell walls. They store food and help in the sideways conduction of water.
- **Xylem Fibres** or **Wood Fibres** They have elongated dead cells with tapering end and thick cell walls. These are mainly supportive in function.

(ii) **Phloem** It transports food from leaves to other parts of the plant both in upward and downward directions. Majorly phloem is made up of following four types of elements

- **Sieve Tubes** These are tubular cells with perforated walls. They have thin layer of cytoplasm. They help in the transport of formed food to storage organs.
- **Companion Cells** These are small, elongated cells having thin walls. The cells help sieve tubes in translocation of food.
- **Phloem Fibres** or **Bast Fibres** These are thick walled sclerenchyma cells, which provides mechanical strength to the tissue.
- **Phloem Parenchyma** These are thin-walled cells, which help in storage of food.

All phloem cells are living except **phloem fibres**. In hilly areas, certain plants have sieve cells in place of sieve tubes. Sieve cells lacks sieve plates.

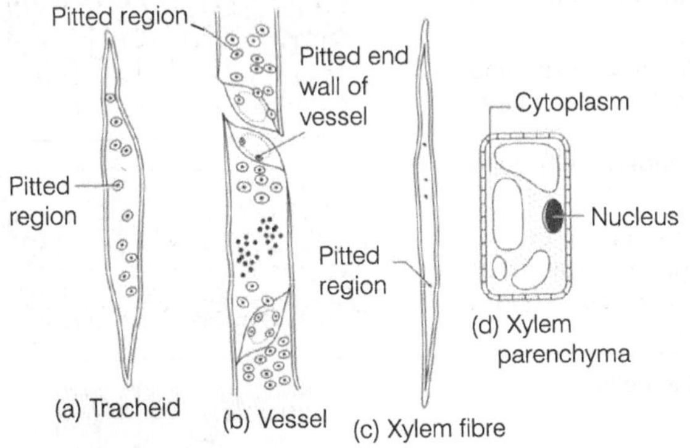

Different components of a xylem

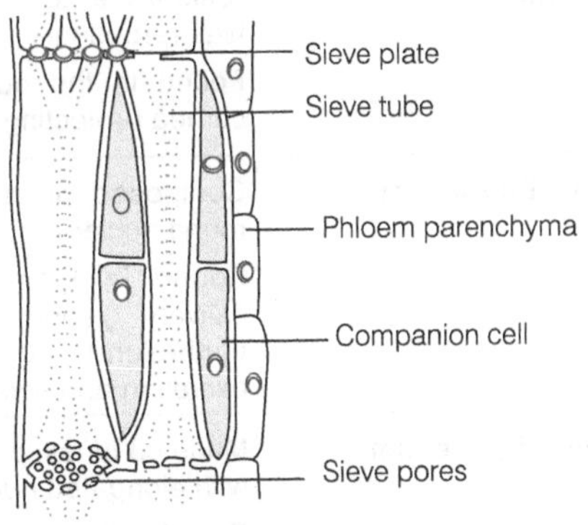

Section of a phloem

III. Specialised Permanent Tissues

This includes two types of specialised tissues; **epidermis** and **cork** or **phellem**.

- **Epidermis** The epidermis forms a single-cell thick, outermost layer covering in various plant organs such as leaves, flowers, stems and roots. It prevents water loss and provide defence.
- **Cork** or **Phellem** It is formed by the cork cambium in older dicot stems, roots and tissues. It is a protective, outer layer which is made up of dead cells and lack intercellular spaces. It prevents water loss and physical damage. It also provides insulation from freezing temperatures.

Animal Tissues

On the basis of their structures and functions, animal tissues are classified into four basic types

Animal Tissues
- **Epithelial**
  - Squamous
    - Simple
    - Stratified
  - Cuboidal
  - Columnar
  - Ciliated
  - Glandular
  - Pseudostratified
- **Connective**
  - Connective tissue proper
    - Areolar
    - Adipose
    - Fibrous
  - Supportive connective tissue
    - Cartilage
    - Bone
  - Fluid connective tissue
    - Blood
    - Lymph
- **Muscular**
  - Striated
  - Unstriated
  - Cardiac
- **Nervous**

1. Epithelial Tissues

- It is the simplest covering and protective tissue of the animal body, which covers most organs and cavities of the body.
- It also forms a barrier to keep different body systems separate from each other.
- Cells are tightly packed, forming a continuous sheet with minimal intercellular space and cementing material.
- Epithelial cells may be flat, cuboidal or columnar in shape.
- Based on the shape and arrangement of the cells, epithelial tissues are further classified into different types which are given in the table below

Types of Epithelial Tissue	Descriptions	
Simple Squamous Epithelium	• Single-layered, tightly packed cells that are thin and flat, resembling tiles with prominent nuclei. • Found in blood vessels, lung, alveoli (for substance transport), oesophagus and mouth lining.	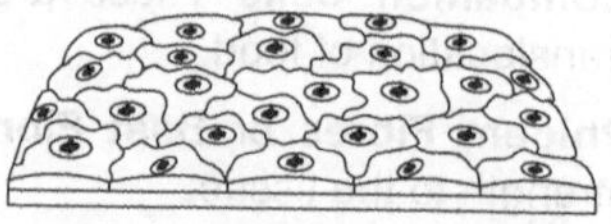
Stratified Squamous Epithelium	• Made of many layers of cells, providing resistance to mechanical injury and waterproofing. • Found in the outer layer of skin and cornea protecting against wear and tear.	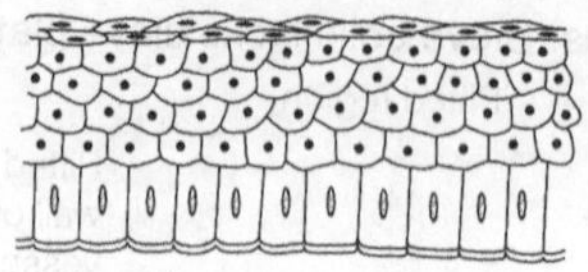
Cuboidal Epithelium	• Composed of cube-shaped cells with round nuclei. • Found in kidney tubules, ducts of salivary glands and gonads (germinal epithelium). Functions in absorption, excretion and secretion.	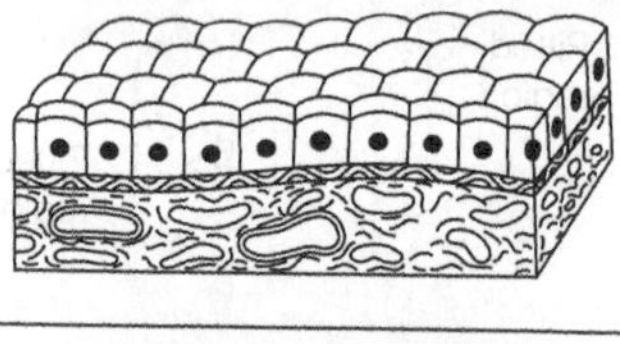
Columnar Epithelium	• Made up of tall, pillar-like cells with elongated nuclei. • Found in the inner lining of the intestine, the respiratory tract where absorption and secretion occur.	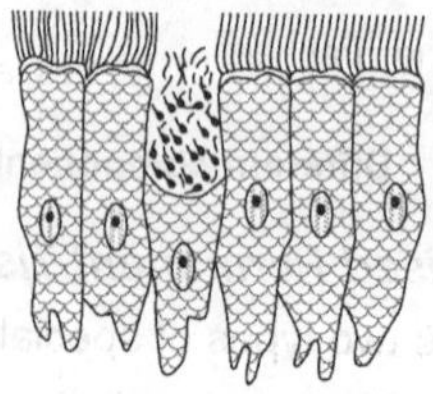
Ciliated Columnar Epithelium	• Columnar cells with hair-like projections (cilia) that move substances like mucus forward to clear the passage. • Found in the respiratory tract, oviducts, sperm ducts and kidney tubules, etc.	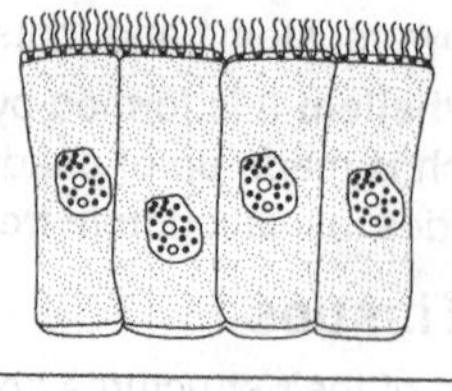
Glandular Epithelium	• Cells that secrete substances at the epithelial surface, sometimes forming multicellular glands. • Found in glands that secrete substances like hormones, enzymes or mucus. e.g. in the lining of stomach and intestine.	

2. Connective Tissues

- These tissues connect or bind various body tissues and body organs with each other.
- The cells are living, widely spaced with ground substance (matrix) filling the intercellular spaces. White and yellow fibres present in the matrix.
- It provides structural support, transport and insulation.

- Connective tissue is classified into three categories as given below

(i) Connective Tissue Proper

It serves for packing and binding the organs. It is further divided into three types, which are as follows

- **Areolar Tissue** It is a supporting and packing tissue found between the organs lying in the body cavity. It fills the space inside the organs, supports internal organs and helps in the repair of tissues.
- **Adipose Tissue** It is located below the skin and in between the internal organs around the kidney and eyeball. It serves as a fat reservoir and keep visceral organs in position. Thus, cells of this tissue are filled with fat globules. It also acts as an insulator due to the storage of fats. Thus, preventing heat loss from the body.

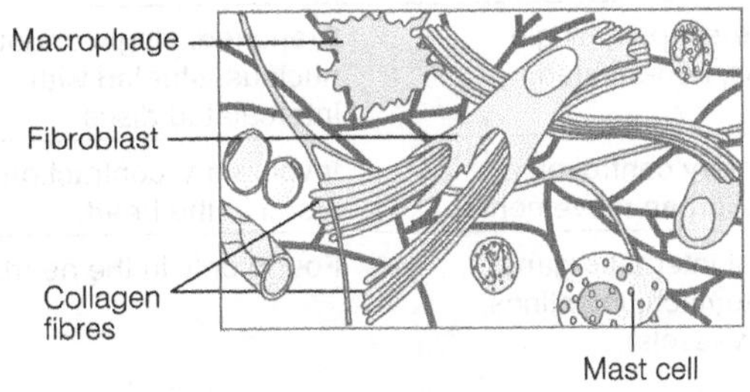

Areolar tissue

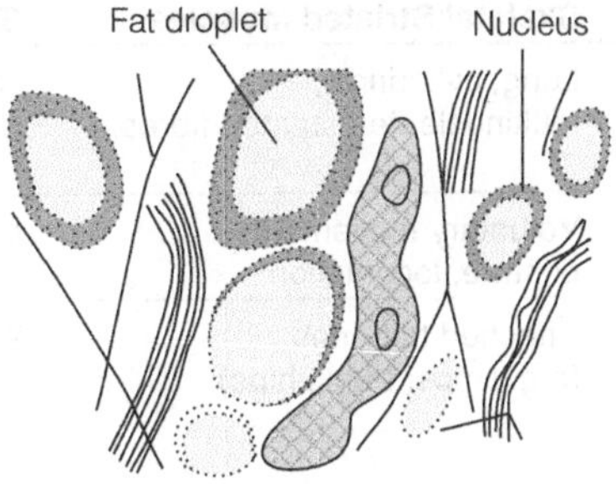

Adipose tissue

- **Fibrous Tissue** It provides strength, support and protection by connecting and binding structures like muscles, bones and organs. It includes **tendons** (connecting muscles to bones) and **ligaments** (connecting bones to bones).

(ii) Supportive Connective Tissues

These tissues provides structural support and provides protection to the vital organs of the body. It is of two main types, i.e. cartilage and bone.

- **Cartilage** is a tough, non-porous, flexible tissue with thickened intercellular substances. It lacks blood vessels and nerves.
  - Cartilage is found at the tip of the nose, external ears, trachea, bronchial tubes between vertebrae and at the end of long bones.
  - It provides smoothness to the bone surface at the joints.

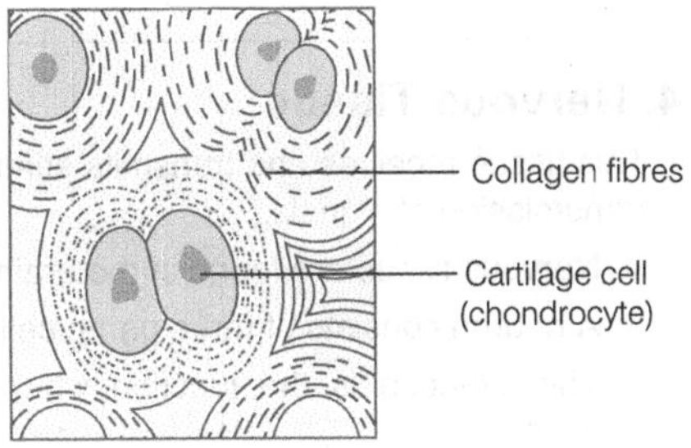

Cartilage

- **Bone** is a hard, porous and non-flexible tissue that has a rich supply of blood vessels and nerves.
  - Its matrix is made up of ossein proteins and is rich in inorganic salts of calcium and phosphorus.
  - Bone consists of living cells called **osteoblasts** and non-living components, including a rigid mass of inorganic salts.
  - It forms the framework that supports the body.

(iii) Fluid Connective Tissue

It helps in the transportation of essential nutrients. It is of two types; **blood** and **lymph**.

- **Blood** is a fluid tissue that continuously circulates in the body.
  - It helps in transport materials such as nutrients, gases, excretory products, hormones and more.
  - Blood consists of two components; plasma (the matrix) and blood corpuscles.
  - The blood corpuscles include
    - **RBCs** (Red Blood Cells) Responsible for oxygen transport. It contains haemoglobin. They helps in gaseous transport.
    - **WBCs** (White Blood Cells) Plays an important role in body's defence system.
    - **Platelets** Aid in blood clotting.

- **Lymph** is a pale-yellow fluid. Its composition is similar to plasma, but it lacks plasma proteins.
  - Lymph contains only WBCs (White Blood Cells).
  - It helps to protect the body, especially against harmful organisms.

3. Muscular Tissue

- It consists of elongated cells called **muscle fibres**. It is responsible for body movement.
- Muscle fibres contain contractile proteins that enable contraction and relaxation.
- There are three main types of muscle tissue, which are given in the table below

Features	Skeletal Striated Muscles	Smooth Unstriated Muscles	Cardiac Heart Muscles
Structure	Long, cylindrical, multinucleated striated fibres.	Spindle-shaped, single nucleus, non-striated.	Branched, single or double nucleus, striated with intercalated discs.
Function	Voluntary movement, posture, locomotion.	Involuntary control of internal organ movements.	Involuntary contraction to pump blood in the heart.
Location	Attached to bones (e.g. limbs, trunk, hips).	Walls of internal organs (e.g. stomach, intestines, blood vessels).	Found only in the heart.

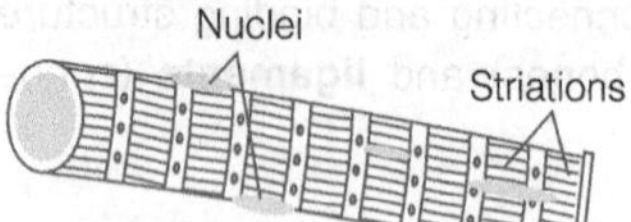

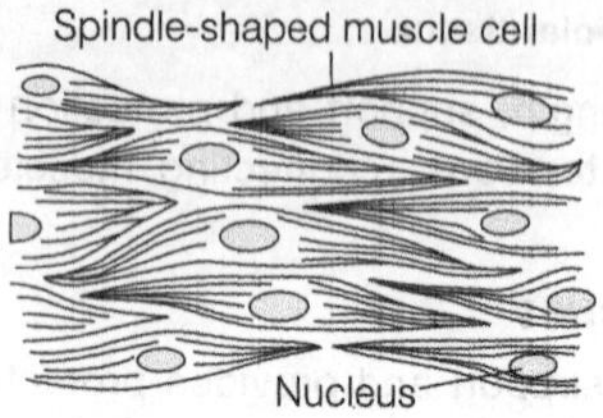

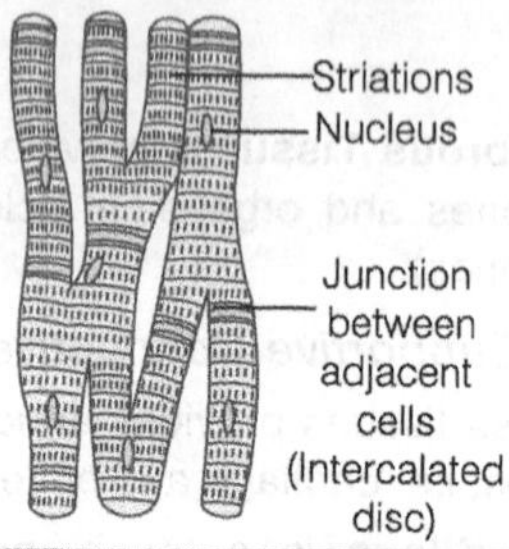

4. Nervous Tissue

- This tissue receives and transmits stimuli throughout the body. The cells called **neurons**, are specialised for rapid transmission of signals.
  - Nervous tissue are found in the brain, spinal cord and nerves.
  - A neuron consists of three parts; cell body, axon and dendrites.
  - The synapse is the junction where one neuron's axon meets another's dendrite, allowing nerve impulse transfer.

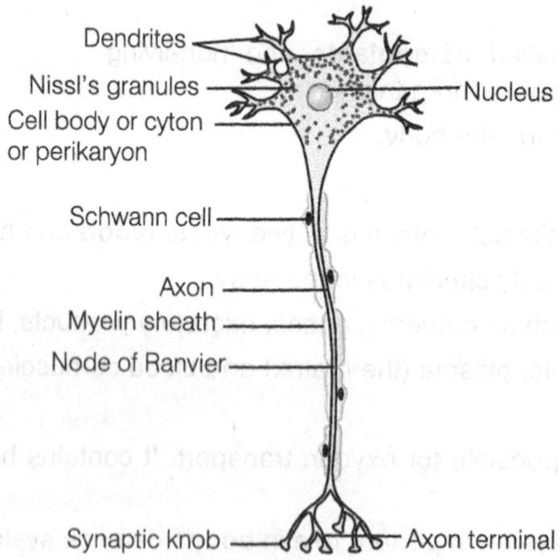

Structure of a neuron

EXAM ORIENTED QUESTIONS

TYPE - 1 01 Mark

Multiple Choice Questions

Q.1 The diagrams below shows the structure in a human being with each other representing a level of organisation of life.

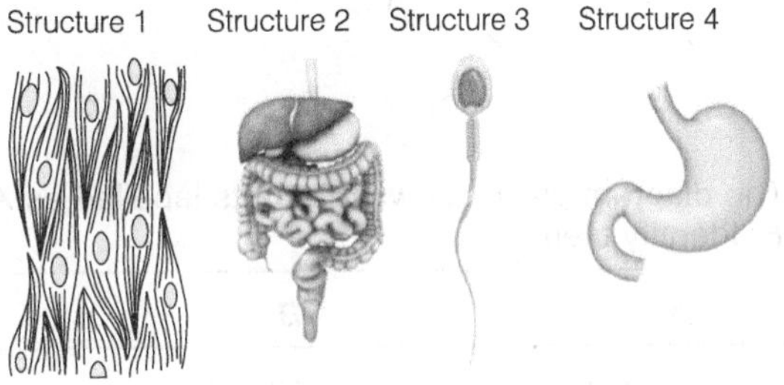

Which of the following correctly identifies the level of organisation of life that these structures belongs to?

S. No.	Structure 1	Structure 2	Structure 3	Structure 4
(a)	Cell	Organ	Tissue	System
(b)	Cell	System	Tissue	Organ
(c)	Tissue	System	Cell	Organ
(d)	Tissue	Organ	Cell	System

Ans. (b)

Q.2 Girth of stem increases due to
(a) apical meristem
(b) lateral meristem
(c) intercalary meristem
(d) vertical meristem

Ans. (b)

Q.3 The tissue which contains photosynthetic pigment is
(a) chlorenchyma (b) aerenchyma
(c) sieve tubes (d) sieve elements

Ans. (a)

Q.4 Parenchyma cells are
(a) relatively unspecified and thin-walled
(b) thick-walled and specialised
(c) lignified
(d) None of the above

Ans. (a)

Q.5 The diagram shows part of a xylem vessel.

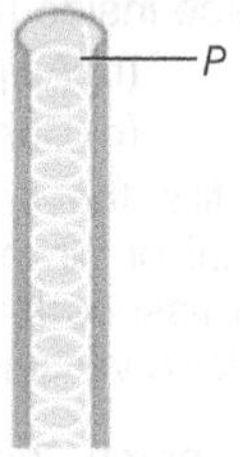

What is the function of the spiral structure '*P*'?
(a) Absorption (b) Photosynthesis
(c) Support (d) Transport

Ans. (d) The tracheid or lignin surrounded the secondary wall of xylem in the form of spiral structure are employed purely in the transportation of water and nutrient from soil towards the plants.

Q.6 The characteristic features of sclerenchyma are
(a) living cells with thin walls
(b) dead cells with thin walls
(c) living cells with highly thickened walls
(d) dead cells with thickened walls

Ans. (d)

Q.7 The diagrams show cells from four tissues.

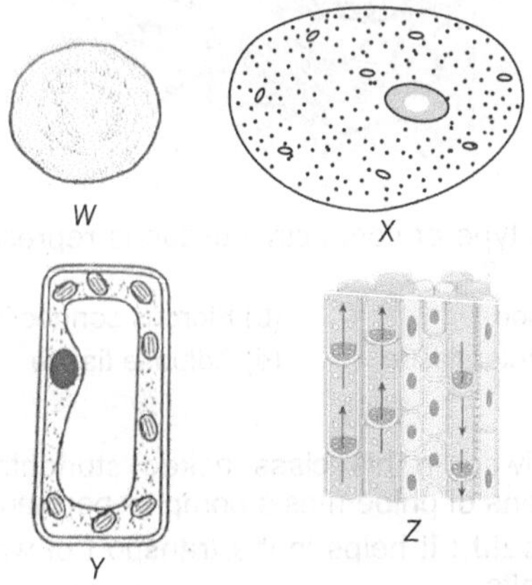

Which cells are adapted for transport?
(a) *W* and *Y* (b) *W* and *Z*
(c) *X* and *Y* (d) *X* and *Z*

Ans. (b) Here, cell Z is plant cell that is modified to form xylem tissue that conducts water and mineral salts from the roots to other parts of the plant. W is a red blood cell that absorbs nutrients and transports oxygen.

Q.8 Hair-like projections present in the respiratory tract are

(a) cilia (b) squamous epithelium
(c) mucus (d) neuron

Ans. (a)

Q.9 Which of the following helps in the repair of tissue and fills up the space inside the organ?

(a) Tendon (b) Adipose tissue
(c) Areolar tissue (d) Cartilage

Ans. (c) Areolar tissue fills the spaces, inside the organ, supports the internal organ and repair tissues. These are the connective tissues found between the muscle and skin, around blood vessels, nerves, etc.

Q.10 Ram is trying to match the blood cells with their specific functions.

Blood Cells	Functions
P	Gaseous transport
Q	Helps in defence mechanism.

Choose the correct option.

(a) *P*- RBCs, *Q*- WBCs (b) *P*- RBCs, *Q*- Platelets
(c) *P*- WBCs, *Q*- RBCs (d) *P*- Plasma, *Q*- Lymph

Ans. (a)

Q.11 The diagram given below represents a type of connective tissue. Observe the diagram carefully and answer the following question.

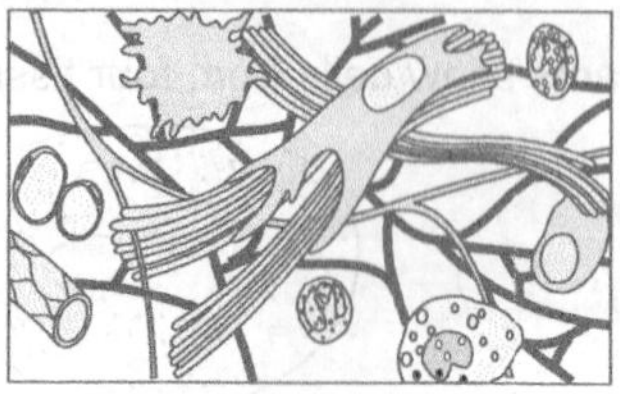

Which type of connective tissue is represented in the diagram?

(a) Blood (b) Fibrous connective tissue
(c) Areolar tissue (d) Adipose tissue

Ans. (c)

Q.12 Mr. Tiwari in his class asked students about the functions of phloem as a complex permanent tissue.

Ram said : It helps in the transport of water, mineral and salts.

Vayu said : It helps in the storage of small amount of food.

Keya said : It helps in the translocation of food materials from leaves to other parts of the plants.

Neha said : It constitutes break of the plant body.

Who is correct?

(a) Ram and Vayu (b) Vayu and Keya
(c) Keya and Neha (d) Only Vayu

Ans. (b)

Q.13 In animal tissues, the nerve cells .....*P*..... and the muscle cells.....*Q*.....

(a) *P*-conducts signals, *Q*-contract and relax
(b) *P*-store nutrients, *Q*-digest food
(c) *P*-form protective layer, *Q*-conduct signals
(d) *P*-contract and relax, *Q*-conduct signals

Ans. (a)

Q.14

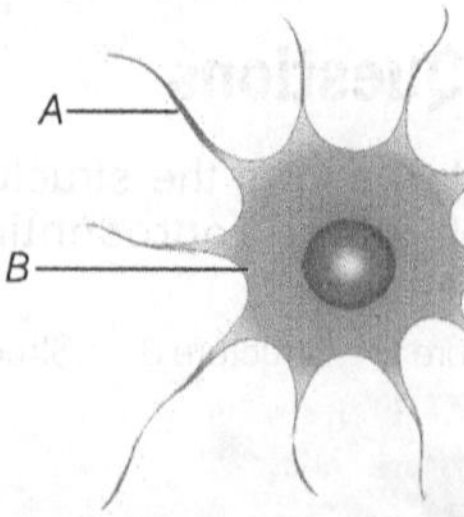

The diagram given shows the parts labelled as *A* and *B*. Identify them.

	A	*B*
(a)	Nucleus	Calculi
(b)	Osteocytes	Calculi
(c)	Canaliculi	Nucleus
(d)	Nucleus	Osteocytes

Ans. (c)

Q.15 While doing work and running, you move your organs like hands, legs, etc. Which among the following is correct?

(a) Smooth muscles contract and pull the ligament to move the bones
(b) Smooth muscles contract and pull the tendon to move the bones
(c) Skeletal muscles contract and pull the ligament to move the bones
(d) Skeletal muscles contract and pull the tendon to move the bones

Ans. (d) While doing work and running, skeletal muscles contract and pull the tendon (which connects muscles to bones) to move the bone.

Q.16 A person met with an accident in which his two long bones of hand were dislocated. Which among the following may be the possible reason?

(a) Tendon break
(b) Break of skeletal muscle
(c) Ligament break
(d) Areolar tissue break

Ans. (c) Ligaments connect the two bones. Therefore, breakage of ligament causes the dislocation of bones.

TYPE - 2 01 Mark

Matching Type Questions

Q.1 Match the following columns.

Column I	Column II
A. Fluid connective tissue	I. Smooth muscles
B. Striated muscle	II. Cartilage
C. Surface of joints	III. Adipose tissue
D. Storage of fat	IV. Blood
E. Unstriated muscles	V. Skeletal muscle

Ans. A–IV, B–V, C–II, D–III, E–I

Q.2 Different types of tissues are shown in the diagram given below. Match the tissue A to E with their respective functions.

Different Types of Tissues	Functions
A. 	I. Helps in storage and photosynthesis.
B. 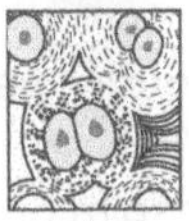	II. Provide mechanical support and flexibility.
C. 	III. Helps in the pumping of heart.
D. 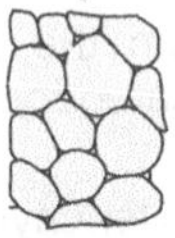	IV. It conducts water in plants.
E. 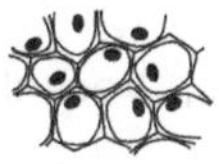	V. Provides smoothness to the bone surface at the joints.

Ans. A–III, B–V, C–IV, D–I, E–II

TYPE - 3 01 Mark

Assertion-Reason Type Questions

Direction (Q. Nos. 1-5) In the following questions statements are given as Assertion (A) and Reason (R).

(a) A is true, but R is false.
(b) A is false, but R is true.
(c) Both A and R are true.
(d) Both A and R are false.

Q.1 Assertion (A) Xylem transports water and minerals in plants.

Reason (R) Xylem vessels and tracheids have thick, lignified walls that help in the conduction of water.

Ans. (c)

Q.2 Assertion (A) The epidermis protects plants from water loss and external damage.

Reason (R) The epidermis is made up of dead cells.

Ans. (a) A is true, but R is false. R can be corrected as
The epidermis is made up of living cells and not dead cells.

Q.3 Assertion (A) Ciliated epithelium tissue is responsible for the secretion of enzymes in the digestive system.

Reason (R) Ciliated epithelium tissue has hair-like structures called cilia.

Ans. (b) A is false, but R is true. A can be corrected as
Ciliated epithelium tissue helps in the movement of substances like mucus or eggs in the body.

Q.4 Assertion (A) Connective tissue provides structural support and connects different parts of the body.

Reason (R) Blood is the example of fluid connective tissues.

Ans. (c)

Q.5 Assertion (A) Nervous tissue is responsible for transmitting electrical impulses throughout the body.

Reason (R) Nervous tissue is made up of specialised cells known as neurons.

Ans. (c)

TYPE - 4 01 Mark

Very Short Answer Type Questions

Q.1 Which tissue is responsible for the growth of the plant?

Ans. Meristematic tissue.

Q.2 Name the substance by which the cell wall of parenchyma is made.

Ans. Cellulose

Q.3 What are the two types of parenchyma?

Ans. Two types of parenchyma are aerenchyma and chlorenchyma.

Q.4 *X* is the tissue which is responsible for the conduction of food in a plant. Identify *X*.

Ans. Phloem

Q.5 Which type of xylem tissue is considered as a living tissue?

Ans. Xylem parenchyma.

Q.6 Name the protective tissue which is made up of cork cambium.

Ans. Cork or phellem is made up of cork cambium.

Q.7 Name the types of tissues present in animals?

Ans. Animals have four types of tissues; **epithelial**, **connective**, **muscular** and **nervous tissue**.

Q.8 Which type of tissue is present in the inner lining of oesophagus and mouth?

Ans. Simple squamous epithelium.

Q.9 Write the function of fibrous connective tissue.

Ans. Fibrous connective tissue provides **strength**, **support** and **protection** by connecting and binding structures like muscles, bones and organs.

Q.10 Which type of cells are present in muscular tissue?

Ans. **Elongated cells** which are also known as **muscle fibres** are present in muscular tissue.

Q.11 Name the cells which are responsible for rapid transmission of signals?

Ans. Neurons

Q.12 In which organs nervous tissues are present in human body?

Ans. In human, nervous tissues are present in **brain**, **spinal cord** and **nerves**.

Q.13 A type of plant tissue (parenchyma) is shown in the diagram below. Observe the diagram carefully and fill the blank spaces. **(1 Mark each)**

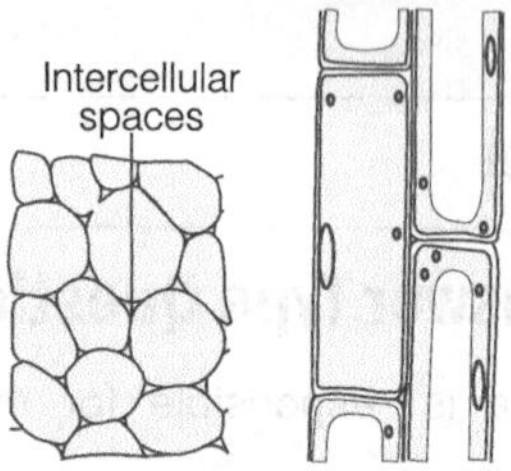

Parenchyma tissue is the type of .....(i)..... tissue. These are simple living cells with little specialisation, thin cell wall made up of .....(ii)..... and single large vacuole. Cells of these tissues are loosely packed with large .....(iii)..... spaces between them. It performs the function of .....(iv)..... and .....(v)..... in plants.

Ans. (i) simple permanent tissue
(ii) cellulose
(iii) intercellular spaces
(iv) photosynthesis
(v) storage

Q.14 Name the following. **(1 Mark each)**

(i) Tissue present in the inner lining of the intestine.
(ii) The tissue present at the apex of roots.
(iii) The type of plant tissue which is fully differentiated.
(iv) A supporting tissue which consists of isodiametric living cells.
(v) Tissue present at the joint between two bones.

Ans. (i) Glandular epithelium
(ii) Apical meristem
(iii) Permanent tissue
(iv) Parenchyma
(v) Ligament

Q.15 Correct and rewrite the following statements by changing the underlined words. **(1 Mark each)**

(i) Cambium meristem is present on the either side of the nodes of stem.
(ii) Xylem consists of tracheids, sieve tubes, xylem parenchyma and xylem fibres.
(iii) WBCs helps in transport of respiratory gases.
(iv) The matrix of bone is made up of fat.
(v) Cardiac muscles are cylindrical, uninucleated and unbranched.

Ans. (i) **Intercalary meristem** is present on the either side of the nodes of stem.
(ii) Xylem consists of **tracheids**, **vessels**, **xylem parenchyma** and **xylem fibres**.
(iii) **RBCs** helps in transport of respiratory gases.
(iv) The matrix of bone is made up of **ossein protein**.
(v) Cardiac muscles are cylindrical, uninucleated and branched.

Q.16 Choose the odd one out from the following terms given below and name the category to which other three belong. **(1 Mark each)**

(i) Parenchyma, Cartilage, Collenchyma, Sclerenchyma
(ii) Xylem fibres, Tracheids, Vessels, Companion cells
(iii) Squamous epithelium, Adipose tissue, Columnar epithelium, Cuboidal epithelium
(iv) Bone, Blood, Areolar tissue, Columnar epithelium
(v) Skeletal muscles, Cardiac muscles, Smooth muscles, Neuron

Ans. (i) Odd term is **cartilage** because it is part of animal tissue, while rest three are examples of **plant tissue**.
(ii) Odd term is **companion cell** because it is the part of phloem, while rest three are **parts of xylem**.
(iii) Odd term is **adipose tissue** because it is the part of connective tissue, while rest three are **type of epithelial tissues**.

(iv) Odd term is columnar epithelium because it is the part of epithelium tissue, while rest three are examples of connective tissue.

(v) Odd term is neuron because it is the part of nervous tissue, while rest three are the type of muscular tissue.

Q.17 Give the biological/technical terms for the following. **(1 Mark each)**

(i) The complex conducting tissue which help the sieve tubes in translocation of food.

(ii) The category of plant tissues that have lost their ability to multiply.

(iii) The kind of plant cells with thin walls and a single large vacuole.

(iv) Elongated cells which are thickened at corners.

(v) Tissues which provide the upward movement of water and dissolved materials from the roots to other parts of the plant.

Ans. (i) Companion cells (ii) Permanent tissue

(iii) Parenchyma cells (iv) Collenchyma

(v) Tracheids and vessels

Q.18 State the exact location of the following. **(1 Mark each)**

(i) Apical meristem

(ii) Lateral meristem

(iii) Parenchyma tissue

(iv) Squamous epithelial cells

(v) Cuboidal epithelium

Ans. (i) Apical meristem is present at the **tip of stems** and **roots**.

(ii) Lateral meristems is present below the back and on the **lateral sides of roots** and **stems**.

(iii) Parenchyma tissue is present in the **cortex, pith** and **roots**.

(iv) Squamous epithelial cells are present in **oesophagus** and **lining of mouth**.

(v) Cuboidal epithelia are found in the **lining of kidney tubules** and **ducts of salivary gland**.

Q.19 Mention one difference between each of the following pairs on the basis of what is given in the bracket. **(1 Mark each)**

(i) Simple tissue and Complex tissue (structure)

(ii) Parenchyma and Sclerenchyma (cell wall)

(iii) Meristematic tissue and Permanent tissue (dividing capacity)

(iv) Blood and Lymph (composition)

(v) Tendon and Ligament (location)

Ans. (i)

Simple Tissue	Complex Tissue
It is made up of only one type of cells which resemble each other, e.g. parenchyma.	It is made up of more than one type of cells which look different from each other, e.g. xylem.

(ii)

Parenchyma	Sclerenchyma
Cell wall is very thin and made up of cellulose.	Cell wall is uniformaly thick due to the deposition of lignin.

(iii)

Meristematic Tissue	Permanent Tissue
Cells divide repeatedly to form new cells.	Cells normally do not divide and attain specialised functions.

(iv)

Blood	Lymph
It consists of plasma, RBCs, WBCs and platelets.	It consists of blood, plasma and white blood cells.

(v)

Tendon	Ligament
It attaches muscles to bone.	It attaches bone to bone.

Q.20 Give reason for the following. **(1 Mark each)**

(i) The shells of walnut are hard and the pulp and skin of pears is gritty. Why?

(ii) Palm trees are tall, but lack increase in diameter. Why?

(iii) Why we cannot consider a cluster of eggs placed in a basket as a tissue?

Ans. (i) The shells of walnut are hard, but pulp and skin of pears is gritty because they are made up of **sclerenchyma cells**, known as **stone cells**, which are hard and cell walls thickened due to **lignin deposition**.

(ii) Palm trees are tall, but lack increase in diameter because they lack lateral meristem or cambium which are responsible for increase in girth (diameter) of the stem.

(iii) We cannot consider a cluster of eggs placed in a basket as a tissue because a tissue is a group of cells performing specific functions together.

TYPE - 5 02 Marks

Short Answer Type Questions

Q.1 The tissue system in multicellular organisms promotes division of labour. Justify the statement.

Ans. The tissue system in multicellular organisms promotes division of labour by organising cells into specialised tissues, each performing a specific function. This specialisation allows different tissues to work together more efficiently with each tissue contributing to the overall function of the organism.

Q.2 Write the name of tissues found in plants.

Ans. There are two types of tissues found in plants, which are as follows

(i) Meristematic tissue (ii) Permanent tissue

Q.3 Write any two characteristic features of cells of meristematic tissues.

Ans. Two characteristic features of cells of meristematic tissues are as follows

(i) Cells of meristematic tissue is small and thin with large nuclei, these are cubical in shape.

(ii) Cells are tightly packed with almost no intercellular spaces and vacuoles.

Q.4 Differentiate between aerenchyma and chlorenchyma.

Ans. Differences between aerenchyma and chlorenchyma are as follows

Aerenchyma	Chlorenchyma
It is a specialised tissue with large air spaces, found in aquatic or water logged plants.	It is a type of parenchyma tissue that contains chloroplasts and is involved in photosynthesis.
It helps in the exchange of gases and provides buoyancy in aquatic plants.	It is responsible for photosynthesis due to its chloroplasts.

Q.5 What are the two types of complex permanent tissues? Explain the main function of complex permanent tissue.

Ans. The two types of complex permanent tissues are xylem and phloem.

The main function of complex permanent tissue is transportation of water and minerals.

Q.6 Write two characteristic features of epithelial tissue.

Ans. Two characteristic features of epithelial tissue are as follows

(i) It acts as a barrier by keeping different body systems separate from each other.

(ii) Cells are tightly packed, forming a continuous sheet with minimal intercellular space and cementing material.

Q.7 The table applies to four cells. Which one is a xylem vessel?

	Cell Wall	Nucleus
A.	Absent	Absent
B.	Absent	Present
C.	Present	Absent
D.	Present	Present

Ans. A is correct. The xylem vessel has no cell wall or nucleus as they are modified to conduct water and mineral salts from the roots to other parts of the plant. They are hollow tubes with no protoplasm, so that water can flow continuously through them.

Q.8 What type of tissue is blood and what are its components?

Ans. Blood is a **connective tissue**. It includes following components; **platelets**, **RBCs**, **WBC** and **blood plasma**.

Q.9 Identify the image given below and answer the following question.

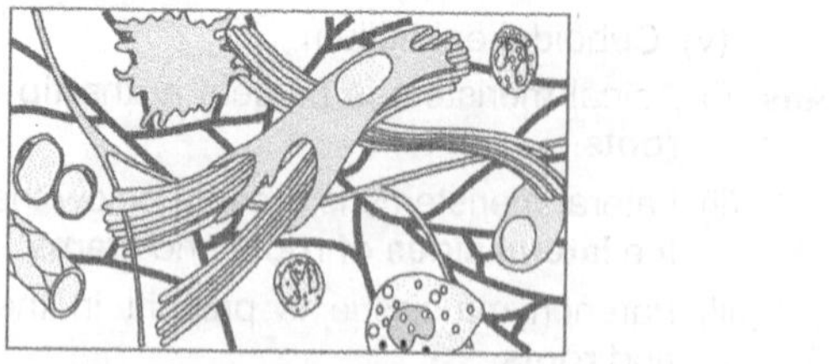

Write the function of this tissue.

Ans. The above image represents areolar tissue. It binds skin to muscles and fills spaces between organs.

Q.10 Explain the composition of lymph and its function.

Ans. Lymph is a pale-yellow fluid that contains blood plasma, white blood cells (mainly lymphocytes). The main function of lymph is as follows

Lymph helps in immune defence, transporting white blood cells to fight infections and removes waste and excess fluids from tissues.

Q.11 Explain the structure of skeletal muscles.

Ans. Skeletal muscles are made up of **long, cylindrical fibres** called **muscle fibres**. These fibres are multinucleated and have striated (striped) appearance due to the arrangement of contractile proteins.

It mostly attaches to the bones and helps in the body movement.

Q.12 Name the tissue which is found in spinal cord and name the three parts of neuron.

Ans. Nervous tissue is present in the spinal cord. Axon, cell body and dendrites are the three parts of a neuron.

Q.13 Given below *A* and *B* are animal tissues. Identify them and write one function of each.

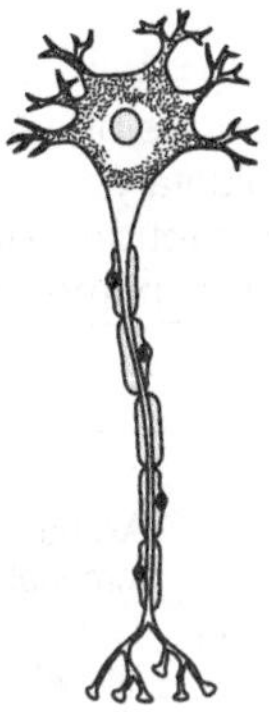

(*A*)

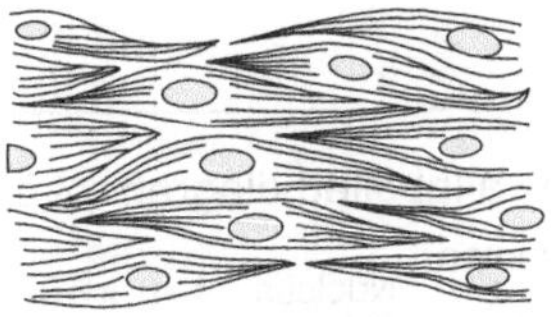

(*B*)

Ans. *A*–Neuron (Nervous tissue)

B–Unstriated muscles (Muscular tissue)

Functions

A–It receives stimulus and transmits it from one part of the body to other part of body.

B–It is responsible for movement in our body. For example, movement of food in alimentary canal.

Q.14 Animals living in colder regions and fishes of cold water have thicker layer of sub-cutaneous fat. Describe why?

Ans. Animals of colder regions and fishes of cold water have thicker layer of sub-cutaneous fat because fat acts as an insulator and prevents the loss of heat from their body during cold climatic conditions. Thus, it helps in maintaining the temperature of the body.

Q.15 We can control some of the actions of our body, but some are not in our control. Comment on this statement.

Ans. Some of the actions like moving our limbs, fingers, neck, etc., can be controlled by our will. We can move these parts of our body whenever we want to. Such actions are called voluntary actions and are performed by the voluntary muscles.

While, the other actions such as contraction and relaxation of heart, blinking of eye, etc., are not under our will. Hence, cannot stop functioning if we want to do so. These actions are called involuntary actions and are performed by involuntary muscles.

TYPE - 6 — 03 Marks

Short Answer Type Questions

Q.1 Explain all the types of meristematic tissue.

Ans. Meristematic tissue is classified into three types based on its location; apical meristem, intercalary meristem and lateral meristem.

(i) **Apical Meristem** It is found at the growing tips of stems and roots. It helps to increase the length of stems and roots.

(ii) **Intercalary Meristem** It is found at the base of leaves or internodes. Important for the longitudinal growth of plants.

(iii) **Lateral Meristem** It is found on the lateral sides of the stems and roots. It helps to increase the thickness (girth) of stems and roots.

Q.2 What is permanent tissue? Name all the types of permanent tissue and their functions.

Ans. Permanent tissue is a type of plant tissue which consist of non-dividing cells with a specific shape, size and function, formed from meristematic tissue.

They can be living or dead and are classified into simple and complex tissues. They perform the following functions

(i) Simple permanent tissue perform basic functions like **storage**, **support** and **protection** in plants.

(ii) Complex permanent tissue helps in the **transportation of water** and **mineral salts**.

Q.3 Water hyacinth floats on water surface, which tissue helps in this mechanism? Also explain the type of cells present in it.

Ans. The aerenchyma tissue helps water hyacinth to float on the water surface. This tissue contains large air spaces, which provide buoyancy and allow the plant to float.

The cells in aerenchyma are mostly parenchyma cells with large intercellular air spaces, which help in both buoyancy and the exchange of gases.

Q.4 Explain the tissue which helps in the water transportation in plants. Also explain its parts.

Ans. Xylem tissue helps in the water transportation in plants. It is a vascular and mechanical tissue (wood) with thick-walled tubular cells. It consists of four parts

(i) **Tracheids** Elongated, dead cells in plants that conduct water and minerals.

(ii) **Vessels** Cylindrical, tube-like structures in plants, forming continuous channels for efficient water conduction.

(iii) **Xylem Parenchyma** Small, thick-walled cells which helps in storing starch.

(iv) **Xylem Fibres** Non-living, thick-walled fibres providing mechanical support. All xylem elements, except parenchyma, are dead at maturity.

Q.5 **Explain the function of phloem and sieve tubes.**

Ans. Phloem is a complex tissue responsible for the transport of food (mainly sugars) from leaves to other parts of the plant. It has four components; sieve tubes, companion cells, phloem fibres and phloem parenchyma.

Sieve tubes are slender, tube-like structures made of thin-walled cells with perforated end walls (sieve plates). The nucleus degenerates at maturity. These tube helps to transports the nutrients.

Q.6 **Which tissues are known as the protective tissues of plants? Explain.**

Ans. The tissues known as protective tissue of the plants are as follows

Epidermis It forms a single cell thick outermost layer covering of various plant organs, such as leaves, flowers, stems and roots. It prevents water loss and provide protection against physical damage.

Cork or Phellem It is formed by the cork cambium in older dicot stems and roots. It is a protective, outer layer which is made up of dead cells and lack intercellular spaces. It prevents water loss and physical damage.

Q.7 **Differentiate columnar and glandular epithelium on the basis of their location and functions.**

Ans. Differences between columnar and glandular epithelium are as follows

Features	Columnar Epithelium	Glandular Epithelium
Location	Found in the lining of the stomach, intestines and respiratory tract.	Found in glands like sweat glands, salivary glands and endocrine glands.
Functions	Involved in absorption, secretion and protection.	Specialised for secretion of substances like hormones, enzymes and mucus.

Q.8 **Differentiate all three types of muscular tissues on the basis of their location and functions.**

Ans. Differences between all the three muscular tissues are as follows

Types of Muscle Tissues	Location	Functions
Skeletal Muscle	Attached to bones (e.g. arms, legs).	Responsible for voluntary movements, posture and body position.
Smooth Muscle	Found in walls of internal organs (e.g. stomach intestines, blood vessels).	Involved in involuntary movements like digestion, circulation and constriction of blood vessels.
Cardiac Muscle	Found in the heart.	Responsible for the involuntary contraction of the heart to pump blood.

Q.9 **Draw a labelled diagram of a neuron.**

Ans.

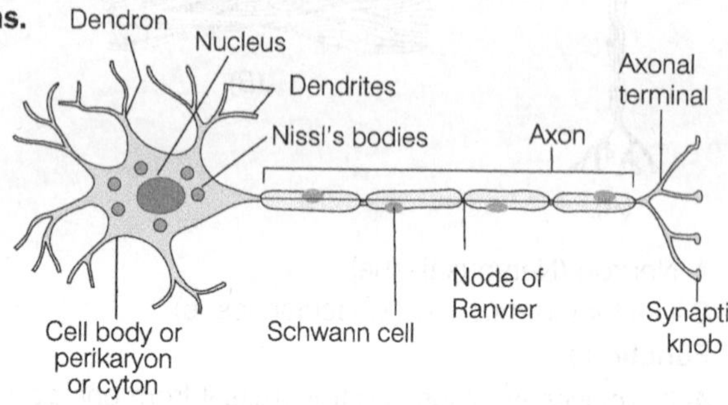

TYPE - 7

03 Marks

Structured Based Questions

Q.1 **Study the diagram given below and answer the questions that follows.**

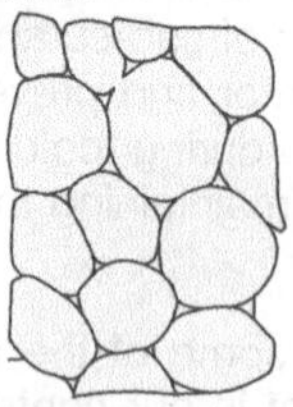

(i) Identify the given tissue.

(ii) Infer the characteristic features of these cells.

(iii) Suggest any two parts of the plant where such cells are present.

Ans. (i) The given tissue is parenchyma.

(ii) The characteristic features of parenchymatous cells are

They consists of thin-walled unspecialised cells which are loosely packed, e.g. having simple intercellular spaces. Each cell has a prominent nucleus.

(iii) Parenchymatous cells are found in

(a) Root (b) Stem

2. **Observe the diagram and answer the following questions.**

(i) **Name the muscles which helps in locomotion.**

(ii) **Explain the structure of these muscles.**

(iii) **Name the organs in which these muscles are present.**

Ans. (i) Skeletal muscles help in locomotion.

(ii) These muscles are long, cylindrical, multinucleated cells with striations (stripes), allowing the voluntary movement.

(iii) Skeletal muscles are present in limbs, legs and other body parts attached to bones.

3. **Observe the following figure and answer the following questions.**

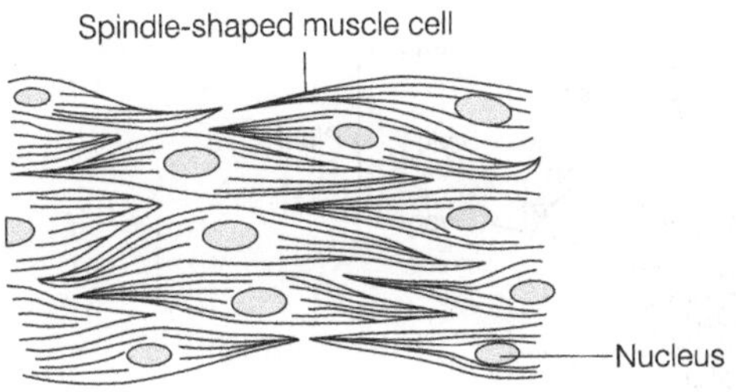

(i) **What is shown in figure?**

(ii) **What is the function of this tissue?**

(iii) **Name some organs where this tissue is located.**

Ans. (i) The figure shows smooth muscle cells.

(ii) Smooth muscle tissue facilitates the movements in involuntary organs.

(iii) Smooth muscles are found in alimentary canal, lining of blood vessel, bronchi of lungs, etc.

4. **Study the diagram given below and answer the questions that follows.**

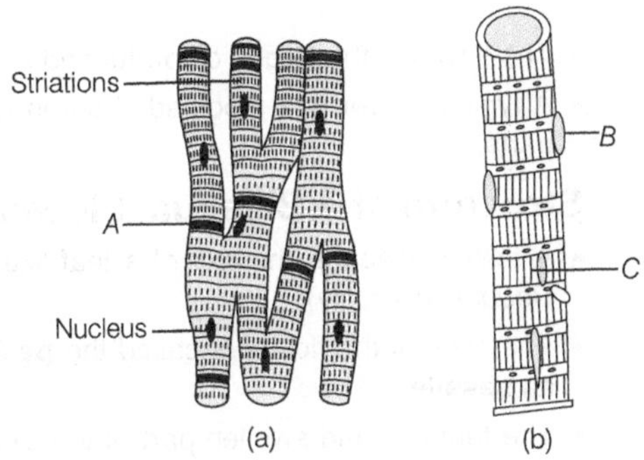

(i) **Label the parts *A*, *B* and *C*.**

(ii) **Which one of them acts as impulse booster?**

(iii) **Give the location of (a) and (b).**

Ans. (i) The parts *A*, *B* and *C* are labelled as

A-Intercalated disc; *B*-Nucleus; *C*-Striation

(ii) Intercalated disc acts as an impulse booster.

(iii) Cardiac muscle (a) are found in heart and skeletal muscles (b) are found in limbs.

THE FLOWER

- The flower is the bright, colourful and attractive reproductive part of the angiosperms.
- A typical flower is a modified shoot in which internodes are highly condensed and leaves are modified into floral parts.

Structure of a Bisexual Flower

- A flower arises in the axil of a leaf-like structure called a **bract**, that may be green or differently coloured (e.g. *Bougainvillea*, lily).
- The stalk of the flower is called the **pedicel** and provides support to the flower. A flower without a stalk is known as **sessile**.
- The terminal and swollen part of the axis of the flower is called the **receptacle** or **thalamus** where all floral parts are attached. It provides support to the flower's structures.

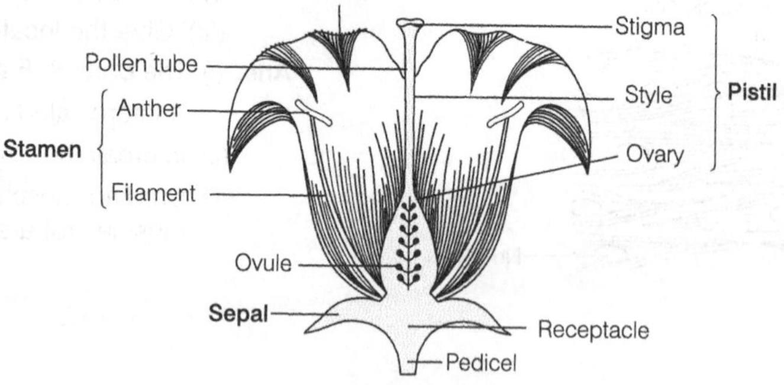

Structure of a flower

Parts of a Flower

- A typical flower consists of four distinct parts (whorls), i.e. the **calyx**, the **corolla**, the **androecium** and the **gynoecium.**
- Out of these, the calyx and corolla are considered as **non-essential** (non-reproductive) **parts**, whereas the androecium and gynoecium are considered as **essential** (reproductive) **parts** because they take part in the process of reproduction.

1. Calyx

- It is the outermost whorl of a flower. It is made up of units called **sepals** (usually 5 in number).
- The sepals are generally green, leaf-like structure which protect the flower in the budding stage.
- These sepals can be fused with each other thus called **gamosepalous** (e.g. marigold, China rose, tulip, sunflower and *Petunia*) or may be free from each other and are called **polysepalous** (e.g. *Brassica*).

2. Corolla

- It is second whorl of the flower. Corolla is composed of **petals** which are coloured and leaf-like structures.
- The colourful and fragrant petals attract insects for pollination and also protect stamens and pistils.

- The petals are generally arranged in a single whorl, but sometimes they may be a double whorl (e.g. poppy) or they may be arranged spirally (e.g. water lily).
- Just like calyx, corolla may also be **gamopetalous** (petals united, e.g. *Petunia*) or **polypetalous** (petals free, e.g. *Hibiscus*).

3. Androecium

- The third whorl of a flower is composed of **stamens**.
- Each stamen represents the **male reproductive organ** and consists of a **stalk**, i.e. **filament** and an **anther**.
- The anther is usually bilobed (*bi*-two, *lobes*-chamber) structure.
- Each lobe of anther has two chambers, called as **pollen sacs**. The pollen grains are produced in pollen sacs.
- The filaments attached to anthers help in making it more accessible for pollination.

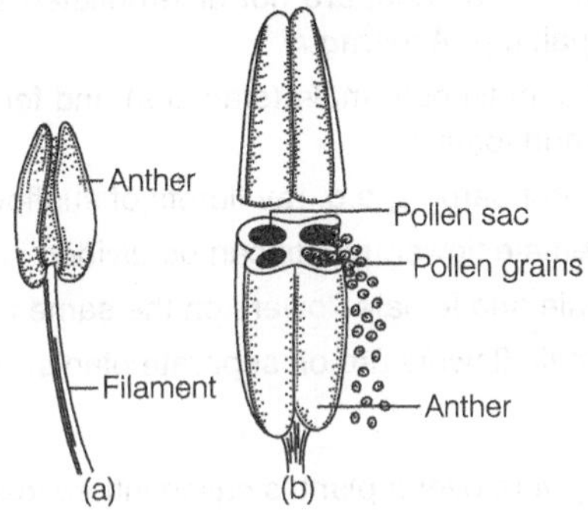

(a) A typical stamen, (b) Anther showing pollen grains

- On the basis of the arrangement of stamens, flowers can be of following types
  - **Polyandrous** All stamens are free from each other. Their filaments may be of same or different sizes, e.g. *Petunia*.
  - **Monadelphous** Only anthers are free, but their filaments are united to form one group, e.g. China rose (shoe flower), cotton.
  - **Diadelphous** The filaments of stamens are united in two bundles, but their anthers are free, e.g. pea, *Sesbania*, etc.
  - **Polyadelphous** The filaments of the androecium unite to form several groups, e.g. *Bombax,* etc.

4. Gynoecium

- Pistil or gynoecium is the fourth whorl, which constitutes **female reproductive part** of the flower.
- It is made up of one or more **carpels** (single female unit). A carpel consists of three parts, i.e. stigma, style and ovary.
- The **stigma** is usually present at the tip of style and is the receptive surface for pollen grains.
- **Style** is a slender stalk that bridges ovary to stigma.
- **Ovary** is the enlarged basal part of gynoecium.
- Each ovary bears one or more ovules attached to a flattened, cushion-like **placenta**.
- When gynoecium contains one carpel, it is **monocarpellary**, if it contains two carpels, then it is **bicarpellary** and if more than two carpels, then it is **polycarpellary**.
- If the carpels are free, the gynoecium is called **apocarpous** and if the carpels are united, it is called **syncarpous**.
- Ovary having single chamber is called **unilocular** and that having many chambers is called **multilocular**.
- The embryo sac is located within the ovule, which is found inside the ovary of a flower.

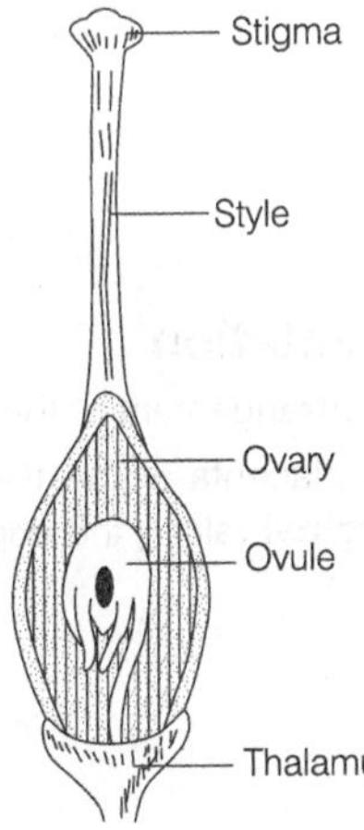

Gynoecium (Single carpel)

Types of a Flower

1. On the basis of the whorls, flowers are of two types

- **Complete Flower** A flower that has all four floral whorls is called complete flower, e.g. rose, *Petunia, Hibiscus.*
- **Incomplete Flower** A flower that lacks one or more of these whorls is called incomplete flower, e.g. *Begonia*, orchid.

2. Flowers are also classified into following types based on the presence of male or female reproductive parts

- **Unisexual flowers** contain only one sex (either male or female).
  - **Staminate Flowers** Male flowers that have only stamens (no carpels), e.g. cucumber.
  - **Pistillate Flowers** Female flowers that have only carpels (no stamens), e.g. mulberry.
  - **Perianth Flowers** If in a flower petal and sepal are not differentiated such a structure is called **perianth**, the individual perianth lobe is called tepal, e.g. *Asparagus.*
- **Bisexual** (or hermaphrodite) **flowers** contain both male (stamens) and female (carpels) reproductive organs, e.g. mustard, *Petunia, Hibiscus,* rose, lily and tomato.
- **Neuter flowers** have neither stamens nor carpels, e.g. ray florets of sunflower.

3. Based on the presence of male and female flower, plants can be divided into two types

- **Monoecious** Plants that have both male and female flowers on the same plant, e.g. maize, cucumber.
- **Dioecious** Plants where male and female flowers are on separate plants, e.g. papaya, palm.

Inflorescence

- The arrangement and distribution of flowers over a plant is called inflorescence.
- The inflorescence can be of following types
  - **Racemose Inflorescence** Flowers are borne on main axis that continues to grow with the older flowers at the base and younger ones at the top (acropetal pattern), e.g. mustard, radish, *Sesbania, Trifolium.*
  - **Cymose Inflorescence** The main axis grows limited and the flowers are borne in a pattern where the terminal flower blooms first with lateral branches growing to form new flowers (basipetal pattern), e.g. *Solanum, Begonia*, teak.

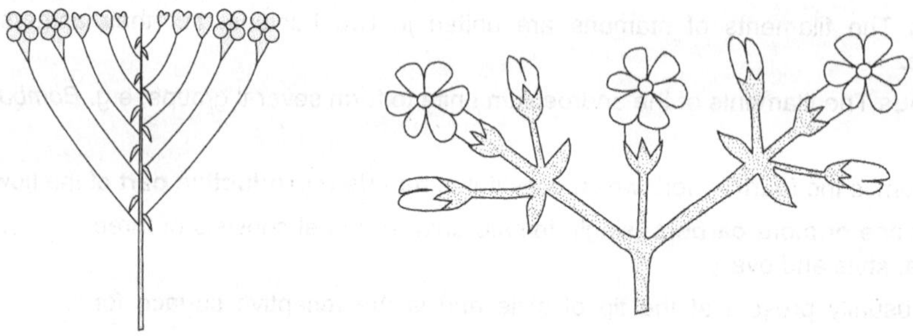

Racemose inflorescence   Cymose inflorescence

Placentation

- The arrangement of the ovule inside the ovary through the placenta is called placentation.
- The placenta is the tissue that connects the ovules to the ovary wall and the arrangement can vary, such as **marginal** (along the edge), **axial** (along the central axis) or **parietal** (on the ovary wall).

EXAM ORIENTED QUESTIONS

TYPE - 1 01 Mark

Multiple Choice Questions

Q.1 The four whorls or appendages of a flower are attached to which of the following structure?

(a) Petals (b) Receptacle

(c) Placenta (d) Style

Ans. (b)

Q.2 Choose the incorrect statement about a flower.

(a) A flower has four whorls arranged successively i.e. calyx, corolla, androecium and gynoecium

(b) Members of calyx and corolla are called sepals and petals, respectively

(c) In polysepalous, the sepals are arranged in a free manner, whereas in gamosepalous, the sepals are united

(d) Tulip is an example of polysepalous

Ans. (d) Tulip is an example of gamosepalous.

Q.3 Parts of a flower that attracts insects for pollination is/are

(a) petals and sepals (b) anther and stigma

(c) petals only (d) sepals only

Ans. (c) Petals are the part of flower that attracts insects for pollination. The petals are responsible for providing unique shape, colour, fragrance to the flower to attract pollinators.

Q.4 The calyx and corolla are considered as .....*P*..... , whereas the androecium and gynoecium are considered as ......*Q*...... .

(a) *P* - essential part, *Q* - non-essential part

(b) *P* - essential part, *Q* - reproductive part

(c) *P* - non-essential part, *Q* - essential part

(d) *P* - reproductive part, *Q* - non-reproductive part

Ans. (c)

Q.5 Which of these is essential part of the flower?

(a) Anther (b) Calyx

(c) Petal (d) Sepal

Ans. (a)

Q.6 Which flower structure produces pollen?

(a) Anther (b) Carpel

(c) Petal (d) Stigma

Ans. (a) The anther cells in the pollen sacs undergoes meiosis to produce pollen grains that contains the male gametes.

Q.7 Which of the following flower(s) is/are staminate flower?

(i) Cucumber

(ii) Ray floret of sunflower

(iii) Rose

(iv) Poppy

(a) Only (iii) (b) Only (ii)

(c) Both (i) and (ii) (d) Only (i)

Ans. (c)

Q.8 Ankita tried to match the different types of stamen according to the number of groups in which they are present. She tabulated the pairs as follows.

Stamens	No. of Groups
P	Stamens are united in one group.
Q	Stamens are united in two or more groups.

Identify the correct pair.

(a) *P*- Monadelphous, *Q*- Polyadelphous

(b) *P*- Polyadelphous, *Q*- Diadelphous

(c) *P*- Diadelphous, *Q*- Monadelphous

(d) *P*- Polyadelphous, *Q*- Monadelphous

Ans. (a)

Q.9 The diagram shows Longitudinal Section (LS) of a flower.

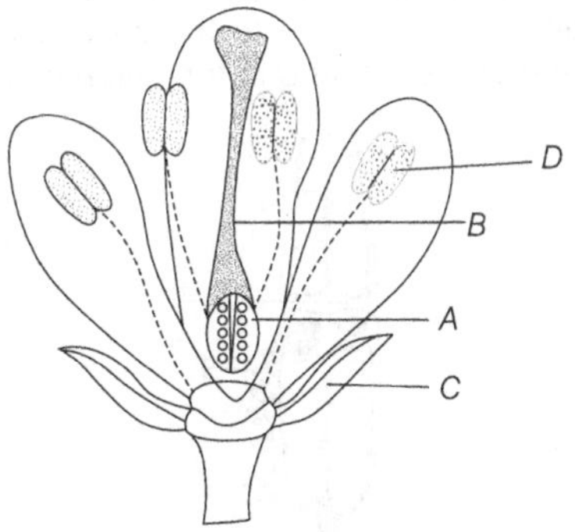

Inside which parts gametes are produced?

(a) *A* and *B* (b) *A* and *D*

(c) *B* and *C* (d) *B* and *D*

Ans. (b) The ovary (*A*) and the anther (*D*), respectively are the structure where gametes are produced.

Q.10 In a laboratory session, Ms. Malhotra instructs her students to study different types of inflorescence. She presents a diagram showing a flower cluster with the terminal flower blooming first, followed by the lateral ones.

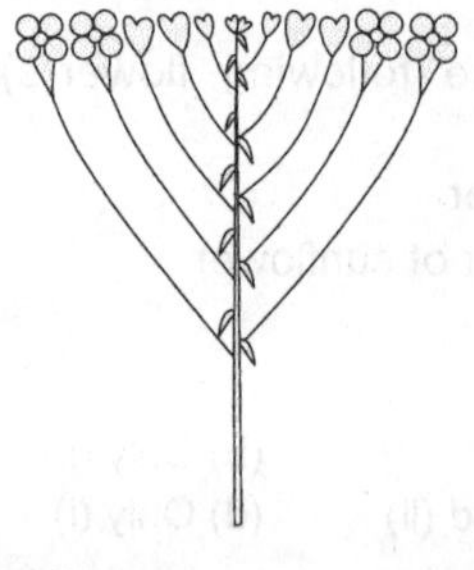

Based on the diagram and characteristics observed, identify the type of inflorescence depicted.

(a) Cymose inflorescence (b) Racemose inflorescence
(c) Capitulum (d) Spike

Ans. (b)

11. Biology teacher while teaching the structure of flower asked students about the type of flower.

Raja said : Staminate flowers are male flowers that have only stamens.

Veena said : Neuter flowers have both stamens and carpels.

Anirudh said : Pistillate flowers are female flowers that have only carpels.

Asha said : Bisexual flowers have neither stamens nor carpels.

Who were correct?

(a) Raja and Veena (b) Veena and Anirudh
(c) Veena and Asha (d) Raja and Anirudh

Ans. (d)

12. During a practical exam, an image of a cross-section of an anther was shown to the students. Identify the parts marked as *A* and *B* in the given image.

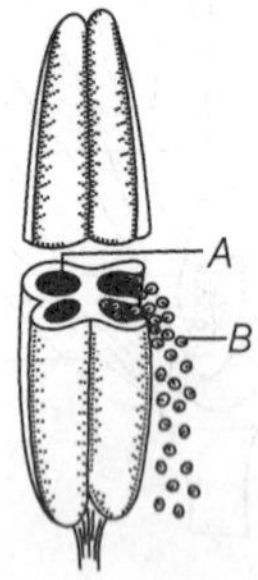

	A	*B*
(a)	Filament	Anther
(b)	Pollen sac	Pollen grain
(c)	Filament	Pollen sac
(d)	Pollen sac	Anther

Ans. (b)

13. Which among the following is incorrect about racemose and cymose?

(a) In racemose inflorescence, the youngest flower remains at the top of the floral axis.

(b) In cymose inflorescence, the floral main axis remains at the top of the floral axis.

(c) In racemose inflorescence, indefinite number of flowers are formed.

(d) In cymose inflorescence, the axillary branches have limited growth and terminate in a flower.

Ans. (b) In racemose inflorescence, the youngest flower remains at the top of the floral axis and indefinite number of flowers are formed. In cymose inflorescence, the floral main axis is limited.

14. The placenta is the tissue that connects the ovules to the ovary wall and the arrangement can vary such as ...*P*... along the edge and ...*Q*... along the central axis and ...*R*... on the ovary wall.

	P	*Q*	*R*
(a)	parietal	axial	marginal
(b)	marginal	parietal	axial
(c)	marginal	axial	parietal
(d)	axial	parietal	marginal

Ans. (c)

TYPE - 2 01 Mark

Matching Type Questions

1. The diagram of a flower is given below. Choose the correct match for parts *A* to *E*.

Floral Parts	Functions
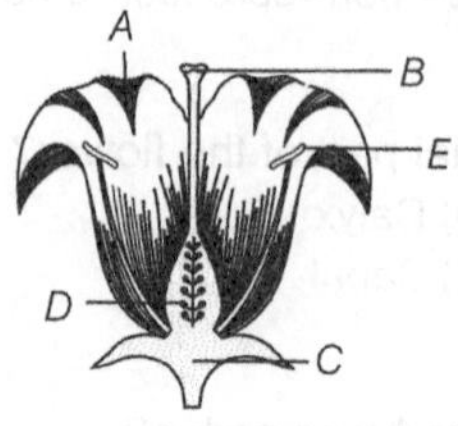	I. Produces pollen. II. Develops into a seed after fertilisation. III. Attracts pollinators to the flower. IV. The part of the flower stalk where floral organs are attached. V. Receives pollen during pollination.

Ans. A-III, B-V, C–IV, D-II, E-I

Q.2 Match the following columns.

Column I	Column II
A. Monadelphous	I. Pollens
B. Fused sepals	II. Present inside ovary
C. Ovules	III. Marigold
D. Stamen	IV. Shoe flower

Ans. A–IV, B–III, C–II, D–I

TYPE - 3 01 Mark

Assertion-Reason Type Questions

Direction (Q. Nos. 1-5) In the following questions statements are given as Assertion (A) and Reason (R).

(a) A is true, but R is false.
(b) A is false, but R is true.
(c) Both A and R are true.
(d) Both A and R are false.

Q.1 Assertion (A) The androecium, being the male reproductive whorl of a flower, significantly influences the reproductive success of angiosperms.

Reason (R) The stamens within the androecium generate microspores (pollen grains).

Ans. (c)

Q.2 Assertion (A) The stigma of gynoecium is usually present at the tip of style.

Reason (R) It is the receptive surface of pollen grains.

Ans. (c)

Q.3 Assertion (A) In racemose inflorescence, the main axis continues to grow indefinitely.

Reason (R) In this type of inflorescence, flowers are borne in a basipetal order.

Ans. (a) A is true, but R is false. R can be corrected as In racemose inflorescence flowers are borne in a acropetal order.

Q.4 Assertion (A) The sepals are usually green in colour

Reason (R) The sepals helps to protect flower in the budding stage

Ans. (c)

Q.5 Assertion (A) A flower with all four whorls is a complete flower.

Reason (R) Female flowers that have only carpels is called Nerter flowers

Ans. (a)

TYPE - 4 01 Mark

Very Short Answer Type Questions

Q.1 Name the structure of the flower which is responsible for the protection of a flower bud.

Ans. Sepal

Q.2 In which flower the sepals are fused with each other?

Ans. China rose and sunflower.

Q.3 Give one example of a flower in which the petals are united (Gamopetalous).

Ans. *Petunia.*

Q.4 What are the two primary components of stamen?

Ans. Anther and filament.

Q.5 Name the type of androecium which is found in *Bombax*.

Ans. Polyadelphous

Q.6 *X* is the part of the flower which is responsible for the formation of an ovule. Identify the part *X*.

Ans. Ovary

Q.7 Identify the term which is used for the arrangement of flower on the axis of the plant.

Ans. Inflorescence

Q.8 In the flower *X* the axis is laterally flattened and making a disc like inflorescence. Identify the flower.

Ans. Sunflower

Q.9 Identify the inflorescence in which older flowers are found at the base, whereas the new flowers present at the apex.

Ans. Racemose

Q.10 Name the cushion-like structure present in an ovary.

Ans. Placenta

Q.11 Given alongside is the diagram of an anther. Observe the given diagram carefully and fill the blank spaces.

(1 Mark each)

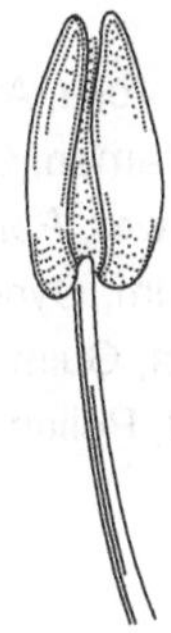

The third whorl of a flower is composed of .....(i)..... . It represents the male reproductive organ and consists of a .....(ii) ..... and an .....(iii)..... . Each anther is usually .....(iv)..... . Each lobe has two chambers, called as .....(v)..... . Pollen grains are of different shapes and sizes.

Ans. (i) stamens (ii) filament
(iii) anther (iv) bilobed
(v) pollen sacs

Q.12 Name the following. **(1 Mark each)**

(i) A specialised shoot having leaves modified into floral structures.

(ii) The two parts of a flower which play a key role in reproduction.

(iii) The gynoecium of a flower in which carpels are free.

Ans. (i) Flower (ii) Androecium and gynoecium
(iii) Apocarpous

Q.13 Correct and rewrite the following statements by changing the underlined words. **(1 Mark each)**

(i) The essential whorls of a flower play a vital role in transportation.

(ii) *Hibiscus* shows diadelphous condition.

(iii) The pistil is made up of units called rachis.

(iv) A flower lacking one or more sets of floral whorls is a complete flower.

(v) Ray florets of sunflower is an example of staminate flower.

Ans. (i) The essential whorls of a flower, i.e. androecium and gynoecium play a vital role in reproduction.

(ii) *Hibiscus* or China rose represents monadelphous condition.

(iii) The pistil is made up of units called carpels.

(iv) A flower lacking one or more sets of floral whorls is an incomplete flower.

(v) Ray florets of sunflower is an example of a neuter flower.

Q.14 Choose the odd one out from the following terms given below and name the category to which other three belong. **(1 Mark each)**

(i) Petals, Calyx, Corolla, Androecium

(ii) Style, Stigma, Stamen, Ovary

(iii) Marigold, Sunflower, *Petunia, Brassica*

(iv) Calyx, Androecium, Gynoecium, Thalamus

(v) Coconut, Papaya, Gulmohar, Maize

(vi) Anther, Filament, Pollen grain, Stigma, Pollen sac

Ans. (i) The odd term is androecium, while rest three are not essential whorls of the flower.

(ii) The odd term is stamen, while rest three are the parts of carpel.

(iii) The odd term is *Brassica* (polysepalous), while rest three exhibit gamosepalous condition where sepals are fused with each other.

(iv) The odd term is thalamus, while rest three are distinct whorls of a flower.

(v) The odd term is gulmohar, while rest three are examples of unisexual flower.

(vi) Stigma is the part of gynoecium, while the other are part of androecium of a flower.

Q.15 Differentiate between the following pairs on the basis of what is mentioned in brackets. **(1 Mark each)**

(i) Calyx and Corolla (function)

(ii) Gamopetalous and Polypetalous (condition of petals)

(iii) Style and Filament (function)

(iv) Apocarpous and Syncarpous (condition of carpel)

Ans. (i)

Calyx	Corolla
It protects the inner parts of a flower during the bud stage.	It attracts insects for pollination.

(ii)

Gamopetalous	Polypetalous
Petals are fused fully or partially.	Petals are free from each other.

(iii)

Style	Filament
It is a part of carpel that holds stigma and the pollen tube passes through it to reach ovule.	It is a part of androecium that holds anther.

(iv)

Apocarpous	Syncarpous
More than one carpel or all of them are free from each other.	More than one carpel or all of them are fused with each other.

TYPE - 5

02 Marks

Short Answer Type Questions

Q.1 Mention the types of sepals and petals found in *Petunia*.

Ans. In *Petunia*, the sepals are gamosepalous and petals are gamopetalous.

Q.2 Explain the terms gamopetalous and polypetalous.

Ans. **Gamopetalous** Petals are fused together to form a tube-like structure (e.g. morning glory).

Polypetalous Petals are separate and not fused (e.g. buttercup).

Q.3 Mention the exact location of the following.

(i) Pollen grains (ii) Calyx

Ans. (i) Pollen grains are found inside the pollen sacs in the anther of a flower.

(ii) Calyx is the first whorl of a flower whose individual unit is called sepal.

TYPE - 6

03 Marks

Short Answer Type Questions

Q.1 Write a short note on the types of flower on the basis of presence or absence of reproductive part.

Ans. There are two types of flower on the basis of presence and absence of reproductive part.

Complete (Hermaphroditic) **Flowers** These flowers contain both male (stamens) and female (pistils) reproductive organs, e.g. rose, lily.

Incomplete Flowers These flowers have either male or female reproductive organs, not both. They are of two types

- **Staminate** Male flowers with only stamens, e.g. pumpkin.
- **Pistillate** Female flowers with only pistils, e.g. cucumber.

Q.2 Give a detailed account of gynoecium.

Ans. The gynoecium is the female reproductive part of a flower, composed of one or more carpels. Each carpel consists of three parts

(i) **Stigma** The sticky, receptive surface where pollen grains land during pollination.

(ii) **Style** The slender stalk that connects the stigma to the ovary, facilitating the movement of pollen tubes.

(iii) **Ovary** The basal swollen part that contains ovules, which develop into seeds after fertilisation.

Q.3 Draw the diagram of a typical stamen.

Ans.

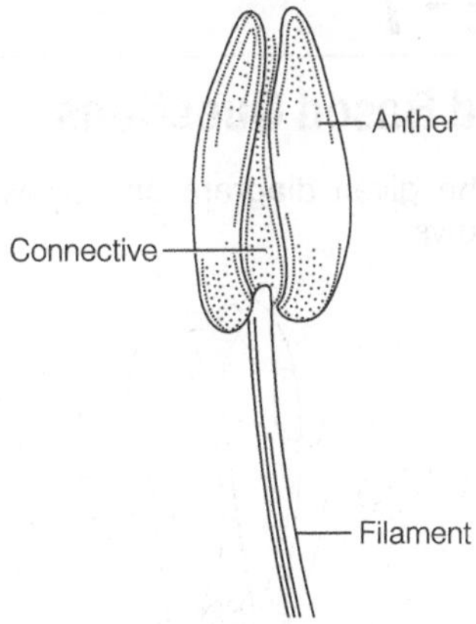

A typical stamen

Q.4 How are flowers classified based on the carpels of ovary?

Ans. Flowers are classified into following categories based on the carpels of the ovary into

(i) **Monocarpellary** Flowers with a single carpel, e.g. pea.

(ii) **Multicarpellary** Flowers with multiple carpels, which can be

- **Syncarpous** Carpels are fused (e.g. tomato).
- **Apocarpous** Carpels are free (e.g. lotus).

Q.5 Where are the following structures located and what are their functions?

(i) Ovule

(ii) Anther

(iii) Receptacle

Ans. (i) **Ovule** It is found inside the ovary of the flower.

Function The ovule is the structure that develops into a seed after fertilisation.

(ii) **Anther** It is located at the tip of the stamen, the male reproductive organ of the flower.

Function The anther produces and releases pollen grains, which contain male gametes (sperm cells) essential for fertilisation in plants.

(iii) **Receptacle** It is the thickened part of the stem where the floral organs (sepals, petals, stamens and pistils) are attached.

Function It supports and holds the flower in place, providing a base for the attachment of the other floral parts.

TYPE - 7

03 Marks

Structured Based Questions

Q.1 **Study the given diagram and answer the questions that follows.**

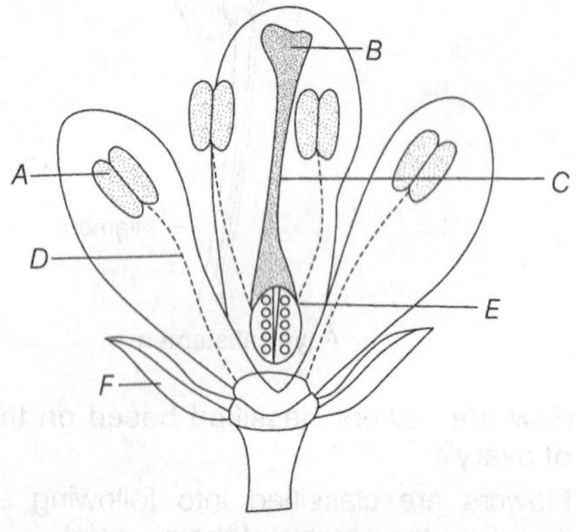

(i) **Name the parts marked as *A-F*.**

(ii) **State giving reason whether the above shown flower is bisexual or unisexual.**

(iii) **Which part produces pollen grains?**

Ans. (i) The parts marked as *A–F* are

A-Anther

B-Stigma

C-Style

D-Filament

E-Ovary

F-Calyx

(ii) The shown flower is bisexual, since both androecium and gynoecium are present in it.

(iii) Part *A* (Anther) produces pollen grains.

Q.2 **In the given diagram, a flower is being pollinated by a bee. Observe the diagram carefully and answer the following questions.**

(i) **Which part of a flower is responsible to attract the bee?**

(ii) **Name the essential whorl of the flower.**

(iii) **Which part is responsible for the formation of pollens?**

Ans. (i) Petals are responsible for attracting the bee.

(ii) Androecium and gynoecium are essential whorl of the flower.

(iii) Stamen is responsible for the formation of pollens.

Q.3 **Study the given diagram and answer the questions that follows.**

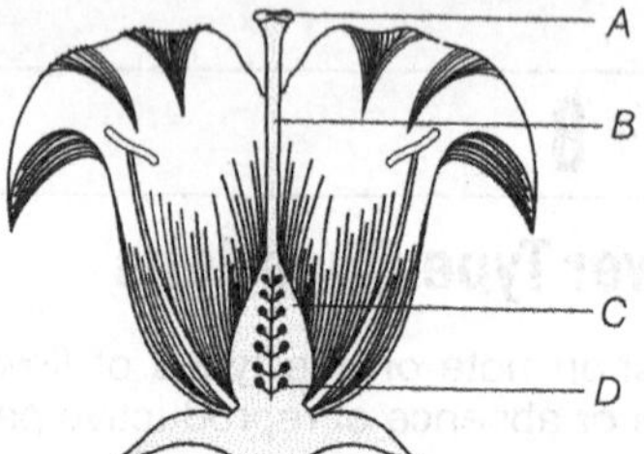

(i) **What do parts labelled as *A*, *B* and *C* constitue?**

(ii) **Name the part labelled as *D*.**

(iii) **State any one characteristic feature of the flower shown above.**

Ans. (i) The parts labelled as *A* (Stigma) and *B* (Style) and *C* (Ovary) constitute the carpel.

(ii) The part labelled as *D* is ovule.

(iii) The given flower is bisexual as it contains both stamens and carpels.

04

POLLINATION AND FERTILISATION

Pollination

- The process of transfer of pollen grains from the anther of the stamen to the stigma of the same flower or different flower is termed as **pollination**.
- Pollen grains contain the **male gametes** and ovary contains the **female gamete**.
- There are two types of pollination that occurs in plant, i.e. self-pollination and cross-pollination.

Self-pollination

- When the pollen from the anther of a flower is transferred to the stigma of the same flower or to the stigma of another flower of the same plant, it is known as self-pollination.
- Generally, it is not dependent on any external agency for pollination.
- Self-pollination can be of the following two types
  - **Autogamy** It involves the transfer of pollen grains from anther to the stigma of same flower, e.g. wheat, rice, etc.
  - **Geitonogamy** It involves the transfer of pollen grains from the anther of a flower to the stigma of another flower of the same plant, e.g. *Cucurbita*.

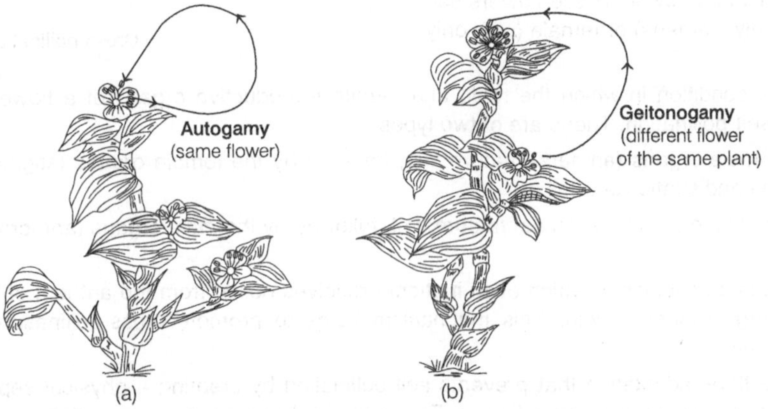

Self-pollination

Adaptations for Self-pollination

Plants require some adaptations to fulfil the needs for self-pollination, which are as follows

- **Bisexuality** In plants where a flower has both male and female parts, such flowers can be pollinated by self-pollination. Self-pollination can also occur in plants that have separate male and female flowers, but both types are on the same plant.
- **Homogamy** When male and female reproductive parts, i.e. the anther and stigma, mature at the same time in a flower, e.g. *Mirabilis*.
- **Cleistogamy** It occurs in flowers that remain closed, preventing cross-pollination and ensuring self-pollination (i.e. the pollen fertilises the same flower), e.g. pea.

Advantages of Self-pollination

- It ensures that pollination takes place when both male and female reproductive parts mature at the same time.
- Parental characters are preserved indefinitely.
- Production of nectar and scent by flowers is not required.
- There is no wastage of pollen grains. Small number of pollens will ensure pollination.

Disadvantages of Self-pollination

- Repeated self-pollination can make the plant weaker over time.
- The weaker or defective characters are inherited and cannot be eliminated.
- Production of new varieties and species of plants are not possible because the same genetic traits are passed on to the next or upcoming generations.

Cross-pollination or Allogamy

- It involves the transfer of pollen grains from the anther of one plant to the stigma of different flower of the another plant.
- This is the only type of pollination which brings genetically different types of pollen grains to the stigma of same species, e.g. papaya, maize, etc.
- Cross-pollination or allogamy takes place in unisexual as well as in bisexual (monoecious) flowers.

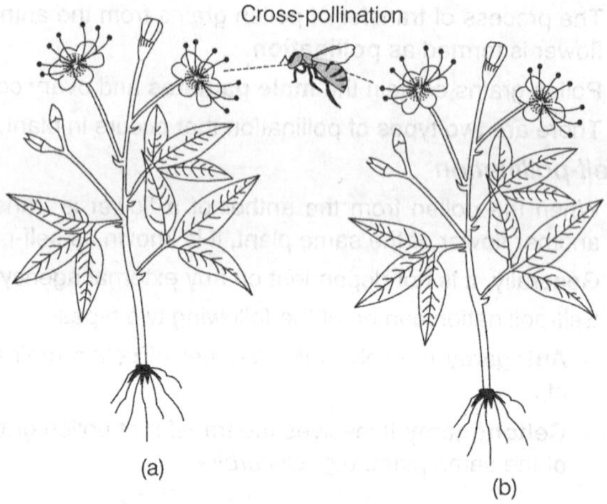

Cross-pollination

Adaptations for Cross-pollination

Nature favours cross-pollination and plants exhibit various adaptation, which are as follows

- **Unisexuality** Presence of either male or female reproductive organs, in a flower. These flowers can either male (with only stamens) or female (with only pistils).
- **Dichogamy** It is a condition in which the male and female reproductive organs of a flower mature at different times, preventing self-pollination. These are of two types
  - **Protandry** The male organs (anthers) mature first, followed by the female organs (stigmas), e.g. *Salvia*, lady finger, sweet pea and sunflower.
  - **Protogyny** The female organs (stigmas) mature first, followed by the male organs (anthers), e.g. custard apple, peepal.
- **Self-sterility** This is a condition in which even if stigma receives pollen from the anthers of the same flower, the pollen fail to undergo further growth. This mechanism helps to promote cross-pollination, e.g. ray florets of sunflower, orchids, etc.
- **Herkogamy** It is a floral adaptation that prevents self-pollination by creating a physical separation between the stamen and the stigma within the same flower. For example, hood covering the stigma acts as a mechanical barriers in flower of pansy, *Iris*, etc.
- **Heterostyly** It is a condition where a plant species has flowers with different lengths of styles and stamens, promoting cross-pollination by encouraging pollen transfer between flowers with complementary structures, e.g. primrose, *Oxalis*.

Advantages of Cross-pollination

- Stronger and healthier offspring are produced.
- Production of a large number of viable seeds.
- New varieties with useful characters are produced.
- Plants produced from cross-pollinated flowers are more resistant to diseases and other unfavourable conditions.

Disadvantages of Cross-pollination

- It does not ensure fertilisation because the pollen that lands on the stigma may not be viable or functional.
- Cross-pollinating plants waste a large amount of energy in the formation of large number of pollen grains, production of scent or odour and showy, bright-coloured petals.
- It involves different external agencies, if somehow these agencies are absent then, there are negligible chances of pollination.

Agents of Cross-pollination

- In cross-pollination pollen grains are transferred from the anther of one flower to the stigma of another flower by the help of **abiotic agents** such as wind, water and **biotic agents** such as insects and birds.
- The adaptive features of flowering plants along with their agent of pollination are discussed below

1. Wind Pollination or Anemophily

It takes place through the wind. The flowers that are pollinated by wind shows the following characteristics

- Flowers are small, colourless and nectarless.
- The anthers are well-exposed for the easy dispersal of pollen grains.
- Pollen grains are small, light, dry, dusty, non-sticky and sometimes even winged.
- Pollen grains are produced in large numbers.
- The stigmas are large, hairy and feathery or branched to catch the air-borne pollen grains.
- Common examples of wind pollinated flowers are grasses, sugarcane, bamboo, coconut, maize, pine, etc.

2. Water Pollination or Hydrophily

It is seen in aquatic plants. The flowers that are pollinated by water show the following characteristics

- Flowers are small, colourless, inconspicuous, odourless and nectar less.
- The stigmas are long and sticky, e.g. *Vallisneria, Hydrilla* and *Zostera.*
- The pollen grains have the same specific gravity as that of water, so that they can float on water.
- Pollen grains are produced in large quantity and have mucilaginous covering.
- In some cases, the male flowers detach and float on water till they meet the female flowers, e.g. *Vallisneria.*

3. Insect Pollination or Entomophily

It takes place through insects. The flowers that are pollinated by insects show the following characteristics

- In the case of small flower a large number of flowers are clustered into an inflorescence to make them conspicuous, e.g. *Dahlia.*
- Flowers are large, colourful, fragrant and rich in nectar to attract insects, e.g. *Salvia.*
- The surface of both the pollen grains and the stigma is sticky, e.g. China rose, lotus, roses, etc.

4. Bird Pollination or Ornithophily

The flowers that are pollinated by birds show following characteristics

- Flowers are coloured, produce plenty of nectar.
- Flowers are scentless as birds lack a good sense of smell.
- Example of bird pollinated flowers are *Bignonia, Canna.*

5. Elephophily

It refers to pollination facilitated by elephants, as seen in *Rafflesia.*

6. Chiropterophily

It is pollination by bats, found in plants like *Bauhina.*

Artificial Pollination

Humans practice **artificial pollination**, where desired pollen is transferred manually to produce new plant varieties. It is practiced in crop improvement programmes. For this the anthers from a flower bud are removed **(emasculation)** and then covered with bag **(bagging)** to prevent the stigma from getting the pollen from other flowers.

Fertilisation

- A successful pollination is followed by fertilisation in plants. It is the fusion of male and female gametes resulting in the formation of a **zygote**.
- In flowering plants, the pollen grain carries the male gamete, while the female gamete is present in the ovule inside the ovary.

Structure of Pollen Grain

- It is a cell enclosed by double layer, i.e. an outer layer called the **exine** and an inner layer called the **intine**.
- The exine at certain places has pores called **germ pores** through which pollen tube germinates.
- A mature pollen grain contains two cells, i.e. **vegetative cell** (bigger), which contains food reserves and **generative cell** (small), which floats on the cytoplasm of the vegetative cell.

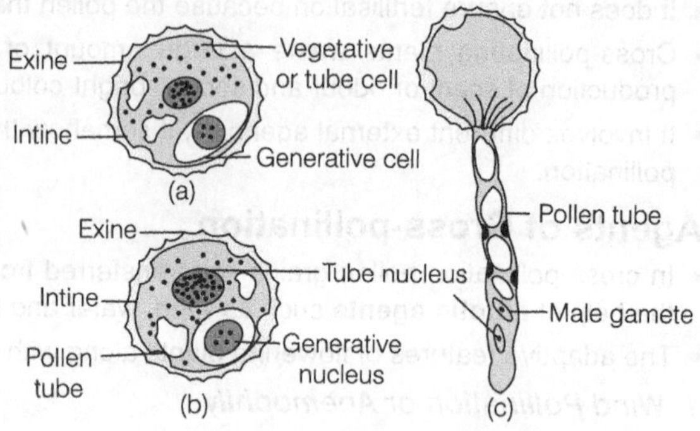

(a-b) Mature pollen grain, (c) Pollen germination

Structure of an Ovule

It is a small structure present in the ovary. It has following characteristic features

- It is attached to the placenta by a stalk called **funicle**.
- Each ovule has one or two protective envelopes called **integuments**.
- **Micropyle** is an opening present at the tip, where integument is absent. Pollen tube enters through micropyle.
- The integuments enclose a mass of cells called the **nucellus**, which have food reserves.
- **Embryo sac** or **female gametophyte** is located in the nucellus.The embryo sac contains the following structures
  - A female gamete called **egg cell**.
  - One large central cell that contains two **polar nuclei**, which fuse to form the secondary nucleus in the centre.
  - Two **synergids** and three **antipodal cells** (7 celled ovule).

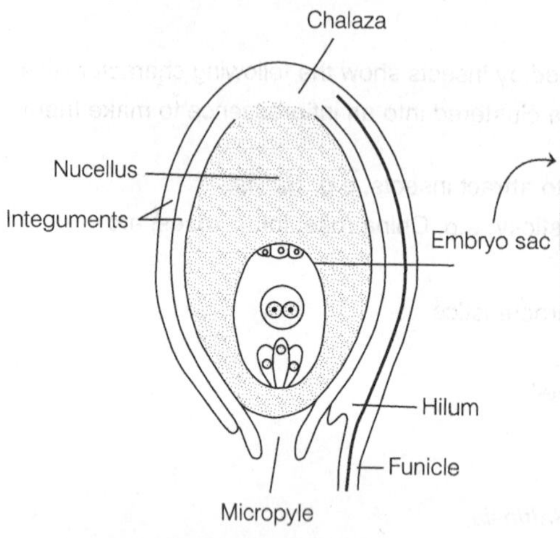

LS of ovule

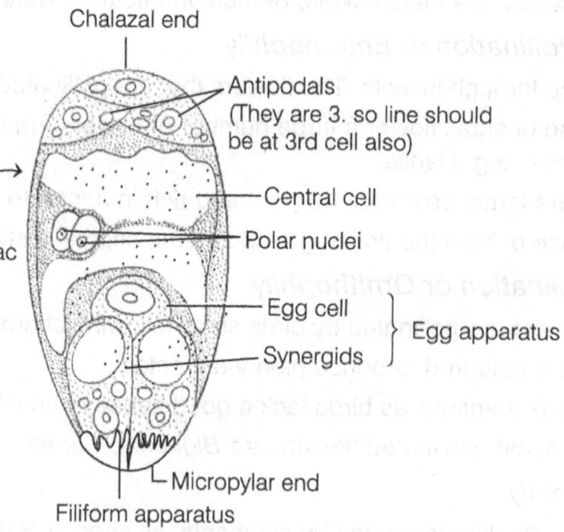

A mature embryo sac

Events During Fertilisation

The process of fertilisation contains following events

- **Pollen Germination** After compatible pollination, the **pollen grain** absorbs water and nutrients from stigma, leading to the formation of a **pollen tube** through one of the germ pores.
- **Pollen Tube Growth** The **generative cell** and **tube nucleus** move into the pollen tube which grows through the stigma and style by secreting enzymes that digest surrounding tissues.

- During pollen tube growth the generative cell divides to form **two male gametes.**

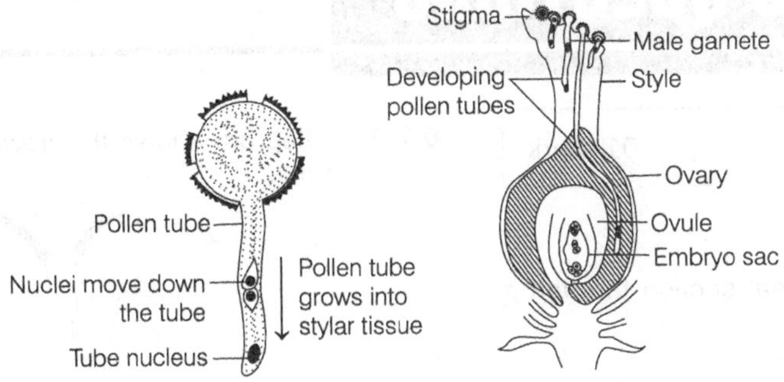

Germination of pollen grain on stigma

Entry of Pollen Tube into Ovule

- The pollen tube enters into the ovule through the micropylar end.
- As the pollen tube tip dissolves the tube nucleus disintegrates and two male gametes are released into the embyro sac.

Double Fertilisation

- One male gamete fuses with the egg cell to form the **zygote** (syngamy).
- The other male gamete fuses with the two polar nuclei to form PEN or **Primary Endosperm Nucleus** (triple fusion).
- Since, two fusions, i.e. syngamy and triple fusion occur in an embryo sac, therefore, this type of fertilisation is called **double fertilisation**.
- The representation for double fertilisation is
  Egg cell (n) + Male gamete (n) = **Zygote** ($2n$) (syngamy).
  Secondary nucleus ($2n$) + Male gamete (n) = **Endosperm** ($3n$) (triple fusion).

Post-fertilisation Changes in the Ovule

A large number of changes takes place in the ovule which are as follows

- Sepals fall down or persist in few (as in brinjal, tomato).
- Petals, stamen, stigma and style fall down.
- Zygote develops into an embryo.
- Primary endosperm nucleus develops into the endosperm, providing nourishment.
- Ovule becomes the seed and ovary becomes the fruit.
- The integument forms seed coat, i.e. outer testa and inner tegmen.

Fruits and Seeds

A **fruit** is defined as ripened or mature ovary. Fruits contain one or more seeds. The mature ovule after fertilisation is known as **seed**. The seed is covered from outside by a hard and protective **seed coat**.

Significance of Fruits

- Fruits protect immature seeds from unfavourable conditions.
- These are colourful, attractive and tasty.
- Many fruits are part of industries and are eaten as food.
- These are rich source of vitamin, minerals and sugars, etc.
- Some fruits have medicinal properties such as watermelon that helps in reducing blood pressure.

Significance of Seeds

- These help in the development of new flowering plants.
- Seeds can be stored as food source for long time.
- These help in overcoming unfavourable conditions as they have adaptive strategies.
- Seeds are the basis of agriculture.

EXAM ORIENTED QUESTIONS

TYPE - 1 01 Mark

Multiple Choice Questions

Q.1 The diagram shows a longitudinal section through a flower.

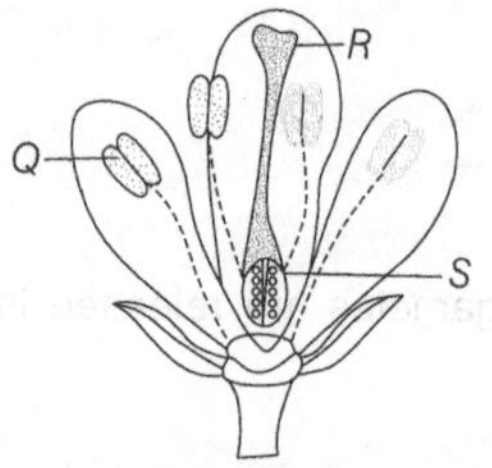

When self-pollination occurs, pollen is transferred from

(a) *Q* to *R* (b) *Q* to *S* (c) *R* to *Q* (d) *R* to *S*

Ans. (a)

Q.2 Transfer of pollen grains from anther to the stigma of another flower on the same plant is

(a) autogamy (b) cross-pollination
(c) geitonogamy (d) xenogamy

Ans. (c)

Q.3 Which of the following statement about bisexuality in plants is correct?

(a) Bisexual flowers have only male parts
(b) Bisexual flowers are pollinated exclusively by cross-pollination
(c) Bisexual flowers contain both male and female parts, allowing self-pollination
(d) Plants with separate male and female flowers on the same plant cannot undergo self-pollination

Ans. (c)

Q.4 Allogamy refers to the process of

(a) fertilisation within the same flower
(b) fertilisation between flowers of different plants of the same species
(c) fertilisation between flowers of the same plant
(d) asexual reproduction

Ans. (b)

Q.5 Maize is pollinated by

(a) bird (b) wind (c) bees (d) water

Ans. (b)

Q.6 Insect pollinated flowers are

(a) nectar producing (b) colourful
(c) fragrance producing (d) All of these

Ans. (d)

Q.7 The diagram shows the flower of a common species of grass.

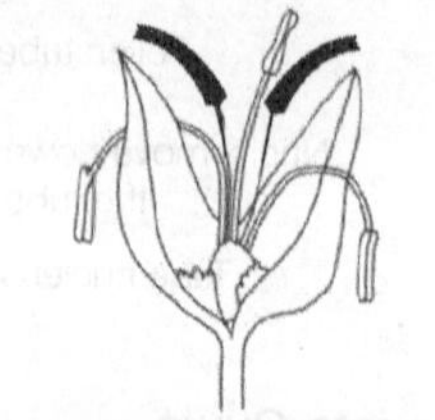

Which characteristic is the flower likely to have?

(a) Anthers with short filaments
(b) Nectaries producing nectar
(c) Short, unbranched stigmas
(d) Small, smooth pollen grains

Ans. (d)

Q.8 A teacher asked her students to give an example of the plant which are pollinated by elephophily and an entemophily, respectively.

Reema said: *Rafflesia* and *Salvia*

Ankur said: Maize and *Salvia*

Rajat said: *Arisaema* and *Salvia*

Mohit said: *Rafflesia* and *Arisaema*

Who is correct?

(a) Reema (b) Both Reema and Mohit
(c) Ankur (d) None of these

Ans. (a) In the given responses, Reema provided both correct examples as

Elephophily refers to pollination carried out by elephants. This is a rare form of pollination and an example of a plant pollinated by elephants is *Rafflesia*.

Entomophily refers to pollination carried out by insects. Plants that rely on insects for pollination, such as *Salvia*, are examples of entomophilous plants.

Q.9 Which of the following diagram show parts of an insect pollinated flowers?

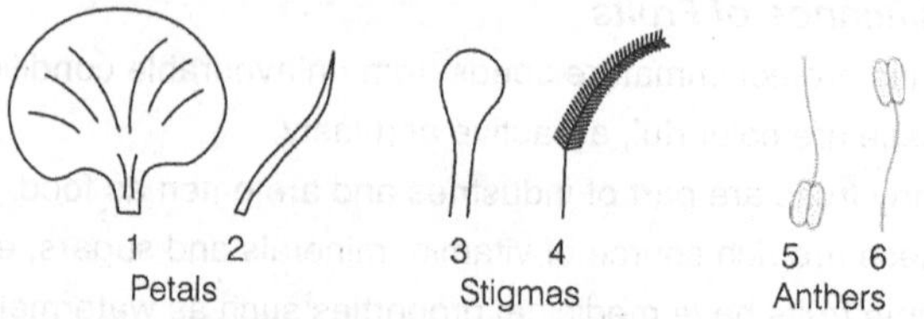

(a)	1	3	6
(b)	1	4	5
(c)	2	3	5
(d)	2	4	6

Ans. (a) In insect pollination, large brightly coloured petals are attractive to insects. Anthers that are found within the corolla are near enough to brush up against pollinators when they visit. Large, feathery stigma is typical of wind pollinated flowers.

Q.10 The diagram given below represents pollen germination. Observe the diagram given below and answer the following question.

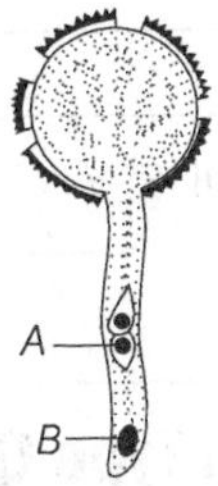

In the given diagram structures *A* and *B* represents respectively

(a) pollen tube and nucleus
(b) tube nucleus and pollen
(c) gamete and tube cell
(d) male gamete and tube nucleus

Ans. (d)

Q.11 The number of antipodal cells in the embryo sac is

(a) 4 (b) 3 (c) 5 (d) 0

Ans. (b)

Q.12 Which of the following cells in the embryo sac plays a role in the formation of zygote after fertilisation?

(a) Synergids (b) Polar nuclei
(c) Egg cells (d) Antipodal cells

Ans. (c)

Q.13 The diagram shows a section through the carpel of a flower.

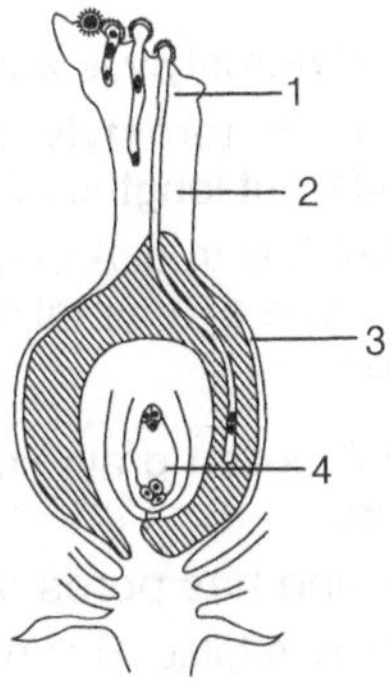

Where do pollination and fertilisation occur?

	Pollination	Fertilisation
(a)	1	2
(b)	1	4
(c)	2	3
(d)	3	4

Ans. (b) The stigma (1) recieves pollen grains during pollination. While, fertilisation occurs in the ovary (4), which has ovules containing the female gamete.

Q.14 The diagram shows a section through a flower.

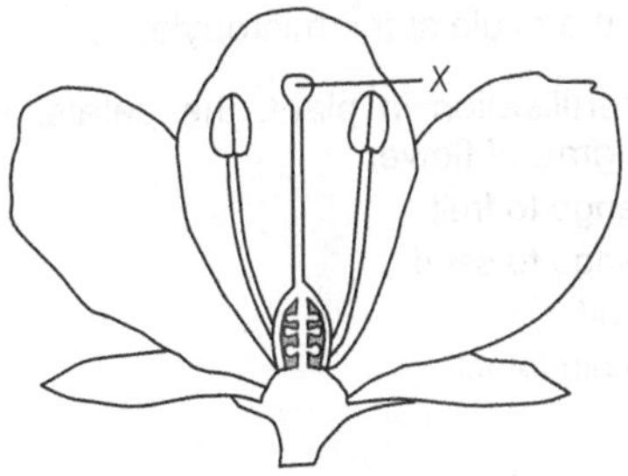

What passes down the tube *X*?

(a) Female gamete (b) Male gamete
(c) Nectar (d) Pollen grain

Ans. (b)

Q.15 Choose the correct statement showing the example of fertilisation.

(a) A pollen nucleus passing through the pollen tube
(b) The transferring of pollen from one flower to another
(c) A sperm nucleus fusing with an egg nucleus
(d) Sperms entering a female animal during copulation

Ans. (c) Fertilisation is the process by which the male gamete (sperm) fuses with the female gamete (egg nucleus) to form a zygote.

Q.16 The diagram shows a cross-section through the carpel of a flower just before fertilisation. Where are the male and female gametes just before fertilisation?

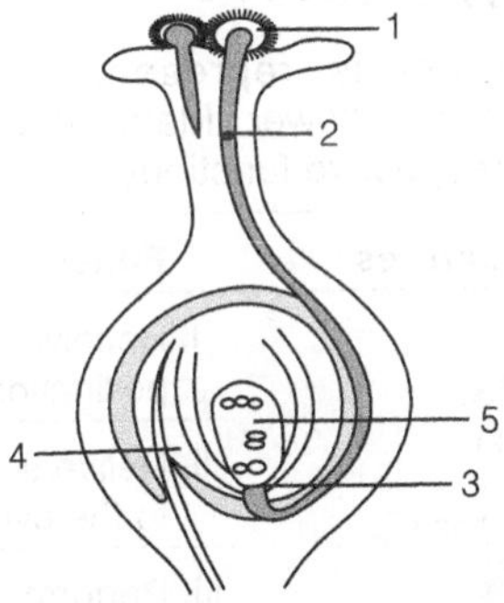

	Male Gamete	Female Gamete
(a)	1	5
(b)	1	4
(c)	2	4
(d)	3	5

Ans. (d) The pollen grains germinates to form a pollen tube, which grows down through the tissues of the style of the stigma and the ovary wall. As the pollen tube grows, its nucleus divides to form two male gametes that are released into the ovule, when the pollen tube enters the ovule at the micropyle.

Q.17 After fertilisation in plant, the petals, stamens, style and stigma of flower
(a) change to fruit
(b) change to seed
(c) fall off
(d) remain intact

Ans. (c)

Q.18 Select the appropriate pair for *P* and Q based on their respective outcomes after fertilisation.

Structures During Fertilisation	Structures After Fertilisation
P	Forms seed coat after fertilisation.
Q	Develops into an embryo.

(a) *P* - Integuments, *Q*- Zygote
(b) *P* - Endosperm, *Q*- Seed coat
(c) *P* -Petals, *Q*- Nucleus
(d) *P* - Zygote, *Q*- Seed

Ans. (a)

TYPE - 2 01 Mark

Matching Type Questions

Q.1 The diagram is representing the process of fertilisation in a flower. Match the structures *A* to *E* with their respective functions.

Floral Structures	Functions
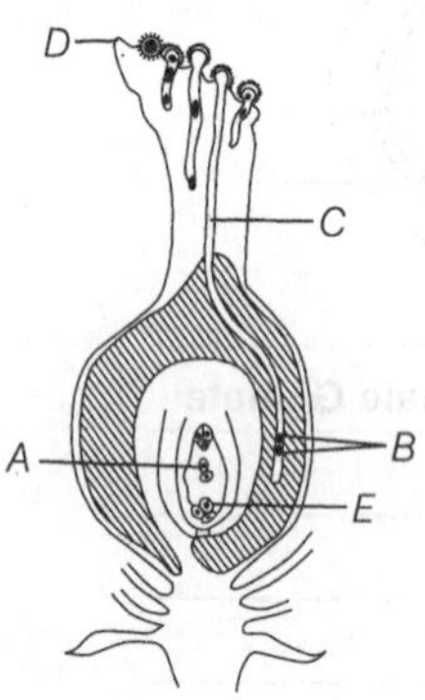	I. Receives the pollen during pollination.
	II. Delivers the male gametes to the ovule.
	III. Performs double fertilisation.
	IV. Fertilised by the male gamete (sperm) to form the zygote.
	V. Form the primary endosperm nucleus.

Ans. A-V, B- III, C- II, D-I, E- IV

Q.2 Match the following columns.

	Column I	Column II
A.	Outer integuments	I. Fruit
B.	Inner integuments	II. Testa
C.	Ovary	III. Seed
D.	Ovules	IV. Tegmen
E.	Ovary wall	V. Pericarp

Ans. A–II, B–IV, C–I, D–III, E–V

TYPE - 3 01 Mark

Assertion-Reason Type Questions

Direction (Q. Nos. 1-5) In the following questions statements are given as Assertion (A) and Reason (R).
(a) A is true, but R is false.
(b) A is false, but R is true.
(c) Both A and R are true.
(d) Both A and R are false.

Q.1 Assertion (A) Pollination is the transfer of pollen from the anther to the stigma of the same or different flowers.

Reason (R) For fertilisation to occur in flowering plants, pollen must reach the stigma, where it can fertilise the ovules.

Ans. (c)

Q.2 Assertion (A) Cleistogamy is a form of self-pollination where flowers remain closed.

Reason (R) Cleistogamy allows the genetic diversity.

Ans. (a) A is true, but R is false. R can be corrected as Cleistogamy does not promote genetic diversity.

Q.3 Assertion (A) Heterostyly is a type of self-pollination.

Reason (R) In heterostyly a plant species has flowers with different lengths of styles and stamens.

Ans. (b) A is false, but R is true. A can be corrected as Heterostyly is a type of adaptation promoting cross-pollination.

Q.4 Assertion (A) A pollen grain contains two layers, i.e. exine and intine.

Reason (R) Intine has pores at certain stages.

Ans. (a) A is true, but R is false. R can be corrected as Exine has pores at certain stages.

Q.5 Assertion (A) An ovule is a female gamete found in the ovary.

Reason (R) It is attached with the ovary by a structure called placenta.

Ans. (c)

TYPE - 4

01 Mark

Very Short Answer Type Questions

Q.1 Name the process in which an anther and stigma mature at the same time.

Ans. Homogamy.

Q.2 Identify the term used for a flower that has only male reproductive parts (stamens) or only female reproductive parts (carpels).

Ans. Unisexuality.

Q.3 What are the two types of dichogamy?

Ans. The two types of dichogamy are protandry and protogyny.

Q.4 Name the term used when female reproductive part matures first in a flower.

Ans. Protogyny.

Q.5 How the process of herkogamy prevents self-pollination?

Ans. In herkogamy, flowers possesses certain structural or mechanical barriers which do not allow self-pollination.

Q.6 Give two examples of plants which are pollinated by insects.

Or Name two enthomophilous flowers.

Ans. *Salvia* and sunflower.

Q.7 Define fertilisation.

Ans. Fertilisation is the process where the male and female gametes fuse to form a zygote.

Q.8 State the function of micropyle.

Ans. Micropyle helps in the absorption of water that is available to the embryo for germination.

Q.9 How many cells are there in an embryo sac?

Ans. 7 cells.

Q.10 Where is embryo sac located?

Ans. Nucellus.

Q.11 Name the structure which is formed by the fusion of male gamete and two polar nuclei.

Ans. Primary Endosperm Nucleus (PEN).

Q.12 What is the fate of ovary after fertilisation?

Ans. After fertilisation, the ovary develops into a fruit.

Q.13 On what factor does the length of a pollen tube depends?

Ans. The length of a pollen tube depend upon the distance between the pollen grain on the upper surface of the stigma and ovule.

Q.14 Give the correct sequence of events that occurs during sexual reproduction in a flower.

Ans. The correct sequence of events are

Pollination → Fertilisation → Embryo formation → Seedling.

Q.15 Observe the given diagram carefully and fill the blank space with correct words. **(1 Mark each)**

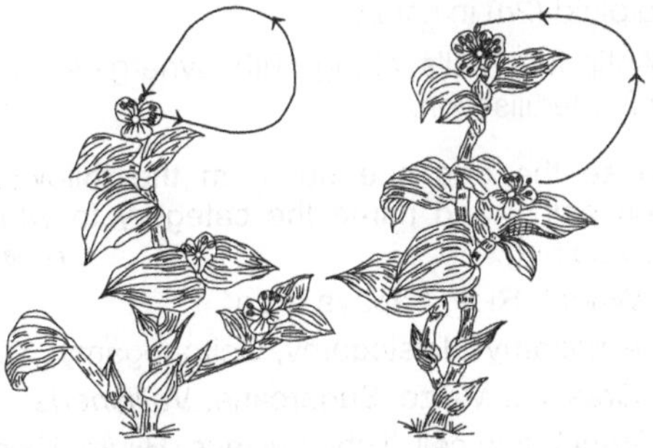

(a) (b)

The transfer of pollen grains from the anther to the stigma of the same flower or of different flowers is termed as ......(i)...... . When the pollen from the anther of a flower is transferred to the stigma of the same flower or to the stigma of another flower of the same plant, it is known as ......(ii)...... . ...(iii)...... involves the transfer of pollen grains from anther to the ......(iv)...... of same flower, while. ......(v)...... involves the transfer of pollen grains from the anther of a flower to the stigma of another flower of the same plant.

Ans. (i) pollination (ii) self-pollination

(iii) Autogamy (iv) stigma

(v) geitonogamy

Q.16 Name the following. **(1 Mark each)**

(i) Transfer of pollen grains from anther to the stigma.

(ii) Condition in which anther and stigma attain maturity at the same time.

(iii) The strategy evolved to prevent self-pollination in flowers.

(iv) Transfer of pollen grains from anther to stigma of another plant.

Ans. (i) Pollination

(ii) Homogamy

(iii) Self-incompatibility/Protogyny

(iv) Cross-pollination or Allogamy

Q.17 Correct and rewrite the following statements by changing the underlined words. **(1 Mark each)**

(i) Allogamy does not require any external agent.

(ii) Showy and bright coloured petals do not play any role in cross-pollination.

(iii) The secondary nucleus that participates in triple fusion is triploid in nature.

(iv) Antipodal cells along with central cell degenerate after fertilisation.

Ans. (i) Autogamy does not require any external agent.

(ii) Showy and bright coloured petals do not play any role in self-pollination.

(iii) The secondary nucleus participates in triple fusion is diploid (2*n*) in nature.

(iv) Antipodal cells along with synergids degenerate after fertilisation.

Q.18 Choose the odd one out from the following terms given below and name the category to which other three belong. **(1 Mark each)**

(i) Wheat, Rice, Papaya, Pea

(ii) Autogamy Cleistogamy, Geitonogamy, Xenogamy

(iii) Grasses, Maize, Sugarcane, *Vallisneria*

(iv) Vegetative cell, Tube nucleus, Hilum, Exine

(v) Protandry, Protogyny, Herkogamy, Bisexuality

Ans. (i) The odd term is papaya because it shows cross-pollination, while rest three show self-pollination.

(ii) The odd term is cleistogamy because it is a condition where flowers are closed, while rest three are types of pollination.

(iii) The odd term is *Vallisneria* because it is pollinated by water, while rest three get pollinated by wind, i.e. anemophilous.

(iv) The odd term is hilum because it is the part of female reproductive organ, while rest three are components of pollen grain.

(v) The odd term is bisexuality because it is related to self-pollination, while rest three are related to cross-pollination.

Q.19 Give biological/technical terms for the following.

(i) Flowers that do not open **(1 Mark each)**

(ii) Flowers pollinated by elephant

(iii) Outer layer of pollen grain

(iv) Cell that forms the pollen tube

(v) Structure formed from a matured ovary

Ans. (i) Cleistogamous

(ii) Elephophily/Elephophilous flowers

(iii) Exine

(iv) Vegetative cell

(v) Fruit

Q.20 Mention one difference in each of the following pairs on the basis of what is given in the bracket. **(1 Mark each)**

(i) Autogamy and Geitonogamy (definition)

(ii) Protandry and Protogyny (maturation of anther and stigma)

(iii) Herkogamy and Heterostyly (presence or absence of barrier)

(iv) Anemophily and Hydrophily (type of stigma)

(v) Insect pollinated flowers and Wind pollinated flowers (essential whorls)

Ans.

(i)

Autogamy	Geitonogamy
It refers to the transfer of pollen grains from the anthers of a flower to the stigma of the same flower.	It refers to the transfer of pollen grains from the anther of a flower to the stigma of another flower of the same plant.

(ii)

Protandry	Protogyny
It is the maturing of anther earlier than stigma.	In this, the stigma matures earlier than anther.

(iii)

Herkogamy	Heterostyly
Mechanical barrier is present to prevent the pollen to reach the stigma of the same flower, e.g. pansy.	No mechanical barrier is present instead the stigma and anther are present at different heights, e.g. *Oxalis*.

(iv)

Anemophily	Hydrophily
Stigmas are large, hairy and feathery.	Stigmas are long and sticky.

(v)

Insect Pollinated Flowers	Wind Pollinated Flowers
Essential whorls are not much exposed to air, e.g. *Salvia*.	Essential whorls are exposed to air, e.g. wheat.

TYPE - 5 02 Marks

Short Answer Type Questions

Q.1 Give an example of each of the following.

(i) Cleistogamy (ii) Heterostyly

Ans. (i) Cleistogamy- Pea

(ii) Heterostyly- Primrose

Q.2 State any two disadvantages of self-pollination.

Ans. Two disadvantages of self-pollination are as follows.

(i) Repeated self-pollination can make the plant weaker over time.

(ii) The weaker or defective characters are inherited and cannot be eliminated.

Q.3 **Name the type of pollination which shows genetic diversity and define it.**

Ans. Cross-pollination shows genetic diversity. It is the process of transferring pollen from the anthers of one plant's flowers to the stigma of a flower on a different plant of the same species.

Q.4 **What are the two categories of pollinating agents? Give examples of these agents.**

Ans. The two categories of pollinating agents are **biotic** and **abiotic** agents.

Examples of **biotic agents** are **insects**, **snails**, **bat** and **birds**.

Examples of **abiotic agents** are **wind** and **water**.

Q.5 **What is ornithophily, give an example?**

Ans. Ornithophily is the pollination carried out by birds, e.g. *Bignonia*.

Q.6 **State the differences between self-pollination and cross-pollination.**

Ans. Differences between self-pollination and cross-pollination are as follows

Self-pollination	Cross-pollination
Pollen is transferred within the same flower or between flowers of the same plant.	Pollen is transferred between flowers of different plants of the same species.
Requires less energy and fewer resources.	Requires external agents like wind, water or animals.
Does not promote genetic diversity.	Promotes genetic diversity.
Ensures fertilisation even when pollinators are absent.	Depends on external factors for successful fertilisation.

Q.7 **Consider the following three flowers namely *X*, *Y* and *Z*. Which flower(s) would develop into a fruit and why?**

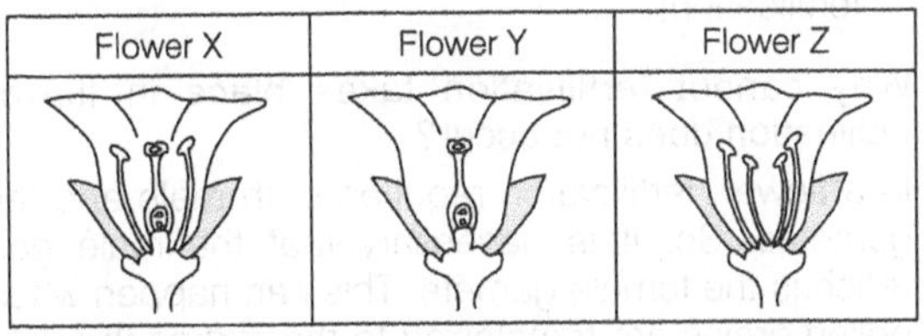

Ans. Out of the three flowers given, only *X* flower would develop into a fruit because it bears both stamens and carpels, which helps in plant reproduction.

Q.8 **Give two characteristic features of an ovule.**

Ans. Two characteristic features of an ovule are as follows.

(i) It is enclosed by one or two integuments, leaving a small opening called the micropyle for pollen tube entry during fertilisation.

(ii) The ovule contains the embryo sac, where the female gamete (egg cell) is located.

Q.9 **Draw a diagram showing germination of pollen on stigma of a flower and mark on it following organs/parts.**

(i) Pollen grain **(ii) Stigma**

(iii) Pollen tube **(iv) Female germ cell**

Ans.

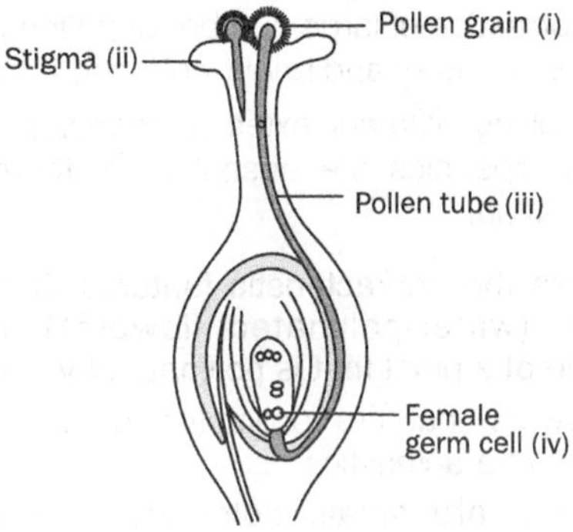

Q.10 **Mention any two economic importance of fruits.**

Ans. Two economic importance of fruits are

(i) Fruits are good source of vitamins, minerals, organic acids and sugars.

(ii) Some fruits have medicinal properties such as watermelon helps in reducing blood pressure.

TYPE - 6 (03 Marks)

Short Answer Type Questions

Q.1 **Name the type of self-pollination which occurs from the anther of one flower to the stigma of another flower on the same plant. Also state two advantages of self-pollination.**

Ans. Geitonogamy is the type of self-pollination which occurs from the anther of one flower to the stigma of another flower on the same plant.

Two advantages of self-pollination are as follows

(i) It is more reliable in bisexual flowers where stamens and carpels mature at the same time.

(ii) Parental characters are preserved indefinitely.

Q.2 State three advantages and disadvantages of cross-pollination.

Ans. Advantages and disadvantages of cross-pollination are as follows

Advantages of Cross-pollination

(i) Stronger and healthier offspring are produced.

(ii) Production of a large number of viable seeds.

(iii) New varieties with useful characters are produced.

Disadvantages of Cross-pollination

(i) It does not ensure fertilisation as the landed pollen may not remain functional.

(ii) Cross-pollinating plants waste lots of their energy in the formation of large number of pollen grains, scent odour or showy and bright-coloured petals.

(iii) It involves different external agencies, if somehow these agencies are absent then, there will be no pollination.

Q.3 What are the characteristic features of hydrophilous flowers (water-pollinated flowers)? Provide an example of a plant that is pollinated by water.

Ans. The flowers that are pollinated by water show the following characteristics

- Flowers are small, colourless, inconspicuous, odourless and nectar less.
- The stigmas are long and sticky.
- The pollen grains have the same specific gravity as that of water, so that they can float on water.
- Pollen grains are produced in large quantity and have mucilaginous covering.
- In some cases, the male flowers detach and float on water till they meet the female flowers.

Vallisneria and *Hydrilla* are the examples of water pollinated plants.

Q.4 Give biological reasons for the following.

(i) Repeated self-pollination is not preferred by the plant breeders.

(ii) Some flowers are brightly coloured.

(iii) Some pollen grains are rough, spiny and sticky.

Ans. (i) Plant breeders usually do not prefer repeated self-pollination as it leads to loss of vigour and vitality of the future generations.

(ii) Flowers like *Hibiscus* are brightly coloured to attract the insects for cross-pollination.

(iii) Some pollen grains are rough, spiny and sticky in nature so that they can easily stick to the body of the insect as well as to the stigma. This aids in the process of cross-pollination.

Q.5 The diagram shows a germinating pollen grain. Observe the diagram and label the parts 1 to 6.

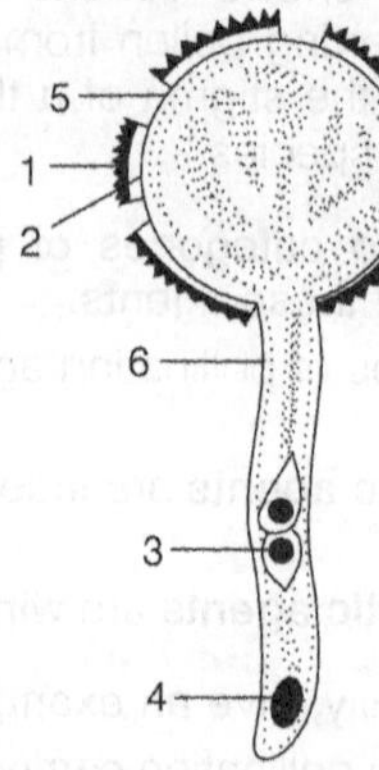

Ans. The parts 1 to 6 are labelled as

1. Exine,
2. Intine,
3. Male gamete,
4. Tube nucleus,
5. Germ pore,
6. Pollen tube

Q.6 What is an embryo sac and how many structures are present in it?

Ans. The embryo sac is the female gametophyte in flowering plants, where fertilisation occurs and the zygote is formed.

The structures present in the embryo sac are as follows

(i) **One egg cell** (female gamete).

(ii) **Two synergids** (located near the micropyle, guiding the pollen tube).

(iii) **Three antipodal cells** (at the opposite end of the micropyle).

(iv) **One central cell** (containing two polar nuclei that fuse to form the primary endosperm nucleus after fertilisation).

Q.7 Why cannot fertilisation takes place in flowers if pollination does not occur?

Ans. In a flower, fertilisation requires both male and female gametes. So, it is necessary that the male gamete reaches the female gamete. This can happen when the pollen grains are transferred to the stigma through any means of pollination.

Hence, fertilisation cannot take place in flowers if pollination does not occur.

Q.8 Draw a labelled diagram of an embryo sac.

Ans.

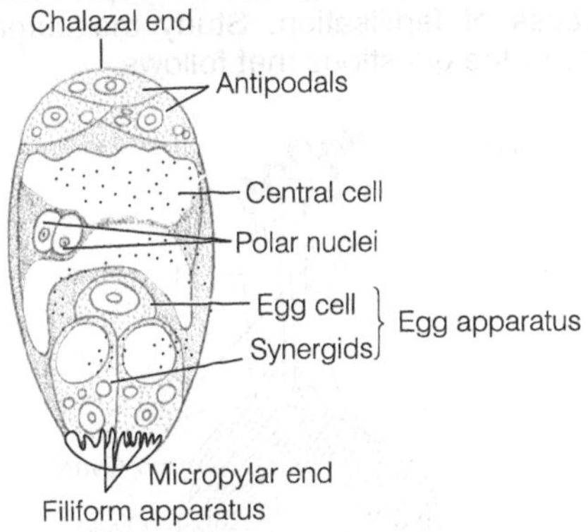

Q.9 What is double fertilisation? Name the structure which is formed by triple fusion.

Ans. Double fertilisation is a process in flowering plants where two male gametes from a pollen grain fertilise two different structures within the female gametophyte.

One male gamete fuse with the egg cell to form zygote, while the other male gamete fuses with other two polar nuclei to form primary endosperm nucleus.

Q.10 The diagram given below shows the process of double fertilisation in a plant. Study the diagram carefully and identify the incorrectly labelled parts.

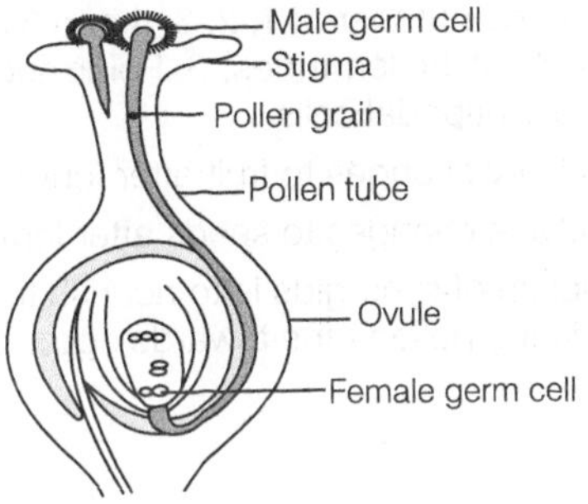

Ans. The incorrectly labelled parts are:

Male germ cells should be pollen grain.

Pollen grain should be male germ cell.

Ovule should be ovary.

TYPE - 7 — 03 Marks

Structured Based Questions

Q.1 Observe the figure given below and answer the following questions.

(i) Which type of pollination is shown in the figure?

(ii) Name the term used for such type of pollination.

(iii) Give an example of the plants which are pollinated by birds.

Ans. (i) Bird pollination is shown in the given figure.

(ii) Ornithophily

(iii) *Begnonia* and *Canna* are the plants pollinated by birds.

Q.2 After the doctor's prescription, Rohani starts to eat an apple every day. she is advised to do so because apples are rich in vitamins and antioxidants, which help improve her overall health. Observe the diagram given below and answer the following questions.

(i) Which part of the flower becomes fruits?

(ii) Which part is developed into seeds?

(iii) Name the part of an ovary which convert into seed coat.

Ans. (i) The ovary develops into the fruit after fertilisation.

(ii) The ovules inside the ovary develop into seeds after fertilisation.

(iii) The integuments of the ovary develop into the seed coat.

Q.3 Study the figure given below and answer the questions that follows.

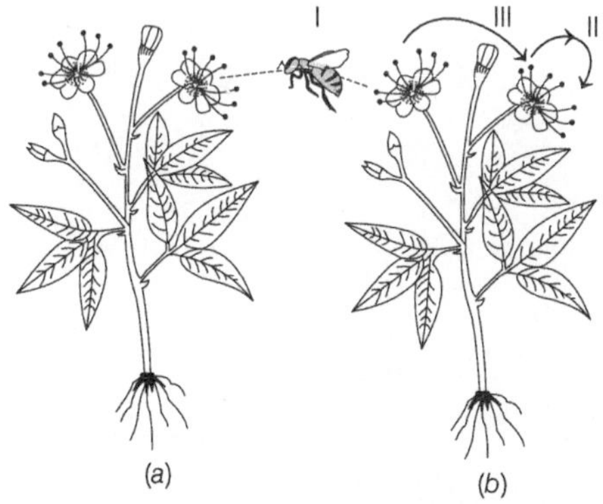

(i) Identify the processes I, II and III.

(ii) Which type of process occurs in a unisexual and cleistogamous flower, respectively?

(iii) State any two characteristic features of the type of flowers involved in process I.

Ans. (i) The processes I, II and III are as
I–Cross-pollination, II–Self-pollination and III–Geitonogamy

(ii) In unisexual flower, process I (cross-pollination) occurs, while in a cleistogamous flower, process II (self-pollination) occurs.

(iii) Two characteristic features of the type of flowers involved in process I are as follows

- Sticky, large, spiny pollen grains.
- Bright coloured flowers.

Q.4 Study the diagram given below and answer the questions that follows.

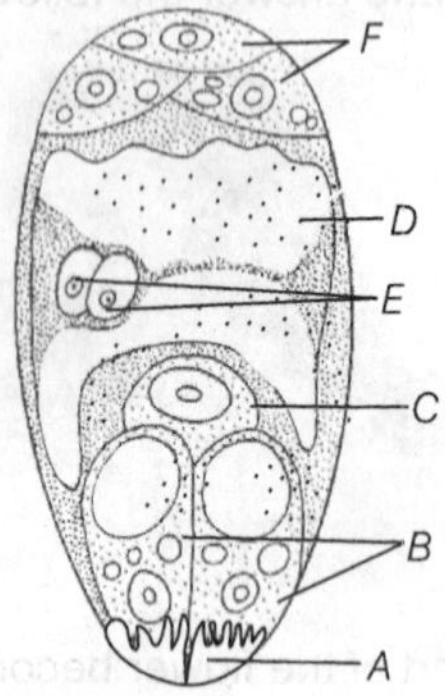

(i) **What is shown in the given diagram?**

(ii) **Identify this labels *A–F* marked in the diagram.**

(iii) **Where is this structure located?**

Ans. (i) The given diagram shows a mature embryo sac.

(ii) The marked parts *A-F* are labelled as
A–Filiform apparatus, *B*–Synergids, *C*–Egg cells, *D*–Central cell, *E*–Polar nuclei, *F*–Antipodal cells

(iii) This structure (embryo sac) is located in the nucellus, in female flower.

Q.5 Given below is a diagrammatic representation of the process of fertilisation. Study the same and then answer the questions that follows.

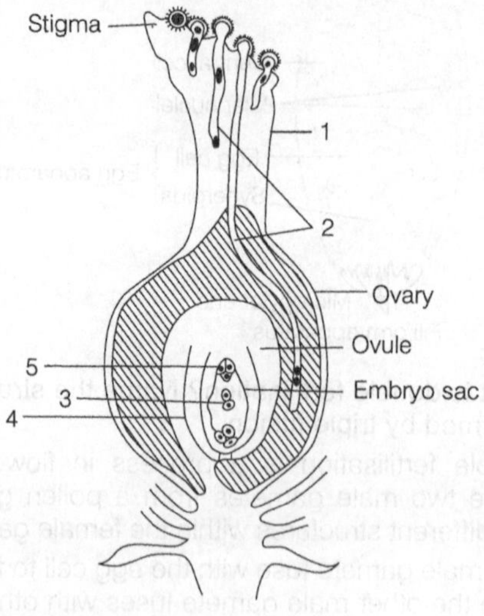

(i) **Name the parts numbered 1, 2, 3, 4 and 5.**

(ii) **What happens to (a) Ovary, (b) Ovule after fertilisation?**

(iii) **What is the function of the synergids?**

Ans. (i) The parts numbered 1, 2, 3, 4 and 5 are
1–Style, 2–Pollen tubes, 3–Polar nuclei, 4–Embryo sac 5–Antipodal cells

(ii) (a) Ovary changes to fruit after fertilisation.
(b) Ovule changes to seeds after fertilisation.

(iii) Function of synergids is to nourish the egg cell and guide the pollen tube towards egg.

STRUCTURE AND GERMINATION OF SEED

Seed

- A seed is a mature **ovule**, which develops after fertilisation. It contains embryo which develops into a new plant.
- The seeds of different plants vary in size and shape, but their basic structure is same in all plants. A mature seed mainly consists of three parts
  - **Seed Coat** Covering of the seed.
  - **Embryo** The miniature plant inside the seed.
  - **Cotyledons** These are the seed leaves which store food for the embryo.

Types of Seed

The seeds can be classified on the basis of number of cotyledons and the presence or absence of endosperm (nutritive tissue), as given below

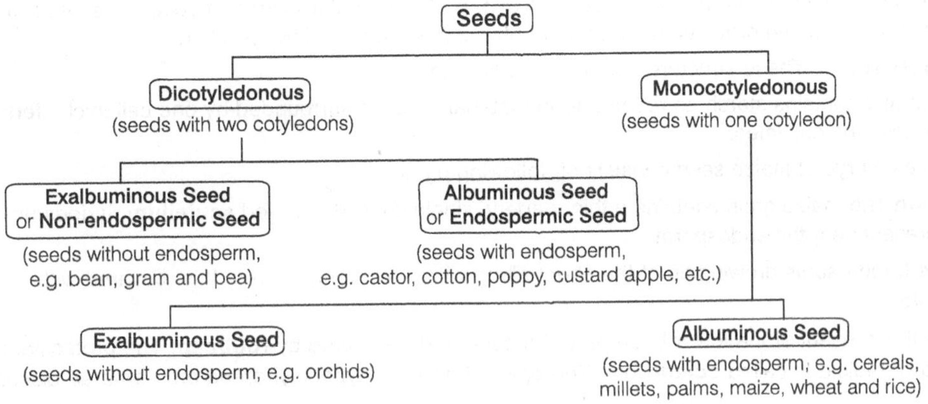

Structure of Dicotyledonous Seed (Bean)

Bean seeds are normally kidney-shaped which are convex on one side and concave on the other. The detailed structure of a dicot seed (bean) is as follows

- **Seed Coat** Each seed is enclosed by a protective covering called the seed coat, which develops from the integuments of the ovule. The seed coat is differentiated into the following layers
  - **Testa** It is the outer, thick layer which protects the seed from pathogens like bacteria, fungi, insects, etc., and from injuries.
  - **Tegmen** It is inner, thin membranous covering which protects the inner part of the seed.
- **Hilum** It marks the point of attachment of the ovule to the ovary and appears as a **scar** on the concave side of the seed.
- **Micropyle** It is a small pore located near the hilum, through which oxygen, water and other substances enter the seed.
- **Raphe** It is a ridge-like structure present around the median groove. It represents the portion of the stalk which remains fused with the testa.

- **Embryo** It is young miniature plant along with cotyledons, enclosed within the seed coat. It consists of two main parts, as described below
  - **Cotyledons** These are the seed leaves, fleshy structures that store food and provide nourishment to the embryo.
  - **Embryonal Axis** It is the young plant between the cotyledons, consisting of the **plumule** (forms the shoot), **radicle** (forms the root), **epicotyl** (above the plumule) and **hypocotyl** (above the radicle).

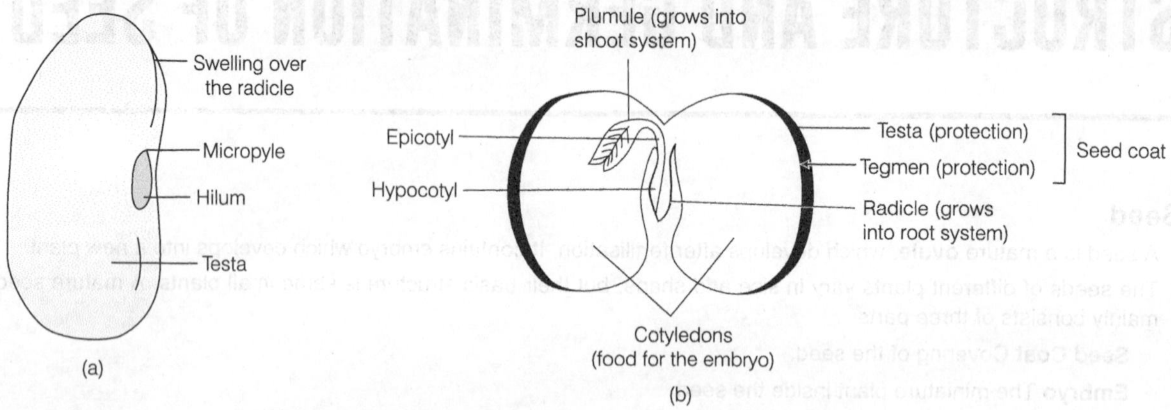

(a) External structure of bean seed, (b) Internal structure of bean seed

Structure of Monocotyledonous Seed (Maize)

The maize grain is flat, almost triangular structure. The structural components of a monocot seed are detailed below

- **Seed Coat** In a monocot seed, the seed coat is a thin, protective outer layer that covers the seed. It is fused with the pericarp (fruit wall) and protects the seed from physical damage and dehydration.
- **Hilum and Micropyle** These structures are not clearly visible.
- **Endosperm** and contains starch as reserve food material which is surrounded by one cell thick **aleurone layer**. It is rich in protein and enzymes.
- **Embryo** The embryo of maize seed consists of following parts
  - **Cotyledon** The maize grain contains a thin, papery, single cotyledon called **scutellum**. It does not contain food and is present near the endosperm.
  - **Plumule** It represents growing tip of the shoot along with embryonic leaves. It is covered with a sheath called **coleoptile**.
  - **Radicle** It is present at the lower base part of a seed and is covered by **root cap**. The protective membranous covering of radicle is called **coleorhiza**. The epicotyl and the hypocotyl areas are same as discussed in dicot seeds.

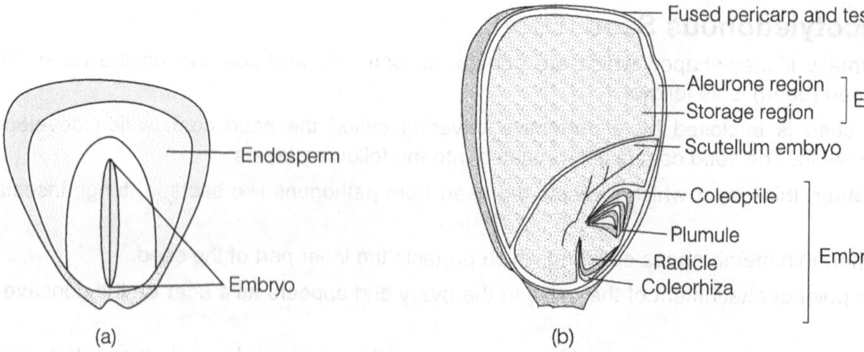

(a) External structure and (b) Internal structure of a maize seed

Differences between Dicot Seed and Monocot Seed

Dicot Seed (Bean)	**Monocot Seed** (Maize)
Seed coat is thick and brown.	Seed coat is fused with pericarp.
Hilum and micropyle can be seen separately.	Hilum and micropyle cannot be differentiated.
Two cotyledons are present.	Only one cotyledon is present.
Endosperm is absent.	Endosperm is present and is well-developed.

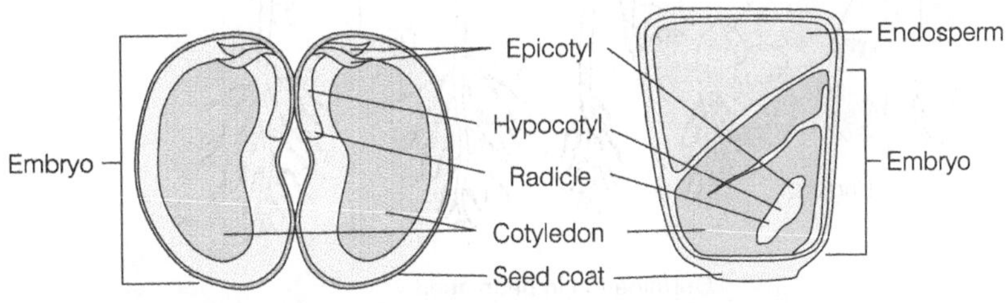

Dicot seed　　Monocot seed

Seed Germination

- The process of seeds developing into new plants is called **germination of seeds**.
- The most common example of germination is the sprouting of a seedling from a seed of an angiosperm or gymnosperm.

Necessary Conditions for Germination

The following conditions are necessary for seed germination

- **Water** The seed absorbs water from its environment, typically from the soil, in natural conditions. This causes the seed to swell, rupturing the seed coat and allowing the radicle to grow. Water also activates enzymes that break down stored food and helps in transport of nutrients.
- **Oxygen** Seeds require oxygen for respiration during germination. Without it, germination may fail.
- **Temperature** A suitable temperature is essential for seed germination. Most seeds germinate within the range of 25-35°C (optimum temperature). While temperatures below 0°C or above 48°C inhibit germination.

Types of Seed Germination

The process of germination is categorised into two types depending upon the behaviour of cotyledons during germination, i.e. epigeal germination and hypogeal germination.

1. Epigeal Germination

- This type of germination takes place above the ground and usually occurs in dicot seeds.
- The cotyledons are first pushed above the ground by the rapid elongation of hypocotyl. Although the length of epicotyl remains the same in epigeal germination.
- Cotyledons soon turn green and start photosynthesising, e.g. *Phaseolus, Ricinus* (castor), *Dolichos* (bean), *Helianthus* (sunflower), *Brassica* (mustard), *Allium* (onion), etc.
- The various stages of epigeal germination of bean seed are as follows
  - The seeds swell up after absorbing water.
  - The radicle elongates, extends downward into the soil.
  - Hypocotyl elongates, plumule reaches the surface of the soil.

- Cotyledons come out of the soil and thus seed germination takes place.

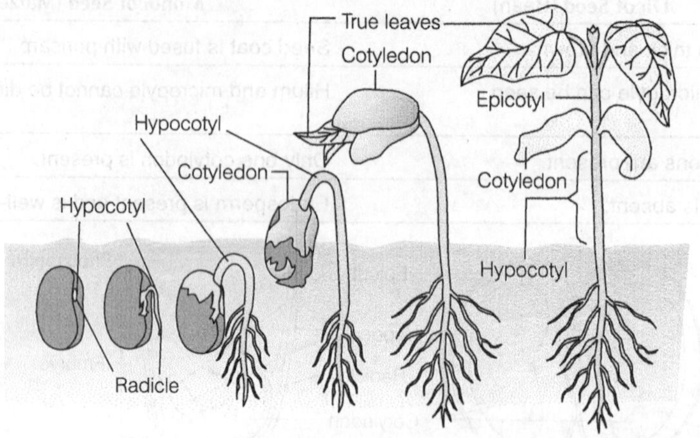

Germination in bean seed

2. *Hypogeal Germination*

- In this type of germination, the epicotyl elongates faster than hypocotyl at the time of seed germination.
- This keeps cotyledons inside the soil or may bring them just above the soil surface. However, they remain non-green, dry up gradually and fall off.
- Some dicot seeds like pea, mango, coconut and most of the monocot seeds like maize, rice show hypogeal germination.

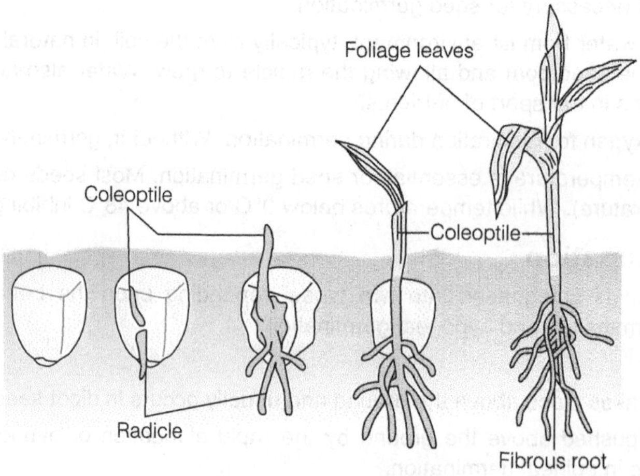

Germination in maize seed

- The various stages of hypogeal germination of maize grain are as follows
  - The seed absorbs water and swells up. The epithelial layer of the scutellum secretes enzymes which convert starch in the endosperm into sugar and transfer it to the cotyledon.
  - The radicle grows down and plumule grows up.
- The epicotyl enlarges and cotyledons remain in the soil. So, the germination is hypogeal.

Differences between Epigeal and Hypogeal Germination

Epigeal Germination	Hypogeal Germination
Hypocotyl elongates at a faster rate.	Epicotyl elongates at a faster rate.
Cotyledons are pushed above the ground.	Cotyledons remain under the ground.
Cotyledons play a role in photosynthesis.	Cotyledons have no role in photosynthesis.
Usually found in monocotyledonous seeds.	Usually found in dicotyledonous seeds.

Experiments Related to Seed Germination

There are few experiments by which we can understand the importance of factors, which are necessary for seed germination.

Experiment 1

Aim To prove that water is necessary for seed germination.

Procedure In the experiment, four petridishes A, B, C and D were prepared as follows

Petridish A with soaked seeds on wet cotton, petridish B with soaked seeds on dry cotton, petridish C with unsoaked seeds on dry cotton and petridish D with soaked seeds submerged in water.

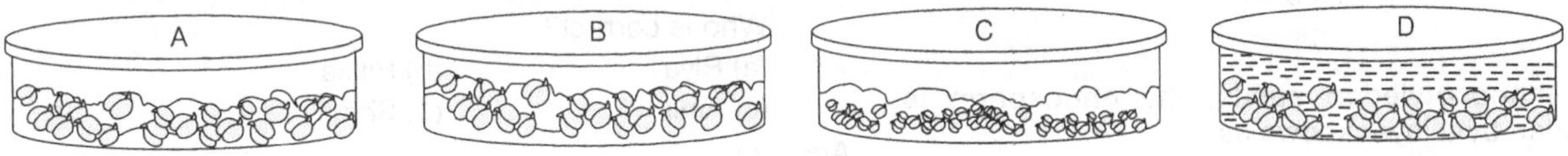

(a) Soaked seeds placed on moist cotton (b) Soaked seeds placed on dry cotton (c) Unsoaked seeds placed on dry cotton (d) Soaked seeds submerged in water

Experimental setup to show that water is necessary for seed germination

Observation

Seeds kept on **petridish A** germinate.

In **petridish B**, seeds germinate, but later they shrivel up and die.

In **petridish C**, no change is seen in seeds.

In **petridish D**, the seeds start germinating, but eventually rot.

Experiment 2

Aim To prove that oxygen is necessary for seed germination.

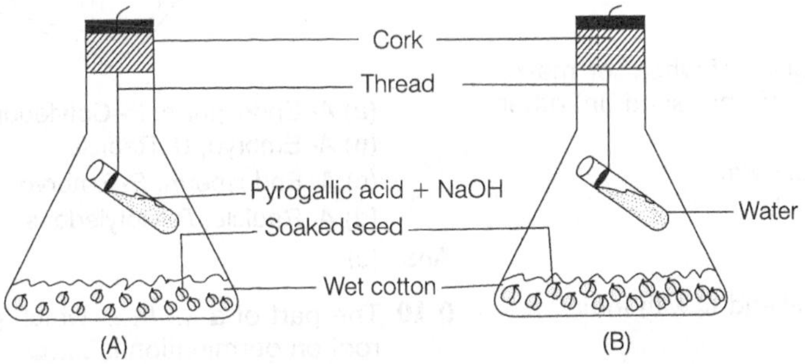

Experimental setup to show that oxygen is necessary for seed germination

Procedure Take two conical flask and mark them as A and B. Spread moist cotton at the bottom of the flasks and place some soaked seeds on wet cotton. Hang a test tube containing **pyrogallic acid** dissolved in **sodium hydroxide** with the help of a thread in a flask marked as A and seal it with a cork. Seal the other flask marked as B, in the same way, but with the test tube containing water. Place both the flasks at room temperature and observe them after 3-4 days.

Observation The seeds in the flask A do not germinate because there is no oxygen, as pyrogallic acid absorbs it, while the seeds in the flask B germinate showing the importance of oxygen for germination.

EXAM ORIENTED QUESTIONS

TYPE - 1 01 Mark

Multiple Choice Questions

Q.1 In pea, castor and maize, the number of cotyledons are
(a) 2, 2 and 1, respectively (b) 1, 2 and 2, respectively
(c) 2, 1 and 2, respectively (d) 1 , 2 and 1, respectively

Ans. (a)

Q.2 An example of exalbuminous dicot seeds is
(a) poppy (b) custard apple
(c) millets (d) gram

Ans. (d)

Q.3 In the monocotyledon seeds, the endosperm is surrounded by a layer known as
(a) testa (b) aleurone
(c) tegmen (d) epithelium

Ans. (b)

Q.4 The aleurone layer primarily contains
(a) lipids (b) starch
(c) proteins (d) fatty acids

Ans. (c)

Q.5 Endosperm is consumed by developing embryo in the seed of
(a) coconut (b) castor
(c) pea (d) maize

Ans. (c)

Q.6 The scutellum observed in a grain of wheat or maize is comparable to which part of the seed in other monocotyledons?
(a) Cotyledon (b) Endosperm
(c) Aleurone layer (d) Plumule

Ans. (a)

Q.7 Match the structures of seeds *P* and *Q* with their respective functions.

Structure of Seed	Functions
P	It stores food.
Q	Outer covering which protects the seed.

Choose the correct option.
(a) *P* - Seed coat, *Q*- Radicle
(b) *P* - Embryo, *Q*- Cotyledon
(c) *P* - Cotyledon, *Q*- Seed coat
(d) *P* - Embryo, *Q*- Plumule

Ans. (c)

Q.8 Mr. Singh asked his students to give an example of two seeds in which aleurone layer is present.
Riya said : Sunflower and rice
Amit said : Rice and maize
Shruti said : Sunflower and maize
Ritika said : Wheat and peas
Who is correct?
(a) Riya (b) Ritika
(c) Amit (d) Shruti

Ans. (c)

Q.9 The teacher shows her students a seed and asks them to identify two parts labelled as *A* and *B* in the given diagram of the seed.

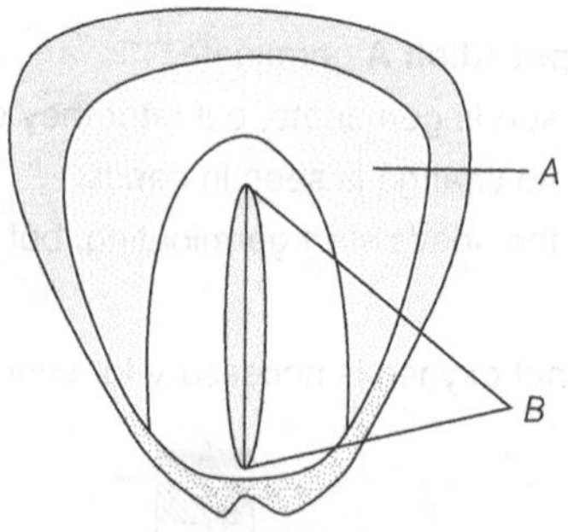

(a) *A*- Endosperm, *B*- Cotyledon
(b) *A*- Embryo, *B*- Radicle
(c) *A*- Endosperm, *B*- Embryo
(d) *A*- Radicle, *B*- Cotyledons

Ans. (c)

Q.10 The part of a .....*P*..... which grows and develops into root on germination is .....*Q*..... .
(a) *P*- cotyledon, *Q*- plumule
(b) *P*-root, *Q*- seed
(c) *P*- shoot, *Q*- radicle
(d) *P*- seed, *Q*- radicle

Ans. (d)

Q.11 The diagram shows three stages in the germination of a seedling. Which part is the plumule?

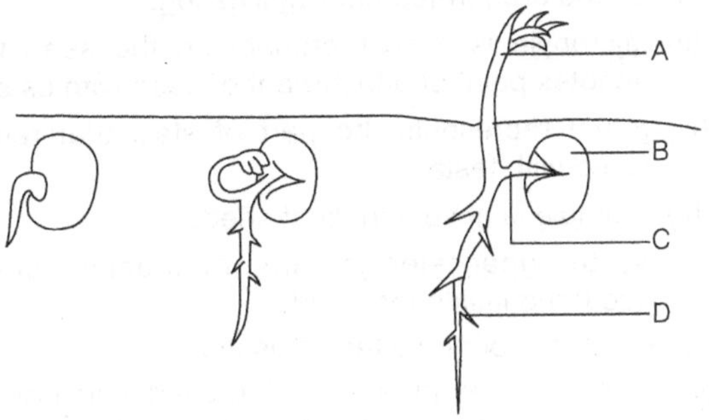

(a) A (b) B
(c) C (d) D

Ans. (a) During germination, the plumule protected by the cotyledons grow upwards against the gravity to form the young shoot.

TYPE - 2 01 Mark

Matching Type Question

Q.1 Match the terms in Column I with their correct description in Column II.

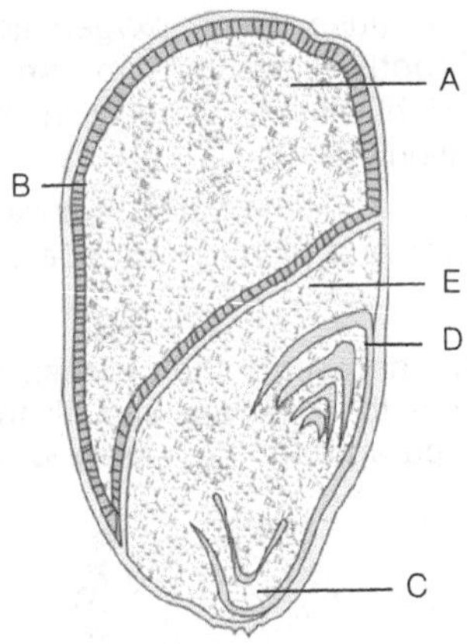

Column I	Column II
	I. It is a layer of cells in the seed that produces enzymes to breakdown stored food during germination.
	II. A protective sheath that covers the young shoot in monocot seeds during germination.
	III. Tissue in seeds that stores food for the developing embryo.
	IV. A single cotyledon in monocot seeds that absorbs nutrients from the endosperm.
	V. A protective covering around the radicle of monocot seeds, aiding in the initial stages of root growth.

Ans. A-III, B-I, C-V, D-II, E-IV

TYPE - 3 01 Mark

Assertion-Reason Type Questions

Direction (Q. Nos. 1-5) In the following questions statements are given as Assertion (A) and Reason (R).

(a) A is true, but R is false.
(b) A is false, but R is true.
(c) Both A and R are true.
(d) Both A and R are false.

Q.1 Assertion (A) Seeds help plants to survive unfavourable conditions and aid in the dispersal of species.

Reason (R) A seed is a mature ovule that develops after fertilisation and contains food reserves for the growth of the embryo.

Ans. (c)

Q.2 Assertion (A) Albuminous seeds contains little amount of endosperm.

Reason (R) Castor and custard apple are albuminous seeds.

Ans. (b) A is false, but R is true. A can be corrected as Albuminous seeds contains large amount of endosperm.

Q.3 Assertion (A) Cotyledons are the part of embryo in a seed.

Reason (R) It provides nourishment to the embryo during its development.

Ans. (c)

Q.4 Assertion (A) Bean seeds have two cotyledons.

Reason (R) These seeds are kidney-shaped which appear concave on both sides.

Ans. (a) A is true, but R is false. R can be corrected as Kidney-shaped seeds appear convex on one side and concave on the other side.

Q.5 Assertion (A) In dicot seeds seed coat is thicker and develops from the integuments.

Reason (R) Testa and tegmen are two layers which surrounds the seed coat.

Ans. (c)

TYPE - 4 01 Mark

Very Short Answer Type Questions

Q.1 Name the structure which develops from the ovule after fertilisation.

Ans. Seed

Q.2 How are seeds classified based on the presence of endosperm?

Ans. On the basis of presence and absence of endosperm seeds are classified into two categories, i.e. albuminous and exalbuminous.

Q.3 *X* is the outer layer of seed which protects the seed from pathogens and injuries. Identify the *X*.

Ans. Testa

Q.4 Name the part of an embryo which develops into shoot.

Ans. Plumule

Q.5 In which type of seed aleurone layer is present?

Ans. Monocot seed.

Q.6 Name the term which is used when the embryo is inactive.

Ans. Dormancy

Q.7 Identify the term used for the temperature at which germination occurs.

Ans. The term used for the temperature at which germination occurs is optimum temperature.

Q.8 Which type of germination occurs in bean seed?

Ans. Epigeal germination.

Q.9 What will happen if seeds are soaked overnight on wet cotton?

Ans. The seeds will absorb water and swell, starting the germination process.

Q.10 What happens if soaked seeds are completely submerged in water?

Ans. The seeds would not get enough oxygen to grow and will not germinate.

Q.11 Name the following. **(1 Mark each)**

(i) Structure that contains embryo and may or may not have a nutritive tissue.

(ii) Protective covering that develops from integuments of ovule.

(iii) Ridge-like structure present around the median groove.

(iv) Young miniature plants having cotyledons and embryonal axis.

(v) Part of embryo that gives rise to shoot.

Ans. (i) Seed

(ii) Seed coat

(iii) Raphe

(iv) Embryo

(v) Plumule

Q.12 Correct and rewrite the following statements by changing the underlined words. **(1 Mark each)**

(i) Seeds are formed after pollination.

(ii) Micropyle is a scar present on the seed which denotes point of attachment of seed with its stalk.

(iii) Hilum represents the part of stalk that remains fused with testa.

(iv) Plumule is absent in dicot seeds.

(v) Water deaccelerates the metabolic activities occurring inside the seed.

Ans. (i) Seeds are formed after fertilisation.

(ii) Hilum is a scar present on the seed which denotes point of attachment of seed with its stalk.

(iii) Raphe represents the part of stalk that remains fused with testa.

(iv) Endosperm is absent in dicot seeds.

(v) Water accelerates the metabolic activities occurring inside the seed.

Q.13 Choose the odd one out from the following terms given below and name the category to which other three belong. **(1 Mark each)**

(i) Seed coat, Hilum, Aleurone layer, Sepals

(ii) Water, Oxygen, Sunlight, Temperature

(iii) Petals, Embryo, Cotyledons, Plumule

Ans. (i) Odd term is sepals because it is a whorl of a flower, while seed coat, hilum and endosperm are structural parts of the seed.

(ii) Odd term is sunlight because water, oxygen and temperature are directly involved in seed germination, while sunlight is not essential in the early stages of germination.

(iii) Odd term is petals because it is the part of a flower, while embryo, cotyledons and plumule are specific parts of the dicot seed.

Q.14 The diagram given below represents the process of seed germination. Observe the diagram and fill the blank spaces in the given paragraph. **(1 Mark each)**

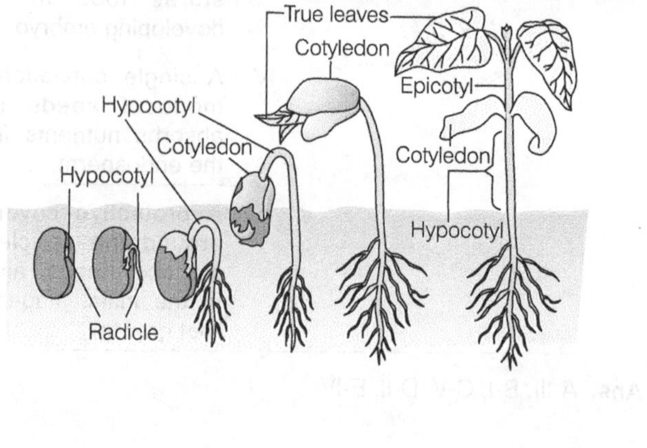

When environmental conditions such as moisture .....(i)..... and .....(ii)..... become favourable, the seed breaks .....(iii)..... and begins germination.

It is the process by which a seed develops into a new plant, starting with the growth of the embryo inside the seed. Suitable temperature is must for the .....(iv)..... . Most of the seeds cannot germinate when the temperature is below 0°C or above 48°C. .....(v)..... temperature range for seed germination is about 25-35°C.

Ans. (i) temperature (ii) light (iii) dormancy (iv) germination (v) Optimum

Q.15 Rearrange the following in logical sequence beginning with the term which is underlined. **(1 Mark each)**

(i) <u>Zygote</u>, Embryo, Seed, Endosperm

(ii) Seed, Embryo, <u>Fusion of gametes</u>, Zygote

Ans. (i) Zygote, Embryo, Endosperm, Seed.

(ii) Fusion of gametes, Zygote, Embryo, Seed.

Q.16 Give one example of each of the following. **(1 Mark each)**

(i) Monocot albuminous seed.

(ii) Seed with one cotyledon.

(iii) Seed with fused seed coat and pericarp.

(iv) Exalbuminous dicot seed.

(v) Hypogeal germination

Ans. (i) Wheat (ii) Rice (iii) Maize (iv) Bean (v) Maize

TYPE - 5 — 02 Marks

Short Answer Type Questions

Q.1 Give any two examples each of endospermic seed and non-endospermic seed in monocots and dicots both.

Ans. Endospermic or Albuminous Seeds

(i) Monocots : Maize, wheat

(ii) Dicots : Castor, cotton

Non-endospermic or Exalbuminous Seeds

(i) Monocots : Orchids, *Vallisneria*

(ii) Dicots : Bean, gram

Q.2 Explain the two main parts of a seed.

Ans. Seed Coat The outer protective layer that surrounds the seed, providing protection against physical damage and dehydration.

Embryo The young, developing plant that consists of the cotyledons, embryonal axis (which includes the plumule and radicle) and other structures essential for growth.

Q.3 State the exact location of the following.

(i) Seed coat

(ii) Raphe

(iii) Tegmen

(iv) Aleurone layer

Ans. (i) **Seed Coat** It is the protective covering around the seed.

(ii) **Raphe** Ridge-like structure around the median groove of seed.

(iii) **Tegmen** Inner thin membrane of seed next to testa.

(iv) **Aleurone Layer** It surrounds the endosperm in a monocot seed.

Q.4 In the following figure showing a germinating gram seed. Name the parts labelled as *A*, *B* and *C*.

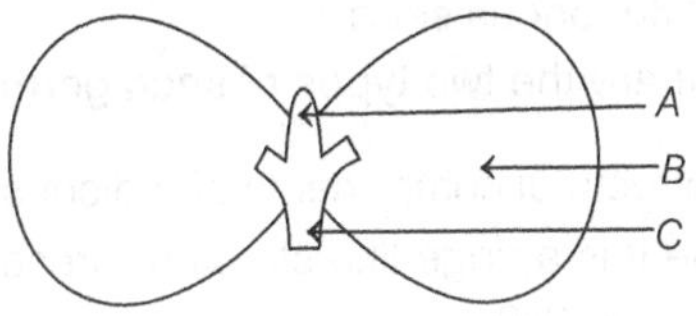

Why is part '*B*' considered to be important during germination?

Ans. The part labelled as *A*, *B* and *C* are plumule, cotyledon and radicle, respectively.

Part *B* of germinating gram seed contain the reserve food material that provides nourishment to the developing seedling, therefore it is considered to be important during germination.

Q.5 What does the seed constitute?

Ans. A seed constitutes the following structures

(i) **Embryo** includes the radicle, plumule and cotyledons.

(ii) **Cotyledons** store or absorb nutrients for the developing embryo.

(iii) **Endosperm** provides nourishment to the embryo in some seeds (e.g. monocots like maize).

(iv) **Seed coat** is the outer protective covering, formed from the integuments of the ovule.

Q.6 The tiger lily plant is a monocotyledon.

List two features visible which shows it is a monocotyledon.

Ans. Two visible features in tiger lily plant show that it is a monocotyledon are given below.

(i) **Parallel Venation** The leaves exhibit veins that run parallel to each other.

(ii) **Flower Parts in Multiples of Three** The flower has petals, sepals or other parts arranged in groups of three or multiples of three.

Q.7 Which type of seed is represented by the given diagram? Also give an example of it.

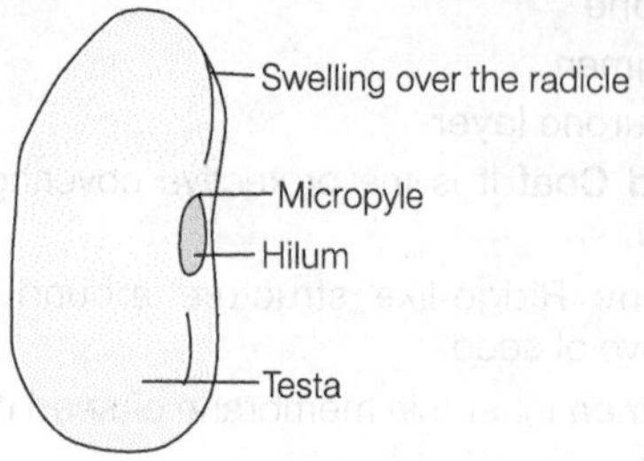

Ans. The given diagram represents a dicot seed, e.g. sunflower and bean seeds.

Q.8 Answer the following questions.

(i) Write about any two structural components of a dicotyledonous seed.

(ii) What are the two types of seed germination?

Ans. (i) Two structural components of a dicot seeds are

Raphe It is a ridge-like structure present around the median groove.

Seed Coat A protective covering that originates from the integuments of ovule. It is divided into testa and tegmen.

(ii) Two types of seed germination are hypogeal seed germination and epigeal seed germination.

Q.9 Define seed germination.

Ans. Seed germination is the process by which a seed develops into a new plant under favourable conditions.

Q.10 Why oxygen is necessary for seed germination?

Ans. Oxygen is necessary for seed germination because it supports respiration in the growing embryo, providing energy for rapid cell growth. Without oxygen, germination may fail.

Q.11 What is viviparous germination?

Ans. Viviparous germination is a special mode of seed germination that occurs inside the fruit, while it is still attached to the parent plant. This type of germination is observed in mangrove plants like *Rhizophora*.

Q.12 Answer the following questions.

(i) What happens in flask *A*, which contains soaked seeds, moist cotton and a test tube with pyrogallic acid dissolved in sodium hydroxide?

(ii) What happens in flask *B*, which contains soaked seeds, moist cotton and a test tube with water?

Ans. (i) Seeds do not germinate due to the absence of oxygen, as pyrogallic acid absorbs it.

(ii) Seeds germinate because oxygen is available for respiration.

TYPE – 6   03 Marks

Short Answer Type Questions

Q.1 Difference between dicot and monocot seeds.

Ans. Differences between dicot and monocot seeds are as follows

Dicot Seeds	Monocot Seeds
The seed coat of dicot seeds typically has two layers, which are thicker.	The seed coat of monocot seeds is generally thinner and often consists of a single layer.
In dicot seeds, the hilum is located on the concave side of the seed.	In monocot seeds, the hilum is located near the edge of the seed.
Dicot seeds have two cotyledons, which serve as the seed, leaves and store food.	Monocot seeds have only one cotyledon which serves the same function as the dicot cotyledons.

Q.2 With regard to germination in bean seed, answer the following questions.

(i) Name the seed part that grows into the seedling.

(ii) Name the seed part that provides nutrition for the growing seedling.

(iii) Draw a neat labelled diagram of a mature bean seed.

Ans. (i) The embryo grows into the seedling.

(ii) The cotyledons provide nutrition for the growing seedling.

(iii)

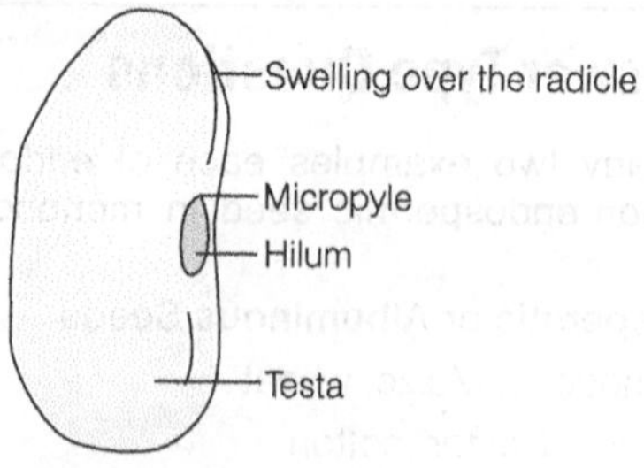

External structure of a bean seed

Q.3 Answer the following questions briefly.

(i) How are seeds broadly classified?

(ii) What do you call the seed having endosperm in them?

(iii) Why are orchid seeds called exalbuminous?

Ans. (i) Seeds are broadly classified as monocots and dicots.

(ii) Endospermic or albuminous seeds.

(iii) Orchid seeds are termed as exalbuminous as they lack endosperm.

Q.4 What is seed dormancy? Explain it.

Ans. A period during which a seed remains inactive is known as seed dormancy, it prevents premature germination.

During dormancy, all chemical activities within the seed continue at a very slow rate, but the seed remains in a state of rest.

Even though the seed is not actively growing, it still consumes small amounts of oxygen and releases carbon dioxide in minimal amounts.

Q.5 **Differentiate between epigeal and hypogeal germination.**

Ans. Differences between epigeal and hypogeal germination are as follows

Epigeal Germination	Hypogeal Germination
Hypocotyl elongates at a faster rate.	Epicotyl elongates at a faster rate.
Cotyledons are pushed above the ground.	Cotyledons are remain under the ground.
Cotyledons play role in photosynthesis.	Cotyledons have no role in photosynthesis.

Q.6 **Give biological reasons for the following.**

(i) **Maize is called a grain and not a seed/fruit.**

(ii) **Seeds have a hard protective covering around them.**

(iii) **Seeds grown deep in soil fail to germinate.**

Ans. (i) Maize is called a grain because it is a caryopsis, where the seed is fused with the fruit wall, making it a single unit that functions as a grain.

(ii) Seeds have a hard protective covering (seed coat) to protect the embryo from mechanical damage, desiccation and microbial infection.

(iii) Seeds grown too deep fail to germinate because they cannot access sufficient oxygen for respiration or energy to push the shoot through the soil surface.

Q.7 **State the differences between a maize grain and a bean seed.**

Ans. The differences between a maize grain and a bean seed are as follows

Maize Grain	Bean Seed
It has only one cotyledon.	It has two cotyledons.
Endosperm is absent.	Endosperm is present.
It has small embryo and the micropyle and hilum are invisible.	It has a large embryo and the micropyle and hilum are visible.

Q.8 **Madhav performs an experiment with three petridishes (*A*, *B* and *C*). He places soaked seeds on wet cotton wool for germination and keeps petridish *A* in a fridge at 4°C, petridish *B* at room temperature and petridish *C* in an incubator at 45°C. After 3-4 days, what are the observations in each petridish?**

Ans. In petridish *A*, seeds do not germinate; in petridish *B*, seeds germinate; in petridish *C*, seeds do not germinate or fail to grow due to high temperature.

Q.9 **Based on the observation given in Q. no. 8, explain why seeds of petridish *A* were not germinated?**

Ans. Seeds do not germinate in petridish *A* because the low temperature (4°C) in the fridge slows down or halts the metabolic processes required for germination.

Q.10 **Given below is the experimental setup. Observe it carefully and answer the following questions.**

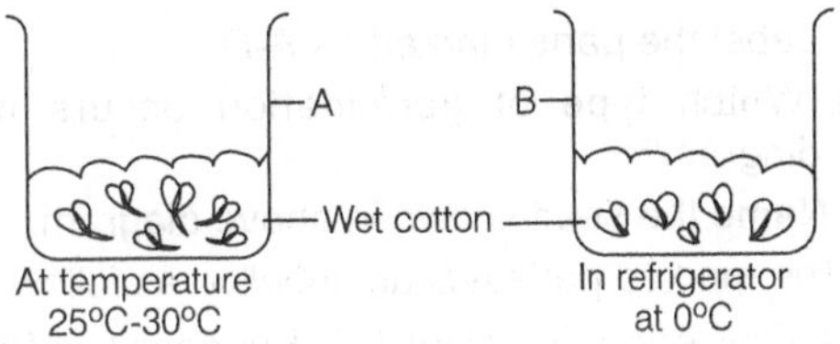

(i) **Write the aim of the experiment shown above.**

(ii) **What will you observe after few days for beakers A and B?**

(iii) **Why is wet cotton kept inside the beakers?**

Ans. (i) To prove that a suitable temperature is necessary for germination.

(ii) After few days, we will observe that the seeds in beaker A have started germinating while, the ones in the beaker 'B' did not germinate.

(iii) Wet cotton is kept inside both beakers for providing necessary moisture for germination.

TYPE - 7   03 Marks

Structured Based Questions

Q.1 Raghav saw his dad disperse seeds on their field and after sometime, he noticed that the seeds began to develop and showed a green appearance on top. Observe the image given along side and answer the following questions.

(i) Which process is shown in the image?

(ii) Which part of the seed develops into the shoot?

(iii) Which part of the seed develops into the root?

Ans. (i) The given image represents the process of seed germination.

(ii) Plumule develops into a shoot.

(iii) Radicle develops into a root.

Q.2 Observe the diagram and answer the following questions.

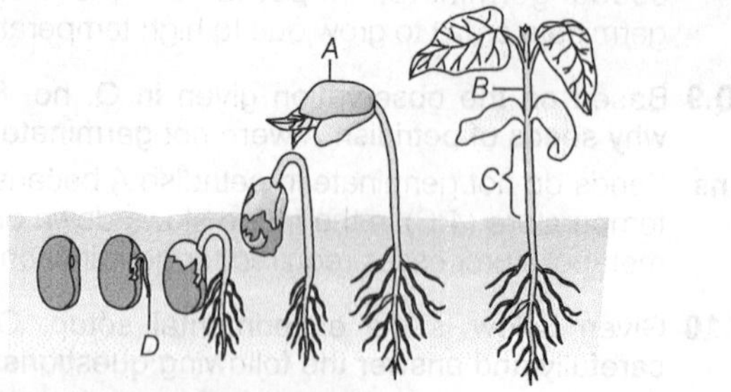

(i) Label the parts marked as *A-D*.

(ii) Which type of germination occurs in above diagram?

(iii) Name the seed shown in above diagram.

Ans. (i) The marked parts *A-D* are labelled as follows

A–Cotyledon, *B*–Epicotyl, *C*–Hypocotyl, *D*-Radicle

(ii) Epigeal germination is the type of germination which occurs in above diagram.

(iii) Bean seed (dicotyledon) is shown in above diagram.

Q.3 Seeds are the product of ripened ovule after fertilisation by pollen.

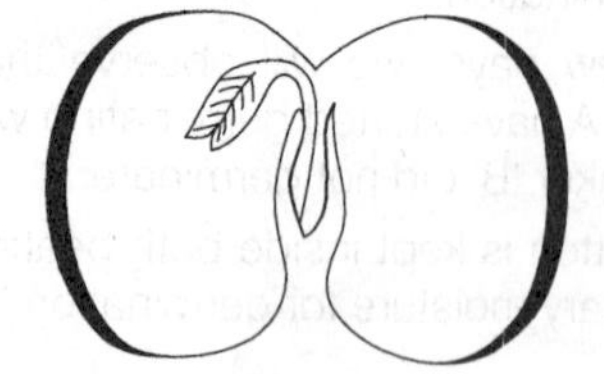

Answer the following questions.

(i) In which seeds, does the embryo absorb the endosperm?

(ii) Where does the seed coat develop from?

(iii) Does micropyle helps in pollination? Comment.

(iv) Why do large seeds have more energy reserves?

Ans. (i) In monocot seeds (e.g. maize), the embryo absorbs the endosperm during germination for nourishment.

(ii) The seed coat develops from the integuments of the ovule, which protect the seed.

(iii) The micropyle does not directly help in pollination; it is the small opening in the seed coat that allows the pollen tube to enter the ovule during fertilisation.

(iv) Large seeds have more energy reserves because they contain greater amounts of stored food (in the form of endosperm or cotyledons), which supports the initial growth of the seedling until it can photosynthesise.

Q.4 Given below is the diagram of a bean seed. Observe the diagram and answer the following questions.

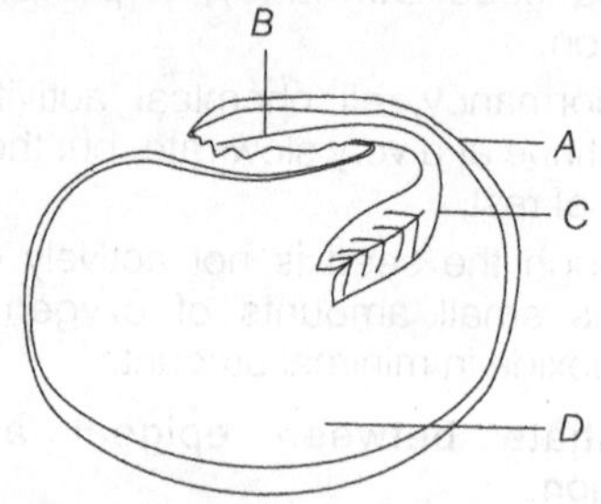

(i) On diagram label parts *A, B, C* and *D*.

(ii) Name the part of the flower in which the seed was formed.

(iii) Name the two parts of seed coat.

Ans. (i) *A*-Testa, *B*-Plumule, *C*-Radicle, *D*-Cotyledon

(ii) The seed is formed in the ovary of the flower.

(iii) Testa and tegmen are the two parts of seed coat.

Q.5 The diagram given below shows three bean seeds that are placed at different levels.

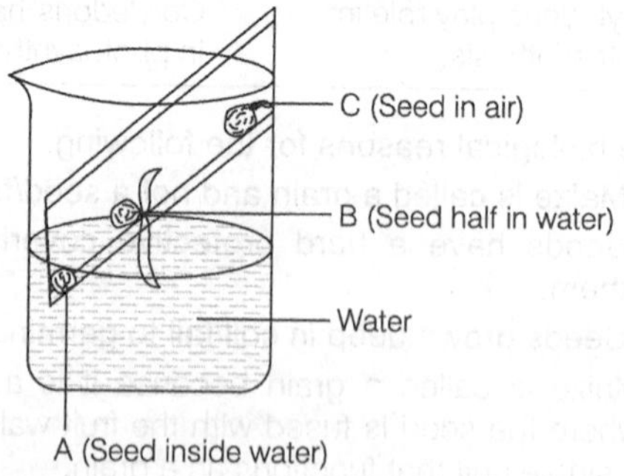

Answer the following questions.

(i) What visible changes as per the activity will you observe in the seeds A, B and C. Also give suitable reasons.

(ii) What type of germination does a bean seed show?

(iii) Mention the parts of a flower that forms fruits and seeds.

Ans. (i) After a few days we will observe that seed A will not germinate due to excess water and less available oxygen.

Seed B will germinate as it gets both water and oxygen in adequate amount.

Seed C will not germinate as it gets only oxygen, but no water.

(ii) A bean seed shows epigeal (cotyledons carried above the soil) type of germination.

(iii) Fruit is formed from the ovary of a flower, while seeds are formed from the ovules of a flower.

06

RESPIRATION IN PLANTS

All living organisms, including plants, require energy to carry out essential life processes. Energy obtained through respiration is used in supporting various vital activities like growth, nutrient transport and reproduction.

Respiration

- It is a metabolic process by which living cells generate energy (ATP) by breaking down glucose in the presence of oxygen, releasing carbon dioxide and water as byproducts.
- Respiration is often compared to burning (such as the combustion of coal) as both release energy and produce carbon dioxide and water vapour as end products.
- However, these two processes differs from each other in following ways
  - **Respiration** is a **controlled** biological process occurring at body temperature, while **burning** is an **uncontrolled** chemical reaction requiring high temperatures.

There are two types of respiration which are as follows

I. Aerobic Respiration

It is the process of breaking down of glucose in the presence of oxygen to produce energy (ATP), carbon dioxide and water. It occurs in all higher organisms.

Aerobic respiration can be summarised in the form of the equation given below

$$\underset{\text{(6 carbon molecules)}}{\text{Glucose}} \xrightarrow[\text{In cytoplasm}]{\text{Glycolysis}} \underset{\text{(3 carbon molecules)}}{\text{Pyruvate}} + \text{Energy}$$

$$\text{Pyruvate} \xrightarrow[\text{In mitochondria}]{\text{Oxygen}} \underset{\text{(6 molecules)}}{\text{Carbon dioxide}} + \underset{\text{(6 molecules)}}{\text{Water}} + \text{Energy}$$

II. Anaerobic Respiration

- It is the process of breaking down of glucose in the absence of oxygen to produce energy (ATP).
- It is termed as fermentation in microorganisms and it is of following types on the basis of the product formed.
  - **Alcoholic Fermentation** It is the incomplete breakdown of sugar into ethanol and carbon dioxide to release energy. This process occurs mainly in yeast, which is used to produce beer, wine, toddy, cheese, etc., by **brewing**. It can be summarised as

$$\underset{\text{(6 carbon molecules)}}{\text{Glucose}} \xrightarrow[\text{In yeast}]{\text{Absence of oxygen}} \underset{\text{(2 carbon molecules)}}{\text{Ethanol}} + \text{Carbon dioxide} + \text{Energy}$$

  Anaerobic respiration is termed as **fermentation** in microorganisms.

  - **Lactic Acid Fermentation** It is the process of incomplete breakdown of sugar into lactic acid and energy, e.g. in yoghurt making anaerobic respiration in some bacteria cause milk to turn sour. Similarly, lactic acid production takes place in human muscles during vigorous physical exercise.

$$\underset{\text{(6 carbon molecules)}}{\text{Glucose}} \xrightarrow[\text{In muscle cells}]{\text{Lack of oxygen}} \underset{\text{(3 carbon molecules)}}{\text{Lactic acid}} + \text{Energy}$$

The breakdown of glucose in anaerobic respiration occurs through glycolysis, while in aerobic respiration, it involves both glycolysis and the Krebs' cycle, these steps are discussed below

1. **Glycolysis** It is the first step in both aerobic and anaerobic respiration, occurring in the **cytoplasm**. It involves the breakdown of one molecule of glucose into two molecules of pyruvate and producing a small amount of ATP. This process does not require oxygen.
2. **Krebs' Cycle** (also known as the citric acid cycle) It occurs in the mitochondria, where each pyruvate is further broken down, releasing carbon dioxide and producing energy rich molecules that are used in the next stage to generate more ATP.

- Significance of glycolysis and Krebs' cycle are as follows
  - Both of these are major pathways for the formation of ATP molecules.
  - Citric acid cycle plays a role in both oxidation (catabolic) and synthetic (anabolic) processes.
- The overall process of breakdown of glucose in both aerobic and anaerobic respiration can be summarised as follows

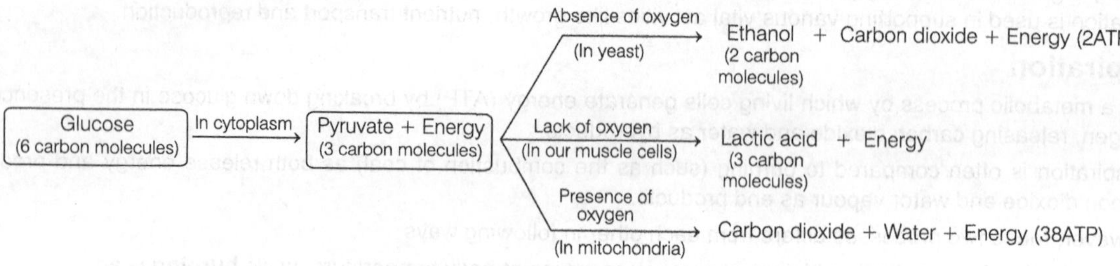

Breakdown of glucose by various pathways

Gaseous Exchange

- Gaseous exchange in plants is the process by which plants exchange gases like oxygen and carbon dioxide with the environment.
- In plants, it occurs primarily through stomata in leaves, lenticels in stem and general surface area of roots.

Experiments on Respiration in Plants

Experiment 1

Aim To demonstrate that oxygen is used in respiration.

Procedure Take two test tubes *A* and *B*. Put some KOH solution in both the test tubes. Now place some germinating seeds in test tube *A* (supported by wire mesh) and heat-killed/boiled germinating seed in test tube *B* along with a disinfectant like formalin to avoid bacterial decay. Connect both test tubes *A* and *B* to a beaker containing coloured water.

The arrangement of experimental setup is done as shown in the figure.

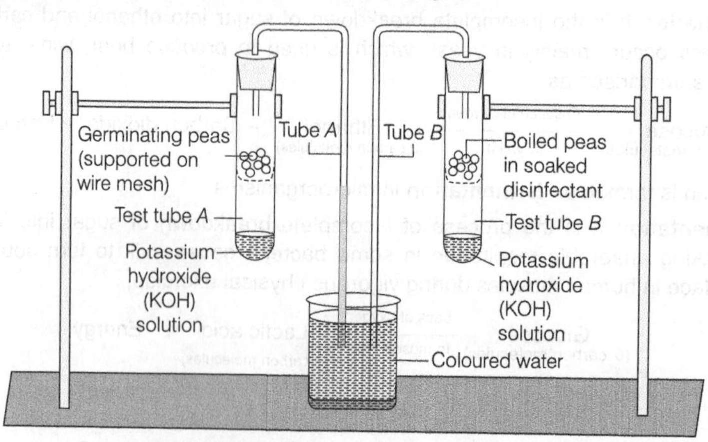

Experiment to demonstrate that oxygen is used up in respiration

Observation After few days, the coloured water rises up in tube *A*.

Inference The oxygen present in test tube *A* was used up by germinating seeds and CO_2 was produced. The CO_2 released by the seeds was absorbed by KOH, creating a vacuum in the system. This resulted in a rise of water level in tube *A*. System *B*, however did not show any change because seeds were boiled and thus inactive. Test tube *B* worked as a control as it did not show any rise in water level.

Experiment 2

Aim To prove that heat is produced during respiration.

Procedure Put some germinating gram seeds in thermoflask *A* and germinated boiled seeds in thermoflask *B*. Insert a thermometer in each flask and plug their mouths with cotton wool. Keep this setup undisturbed for few hours and record any change in temperature.

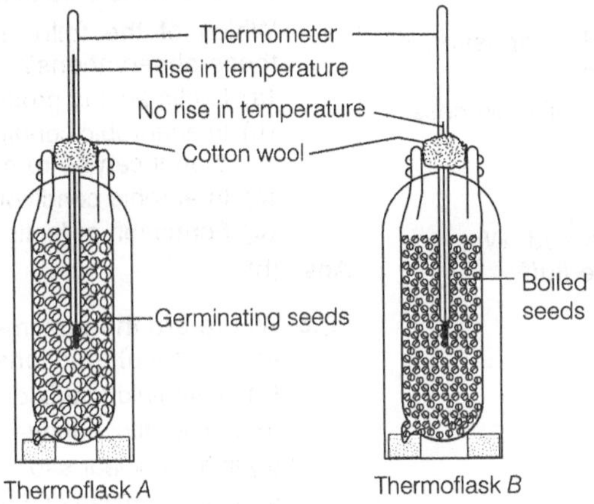

Experimental setup to demonstrate that heat is produced during respiration

Observation There is rise in temperature in flask *A*, but not in flask *B*.

Inference The rise in temperature in thermoflask *A* occur because germinating live seeds respire and produce heat, whereas in flask *B* seeds are killed because of boiling. So, these are not respiring, thus no heat is produced.

Experiment 3

Aim To prove that carbon dioxide is produced by green plants during respiration.

Procedure Place a potted plant and cover it with the help of a bell jar. Apply vaseline on the rims of bell jar to make it airtight. Connect this bell jar with the two conical flasks *A* and *B* containing clear limewater with delivery tubes.

Keep the setup in a dark room or cover the bell jar with a black cloth to prevent photosynthesis

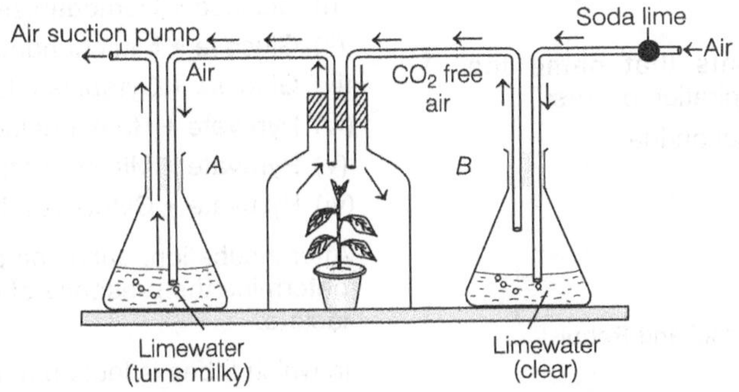

Experiment to show that carbon dioxide is produced by green plants during respiration

Observation Limewater in flask *A* turns milky, but limewater in flask *B* remains clear.

Inference The air passing through flask *B* is free of CO_2, because CO_2 of air is absorbed by the soda lime in the delivery tube. Hence, limewater in flask *B* remains clear and does not turn milky, whereas limewater in flask *A* turns milky proving that CO_2 must have been produced by the plant during respiration.

EXAM ORIENTED QUESTIONS

TYPE - 1

01 Mark

Multiple Choice Questions

Q.1 The difference between respiration and combustion is related to the fact that respiration being

(a) multistep process (b) enzyme controlled process

(c) intracellular process (d) All of these

Ans. (d)

Q.2 The figure given below show a loaf of bread. Which type of respiration is responsible for the fluffy appearance of the bread?

Choose the correct option from those given below.

(a) Krebs' cycle

(b) Glycolysis

(c) Lactic acid fermentation

(d) Alcoholic fermentation

Ans. (d) The type of respiration involved in the formation of bread through the production of CO_2 is alcoholic fermentation. This anaerobic process occurs in yeast, producing ethanol and carbon dioxide, which causes the bread to rise.

Q.3 Mrs. Singh asked her students that name the organelle in which anaerobic respiration occurs.

Rahul said: Cytoplasm and mitochondria.

Anant said: Only cytoplasm

Mridul said: Only mitochondria

Who gave the right answer?

(a) Mridul (b) Rahul

(c) Anant (d) Both Mridul and Rahul

Ans. (c)

Q.4 Where does ethanol formation occur in a yeast cell?

(a) Cell vacuole (b) Cytoplasm

(c) Golgi apparatus (d) Mitochondrion

Ans. (b)

Q.5 Lactic acid is produced when muscle contracts. Frog muscle can contract in the absence of oxygen and lactic acid accumulates until fatigue set in. On return to aerobic conditions, the muscle can contract again and the lactic acid is metabolised.

Which of the following is the best interpretation of these observations?

(a) Lactic acid is produced only in aerobic conditions

(b) In anaerobic conditions, lactic acid is produced faster than it can be removed

(c) In aerobic conditions the muscle will not fatigue

(d) Formation of lactic acid is oxygen-dependent

Ans. (b)

Q.6 Where are the enzymes located which are involved in the chemical reactions which occur during glycolysis?

(a) In the fluid matrix of cytoplasm

(b) In the mitochondrial matrix

(c) In the nuclear sap

(d) On the cristae of a mitochondrion

Ans. (a)

Q.7 How many ATP molecules are produced from one molecule of glucose in plants?

(a) 38 (b) 40

(c) 28 (d) 32

Ans. (a) Total 38 ATP molecules are produced during complete oxidation of one molecule of glucose.

Q.8 Six tubes were setup as shown in the table.

Tubes	Contents
(i)	Glucose + Homogenised animal cells
(ii)	Glucose + Mitochondria
(iii)	Glucose + Cytoplasm lacking organelles
(iv)	Pyruvate + Homogenised animal cells
(v)	Pyruvate + Mitochondria
(vi)	Pyruvate + Cytoplasm lacking organelles

After incubation, each sample was analysed to determine the presence of carbon dioxide and lactate.

In which tubes is lactate most likely to be present?

(a) (i) and (iii) only

(b) (ii), (iii), (v) and (vi) only

(c) (iii) and (vi) only

(d) (iv), (v) and (vi) only

Ans. (c)

Q.9 The total energy gained from one mole of glucose during aerobic respiration is

(a) 2 ATP (b) 4 ATP (c) 38 ATP (d) 40 ATP

Ans. (c)

Q.10 Reena trying to match the types of respiration with the exact amount of energy they produced.

Types of Respiration	Functions
P	2 ATP
Q	38 ATP

Choose the correct option.

(a) *P*- Glycolysis, *Q*- Anaerobic

(b) *P*- Anaerobic, *Q*- Aerobic

(c) *P*- Alcohol fermentation, *Q*- Lactic acid fermentation

(d) *P*- Aerobic, *Q*- Alcohol fermentation

Ans. (b)

Q.11 What is the correct anaerobic respiration in muscles?

	Carbon dioxide produced	Amount of energy released
(a)	No	High
(b)	No	Low
(c)	Yes	High
(d)	Yes	Low

Ans. (b) Anaerobic respiration is the breakdown of glucose in the absence of oxygen. During this process no carbon dioxide is produced.

Glucose $\rightarrow$ Lactic acid + Less energy

Q.12 The amount of energy released from a given quantity of glucose is greater in aerobic respiration than in anaerobic respiration. By approximately how much is the energy yield increased in animals?

(a) 3 times (b) 9 times

(c) 12 times (d) 18 times

Ans. (d)

Q.13 The complete oxidation of one mole of glucose yields 2880 kJ of energy. The addition of one phosphate molecule to ADP requires 30.6 kJ of energy per mole. In aerobic respiration, 38 molecules of ATP are formed as a result of the breakdown of each glucose molecule.

Which figure best represents the efficiency of aerobic respiration in trapping the energy released by the glucose molecule?

(a) 23% (b) 36% (c) 40% (d) 45%

Ans. (c) The total amount of energy used in forming 38 ATP $= 38 \times 30.6 \text{ kJ} = 1162.8 \text{ kJ}$.

Thus, the efficiency of aerobic respiration is $1162.8/2880 \times 100\,\% = 40\%$

TYPE - 2 01 Mark

Matching Type Question

Q.1 Match the following columns.

	Column I	Column II
A.	Lactic acid	I. Mitochondria
B.	Ethyl alcohol	II. Yeast
C.	Krebs' cycle	III. Energy currency
D.	ATP	IV. Cytoplasm
E.	Glycolysis	V. Muscles

Ans. A- V, B- II, C- I, D-III, E- IV

TYPE - 3 01 Mark

Assertion-Reason Type Questions

Direction (Q. Nos. 1-5) In the following questions statements are given as Assertion (A) and Reason (R).

(a) A is true, but R is false.

(b) A is false, but R is true.

(c) Both A and R are true.

(d) Both A and R are false.

Q.1 Assertion (A) All organisms including plants, require energy to carry out essential life processes.

Reason (R) In plants, energy is derived from the breakdown of glucose during respiration, releasing ATP that supports vital activities.

Ans. (c)

Q.2 Assertion (A) Respiration is compared to burning, as both release energy and produce carbon dioxide and water vapour.

Reason (R) Combustion is a controlled biological process.

Ans. (a) A is true, but R is false. R can be corrected as Respiration is a controlled biological process at body temperature, while burning is an uncontrolled reaction requiring high temperature.

Q.3 Assertion (A) Energy is generated in cells through the breakdown of glucose.

Reason (R) During glycolysis, glucose is broken down into pyruvate, this reaction occurs in the mitochondria.

Ans. (a) A is true, but R is false. R can be corrected as During glycolysis, glucose is broken down into pyruvate, this reaction occurs in the cytoplasm.

Q.4 Assertion (A) Anaerobic respiration produces less energy compared to aerobic respiration.

Reason (R) In anaerobic respiration, glucose is only partially broken down due to the absence of oxygen.

Ans. (c)

Q.5 Assertion (A) Stomata are the primary site for gaseous exchange in plants.

Reason (R) Stomata open and close to regulate the exchange of oxygen, carbon dioxide and water vapour.

Ans. (c)

TYPE - 4 01 Mark

Very Short Answer Type Questions

Q.1 Respiration is a metabolic process that occurs in two forms. Name them.

Ans. Aerobic and anaerobic are the two forms of respiration.

Q.2 Write the chemical equation for aerobic respiration.

Ans. $C_6H_{12}O_6 + 6O_2 \longrightarrow 6CO_2 + 6H_2O$ + Energy

Q.3 *X* is the phase of aerobic respiration which does not require oxygen. Identify the *X*.

Ans. Glycolysis

Q.4 Identify the process in which pyruvate is broken down to release energy.

Ans. Krebs' cycle

Q.5 Fill in the blanks with suitable words.

Glucose is incompletety broken down to ...*A*... alcohol in yeast during ...*B*... .

Ans. Glucose is incompletely broken down to (*A*) **ethyl alcohol** in yeast during (*B*) **anaerobic respiration.**

Q.6 In the experiment to show that heat is produced during respiration, which seeds are used?

Ans. Germinating seeds.

Q.7 Why is the experiment demonstrating the production of carbon dioxide is conducted in the dark?

Ans. To prevent photosynthesis, which would use up the CO_2.

Q.8 Name the following. **(1 Mark each)**

(i) A chain of chemical reactions that enable all living organisms to synthesise energy.

(ii) A microorganism that produces lactic acid on fermentation.

(iii) Energy currency of the cell.

(iv) Physiochemical process that does not require any enzyme.

(v) Product obtained from the breakdown of glucose.

Ans. (i) Respiration (ii) Bacteria

(iii) ATP (Adenosine Triphosphate)

(iv) Combustion (v) Pyruvate

Q.9 Correct and rewrite the following statements by changing the underlined words. **(1 Mark each)**

(i) Energy obtained for life activities in an organism is obtained by <u>nutrition</u>.

(ii) Respiratory gases undergo <u>osmosis</u> to move from one place to the other.

(iii) Conversion of glucose to pyruvate occurs in the <u>nucleus</u> of a cell.

(iv) Energy released in aerobic process is <u>equal</u> to that in anaerobic process.

Ans. (i) Energy obtained for life activities in an organism is obtained by respiration.

(ii) Respiratory gases undergo diffusion to move from one place to the other.

(iii) Conversion of glucose to pyruvate occurs in the cytoplasm of a cell.

(iv) Energy released in aerobic process is much higher than that in anaerobic process.

Q.10 Name the two types of metabolic activities in living organisms.

Ans. (i) Anabolic (ii) Catabolic

Q.11 Choose the odd one out from the following terms given below and name the category to which other three belong. **(1 Mark each)**

(i) Glucose, H_2O, CO_2, Energy

(ii) Oxygen, Yeast, Ethanol, Lactic acid

(iii) Stomata, Lenticels, Roots, Nucleus

Ans. (i) Odd term is **glucose** because it is not the product of **aerobic respiration**, while rest three are the products of aerobic respiration.

(ii) Odd term is **oxygen** because it is related to **aerobic respiration**, while rest three are related to **anaerobic respiration**.

(iii) Odd term is **nucleus** because it **does not** helps in **gaseous exchange**, while rest three structures help in **gaseous exchange**.

Q.12 Given below are the diagram of stomata which helps the plant in gaseous exchange. Observe the diagram and fill the blank spaces with correct words. **(1 Mark each)**

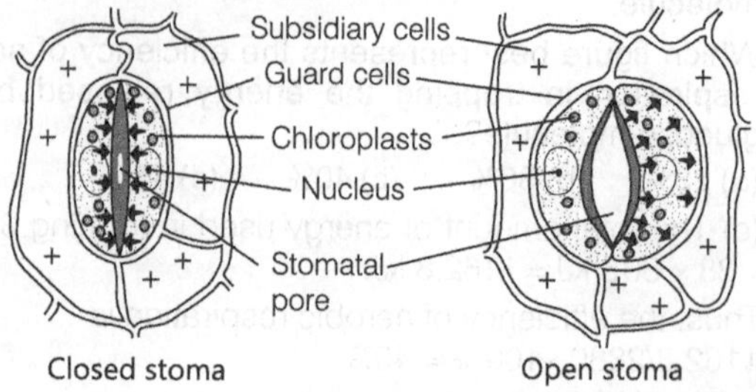

.......(i)....... in plants is the process by which plants exchange gases like ....(ii)....... and carbon dioxide with the environment. It occurs primarily through small openings called ....(iii)....... on the leaves, where carbon dioxide enters for ....(iv)....... and oxygen is released as a byproduct. ....(v)....... on stems and roots also aid in gaseous exchange. The process ensures that the plant has the necessary gases for metabolic functions and maintains balance in its environment.

Ans. (i) Gaseous exchange (ii) oxygen
(iii) stomata (iv) photosynthesis
(v) Lenticels

TYPE - 5 — 02 Marks

Short Answer Type Questions

Q.1 What is respiration? Name any two organisms which respire anaerobically.

Ans. Respiration is a metabolic process by which living cells generate energy (ATP) by breaking down glucose in the presence of oxygen, releasing carbon dioxide and water as byproducts. Fungi and bacteria respire anaerobically.

Q.2 Define aerobic respiration and explain the reaction involved in this process.

Ans. Aerobic respiration is a metabolic process in which cells generate energy (ATP) by breaking down glucose in the presence of oxygen.

The reaction for aerobic respiration is as follows

$$\underset{\text{(Glucose)}}{C_6H_{12}O_6} + 6O_2 \longrightarrow 6CO_2 + 6H_2O + ATP$$

Q.3 Complete the following reactions given.

(i) Pyruvate $\xrightarrow{\text{Krebs' Cycle}}$ .... + ...

(ii) .... $\xrightarrow{\text{Glycolysis}}$ ....

Ans. (i) Pyruvate $\xrightarrow{\text{Krebs' Cycle}}$ Carbon dioxide + Water

(ii) Glucose $\xrightarrow{\text{Glycolysis}}$ Pyruvate

Q.4 In aerobic respiration, how many steps are involved in the breakdown of glucose, explain them?

Ans. The breakdown of glucose in aerobic respiration occurs in two main steps

(i) **Glycolysis** Glucose is broken down into pyruvate in the cytoplasm, producing a small amount of ATP and NADH.

(ii) **Krebs' Cycle** Pyruvate is further broken down in the mitochondria, releasing carbon dioxide and transferring high-energy electrons to NAD^+ and FAD forming NADH and $FADH_2$.

Q.5 Explain the role of stomata in gaseous exchange.

Ans. Stomata are small openings on the surface of leaves that facilitate the exchange of gases, including the intake of carbon dioxide for photosynthesis and the release of oxygen and water vapour.

Q.6 Why is it important to keep the experimental setup airtight when demonstrating oxygen consumption in respiration?

Ans. The setup needs to be airtight to ensure that no external air (and thus oxygen) enters, allowing the measurement of only the oxygen consumed by the plant during respiration.

Q.7 It is difficult to demonstrate respiration in plants. Discuss.

Ans. To demonstrate respiration in living entities, evolution of carbon dioxide can be taken as an indicator. In plants, both respiration and photosynthesis occurs during a day time therefore the carbon dioxide that is liberated during respiration gets used up in photosynthesis, hence, there is not evolution of carbon dioxide. Consequently it becomes difficult to demonstrate respiration in green plants as there is no evolution of CO_2 during the day time.

Q.8 Why is KOH used, in one of the test tubes during the experiment demonstrating the production of carbon dioxide during respiration?

Ans. KOH (potassium hydroxide) is used in one of the test tubes to absorb carbon dioxide. This serves as a control to show that if CO_2 is removed, there is no change in limewater, confirming that the CO_2 in the experimental setup comes from plant respiration

TYPE - 6 — 03 Marks

Short Answer Type Questions

Q.1 State the differences between respiration and combustion.

Ans. Differences between respiration and combustion are as follows

Respiration	Combustion
A biochemical process occurring in living cells to release energy.	A chemical reaction between a fuel and oxygen, releasing energy.
Occurs at body temperature (low temperature).	Requires high temperatures to initiate the reaction.
Produces carbon dioxide and water.	Produces carbon dioxide, water and heat.

Q.2 Write a short note on anaerobic respiration.

Ans. Anaerobic respiration is the incomplete breakdown of glucose into simpler substances in the absence of oxygen. This process occurs in yeast, bacteria and human muscles. It is termed fermentation in microorganisms and is of two types

Alcoholic Fermentation In this process, sugar breaks down into ethanol and CO_2 to release energy.

Lactic Acid Fermentation This is the process of incomplete breakdown of sugar into lactic acid and energy.

Q.3 State the differences between anaerobic and aerobic respiration.

Ans. Differences between anaerobic and aerobic respiration are as follows

Anaerobic Respiration	Aerobic Respiration
Anaerobic respiration does not require oxygen.	Aerobic respiration requires oxygen.
It produces less energy, yielding only 2 ATP per glucose molecule.	It produces more energy, yielding up to 38 ATP per glucose molecule.
The byproducts of anaerobic respiration are lactic acid (in animals) or ethanol and carbon dioxide (in plants and yeast).	The byproducts of aerobic respiration are carbon dioxide and water.

Q.4 Given below are chemical reactions (1-4) involving glucose and four other chemical products (A-D).

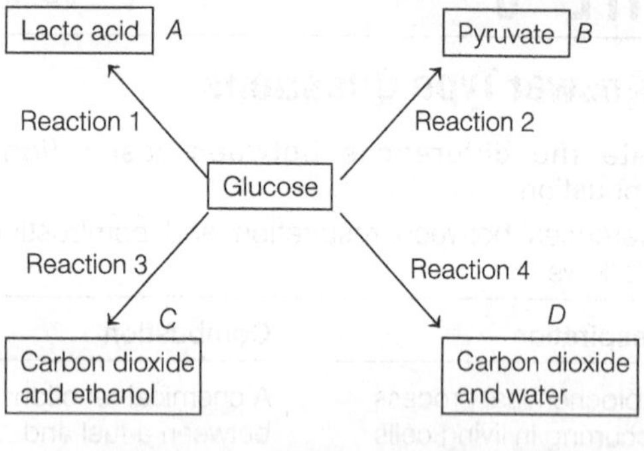

Write the reaction number as per the following.

(i) Anaerobic respiration in plants ....

(ii) End products in aerobic respiration

(iii) Anaerobic respiration in animals

(iv) Product of glycolysis

Ans. (i) 3 (ii) 4

(iii) 1 (iv) 2

Q.5 Answer the following questions briefly.

(i) What happens to the energy released in respiration?

(ii) What are the two phases of aerobic respiration?

(iii) Do all cells use oxygen to produce energy?

Ans. (i) Energy released in respiration is stored as ATP in mitochondria and later used for various metabolic activities in the body.

(ii) The two phases of aerobic respiration are glycolysis and Krebs' cycle.

(iii) No, cells do not always require oxygen to produce energy. For example, in muscle cells, energy is produced anaerobically in the absence of oxygen.

Q.6 What is gaseous exchange in plants and how does it occur?

Ans. Gaseous exchange in plants is the process by which plants exchange gases like oxygen and carbon dioxide with the environment.

It primarily occurs through stomata on the leaves, where carbon dioxide enters for photosynthesis and oxygen is released. Lenticels on stems and roots also assist in gas exchange.

Q.7 Give biological reasons for the following.

(i) Most of the organisms cannot survive without oxygen.

(ii) Respiration is called energy releasing process.

(iii) Glycolysis is considered as an important stage of respiration.

Ans. (i) Most of the organisms require oxygen for cellular respiration in order to produce energy and to carry out vital metabolic activities.

(ii) Respiration involves the breakdown of complex molecules (glucose) into simple ones (carbohydrates) with the release of a huge amount of energy. Thus, it is called an energy releasing process.

(iii) Glycolysis is considered as an important stage of respiration because it is a common process that occurs in both aerobic and anaerobic respiration.

Q.8 Energy required to perform various metabolic activities in the body comes from a vital process.

(i) Name the process responsible for providing energy as per the above statement.

(ii) How is energy liberated after the process?

(iii) How many molecules of ATP are released after oxidation of one molecule of glucose?

Ans. (i) Respiration is the process responsible for providing energy.

(ii) Energy liberated after respiration can be in the form of heat, while the majority of it is also converted to chemical form, i.e. ATP.

(iii) 38 molecules of ATP are released after oxidation of one molecule of glucose.

TYPE - 7

03 Marks

Structured Based Questions

Q.1 Given below is the figure of some bakery product. Take a moment to observe the figure and respond to the following questions based on your observations.

(i) Identify the method by which the dough for bread is prepared.

(ii) In the process of bread formation, which gas is produced?

(iii) List the products that are formed using the same method.

Ans. (i) The dough for bread is prepared through the method of fermentation.

(ii) In the process of bread formation, carbon dioxide gas is produced.

(iii) Alcohol, pizza and cake are the products which are prepared from this method.

Q.2 Ram and Rohan were doing intense exercise, after which they felt soreness and pain in their bodies. Observe the figure and answer the following questions.

(i) Why do they experience body pain after the exercise?

(ii) How can their muscles respire during intense exercise?

(iii) Explain the process with the help of a chemical reaction.

Ans. (i) They experience body pain due to the accumulation of lactic acid in their muscles, which builds up during anaerobic respiration when oxygen is insufficient.

(ii) During intense exercise, their muscles respire anaerobically because they did not get sufficient oxygen.

(iii) The process can be explained through the following chemical reaction

$$\underset{\text{(Glucose)}}{C_6H_{12}O_6} \longrightarrow \underset{\text{(Lactic acid)}}{2C_3H_6O_3} + \text{Energy}$$

Q.3 To study and prove a particular physiological process in plants, the following experiment was setup. Observe the figure and answer the following questions.

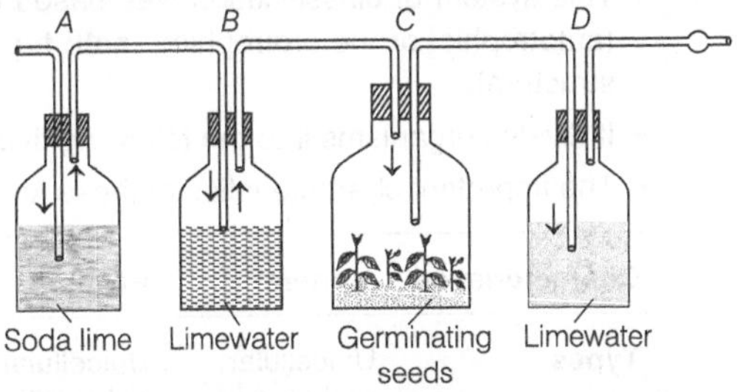

(i) Name the physiological process being studied.

(ii) What is the purpose of using soda lime in bottle *A* and why is limewater placed in bottle *B*?

(iii) Would there be any change taking place in bottle *D*?

Ans. (i) The physiological process being studied is aerobic respiration.

(ii) Soda lime in bottle *A* is used to remove the carbon dioxide from the incoming air. Limewater is placed in bottle *B* to ensure that all the CO_2 present in the air has been absorbed and the air entering bottle *C* is free from CO_2.

(iii) Limewater turns milky.

07

DIVERSITY IN LIVING ORGANISMS

- On Earth, there is a vast diversity of living organisms, ranging from microscopic unicellular forms like bacteria to complex multicellular organisms like plants, animals and humans. This variation among living beings is collectively known as **biodiversity**. To study and organise this diversity, **RH Whittaker** proposed the five kingdom system of classification.

Five Kingdom System of Classification

- This system of classification was based on **cellular organisation** (unicellular or multicellular), **nutritional mode** (autotrophic or heterotrophic), **cell type** (prokaryotic or eukaryotic) and **body organisation** (complexity of structure).
- It divides organisms into the following five kingdoms, i.e. **Monera**, **Protista**, **Fungi**, **Plantae** and **Animalia**.
- The important characteristics of these kingdoms are as follows

Characteristics	Monera	Protista	Fungi	Plantae	Animalia
Types	Unicellular, prokaryotic	Unicellular, eukaryotic	Multicellular, non-green, eukaryotic	Multicellular, eukaryotic	Multicellular, eukaryotic
Modes of Nutrition	Autotrophic or heterotrophic	Autotrophic or heterotrophic	Saprophytic or parasitic sometimes symbiotic	Autotrophic	Heterotrophic
Body	Lack well defined nucleus and cell organelles.	They possesses well defined nucleus, some organisms use pseudopodia or cilia or flagella for movement.	Fungus is made up of long filaments called **hyphae**. The network of hyphae is **mycelium**.	Exhibits high levels of tissue differentiation and have specilised body organs.	Exhibits high level of tissue differentiation and have specialised body organs with well developed organ system.
Examples	Bacteria, blue green algae.	*Amoeba*, *Paramecium*, *Euglena*, *Chlamydomonas* (autotrophic).	Yeast, *Rhizopus*, mushrooms, moulds.	Trees, shrubs and herbs.	Fish, insects, animals, humans, birds.

The kingdoms– **Plantae** and **Animalia** are further discussed in detail below

Kingdom-Plantae

Depending upon various characteristics, kingdom–Plantae is divided into two sub-kingdoms and five divisions:

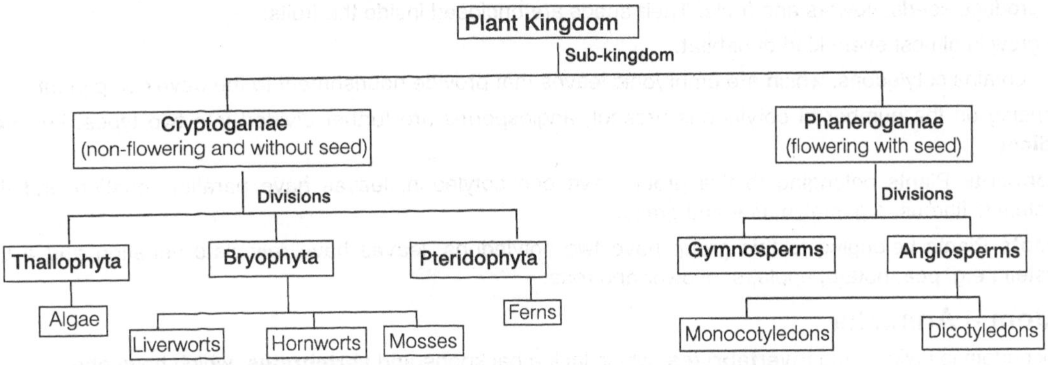

Thallophyta

It includes multicellular algae (i.e. sea weeds and kelps) as its representative organism.

Some common characteristics of thallophytes are as follows

- They have thallus-like body, i.e. the plant body cannot be distinguished into roots, stems and leaves.
- They are largely aquatic (both freshwater and marine) organisms.
- They are autotrophs as they contain chlorophyll.
- Algae may be single-celled (*Chlamydomonas*), colonial (*Volvox*) and filamentous (*Ulothrix, Spirogyra* and *Oedogonium*).

Bryophyta

They include the various mosses and liverworts. Some common characteristics of bryophytes are as follows

- Their plant body is more differentiated than that of algae.
- They lack true roots, stems and leaves, but they may possess root-like, stem-like or leaf-like structures called **rhizoids**, **caulids** and **phyllids**, respectively.
- They usually occur in damp, humid and shaded localities. They are also called **'amphibians of plant kingdom'** because they are terrestrial plants but require water to complete life cycle.
- Example *Riccia*, *Marchantia* (liverwort), *Funaria* (moss), *Sphagnum* (moss), etc.

Pteridophyta

They include all the ferns. Some common characteristics of pteridophytes are as follows

- The plant body is differentiated into true root, stem and leaves.
- The leaves are often made up of the leaflets bearing spores (reproductive structures) on the underside.
- They usually occur in cool, damp, shady places, though some way flourish well in sandy soil condition.
- They are non-flowering plants, e.g. *Selaginella, Equisetum, Dryopteris,* ferns (*Marsilea*), *Adiantum*, etc.

Gymnosperms

Some common characteristics of gymnosperms are as follows

- The plant body is well-differentiated into root, stem and leaves.
- The plants belonging to this group bear naked seeds, i.e. seeds are not enclosed in fruits.
- They produce seeds in cones, with male cones containing pollen and female cones containing ovule.
- They occur as woody trees or bushy shrubs.
- They inhabit in the cold climates, e.g. conifers (*Pinus*), etc.
- The only native gymnosperm which thrive in warmer areas are the cycads, e.g. *Cycas*.

Angiosperms

They include all the flowering plants. The characteristics of angiosperms are as follows

- The plant body is well-differentiated into root, stem and leaves.
- They produce seeds, flowers and fruits. Their seeds are enclosed inside the fruits.
- They grow in almost every kind of habitat.
- Seed contains cotyledons, which are embryonic leaves that provide nourishment to the developing plant.
- Depending on the number of cotyledons present, angiosperms are further divided into two types, i.e. **monocot** and **dicot**.
  - **Monocots** Plants belonging to this group have one cotyledon, leaves have parallel venation and the root system is fibrous, e.g. maize, rice and grass.
  - **Dicots** Plants belonging to this group have two cotyledons, leaves have reticulate venation and a tap root system, e.g. pea, potato, apple, sunflower and rose.

Kingdom – Animalia

- This kingdom is divided into **invertebrates**, which lack a backbone and **vertebrates**, which have one.
- These are further classified into nine major phyla: **Porifera**, **Cnidaria**, **Platyhelminthes**, **Nematoda**, **Annelida**, **Arthropoda**, **Mollusca**, **Echinodermata** and **Chordata**. The first eight phyla consist of invertebrates, while Chordata includes vertebrates.
- The flowchart below provides a clear overview of this classification, highlighting the key characteristics of each group.

Kingdom-Animalia

Invertebrates
Nerve cord present on ventral side, heart on dorsal side, haemoglobin dissolved in blood.

Vertebrates
Notochord/Vertebral column present, heart on ventral side, nerve cord on dorsal side, haemoglobin contained in RBC.

Cellular Level
Phylum–Proifera Aquatic, pore bearers, fixed type, body consists of hollow tube, spongy fibres for protection, e.g. sponges, bath sponge and *Sycon*.

Tissue Level
Phylum–Cnidaria Two-layered body wall enclosing coelentron, radially symmetrical, have tentacles and stinging cells, bisexual, e.g. *Hydra*, jellyfish, sea anemone and corals (exoskeleton made up of calcium carbonate).

Organ or Organ System Level

Acoelomata (No body cavity)

- **Phylum–Platyhelminthes** Bilateral symmetry, free-living as well as parasitic, flat, unsegmented worms, body cavity absent, bisexual, one opening (incomplete digestive system), e.g. *Planaria*-free-living: liver fluke and tapeworm-parasitic.
- **Phylum–Nematoda** Long, soft, cylindrical, unsegmented body, two openings (mouth and anus), parasitic, e.g. *Ascaris*, eel worm and filaria worm.

Coelmata (body cavity present)

- **Phylum– Annelida** Soft, cylindrical, segmented body, two openings, true body cavity, bisexual, excretion through nephridia free-living or parasitic, e.g. earthworm, leech.
- **Phylum–Arthropoda** Largest phylum, body divided into three parts–head, thorax and abdomen, and exoskeleton which moults, jointed legs, e.g. insects, crab, crayfish, millipede, centipede, scorpion, etc.
- **Phylum–Mollusca** Aquatic soft, unsegmented body, hard shell protecting the soft body, gills for breathing, locomotion with a muscular foot, e.g. oyster, slugs clam, snails, squid, mussels and *Octopus*.
- **Phylum–Echinodermata** Unsegmented, marine animals, radially symmetrical, spiny-skinned, head absent, five arms, locomotion with tube feet, e.g. starfish and brittle star.

Phylum–Chordata

Vertebrates are further divided into five classes.

(i) Class–Pisces (Fishes)

The characteristics possessed by Pisces are as follows

- These are exclusively aquatic animals.
- Fins are present, but limbs are absent.
- They are cold-blooded or poikilothermal (i.e. their body temperature fluctuates directly with the temperature of the environment) and have two-chambered heart.
- Most of them lay eggs.

Based on the nature of their skeleton, Pisces is divided into two sub-classes as follows

(a) **Chondrichthyes** (cartilaginous fishes) Sharks, dogfish, skates.

(b) **Osteichthyes** (bony fishes) Carps (*Catla*), roaches, herrings, trouts, seahorse, rohu, etc.

(ii) Class–Amphibia

The characteristics possessed by amphibians are as follows

- They are amphibious in nature, *viz.,* can live on land as well as in water. They were the first chordates to live on land.
- They lack scales and have mucous glands in their skin which secrete mucus that keeps the skin moist.
- Amphibians are cold-blooded and have three-chambered heart.
- Respiration occurs either by skin, gills (in water) or by lungs (on land).
- Sexes are separate and fertilisation is external, e.g. *Rana* (frog), *Bufo* (toad), *Necturus* (mud puppy), *Salamandra* (salamander), *Hyla* (tree frog), etc.

(iii) Class–Reptilia

The characteristics possessed by reptiles are as follows

- These animals possess dry skin, with scales.
- They are cold-blooded animals.
- They have three-chambered heart (two auricles and one ventricle) except crocodile, with four-chambered heart.
- Sexes are separate.
- Fertilisation is internal, e.g. *Chelone* (turtle), *Chameleon, Naja* (cobra), etc.

(iv) Class–Aves

The characteristics possessed by Aves are as follows

- These are warm-blooded or homeothermal.
- They have four-chambered heart.
- Their body is divisible into head, neck, trunk and tail.
- They have a sound producing organ called **syrinx**.
- Birds are egg laying with large amount of yolk and hard calcareous shell.
- Sexes are separate and fertilisation is internal, e.g. *Ciconia ciconia* (white stork), *Aythya fuligula* (male tufted duck), *Struthio camelus* (ostrich), pigeon, crow, sparrow, etc.

(v) Class–Mammalia

The characteristics possessed by mammals are as follows

- Body is divisible into head, neck, trunk and tail. Movable eyelids are present.
- These are warm-blooded animals.
- They have four-chambered heart.
- These are known to be the advanced group of animals with a very well-developed brain.
- Mammalia is the first class to mark the presence of ear **pinna** (external fleshy ear). Middle ear is with three ossicles, i.e. malleus, incus and stapes.
- Limbs are adapted for walking, running, swimming, burrowing and even flying (bats).
- Fertilisation is internal, e.g. *Rattus* (rat), *Homo sapiens* (human), *Felis* (cat), bat, *Canis* (dog), chimpanzee, *Macropus* (kangaroo), whale, dolphins, walrus (aquatic mammals), etc.

EXAM ORIENTED QUESTIONS

TYPE - 1

01 Mark

Multiple Choice Questions

Q.1 Bacteria belong to the kingdom
(a) Monera (b) Protista
(c) Fungi (d) Plantae

Ans. (a)

Q.2 Identify the structure found in Protozoa for locomotion.
(a) Pseudopodia (b) Cilia
(c) Flagella (d) All of these

Ans. (d)

Q.3 Which of the following division of plants show undifferentiated body?
(a) Thallophyta (b) Bryophyta
(c) Pteridophyta (d) Gymnosperms

Ans. (a)

Q.4 During the practical exam, a spot was shown. Students were told to observe the spot and mention the phylum to which it belongs.

(a) Cone, Gymnosperms (b) Spores, Pteridophyta
(c) Cone, Pteridophyta (d) Spores, Gymnosperms

Ans. (a)

Q.5 Which one of these are known for producing seeds?
(a) Pteridophyta and gymnosperms
(b) Bryophyta and gymnosperms
(c) Gymnosperms and angiosperms
(d) Angiosperms and Pteridophyta

Ans. (c)

Q.6 Dicotyledon plants have leaves with .....*P*..... venation and .....*Q*..... root system.
(a) *P*- reticulate, *Q*-fibrous (b) *P*- parallel, *Q*-tap
(c) *P*- reticulate, *Q*-tap (d) *P*-parallel, *Q*-fibrous

Ans. (c)

Q.7 Under which of the following two categories animal kingdom (Kingdom–Animalia) is mainly grouped?
(a) Bilaterally symmetrical and radially symmetrical
(b) Coelomate and acoelomate
(c) Aquatic and terrestrial
(d) Vertebrates and invertebrates

Ans. (d)

Q.8 Radha tried to match the phylum with their characteristics. She tabulated the pairs as follows

Phylum	Characteristics
P	Two layered body wall enclosing coelentron.
Q	Excretion through nephridia.

Identify the pair of phylum.
(a) *P* - Porifera, *Q*-Nematoda
(b) *P* - Cnidaria, *Q*-Annelida
(c) *P* - Arthropoda, *Q*- Mollusca
(d) *P* - Nematoda, *Q*- Porifera

Ans. (b)

Q.9 A biology teacher asked her students to give two examples of animals belonging to the phylum-Arthropoda.

Fatima said: Snails and mussels
Ramu said: Jellyfish and *Hydra*
Sham said: Centipede and prawn
Aliza said: Scorpion and crab

Who were correct?
(a) Aliza and Ramu
(b) Aliza and Sham
(c) Fatima and Ramu
(d) Fatima and Sham

Ans. (b)

Q.10 Which of the following exhibits movement by crawling?
(a) Amphibians
(b) Aves
(c) Mammals
(d) Reptiles

Ans. (d)

TYPE - 2   01 Mark

Matching Type Question

Q.1 Match the following organisms with their characteristic features.

Organisms	Features
 A	I. Have a dual life, spending part of their life in water and part on land.
 B	II. Have dry, scaly skin and lay eggs with leathery or hard shells.
 C	III. Have feathers, a beak without teeth and lay hard-shelled eggs.
 D	IV. Have hair or fur on their bodies and produce milk to feed their young ones.
 E	V. Have a streamlined body, scales and fins.

Ans. A-II, B-IV, C-III, D-I, E-V

TYPE - 3   01 Mark

Assertion-Reason Type Questions

Direction (Q. Nos. 1-5) In the following questions statements are given as Assertion (A) and Reason (R).

(a) A is true, but R is false.
(b) A is false, but R is true.
(c) Both A and R are true.
(d) Both A and R are false.

Q.1 Assertion (A) Fungi are classified as heterotrophic organisms.

Reason (R) Fungi cannot perform photosynthesis and depend on other organisms for food, either through absorption or parasitism.

Ans. (c)

Q.2 Assertion (A) Bryophytes lack true roots.

Reason (R) Bryophytes have caulids instead of roots, which help anchor them to the soil and absorb water.

Ans. (a) A is true, but R is false. R can be corrected as Bryophytes have rhizoids instead of roots, which help anchor them to the soil and absorb water, but do not have the complex structure of true roots.

Q.3 Assertion (A) Bryophytes include *Cycas* and pine.

Reason (R) Body of bryophytes is more differentiated than that of algae.

Ans. (b) A is false, but R is true. A can be corrected as Bryophytes include mosses and liverworts.

Q.4 Assertion (A) Pteridophytes lack flowers and seeds.

Reason (R) Pteridophytes reproduce through spores instead of seeds and do not produce flowers.

Ans. (c)

Q.5 Assertion (A) Pteridophytes have a well-developed root system.

Reason (R) The root system of pteridophytes anchors the plant to the soil and helps in the absorption of water and nutrients.

Ans. (c)

TYPE - 4   01 Mark

Very Short Answer Type Questions

Q.1 Name the five kingdoms proposed in the five-kingdom classification system.

Ans. Monera, Protista, Fungi, Plantae and Animalia.

Q.2 What type of cell structure is found in organisms of kingdom–Monera?

Ans. Prokaryotic

Q.3 Name one example of a plant from the Thallophyta group.

Ans. Kelps

Q.4 What are the seed leaves of an angiosperm called?

Ans. Cotyledons

Q.5 What does the term "Porifera" mean?

Ans. "Porifera" means "pore bearers."

Q.6 What type of body symmetry is found in Platyhelminthes?

Ans. Bilateral symmetry.

Q.7 What type of body segmentation is found in arthropods?

Ans. Segmented body divided into head, thorax and abdomen.

Q.8 Give any two examples of cartilaginous fiish.

Ans. Shark and dogfish.

Q.9 What is the respiratory organ in adult amphibians?

Ans. Lungs and moist skin.

Q.10 What is the unique feature of mammalian skin?

Ans. Skin covered with hair or fur.

Q.11 Given below is the figure of earthworm. Read the information below the figure and fill in the blank spaces. **(1 Mark each)**

Earthworms are often referred to as "farmers' friends" because they improve soil fertility and structure. As they burrow through the soil, they create channels that allow air, water and nutrients to reach plant roots more effectively. Their digestive process breaks down organic matter, enriching the soil with nutrient-rich castings, which enhances soil quality and promotes healthy plant growth. **(1 Mark each)**

Earthworm belongs to the phylum .....(i)...... . Their body is .....(ii)..... and divided into .....(iii)..... They have well developed .....(iv)..... with the alimentary canal open at both ends. They have .....(v)..... body cavity.

Ans. (i) Annelida (ii) cylindrical (iii) segments (iv) digestive system (v) true

Q.12 Name the following. **(1 Mark each)**

(i) Kingdom of prokaryotes.
(ii) Network of hyphae.
(iii) Amphibians of the plant kingdom.
(iv) Seed-bearing structures in gymnosperms.
(v) Name the division of plants to which monocots and dicots belong.

Ans. (i) Monera (ii) Mycelium (iii) Bryophyta (iv) Cones (v) Angiospermae

Q.13 Correct and rewrite the following statements by changing the underlined words. **(1 Mark each)**

(i) Carolus Linnaeus classified organisms into five kingdoms based on certain characters.
(ii) Kingdom–Fungi includes eukaryotic, multicellular, autotrophic organisms.
(iii) Mosses and liverworts are categorised under division–Pteridophyta.
(iv) Alimentary canal is absent in nematodes.
(v) Fishes are cold-blooded with a four-chambered heart.

Ans. (i) **RH Whittaker** classified organisms into **five kingdoms** based on certain characters.
(ii) Kingdom–Fungi includes eukaryotic, multicellular, **heterotrophic** organisms.
(iii) Mosses and liverworts are categorised under division–**Bryophyta**.
(iv) Alimentary canal is completely **present** in nematodes.
(v) Fishes are cold-blooded with a **two-chambered heart**.

Q.14 Choose the odd one out from the following terms and name the category to which the other three belong. **(1 Mark each)**

(i) *Amoeba, Paramecium*, Yeast, *Euglena*
(ii) *Cycas*, Pine, Fir, Mosses
(iii) Oyster, Slug, Scorpion, *Octopus*
(iv) Earthworm, Insects, Snails, Tapeworm
(v) Dogfish, Frog, Lizards, Dolphin

Ans. (i) The odd term is **yeast** because it is a fungus, while the other three *Amoeba, Paramecium* and *Euglena* are protists.
(ii) The odd term is **mosses** because mosses are bryophytes, while the other three *Cycas*, pine and fir are gymnosperms.
(iii) The odd term is **scorpion** because the scorpion is an arthropod, while the other three oyster, slug and *Octopus* are molluscs.
(iv) The odd term is **tapeworm** because it is an acoeiomate, while the other three earthworm, insects and snails have a coelom.
(v) The odd term is **dolphin** because it is warm-blooded, while the other three dogfish, frog and lizards are cold-blooded.

Q.15 Give biological/technical terms for the following. **(1 Mark each)**

(i) Unicellular eukaryotic organisms.
(ii) Mode of nutrition in which one organism depends on the other for food.
(iii) Body can be divided into two equal halves and along one plane.
(iv) Mode of nutrition in which organism prepare their own food.
(v) Organisms that have body cavity present.

Ans. (i) Protista (ii) Heterotrophic (iii) Bilateral symmetry (iv) Autotrophic (v) Coelomata

TYPE - 5 02 Marks

Short Answer Type Questions

Q.1 Who proposed the five-kingdom classification for living organisms? On what basis did he classify organisms into these five kingdoms?

Ans. The five-kingdom classification was proposed by RH Whittaker in 1969.

He classified living organisms into five kingdoms—Monera, Protista, Fungi, Plantae and Animalia; based on several factors, including cellular organisation (unicellular or multicellular), mode of nutrition (autotrophic or heterotrophic) and the presence or absence of a cell wall.

Q.2 Observe the classification below and complete the boxes given.

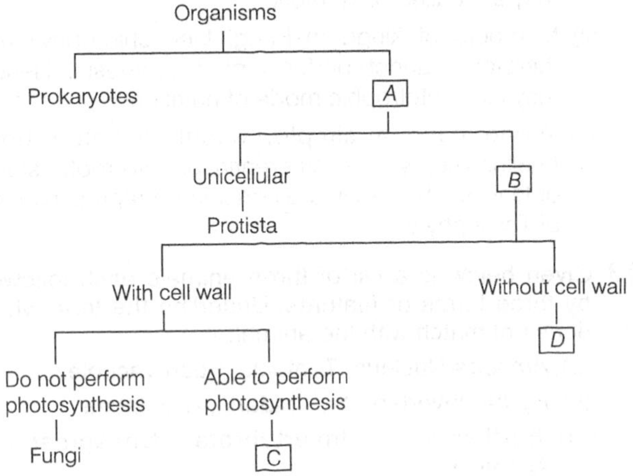

Ans. *A*–Eukaryotes
B–Multicellular
C–Plantae
D–Animalia

Q.3 How do fungi obtain their nutrition?

Ans. Fungi are heterotrophic organisms that obtain their nutrition through absorption. They release digestive enzymes into their surroundings to breakdown organic matter and then absorb the resulting nutrients.

Q.4 We start the classification of plants on the basis of differentiation of the plant body.

(i) Which division lacks a well-differentiated body design?

(ii) Where are such plants predominantly found?

Ans. (i) Thallophyta (algae) lack a well-differentiated body design.

(ii) These plants are predominantly found in both freshwater and marine habitats.

Q.5 State the main function of the following.

(i) Cilia (ii) Spores

Ans. (i) Cilia act as a locomotory organ in *Paramecium*.

(ii) Spores act as reproductive parts in bryophytes and pteridophytes.

Q.6 Mention one difference in each of the following pairs based on what is given in the bracket.

(i) Bryophyta and Thallophyta (plant body).

(ii) Gymnosperms and Angiosperms (seeds).

Ans. (i)

Bryophyta	Thallophyta
Plant body is differentiated into stems and root-like structures rhizoids.	Plant body shows no differentiation and is simple.

(ii)

Gymnosperms	Angiosperms
Plants of these group bear naked seeds.	Plants of these group bear seeds enclosed in a fruit.

Q.7 What are the main characteristics of the phylum – Porifera?

Ans. Phylum–Porifera includes simple, multicellular animals known as sponges. They have a porous body with a large number of small holes called pores. They lack true tissues and organs and their body is supported by a skeleton made of spicules or spongin. Sponges are sessile and filtre-feed by drawing water through their pores and extracting food particles from it.

Q.8 Write any two key features of the phylum–Mollusca.

Ans. (i) They have a soft, unsegmented body, which is often protected by a hard external shell made of calcium carbonate.

(ii) They possess a muscular foot used for locomotion and a mantle that covers the internal organs and secretes the shell in many species.

Q.9 Mention two characteristics of the phylum to which the given organism belongs.

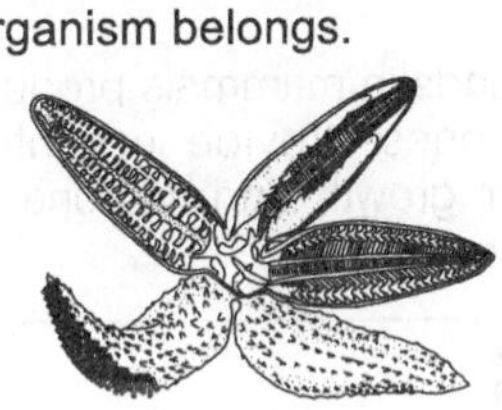

Ans. The given organism (starfish) belongs to the phylum Echinodermata. Two key features of this phylum are

(i) Echinoderms have a spiny, hard outer covering, which provides protection and support.

(ii) They possess a unique water vascular system that aids in movement, feeding and respiration.

Q.10 Given below are four different living organisms. Observe them carefully and answer the questions that follows.

A

B

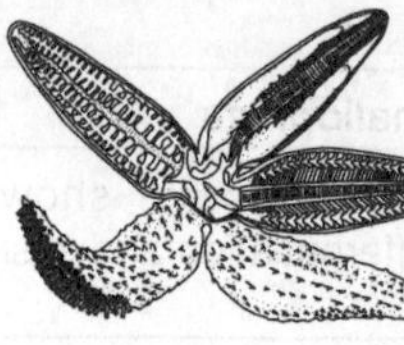

C

D

(i) To which of the phylums does *A*, *B*, *C* and *D* belong?

(ii) Which out of the following phylum

(a) is vertebrate?

(b) have calcareous shell made up of calcium carbonate?

Ans. (i) *A*-Reptilia, *B*-Amphibia, *C*-Echinodermata *D*-Mollusca

(ii) (a) Reptilia (b) Mollusca

Q.11 How do cold-blooded and warm-blooded animals differ? Provide one example of each.

Ans. Cold-blooded animals or poikilothermal also known as ectothermic, they rely on external sources of heat to regulate their body temperature. In contrast, warm-blooded animals or homothermal or endothermic, maintain a constant internal body temperature regardless of external conditions. For example, lizard (cold-blooded), human (warm-blooded).

Q.12 What is the significance of mammary glands in mammals?

Ans. Mammary glands in mammals produce milk to nourish their young ones provide essential nutrients and antibodies for growth and immune protection during early development.

TYPE - 6   03 Marks

Short Answer Type Questions

Q.1 Draw two organisms that belong to the phylum–Protista.

Ans.

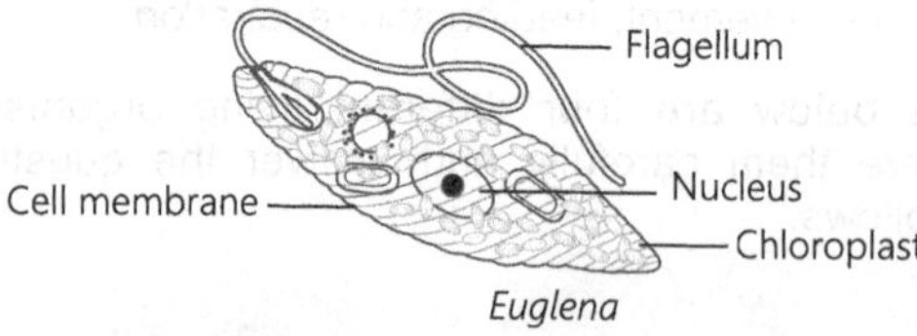

Euglena

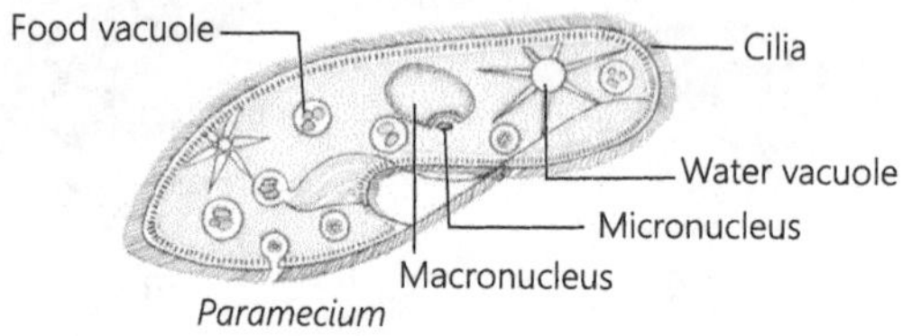

Paramecium

Q.2 Give biological reasons for the following.

(i) Organisms of kingdom–Monera are called prokaryotic.

(ii) Fungi lack autotrophic mode of nutrition.

(iii) Algae are a representative of Thallophyta.

Ans. (i) Kingdom–Monera consists of organisms that are single-celled and lack a well-defined nucleus. Thus, they are called prokaryotic.

(ii) Members of kingdom–Fungi lack chlorophyll and therefore cannot perform photosynthesis. Hence, they lack autotrophic mode of nutrition.

(iii) Algae have a simple, undifferentiated body (thallus-like) with no differentiation into roots, stems or leaves. Thus, they are considered representatives of Thallophyta.

Q.3 Given below is a list of three animals each followed by three terms or features. Underline the term which does not match with the animal.

(i) *Amoeba*-Nucleus, Tentacle, Food vacuole.

(ii) *Hydra*- Invertebrata, Cnidaria, Crustacea.

(iii) Earthworm - Invertebrata, Unsegmented, Annelida.

Ans. (i) *Amoeba*-Nucleus, Tentacle, Food vacuole.

(ii) *Hydra*-Invertebrata, Cnidaria, Crustacea

(iii) Earthworm - Invertebrata, Unsegmented, Annelida.

Q.4 Classify the following organisms based on the presence/absence of a true coelom (acoelomate and coelomate).

Spongilla, Sea anemone, *Planaria*, Liverfluke, *Ascaris, Nereis*, Earthworm, Scorpion, Birds, Fishes, and Horses.

Ans. **Acoelomates** *Spongilla*, Sea anemone, *Planaria*, Liver fluke.

Coelomates *Ascaris, Nereis*, Earthworm, Scorpion, Birds, Fishes and Horses.

Q.5 Vertebrates show a variety in shape and size, from small animals like frogs to large ones like whales.

(i) State one unique feature of vertebrates.

(ii) Name the class of Vertebrata that respire only by lungs.

(iii) Which vertebrates are called the 'first class of terrestrial animals'?

Ans. (i) One unique feature of vertebrates is that they have a true vertebral column and an internal skeleton that helps in smooth muscle movement.

(ii) Class–Reptilia respire only by lungs.

(iii) Reptiles are called the 'first class of terrestrial animals'.

Q.6 State any three reasons why reptiles are successful on land.

Ans. Reptiles are successful on land because

(i) they have dry, keratinised skin that prevents water loss.

(ii) their eggs are surrounded by a hard shell, which protects the developing embryo.

(iii) internal fertilisation occurs, reducing the need for water in the reproductive process.

Q.7 Name three animals belonging to different classes, which breathe by means of lungs, but have no external ears (pinna).

Ans. The three animals that belong to the kingdom of Animalia, which breathe through lungs, but do not have external ears are

Lizard and crocodile (class-Reptilia)

Frog and salamander (class- Amphibia)

Parrot and crow (class-Aves)

Q.8 Observe the organism given below and answer the questions that follows

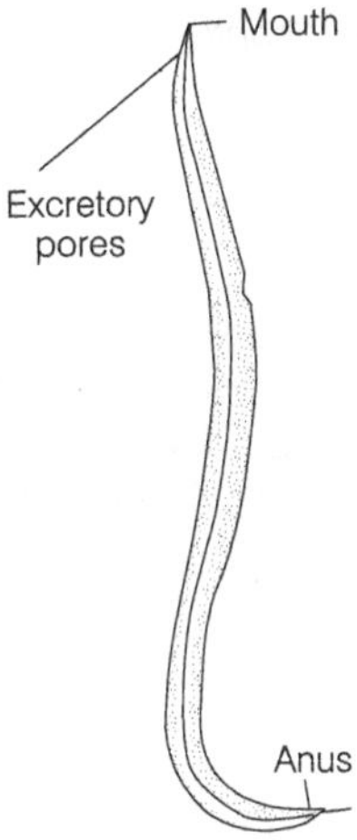

(i) Identify the organism.

(ii) To which phylum does it belongs?

(iii) Give any two important characteristics of the organism.

Ans. (i) *Ascaris* (female)

(ii) Nematoda

(iii) The important characteristic features are

- They are bilaterally symmetrical.
- They have a fluid-filled or false body cavity (without a true coelom).

TYPE - 7

03 Marks

Structured Based Questions

Q.1 A bread kept in a moist, humid place often develops some greenish growth on it. This growth is typically seen as a fuzzy or mold-like substance.

(i) Write the mode of nutrition of these organisms.

(ii) Give two examples of organisms belonging to the same group.

(iii) Write the type of cells present in these organisms.

Ans. (i) The mode of nutrition of these organisms is saprophytic, as they obtain nutrients by breaking down the dead and decaying organic matter.

(ii) Two examples of organisms belonging to the same group are

- Yeast
- *Rhizopus*

(iii) The type of cells present in these organisms are eukaryotic cells, as they are fungi.

Q.2 Observe the given figure and answer the following questions.

(i) Name the group to which the above organism belongs.

(ii) State the mode of nutrition followed by the organism.

(iii) State one point that makes it different from kingdom–Plantae.

Ans. (i) The given organism (*Agaricus*) belongs to the kingdom–Fungi.

(ii) The organism follows a heterotrophic mode of nutrition.

(iii) The organism lacks chlorophyll, which makes it different from kingdom–Plantae.

Q.3 Children love to visit aquariums to explore and observe the fascinating aquatic life. They enjoy watching various swimming organisms in their natural habitat.

(i) The most commonly found swimming organisms in aquariums belong to which phylum?

(ii) Write any two characteristics of this phylum.

(iii) Write any two examples belonging to this phylum.

Ans. (i) The most commonly found swimming organisms belong to the phylum–Chordata.

(ii) Two characteristics of phylum–Chordata are as follows

- Members of phylum–Chordata have a notochord at some stage of their life cycle.
- They have a dorsal, hollow nerve cord.

(iii) Two examples belonging to phylum–Chordata are fish and whales.

Q.4 Students were taken to the biology laboratory by their biology teacher to show them different plant specimens. Teacher explained and showed differentiated plant body lacking vascular tissue. And told that these group of plants requires water to carry out their reproductive activities.

(i) To which group does these plants belongs?

(ii) Write any one important feature of this group.

(iii) Give any two examples of this group.

Ans. (i) Bryophytes

(ii) The bryophytes are called amphibians of a plant kingdom.

(iii) *Riccia* and *Marchantia*

ECONOMIC IMPORTANCE OF BACTERIA AND FUNGI

- Bacteria and fungi are economically significant due to their roles in various industries.
- Bacteria aid in fermentation, nitrogen fixation and antibiotic production, while fungi contribute to enzyme production, fermentation and waste decomposition, enhancing soil fertility and industrial processes.

Useful Role of Bacteria

These are used in different fields which are discussed below

Bacteria in Medicine

1. **Antibiotics** These are chemical substances produced by microbes that kill or inhibit the growth of other microbes. Several antibiotics prepared from bacteria are effective against other harmful bacteria without causing any side effects to organisms.

   Some well-known antibiotics, their sources and the diseases they treat are as follows

Antibiotics	Source Organisms	Diseases Treated
Penicillin	*Penicillium chrysogenum* (a mould)	Tetanus, diphtheria
Streptomycin	*Streptomyces griseus*	Tuberculosis
Chlorotetracycline	*Streptomyces aureofaciens*	Typhoid
Erythromycin	*Saccharopolyspora erythraea/Streptomyces erythraeus*	Rickettsial fever

2. **Serum** It is defined as blood plasma devoid of clotting factors (fibrinogen). It contains antitoxins for a particular pathogen.
   - Preparation of serum requires introduction of a small dose of bacterial toxin into a healthy animal, e.g. cow.
   - The body produces antitoxins to neutralise the effect of toxin. Blood of animal is taken after repeated introduction of the same toxin and after being chilled, it results in a clear straw coloured liquid (serum). Serum is used as a preventive measure against bacterial invasions.
3. **Vaccine** It is a biological preparation developed from weakened (attenuated) or killed forms of bacteria.
   - Vaccines stimulate the body to produce antitoxins, which offer immunity against future attacks by a specific pathogen. They are available for several diseases like cholera, typhoid and smallpox.
   - Two common types of vaccines obtained by bacteria are as follows
     (i) **killed bacteria** (e.g. TAB vaccine for typhoid) and (ii) **living weakend bacteria** (e.g. Bacillus Calmette Guerin or BCG vaccine for tuberculosis).

Bacteria in Agriculture

- Bacteria are used as biofertilisers to enrich the nutrient quality of the soil.
- They also play an important role in the nitrogen cycle.

Nitrogen Cycle

- The nitrogen cycle is the biogeochemical cycle by which free atmospheric nitrogen is converted into its various chemical forms.
- The nitrogen cycle is mainly composed of four important processes, i.e. **nitrogen-fixation**, **ammonification**, **nitrification** and **denitrification**.

1. Nitrogen-fixation

In this process, the atmospheric nitrogen is fixed which is used by the plants. In this step, the molecular nitrogen (N_2) is converted into inorganic nitrogenous compounds like nitrate, nitrite and ammonia.

The organisms that fix nitrogen can be of two types

- **Asymbiotic or Free-living Bacteria** These are the bacteria which are not found in close relationship with another bacteria or organisms in order to convert atmospheric nitrogen into ammonia, e.g. number of cyanobacteria like *Anabaena* and *Nostoc*.
- **Symbiotic Bacteria** These are bacteria that can fix nitrogen by forming close associations with each other or with another organisms, e.g. relationship between *Rhizobium* bacteria with legumes.

2. Ammonification

In next step, the organic matter (proteins and nucleic acids) of the dead remains is decomposed in order to produce ammonia (NH_3) by microorganisms (like *Clostridium*).

3. Nitrification

It is the process in which ammonia produced by the degradation of manures is first oxidised to nitrite by the soil bacterium *Nitrosomonas* or *Nitrococcus*.

This nitrite is further oxidised to nitrate by another soil bacterium, i.e. *Nitrobacter*.

4. Denitrification

It is the process in which the nitrate present in the soil is reduced back to free nitrogen (N_2). The process of denitrification is carried out by denitrifying bacteria (like *Thiobacillus denitrificans, Pseudomonas denitrificans*, etc.).

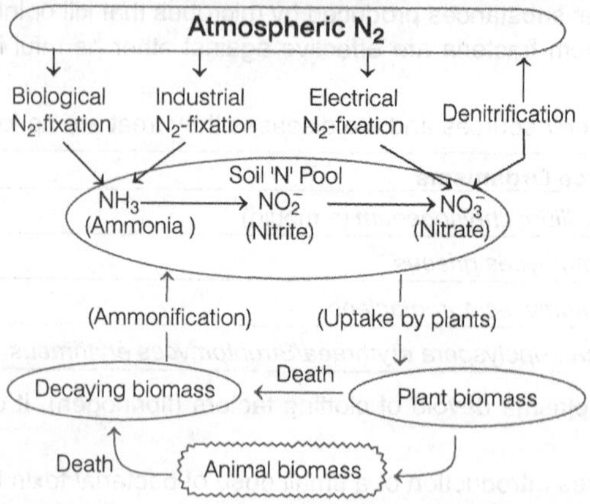

The nitrogen cycle showing relationship between the three main nitrogen polls, i.e. atmospheric, soil and biomass

Bacteria in Various Industries

Bacteria are useful in various industries which are as follows

- **Curing and Ripening of Tea and Tobacco** Fermentation by bacteria is used for curing crude leaves of tea and tobacco. After harvesting, crude leaves are hung in shade and are permitted for the action of certain bacteria (*Bacillus megaterium*). This process helps in the removal of bitterness, adds flavour and taste to tea and tobacco leaves increasing their market value.
- **Tanning of Hides and Leather** Removal of fats, hair and other tissues from the hides of animals is achieved through chemical and mechanical processes with fermentation by bacteria. This process is called **tanning.**

Harmful Activities of Bacteria

These can be grouped under the following

1. Food Spoilage

- Many bacteria spoil cooked food and milk through the process of decay, sometimes to the extent of causing food poisoning. Botulism is a severe form of food poisoning caused by a specific bacterium (*Clostridium perfringens, E. coli, Staphylococcus aureus*) found in tinned and sealed food.
- Therefore, preservation of food and making it free of disease-causing germs is very necessary. One such method is **pasteurisation**, which is a technique of partial sterilisation applied usually to milk.

- Other methods include salting, refrigeration, adding preservatives, boiling or heating at high temperature (sterilisation).

2. Diseases

Bacteria cause various diseases in humans, domesticated animals and cultivated plants, which are as follows

Bacterial Diseases in Plants

Two well-known bacterial diseases of plants are **black rot of mustard and cauliflower** and **bacterial blight of cowpea (lobia)**.

Bacterial Diseases in Animals

Humans

Some common human diseases caused by bacteria are **whooping cough**, **cholera**, **tuberculosis**, **diphtheria**, **typhoid**, **pneumonia**, **tetanus**, etc.

Domesticated Animals *(Cattle)*

Two common bacterial diseases of cattle are:

- **Anthrax** (swelling of body and reduced milk yield)
- **Bovine tuberculosis** (lungs affected, dry husky cough)

3. Bioweapons

- A **bioweapon** or **biological weapon**, is a device that carries and delivers disease-causing biological agents (such as bacteria, viruses or genetically altered organisms), to harm or kill humans, animals or plants.
- Biological agents are used against humans, their crops and animals and this is termed as **biowar** or **biological warfare**.
- These agents are highly infectious which reproduce quickly and easily and have high potency and low cost, e.g. *Bacillus anthracis* (anthrax), *Yersinia pestis* (plague), etc.

Economic Importance of Fungi

Fungi are indispensable in various industries, especially breweries, bakeries and cheese processing.

1. Breweries

- Fungi, particularly yeasts (*Saccharomyces cerevisiae*) are used for producing alcoholic beverages such as beer, wine, whisky, rum and gin through the process of **fermentation**.
- During fermentation (anaerobic respiration), glucose in yeast is converted into ethyl alcohol (ethanol) and CO_2.
- Different raw materials are used for producing alcoholic beverages, e.g. grapes for wine and barley maltose for beer.

2. Bakeries

The fluffiness of bread, cakes and similar products is due to the CO_2 released by yeast during fermentation which forms air spaces, giving the fluffy texture to bread.

3. Cheese Processing

- Cheese is a valuable food with high quantities of fat and proteins along with calcium, phosphorus, vitamin-A and some quantities of vitamin-B.
- Several species of *Penicillium* and *Aspergillus* impart unique flavours to cheese. For example, *Penicillium roqueforti* is used to produce Roquefort cheese.

4. Mushroom Cultivation

- Mushrooms are multicellular, saprophytic fungi that grow on dead or decaying leaves, wood logs and other organic matter. They are an important source of proteins and vitamins.
- Mushrooms can be cultivated in little land areas throughout the year in hills and during winter in plains, in a temperature range of 16-18°C. Three kinds of mushrooms widely cultivated in India and abroad are
  - White button mushroom (*Agaricus bisporus*)
  - Paddy straw mushroom (*Volvariella*)
  - Oyster mushroom (*Pleurotus*)
- Cultivation of mushroom involves five major steps, i.e. **composting, spawning, casing, cropping** and **harvesting** and **preservation**.

EXAM ORIENTED QUESTIONS

TYPE - 1 01 Mark

Multiple Choice Questions

Q.1 Typhoid is treated with the help of ......*P*...... which is obtained from the ......*Q*...... .

(a) *P*-erythromycin, *Q*- *Streptomyces griseus*
(b) *P*-chlorotetracycline, *Q*-*Streptomyces aureofaciens*
(c) *P*-penicillin, *Q*-*Penicillium chrysogenum*
(d) *P*-streptomycin, *Q*-*Streptomyces griseus*

Ans. (b)

Q.2 Shreya tried to match the bacteria with their functions. She tabulated the pairs as follows

Bacteria	Functions
P	Convert ammonia into nitrites.
Q	Fix nitrogen in the soil.

(a) *P-Pseudomonas, Q-Nitrobacter*
(b) *P-Clostridium, Q-Nitrosomonas*
(c) *P-Nitrosomonas, Q-Rhizobium*
(d) *P-Azotobacter, Q-Nitrobacter*

Ans. (c)

Q.3 Which of these is treated by pasteurisation?

(a) Water (b) Oil
(c) Fruit juice (d) Milk

Ans. (d)

Q.4 A serious food poisoning disease is caused due to a bacterium in tinned food. Identify the name of the disease and bacterium responsible.

	Diseases	Causative Organisms
(a)	Dysentery	*Shigella dysenteriae*
(b)	Botulism	*Clostridium botulinum*
(c)	Black leg	*Clostridium chauvoei*
(d)	Vibriosis	*Vibrio tatus*

Ans. (b)

Q.5 A biology teacher asked her students to give two examples of bacterial diseases in humans.

Sham said : Cold and diphtheria
Radha said : Tetanus and pneumonia
Gurpreet said : Whooping cough and tetanus
Sonam said : Flu and typhoid

Who were correct?

(a) Radha and Gurpreet
(b) Sonam and Radha
(c) Gurpreet and Sham
(d) Sham and Sonam

Ans. (a)

Q.6 The process of conversion of sugar into alcohol is called

(a) nitrogen-fixation (b) moulding
(c) fermentation (d) infection

Ans. (c)

TYPE - 2 01 Mark

Matching Type Question

Q.1 Match the structure *A* to *E* with their respective functions.

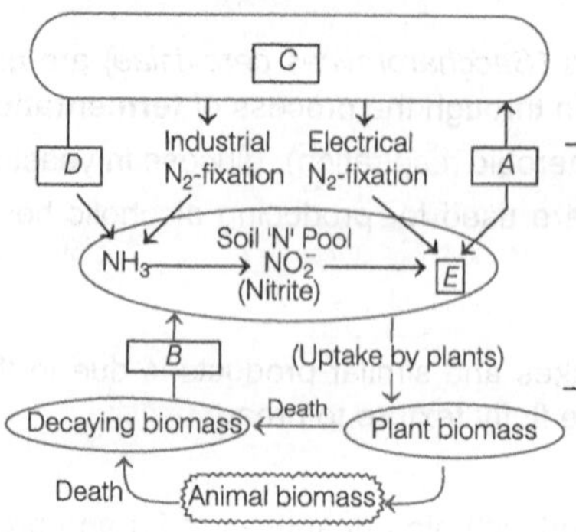

I. Largely inert and cannot be directly used by plants.

II. Process of converting organic nitrogen from dead organisms into ammonia.

III. Process by which certain bacteria convert atmospheric nitrogen (N_2) into ammonia (NH_3).

IV. Process by which nitrates are converted into nitrogen.

V. Aids in protein synthesis and overall growth of plant.

Ans. A-IV, B-II, C-I, D-III, E-V

TYPE - 3
01 Mark

Assertion-Reason Type Questions

Direction (Q. Nos. 1-3) In the following questions statements are given as Assertion (A) and Reason (R).

(a) A is true, but R is false.
(b) A is false, but R is true.
(c) Both A and R are true.
(d) Both A and R are false.

Q.1 Assertion (A) Antibiotics can be used to treat viral infections like the common cold.

Reason (R) Antibiotics are effective against bacteria.

Ans. (b) A is false, but R is true. A can be corrected as Antibiotics are used to treat the bacterial infections like typhoid.

Q.2 Assertion (A) Bacteria are one of the main causes of food spoilage.

Reason (R) Bacteria can breakdown food materials and produce substances like acids, gases and toxins that cause deterioration in food.

Ans. (c)

Q.3 Assertion (A) Yeasts play an important role in the production of alcoholic beverages in breweries.

Reason (R) Yeasts perform fermentation, where they convert sugars into ethanol and carbon dioxide, which are essential for alcohol production.

Ans. (c)

TYPE - 4
01 Mark

Very Short Answer Type Questions

Q.1 Name the vaccine used to prevent tuberculosis.

Ans. BCG vaccine.

Q.2 Which step in tea curing is responsible for the development of flavour?

Ans. Fermentation is responsible for developing the flavour of tea.

Q.3 What is a bioweapon?

Ans. A bioweapon is a weapon that uses disease-causing biological agents, such as bacteria, viruses or toxins, to harm or kill humans, animals or plants.

Q.4 What role do fungi play in bakeries?

Ans. Fungi, especially yeast, play a key role in leavening bread and other baked goods by producing carbon dioxide during fermentation.

Q.5 Which fungus is commonly used in mushroom cultivation?

Ans. *Agaricus bisporus* (white button mushroom) is commonly used in mushroom cultivation.

Q.6 Observe the diagram carefully and fill the blank spaces with correct words.

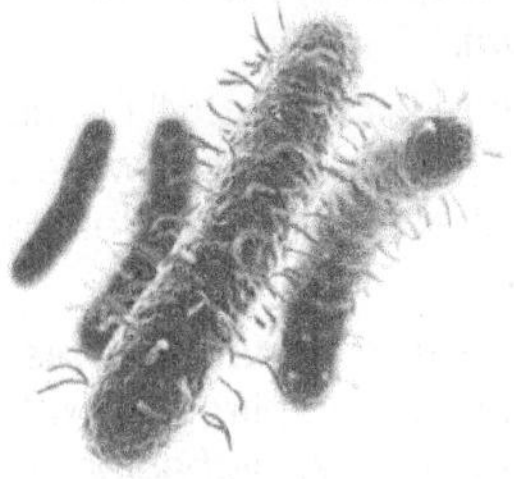

Bacteria are microscopic, single-celled organisms that play essential roles in various ecological processes, such as decomposition and nitrogen fixation. There are various uses of bacteria, one of which is their use in vaccines. **(1 Mark each)**

Vaccine is a biological preparation that is developed from ......(i)...... or ......(ii)...... forms of bacteria. Vaccines stimulate the body to produce ......(iii)......, which offers ......(iv)...... against the future attacks by a specific pathogen. Different diseases have specific vaccines developed for them. For example, ...(v)...... vaccine is for typhoid.

Ans. (i) weakened
(ii) killed
(iii) antitoxins
(iv) immunity
(v) TAB

Q.7 Name the following. **(1 Mark each)**

(i) The bacteria used for producing streptomycin.
(ii) Blood plasma devoid of clotting factor.
(iii) Fermentation of tea leaves to obtain a particular flavour.
(iv) Treating animal hides to prevent decay and to convert them into durable, flexible leather.
(v) The fungus used for the commercial production of alcohol.

Ans (i) *Streptomyces griseus*
(ii) Serum
(iii) Curing of tea
(iv) Tanning of leather
(v) *Saccharomyces cerevisiae*

Q.8 Choose the odd one out from the following terms given below and name the category to which the other three belong. **(1 Mark each)**

(i) Penicillin, Streptomycin, Chlorophyll, Tetracycline

(ii) *Rhizobium, Azotobacter, Pseudomonas, Clostridium*

(iii) Tuberculosis, Malaria, Cholera, Typhoid

(iv) *Agaricus bisporus, Pleurotus, Volvariella, Penicillium.*

Ans. (i) The odd term is chlorophyll because it is a pigment involved in photosynthesis, while the other three penicillin, streptomycin and tetracycline are antibiotics.

(ii) The odd term is ***Pseudomonas*** because it is not primarily involved in nitrogen fixation, while the other three *Rhizobium, Azotobacter* and *Clostridium* are nitrogen-fixing bacteria.

(iii) The odd term is **malaria** because it is caused by a protozoan (*Plasmodium*), while the other three tuberculosis, cholera and typhoid are bacterial diseases.

(iv) The odd term is ***Penicillium*** because it is a fungus used for antibiotic production not for mushroom cultivation, whereas the other three *Agaricus bisporus, Pleurotus* and *Volvariella* are types of mushrooms cultivated in mushroom farming.

Q.9 Arrange and rewrite the terms in each group in the correct order so as to be in a logical sequences beginning with the term that is underlined. **(1 Mark each)**

(i) *Pseudomonas*, <u>*Rhizobium*</u>, *Nitrobacter, Nitrosomonas*

(ii) Spoilage, <u>Bacteria</u>, Food poisoning, Botulism

(iii) <u>Wine, Fermentation</u>, <u>Grapes</u>

(iv) Bread, Fluffy texture, <u>Fermentation</u>, CO_2

(v) <u>Spawning</u>, Casing, Cropping and harvesting, Preservation

Ans. (i) *Rhizobium, Nitrosomonas, Nitrobacter, Pseudomonas*

(ii) Bacteria, Spoilage, Food poisoning, Botulism

(iii) Grapes, Fermentation, Wine

(iv) Fermentation, CO_2, Fluffy texture, Bread

(v) Spawning, Casing, Cropping and harvesting, Preservation

Q.10 Give biological/technical terms for the following.

(i) Suspension of heat-killed pathogens which induce immunity.

(ii) Cyclic event in which atmospheric nitrogen changes from one form to another.

(iii) Device that carries and delivers a disease-causing biological agent.

Ans. (i) Vaccine

(ii) Nitrogen cycle

(iii) Bioweapon

Q.11 Mention one difference in each of the following pairs on the basis of what is given in the braket. **(1 Mark each)**

(i) Erythromycin and Chlorotetracycline (source)

(ii) Streptomycin and Penicillin (source)

(iii) Nitrification and Ammonification (definition)

(iv) *Agaricus bisporus* and Fly agaric (nature)

Ans. (i)

Erythromycin	Chlorotetracycline
It is obtained from *Streptomyces erythreus*.	It is obtained from *Streptomyces aureofaciens.*

(ii)

Streptomycin	Penicillin
It is obtained from *Streptomyces griseus*.	It is obtained from *Penicillium chrysogenum*.

(iii)

Nitrification	Ammonification
It is the conversion of ammonia and ammonium compounds into nitrates and nitrites.	It involves decomposition of organic matter to produce ammonia.

(iv)

Agaricus bisporus	Fly Agaric
It is an edible mushroom.	It is poisonous in nature, and hence it is non-edible.

TYPE - 5 02 Marks

Short Answer Type Questions

Q.1 Mention the source organism of the following antibiotics.

(i) Penicillin

(ii) Streptomycin

(iii) Chlorotetracycline

(iv) Erythromycin

Ans. (i) **Penicillin** *Penicillium chrysogenum* (a fungus)

(ii) **Streptomycin** *Streptomyces griseus* (a bacterium)

(iii) **Chlorotetracycline** *Streptomyces aureofaciens* (a bacterium)

(iv) **Erythromycin** *Saccharopolyspora erythraea* (a bacterium)

Q.2 **State any two features of a good antibiotic.**

Ans. A good antibiotic should have the following two features

(i) It should be able to kill several disease causing microorganisms.

(ii) It should not cause any side effect post usage.

Q.3 **Briefly explain the following terms**

(i) Botulism

(ii) Pasteurisation

Ans. (i) Botulism is a rare condition of food poisoning caused by the bacterium *Clostridium botulinum*.

(ii) Pasteurisation is the heating of milk at a higher temperature of about 60°C for about 30 minutes followed by rapid and sudden cooling.

Q.4 **State the importance of yeast in breweries and bakeries.**

Ans. Yeast, especially *Saccharomyces cerevisiae*, is essential in both breweries and bakeries. In breweries, it is used for fermentation to produce alcoholic beverages like beer and wine by converting glucose into ethyl alcohol (ethanol) and carbon dioxide (CO_2) under anaerobic conditions.

In bakeries, yeast is used to make dough rise by producing CO_2 during fermentation, which creates air pockets in the dough, resulting in soft and fluffy baked goods.

TYPE - 6 03 Marks

Short Answer Type Questions

Q.1 **Write any three applications of bacteria in the field of medicine.**

Ans. Three applications of bacteria in the field of medicine are as follows

(i) **Antibiotics** These are chemical substances produced by some microbes that kill or inhibit the growth of other microbes. Several antibiotics prepared from bacteria are effective against other bacteria, e.g. bacitracin from *Bacillus subtilis* and streptomycin from *Streptomyces griseus*.

(ii) **Vaccine** It is a biological preparation that provides active acquired immunity to a particular disease. A number of vaccines have been developed from weakened or killed forms of bacteria, e.g. the BCG vaccine for tuberculosis (prepared from living weakened bacteria) and the TAB vaccine for typhoid (prepared from killed bacteria).

(iii) **Serum** It is a plasma preparation (containing specific antibodies or antitoxins) from the blood of certain mammals, such as horses or monkeys. Serums are used as a preventive measure against bacterial invasion. For example, blood clotting factor VIII, used for the treatment of haemophilia-A, is produced by genetically modified bacteria.

Q.2 **Name the process in which bacteria present in the soil fix the nitrogen for plant use. Write about these bacteria in brief.**

Ans. The process is known as nitrogen-fixation.

Nitrogen-fixing bacteria play a crucial role in converting atmospheric nitrogen (N_2) into a form that plants can absorb and use, such as ammonia (NH_3), nitrates or nitrites. Some examples are as follows

(i) ***Rhizobium*** They forms a symbiotic relationship with the root nodules of leguminous plants, where it fixes nitrogen in exchange for nutrients.

(ii) ***Azotobacter* and *Clostridium*** These are free-living nitrogen-fixing bacteria present in the soil that fix nitrogen independently of plants.

This process enriches the soil and supports plant growth, reducing the need for chemical fertilisers.

Q.3 **Draw a labelled diagram to illustrate the nitrogen cycle.**

Ans.

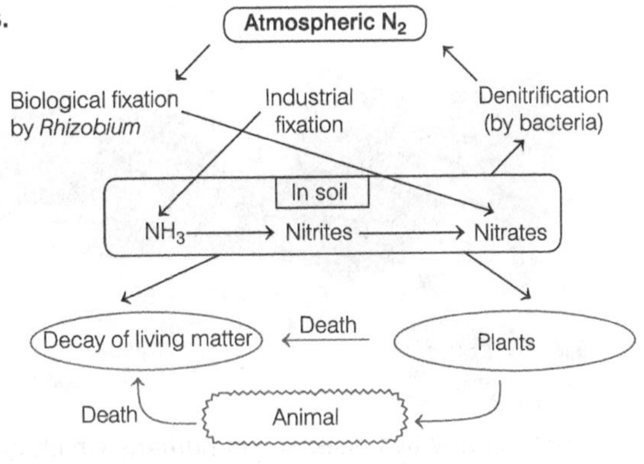

Nitrogen cycle

Q.4 **What are the major steps involved in mushroom cultivation?**

Ans. The major steps of mushroom cultivation are as follows

(i) **Composting** It is prepared by mixing paddy or wheat straw, chicken manure and organic and inorganic fertilisers. The compost is filled in trays.

(ii) **Spawning** The seeds (mycelium) of mushrooms are introduced into the compost.

(iii) **Casing** A thin layer of soil is spread over the compost and the temperature is maintained at 25°C for 3 days. Then, the temperature is lowered to 16-18°C.

(iv) **Cropping and Harvesting** Growth occurs between 2-6 weeks. Fully grown mushrooms are carefully harvested.

(v) **Preservation** Important steps for preserving mushrooms and increasing their shelf-life include vacuum cooling, storing at 15°C and freeze-drying in a solution of brine.

TYPE - 7 — 03 Marks

Structured Based Questions

Q.1 People often become ill when harmful microorganisms enter the body through contaminated food, water or direct contact with infected individuals. These microorganisms can release toxins or invade body tissues, leading to symptoms like fever, swelling and tissue damage, which are commonly associated with infections caused by specific types of microorganisms.

(i) Mention any two diseases in humans which occur by this kind of microorganisms.

(ii) Write one method of prevention and one method of cure that can be taken for such diseases.

(iii) Explain how the preventive measure for such diseases work.

Ans. (i) Tuberculosis, cholera.

(ii) **Prevention Method** Vaccination (e.g. BCG vaccine for tuberculosis).

Cure Method Antibiotics (e.g. penicillin for bacterial infections).

(iii) Vaccines stimulate the immune system to recognise and fight specific bacteria, while maintaining good hygiene and sanitation prevents the spread of bacteria through contaminated food or water.

Q.2 Observe the given figure carefully and answer the questions that follows

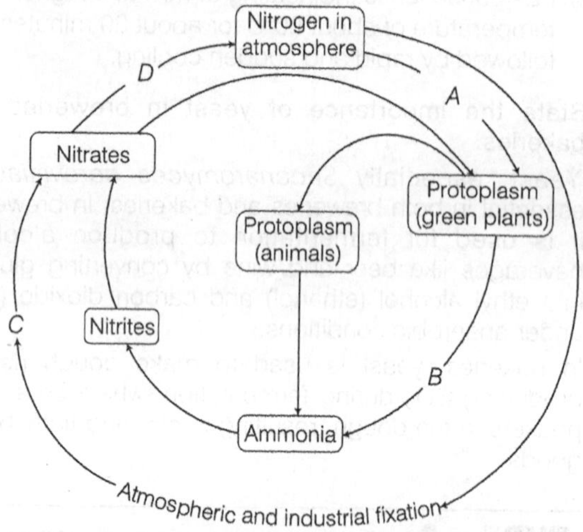

(i) Identify the process *A-D*.

(ii) Name the product obtained by decomposition of organic matter of dead remains.

(iii) State the importance of this cycle.

Ans. (i) The process *A-E* are as follows

A-Nitrogen-fixation *B*-Ammonification
C-Nitrification *D*-Denitrification

(ii) Ammonia is obtained from the organic matter of the dead remains.

(iii) Nitrogen cycle allows the continuous flow of nitrogen in the air, soil and water.

It is important as nitrogen is an essential element for living organisms.

09

NUTRITION IN HUMANS

Food

- It is an essential requirement for all living organisms, as it provides energy needed for daily activities, supports growth, repairs tissues and protects the body from diseases.
- Every food item consumed by an organism, is made up of one or more ingredients, which are derived from plants or animals. These ingredients contain specific substances called **nutrients**.
- Based on its function, food can be classified into different types
  - **Energy-yielding** (carbohydrates and fats) provide energy.
  - **Body-building** (proteins) help in growth and repair.
  - **Protective** (vitamins and minerals) support immunity and protect the body.
  - **Roughage** (fibre) aids digestion and promotes healthy bowel movements.
- **Nutrition** is the biological process by which organisms obtain their food, extract nutrients and use them to produce energy, repair tissues and maintain health.
- **Nutrients** are the chemical components of food, these are vital for carrying out various body functions and maintaining overall well-being. These can be classified into six categories, i.e. carbohydrates, fats, proteins, vitamins, mineral salts.

Carbohydrates

- These are energy releasing compounds made up of oxygen, hydrogen and carbon in which the ratio of hydrogen and oxygen is always 2 : 1.
- The carbohydrates are of three types, depending upon their structure; **monosaccharides** (glucose and fructose), **oligosaccharides** (sucrose) and **polysaccharides** (cellulose).
- The main carbohydrates found in our food are in the form of starch and sugars. These components provide energy to our body.
- Some sources of carbohydrates are **wheat, rice, maize, pearl millet, potatoes, sugar, jaggery** (gud), **honey, fruits** (banana, mango and papaya), etc.
- The major functions of carbohydrates include
  - To provide energy, as they are the main source of energy needed for physical and other activities.
  - To store energy in the form of starch in plants whereas in animals, these are stored as glycogen.
- Cellulose is found in the cell walls of plants. It is not digested by the body because human lack the enzyme to break it down. Undigested cellulose being fibrous in nature and act as roughage.

Fats

- These also provide energy to our body. Infact, fats provide more energy than carbohydrates.
- Fats can be obtained from plants as well as from animals. Some of the **plant sources** of fats are groundnut oil, mustard oil, coconut oil, sunflower oil, soybean oil, til oil and nut oil and some of the **animal sources** of fats are butter, ghee, milk, cream, cheese, eggs and meat.
- The major functions of fats include
  - They mainly act as reserve food and are the basic energy providers of our body.
  - They provide an insulating and protective covering. This covering is present over the entire surface of our body below the skin.

Proteins

- These constitute major part of our food and mainly are used as the **building blocks** in our body. They contain carbon, hydrogen, oxygen and nitrogen.
- Proteins are made up of amino acids. Proteins can be divided into two groups depending on their sources.
  - **Animal Proteins** These are obtained from animal products like **milk, cheese, egg, fish** or **meat.**
  - **Vegetable Proteins** These are obtained from plants like **gram, moong, tuar dal, beans, peas, soybeans,** etc.
- The major functions of proteins are as follows
  - They are essential for growth and repair of body.
  - They act as enzymes or chemical catalyst in metabolic reactions.
  - Antibodies are proteins which work for the defence system of the body.
  - The amount of energy produced on burning of one gram of food substance is called **calorific value.**

Calorific	Values
Carbohydrate	4.5 kcal/gm
Fat	9.2 kcal/gm
Protein	5.7 kcal/gm

Vitamins

- These are a group of nutrients that our body requires in small quantities.
- These are essential for the proper functioning of the body, but do not provide energy (protective food). Deficiency of any vitamin can lead to specific diseases.
- Vitamins may be divided into two classes
  - **Fat Soluble Vitamins** Vitamin-A, D, E and K.
  - **Water Soluble Vitamins** Vitamin-B complex and vitamin-C.

An Overview of Various Vitamins

Name of Vitamins	Sources	Functions	Deficiency Diseases
		Fat Soluble Vitamins	
Vitamin-A (Retinol)	Fish liver oil, egg yolk, milk, animal liver, yellow, red and green fruits. Vegetables like carrot, orange, etc.	Synthesis of retinal pigment, promotes normal vision, growth of bones and teeth, maintenance of epithelia.	**Xerophthalmia** (dryness of cornea and ulceration), **night blindness** (poor vision in dark).
Vitamin-D (Calciferol)	Fish liver oil, milk and its products, egg yolk, butter, sunlight, etc	It regulates the metabolism of calcium and phosphorus for growth of bones and teeth.	**Rickets** in children, weak bones, bone deformities, **osteomalacia** in adults, dental caries, etc.
Vitamin-E (Tocopherol)	Vegetable oils, milk, green vegetables like lettuce, egg yolk, meat, cereals, nuts, etc.	Works as antioxidant, role in healing wound, etc.	Anaemia, sterility, muscular dystrophy.
Vitamin-K (Phylloquinone)	Green leafy vegetables, tomatoes, soybean, wheat, fish, liver, egg, etc.	Helps in the formation of prothrombin in liver for normal clotting of blood, also have role in formation of other blood clotting proteins.	**Haemorrhage** deficiency of prothrombin in blood (delaying in blood clotting).
		Water Soluble Vitamins	
Vitamin-B_1 (Thiamine)	Beans, peas, green vegetables, cereals, whole wheat, yeast, milk, egg yolk, rice, etc.	Helps in increasing appetite, promotes growth of the body.	**Beri-beri** (affects nervous system)

Name of Vitamins	Sources	Functions	Deficiency Diseases
Vitamin-B_2 (Riboflavin)	Milk, liver, kidney, egg yolk, fish, yeast, germinating seeds, avocado. broccoli, spinach, etc.	Required for cell growth and regulates oxidation of food.	**Cheliosis**, i.e. cracking corners of mouth. **Dermatitis**, i.e. dryness of skin.
Vitamin-B_3 (Niacin)	Wheat bran, yeast, liver, vegetables, pulses, almonds, mushrooms, corn, etc.	Helps to maintain healthy skin and supports the proper functioning of the nervous system.	Pellagra, diarrhoea, indigestion, skin lesions, vomiting, dementia.
Vitamin-B_5 (Pantothenic acid)	Honey, egg yolk, tomatoes, sweet potato, yeast, etc.	Used in synthesis of fats, proteins, coenzyme-A, helpful for healthy skin and hair.	Fatigue, insomnia, premature greying of hair, burning feet syndrome, retarded growth.
Vitamin-B_6 (Pyridoxine)	Meat, milk, egg yolk, fish, peas, whole grain, green leafy vegetables, liver, etc.	Involved in carbohydrate, lipid and protein metabolism.	Anaemia, dermititis, paralysis, mental disorder.
Vitamin-B_9 (Folic acid)	Spinach leaves, wheat, peanuts, yeast, liver, kidney, etc.	It is crucial for DNA synthesis and cell division, especially in pregnancy.	Inflammation of bowel, conditions involving ulceration of mouth, anaemia.
Vitamin-B_{12} (Cobalamine)	Liver and kidney are the richest sources. Other sources are egg, milk, fish, intestinal bacteria, etc.	Essential for red blood cell production and nerve health.	Pernicious anaemia, fatigue.
Vitamin-C (Ascorbic acid)	Citrus fruits like lemon, grapes, cherry, tomato, green vegetables, etc.	Healing wounds and damaged bones, necessary for healthy teeth and gums.	Scurvy (Sailor's disease) delayed wound healing, loss of appetite.

Mineral Salts

- These are essential inorganic nutrients required by the body to support various functions, including bone formation, nerve transmission and fluid balance.
- Minerals can be categorised into macroelements and microelements. A brief introduction to these elements is given below

Macroelements

These nutrients are required in large quantities, e.g. Ca, Mg, Cl, etc. Two of these are given below

- **Calcium** (Ca) is useful for bones and teeth formation. It is a major component for nerve function, muscle contraction, coagulation of blood, etc. It is found in dairy products, eggs, wheat, leafy green vegetables and dates, etc. Its deficiency in the blood causes **rickets, muscular spasm, delayed blood clotting, nervous disorders, muscular cramps**, etc.
- **Sodium** (Na) is most important for blood and nerve functioning. It is a principal cation of extracellular fluid (0-7%). In excitable tissues, it is responsible for the impulse transmission. It is found in table salt and its deficiency causes **muscular cramps** along with **neural disorders**.

Microelements

These nutrients are required in smaller quantities which are given below

- **Iodine** (I) is a component of hormones of thyroid gland. It is present in salt (iodised salt), sea food, onions and drinking water. Its deficiency is associated to thyroid gland dysfunction and can lead to **goitre**.
- **Iron** (Fe) is a component of respiratory pigments (like haemoglobin and myoglobin) and respiratory enzyme (like cytochromes). It is found in meat, dried nuts, cereals, beans, apple, banana, honey, dates, green leafy vegetables and pomegranate. Its deficiency causes **anaemia**.

Functions of Mineral Salts

The major functions of mineral salts are as follows

- They are required for proper functioning, normal growth and good health.

- They are needed to build bones and teeth, formation of blood, coagulation of blood and functioning of muscles, nerves, thyroid glands, etc.
- They also control or affect the working of some glands like thyroid.

Water

- It makes up almost 70% of our body weight and various life processes are impossible without it.
- We take in water not only directly by drinking, but also as part of the food we eat.
- Fresh fruits and vegetables, e.g. tomatoes, spinach, oranges, watermelons, etc., also provide a lot of water to our body.
- Water helps our body to absorb nutrients from food. It also helps in excreting out some wastes from body as urine and sweat.
- The loss of lots of water from the body is called **dehydration**. It can happen due to diarrhoea, vomiting, burn or heat stroke. Acute dehydration can even cause death.

Balanced Diet

- The total amount of food which a person eats during entire day is called their **diet.**
- Balanced diet is the diet that contains proper amounts of all the nutrients. It provides the body with all energy and fulfil various nutrient requirements needed for proper functioning.
- A balanced diet is not same for everyone. It depends upon age, sex and type of work that one does. This can be explained by following examples
  - In early childhood, the child grows rapidly. He or she needs more **proteins**.
  - Nursing mothers and pregnant women also need more protein to serve the needs of the growing baby.
  - A hard worker, labourer needs more energy which he can get by eating more **fats** and **carbohydrates**.

A Typical Balanced Diet

Carbohydrates	45–65%
Fats	20–35%
Proteins	10–35%

Nutritional Disorders

- Every organism requires adequate supply of nutrients in their diet for proper growth and development. Any change in this leads to either a nutritional imbalance or a digestive disorder.
- A lack or deficiency of one or more essential nutrients in the diet can lead to **malnutrition**.
- Some of the nutritional disorders are as follows

1. Kwashiorkor

- It is a severe protein deficiency disease, typically affecting young children. It occurs when mothers stop breastfeeding their babies too early and the child is fed a diet lacking in proteins.
- **Symptoms of kwashiorkor** include a protruding belly, dark and scaly skin, stunted growth, low body weight, loss of appetite, repeated diarrhoea and an enlarged liver. Anaemia is also common in affected individuals.
- **Control/Treatment for Kwashiorkor** Children with kwashiorkor should be given a protein-rich diet, including pulses, milk, eggs, fish and meat.

2. Marasmus

- This disease typically affects infants under one year old and results from the deficiency of carbohydrates, fats and proteins in the diet.
- **Symptoms of marasmus** include low body weight, severe weakness where the body appears made of skin, muscles and bones, loose and folded skin, a thin face, thinning limbs, retarded physical and mental growth and prominent ribs.
- **Control/Treatment for Marasmus** A child suffering from marasmus should be provided with a diet rich in proteins and carbohydrates.

EXAM ORIENTED QUESTIONS

TYPE - 1 01 Mark

Multiple Choice Questions

Q.1 Which of the following best describes the role of food for living organisms?
(a) Food is only consumed for taste.
(b) Food provides essential nutrients necessary for growth, repair and proper body function.
(c) Food is only needed to supply energy for movement.
(d) Food is consumed to regulate body temperature.

Ans. (b)

Q.2 Mrs. Bansal asked her students to give examples of carbohydrate rich food.

Krishna said: Rice and potatoes

Ramya said: Eggs and rice

Shreya said: Milk and ghee

Who gave the right examples?
(a) Krishna
(b) Shreya
(c) Ramya and Krishna
(d) Ramya

Ans. (a)

Q.3 Given below is the table full of different food sources, observe the image carefully and answer the following question.

Based on the food items of the plate, which type of nutrient is primarily represented?
(a) Proteins and fats
(b) Carbohydrates
(c) Fats
(d) Carbohydrates and fats

Ans. (b)

Q.4 The table shows nutrients present in four foods.

Foods	Carbohydrate	Fat	Protein
P	✔	✗	✔
Q	✗	✗	✔
R	✗	✔	✗
S	✔	✔	✗

Key : Present =✔, Absent = ✗

Which foods would be partly digested in the stomach?
(a) P and Q (b) P and R
(c) Q and S (d) R and S

Ans. (a)

Q.5 Select from the following a group of eatables each member of which is rich in iron.
(a) Amla, spinach, jaggery
(b) Amla, cabbage, tomato
(c) Cabbage, amla, spinach
(d) Jaggery, amla, tomato

Ans. (a) Amla, spinach and jaggery all are rich sources of iron for the human consumption. The iron rich food helps in making haemoglobin in the blood.

Q.6 Which of the following is a polysaccharide present in human muscle?
(a) Amylose (b) Collagen
(c) Glycogen (d) Myoglobin

Ans. (c)

Q.7 A person ate food *X*. Food *X* was not affected by enzymes until it reached the duodenum.

What was in food *X*?
(a) Fat (b) Mineral ion
(c) Protein (d) Strach

Ans. (a)

Q.8 Undigested cellulose being fibrous in nature and act as ....*P*..... Cellulose absorbs water to keep faecal matter ....*Q*.... .
(a) *P*- dietary, *Q*- hard
(b) *P*- roughage, *Q*- soft
(c) *P*- fibrous, *Q*- eases
(d) *P*- fibres, *Q*- rough

Ans. (b)

Q.9 Radha's teacher observed that Radha is finding difficulty in reading black board. The doctor suggest that Radha needs to increase the food rich in which of the following nutrients?

(a) Vitamin-A (b) Vitamin-B
(c) Vitamin-C (d) Vitamin-D

Ans. (a) Insufficient intake of vitamin-A can lead to the deficiency that leads to poor vision.

Q.10 Riya tried to match the macronutrients with their diseases. She tabulated the pairs as follows.

Macronutrients	Diseases
P	Rickets, muscle cramps
Q	Anaemia

Choose the correct pair.

(a) *P*- Calcium, *Q*- Magnesium
(b) *P*- Potassium, *Q*- Molybdenum
(c) *P*- Calcium, *Q*- Iron
(d) *P*- Iron, *Q*- Magnesium

Ans. (c)

Q.11 Ascorbic acid is the another name for which of the nutrient?

(a) Vitamin-A (b) Vitamin-C
(c) Vitamin-B (d) Vitamin-D

Ans. (b)

Q.12 Poor nutrition can lead to a condition called rickets in which bones fail to develop properly. The table shows some minerals and vitamins present in four foods. Which food would be best for a child who has rickets?

	Calcium	Iron	Vitamin-C	Vitamin-D
(a)	✔	✗	✔	✗
(b)	✔	✗	✗	✔
(c)	✗	✔	✔	✗
(d)	✗	✔	✗	✔

Ans. (b)

Q.13 The table below shows the proteins, fats and carbohydrates content in 20 g of rice.

Foods	Proteins/g	Fats/g	Carbohydrates/g
Rice	0.5	0.1	9.2
White fish	2.1	0.005	0.0

What will be the main end products of digestion of a meal of rice and white fish?

(a) Amino acids and fatty acids
(b) Amino acids and glucose
(c) Fatty acids and glucose
(d) Glucose and glycerol

Ans. (b) During digestion carbohydrate are broken down into simple sugars mainly glucose, and proteins are broken down into amino acids.

TYPE - 2 01 Mark

Matching Type Question

Q.1 Match the following food sources with their correct nutrients.

	Food Sources	Nutrients
A.		I. Good source of vitamin-A
B.		II. Source of fructose sugar
C.		III. Source of carbohydrates
D.		IV. Good source of protein
E.		V. Source of fats

Ans. A-IV, B-III, C-V, D-II, E-I

TYPE - 3 01 Mark

Assertion-Reason Type Questions

Direction (Q. Nos. 1-5) In the following questions statements are given as Assertion (A) and Reason (R).

(a) A is true, but R is false.
(b) A is false, but R is true.
(c) Both A and R are true.
(d) Both A and R are false.

Q.1 Assertion (A) Every food item is made up of ingredients that provide essential nutrients to the human body.

Reason (R) Nutrition is the process through which a living body receives these nutrients.

Ans. (c)

Q.2 Assertion (A) Fats are a major source of energy for the body.

Reason (R) Fats release less energy compared to carbohydrates, providing short-term energy storage.

Ans. (a) A is true, but R is false. R can be corrected as Fats release more energy compared to carbohydrates and serve as long term energy storage.

Q.3 Assertion (A) Proteins are made up of carbon, hydrogen and oxygen.

Reason (R) Eggs and fishes are good source of protein.

Ans. (b) A is false, but R is true. A can be corrected as Proteins are composed of carbon, hydrogen, oxygen, and nitrogen.

Q.4 Assertion (A) Vitamins and minerals are body building food.

Reason (R) Ascorbic acid is a fat-soluble vitamin.

Ans. (d) Both A and R are false. These can be corrected as Vitamins and minerals are protective food and ascorbic acid is a water-soluble vitamin.

Q.5 Assertion (A) Water is crucial for various life processes in the body, making up about 70% of our body weight.

Reason (R) Water helps in digestion, transportation of nutrients, removal of waste and maintaining body temperature.

Ans. (c)

TYPE - 4

01 Mark

Very Short Answer Type Questions

Q.1 Name the category of food in which carbohydrates and fats are placed.

Ans. Energy yielding food.

Q.2 *X* is the type of sugar which does not require digestion it can directly absorb in the body. Identify *X*.

Ans. Monosaccharides.

Q.3 Name the food source which acts like an insulator for the body.

Ans. Fats

Q.4 Identify the disease caused when a mother stops breastfeeding too early, leading to a diet lacking in proteins.

Ans. Kwashiorkor

Q.5 Name the mineral and foods most required for a mother who is on a breast feed.

Ans. Calcium, iron, vitamin-D and protein rich food.

Q.6 Name any two fat soluble vitamins.

Ans. Vitamin-A (retinol) and vitamin-K (phylloquinone) are fat soluble vitamins.

Q.7 *Y* is the disease which is caused by the deficiency of thiamine. Identify the *Y*.

Ans. Beri-beri

Q.8 What are micronutrients? Give an example of it.

Ans. Micronutrients are essential nutrients which required in small amounts, e.g. iron.

Q.9 Name the micronutrient which is essential for red blood cells production.

Ans. Cobalt.

Q.10 What is balanced diet?

Ans. A balanced diet is containing all the essential nutrients in the right proportions to maintain good health and proper body function.

Q.11 Identify the condition caused by an imbalance in the intake of nutrients, either due to insufficient, excessive or imbalanced nutrition.

Ans. Malnutrition is a condition caused by an imbalance in the intake of nutrients, either due to insufficient, excessive or imbalanced nutrition, leading to health problems.

Q.12 Name the following. **(1 Mark each)**

(i) The undigestible, fibrous portion of food.

(ii) The fat-soluble vitamin.

(iii) Deficiency of RBCs or haemoglobin in the blood.

(iv) A vitamin whose deficiency causes beri-beri.

(v) The disease caused by deficiency of iodine.

Ans. (i) Roughage

(ii) Vitamin-A (iii) Anaemia

(iv) Thiamine (vitamin-B_1) (v) Goitre

Q.13 Choose the odd one out from the following terms given below and name the category to which other three belong. **(1 Mark each)**

(i) Vitamin-A, Vitamin-C, Vitamin-D, Vitamin-E

(ii) Riboflavin, Thiamine, Folic acid, Iodine

(iii) Xerophthalmia, Marasmus, Pellagra, Scurvy

(iv) Egg, Rice, Bread, Potato

(v) Calcium, Cobalt, Sodium, Magnesium

Ans. (i) Odd term is vitamin-C because it is a water soluble vitamin, while the rest three are fat soluble vitamins.

(ii) Odd term is iodine because it is a micronutrient, while rest three are vitamins.

(iii) Odd term is marasmus because it is the deficiency of protein, while rest three are the deficiency of vitamins.

(iv) Odd term is egg because it is a protein source, while rest three are the source of carbohydrates.

(v) Odd term is cobalt because it is a micronutrient, while rest three are macronutrients.

Q.14 Given diagram represents a balanced diet. Observe the diagram and fill the blank spaces with correct words. **(1 Mark each)**

A balanced diet contains all the essential nutrients in the right proportions to maintain .....(i)..... and proper body function. Among these nutrients, carbohydrates and proteins play key roles in energy production and bodily repair. Carbohydrates are made up of carbon, hydrogen and oxygen, with hydrogen and oxygen in a .....(ii)..... . They are oxidised in cells to release energy. Proteins composed of carbon, hydrogen, oxygen and nitrogen, with .....(iii)..... being the most important element, play a crucial role in the body. Some proteins also contain .....(iv)..... and phosphorus. During digestion, proteins are broken down into smaller units called .....(v)..... , which are essential for growth and repair.

Ans. (i) good health, (ii) 2:1 ratio, (iii) nitrogen, (iv) sulphur, (v) amino acids.

Q.15 Correct and rewrite the following statements by changing the underlined words. **(1 Mark each)**

(i) Monosaccharides are known as complex sugars.

(ii) Cellulose is an example of disaccharides.

(iii) Proteins are also made up of sulphur and magnesium.

(iv) Tocopherol is a water-soluble vitamin.

(v) Iodine is a macronutrient.

Ans. (i) Monosaccharides are known as simple sugars.

(ii) Cellulose is an example of a polysaccharide.

(iii) Proteins are also made up of sulphur and phosphorus.

(iv) Tocopherol is a fat-soluble vitamin.

(v) Iodine is a micronutrient.

TYPE - 5

02 Marks

Short Answer Type Questions

Q.1 State the differences between carbohydrate and proteins.

Ans. Differences between carbohydrates and proteins are as follows

Carbohydrates	Proteins
Composed of carbon, hydrogen and oxygen.	Composed of carbon, hydrogen, oxygen and nitrogen (may also contain sulphur or phosphorus).
Primary function is to provide energy.	Primary function is to build and repair tissues.

Q.2 Describe the symptoms and treatment of marasmus.

Ans. Marasmus includes following symptoms

(i) Severe weight loss, with the body appearing extremely thin and weak.

(ii) Prominent ribs and visible bones due to loss of fat and muscle.

(iii) Loose and wrinkled skin.

(iv) Stunted physical and mental growth.

(v) Weak immune system and frequent infections.

(Any two)

Treatment A child suffering from marasmus should be provided with a diet rich in proteins and carbohydrates.

Q.3 State the differences between fat soluble and water soluble vitamins.

Ans. Differences between fat soluble and water soluble vitamins are as follows

Fat Soluble Vitamins	Water Soluble Vitamins
Stored in the body's fat tissues and liver.	Not stored in the body; excess is excreted in urine.
Includes vitamins-A, D, E and K.	Includes vitamin-B complex and vitamin-C.

Q.4 What are macronutrients? Give two examples of it.

Ans. Macronutrients are nutrients required by the body in large amounts to provide energy and support growth and bodily functions, e.g. calcium and chlorine.

Q.5 It is advisable for a orthopedic patient to include more milk and milk products in his everyday food. Comment.

Ans. Calcium is considered as a constituent of bones. since, milk and milk products are rich sources of calcium. Hence, doctor advised a orthopedic patient to include more milk and milk products in his every day food.

Q.6 State any two functions of water in human body.

Ans. Functions of water are as follows

(i) Water transports digested food and oxygen throughout the body.

(ii) It aids in the removal of soluble waste.

Q.7 'It is said that vitamins are not digested by any enzymes'. Why?

Ans. Vitamins are used in their original form by the cells and does not requires any enzyme for digestion because they are absorbed directly from the digestive tract and are transported by blood to the cells.

Q.8 Why roughage is considered as an important part of our diet? Explain.

Ans. Roughage is an important part of our diet because

(i) It helps in the movement of food easily through the intestine.

(ii) It helps to make food soft to help avoid constipation.

TYPE - 6 03 Marks

Short Answer Type Questions

Q.1 Describe three main purposes of food requirement in our body.

Ans. The food is required by the body for the following purposes

(i) **Growth** Food provides raw materials for building up new protoplasm or cells for growth.

(ii) **Repair** Food provides raw materials for repair of worn-out cells and for replacement of dead cells.

(iii) **Energy** The oxidation of food during respiration generates energy, which the body utilises for various activities.

Q.2 What are nutrients? Name the different categories of nutrients.

Ans. Nutrients are substances required by living organisms for proper growth, development, repair and maintenance of the body. They provide energy, support bodily functions and protect against diseases.

The different categories of nutrients include carbohydrates, proteins, fats, vitamins, minerals and water.

Q.3 Explain monosaccharides and disaccharides with their examples.

Ans. **Monosaccharides or simple sugars** are soluble in water and have the general chemical formula $C_6H_{12}O_6$. They require no digestion and are directly absorbed into the body, e.g. glucose.

Disaccharides or double sugars have the chemical formula $C_{12}H_{22}O_{11}$. These sugars are not absorbed directly into the body and require digestion, e.g. sucrose.

Q.4 State any three important functions of proteins in human body.

Ans. Functions of proteins are as follows

(i) It acts as building blocks for growth and repair of body cells and tissues.

(ii) Proteins can be oxidised for energy in emergencies.

(iii) Help in the formation of hair, nails and other body structures.

(iv) Aid in the synthesis of antibodies, which protect against germs.

(v) Essential for the growth of children.

(vi) Some proteins also help in transportation such as haemoglobin. (Any three)

Q.5 Write the chemical name of vitamins-D, E and B_{12}.

Ans. The chemical names of the vitamins are as follows

(i) Vitamin-D: Calciferol

(ii) Vitamin-E: Tocopherol

(ii) Vitamin-B_{12}: Cyanocobalamine

Q.6 Give biological reasons for the following.

(i) Fats are considered as the main energy producers. Why?

(ii) Vitamins are not digested by enzymes.

(iii) Humans cannot digest cellulose.

Ans. (i) Fats provide more energy than carbohydrates and proteins because they yield about 9 kcal per gram, which is more than twice the energy produced by carbohydrates (4.5 kcal per gm) or proteins (5.7 kcal per gram).

(ii) Vitamins are organic compounds that are already in their simplest form and do not require digestion. They are directly absorbed into the bloodstream or cells to perform their specific functions.

(iii) Humans lack the enzyme cellulase, which is required to breakdown cellulose into glucose. As a result, cellulose passes through the digestive system undigested, acting as dietary fibre.

Q.7 Write the deficiency of the following nutrients.
(i) Sodium (ii) Iron
(iii) Vitamin-E

Ans. (i) **Sodium** Deficiency can lead to muscle cramps, nausea and dizziness.
(ii) **Iron** Deficiency can cause anaemia, fatigue and weakness.
(iii) **Vitamin-E** Deficiency can result in muscle weakness, vision problems and weakened immune function.

Q.8 How does protein deficiency contribute to diseases and what are the effects of such deficiencies on the body?

Ans. Protein deficiency can cause diseases like kwashiorkor and marasmus.

Kwashiorkor It is a severe protein deficiency disease that typically affects children who do not get enough protein despite adequate calorie intake. It leads to symptoms such as swelling (oedema), especially in the abdomen and legs, delayed growth, skin changes and a weakened immune system, making the body more vulnerable to infections.

Marasmus It is a condition caused by a severe deficiency in both protein and calories. It results in extreme weight loss, muscle wasting and overall weakness. Affected individuals often appear very thin with noticeable rib and bone structure due to the lack of sufficient nutrients needed for proper growth and energy.

TYPE - 7 03 Marks

Structured Based Questions

Q.1 Observe the given image carefully and answer the following questions.

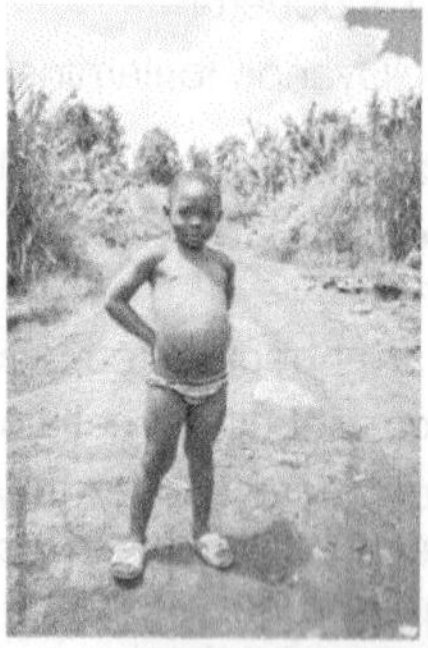

(i) Which disease is shown in the given image?
(ii) The given disease occurs due to the deficiency of which nutrient?
(iii) Describe the treatment of this disease.

Ans. (i) The disease shown in the given image is kwashiorkor.
(ii) This disease occurs due to the deficiency of protein in the diet.
(iii) The treatment of kwashiorkor involves providing a protein-rich diet, including foods like pulses, milk, eggs, fish and meat.

Q.2 The doctor advised Rohan to do Sun basking every morning. Observe the given image and answer the following questions.

(i) Which vitamin deficiency might Rohan be suffering from?
(ii) What are the main sources of this vitamin?
(iii) Write the chemical name of this vitamin.

Ans. (i) Rohan might be suffering from a deficiency of vitamin-D.
(ii) The main sources of vitamin-D include sunlight, fish and egg yolks.
(iii) The chemical name of vitamin-D is calciferol.

Q.3 Advik drinks milk regularly in the morning and takes a balanced diet. Based on the above information, answer the following questions.

(i) Which macronutrient is obtained from milk?
(ii) What are the advantages of taking a balanced diet?
(iii) Which deficiencies can occur due to a diet lacking essential nutrients?

Ans. (i) Milk is a rich source of protein, which is a vital macronutrient for growth, muscle repair and immune function.
(ii) A balanced diet provides all the essential nutrients–proteins, carbohydrates, fats, vitamins and minerals–needed for good health. It helps in maintaining energy levels, promoting growth and preventing diseases.
(iii) A diet lacking essential nutrients can lead to deficiencies, such as protein deficiency causing kwashiorkor or marasmus, and vitamin or mineral deficiencies leading to conditions like anaemia or weakened immunity.

10

DIGESTION IN HUMANS

The food we consume cannot be used by the body in its original form. It must first be transformed into a soluble and absorbable state, so that it can enter to the bloodstream and be distributed throughout the body. This transformation of food occurs through **digestion**.

Digestive System

The entire process of digestion is carried out by the digestive system, which consists of a long tube called the **alimentary canal** (about 7-8 metres long) and **digestive glands** that secrete enzymes to aid in the breakdown of food.

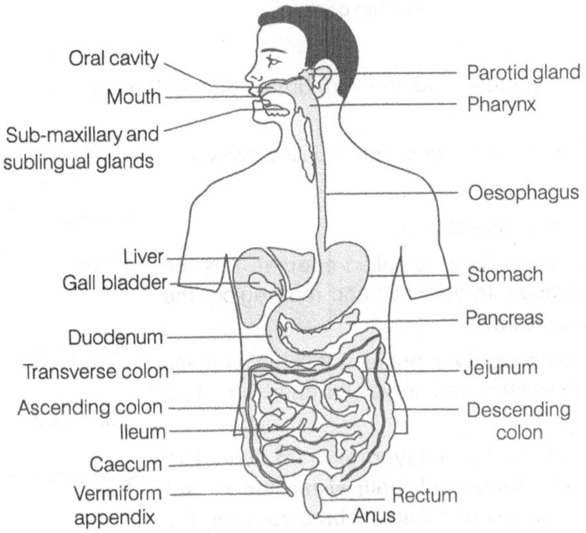

Human digestive system

Alimentary Canal

- It is a long muscular tube that begins at the mouth and ends at the anus.
- It is approximately 7-8 metres in length and is tightly coiled in some areas, particularly in the small intestine.
- Alimentary canal is divided into following parts

(i) Mouth and buccal cavity (ii) Pharynx (iii) Oesophagus (iv) Stomach (v) Small intestine (vi) Large intestine (vii) Anus

Mouth and Buccal Cavity

- Mouth is the first part of the digestive system from where the food enters into the alimentary canal.
- Mouth is a slit-like opening, bounded by two soft, movable **lips**. It opens into a small **vestibule** (space enclosed between lips and teeth), which in turn leads into the **buccal** or **oral cavity**.

REVISION NOTES

Oral cavity further comprises of two main components which are as follows

- **Tongue** It is a highly muscular, sensory organ present at the floor of the buccal cavity. It bears several taste buds that helps in mixing food with saliva. Apart from this, it is also helpful in producing speech.
- **Teeth** These are hard structures embedded in the socket of jaw bones of both lower and upper jaws. Teeth are basically used for the purpose of **grinding, cutting** and **chewing** of food.
  In mammals, four types of teeth are present which are used for different purposes, i.e.
  - **Incisors** are present at the front of the mouth and are used for **cutting** or **clipping**.
  - **Canines** are next to incisors and are used for puncturing or holding or **tearing** the food.
  - **Premolars** and **molars** are the innermost and are used for crushing or grinding the food. The last molar of each side in each jaw is called **wisdom tooth**.

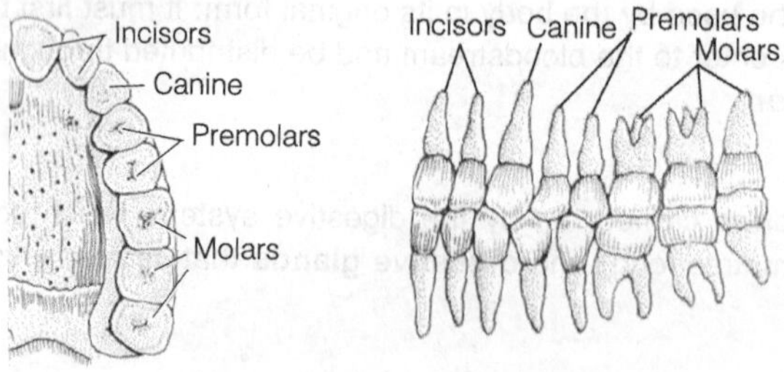

Human dentition

Tooth Structure

- The tooth have almost same structure in all the vertebrates. It is differentiated into three regions namely, **crown, neck** and **the root**.
  - The part of tooth projecting above the gum line is called **crown**.
  - The **neck** is the part present inside the gums.
  - The **root** is present inside the bony socket.
- In the crown region, the outermost layer is called **enamel**. It is the hardest substance of human body. In the neck and root region, the outermost layer is called **cementum**.
- In the centre of the tooth, a **pulp cavity** is present. It contains mass of cells, blood vessels, lymph vessels and nerves for nourishment of tooth.
- The **pulp cavity** is surrounded by a layer of hard ivory-like substance called **dentine**. The fixation of tooth within the socket occurs with the help of thick bundles of collagen fibres covering the cementum.

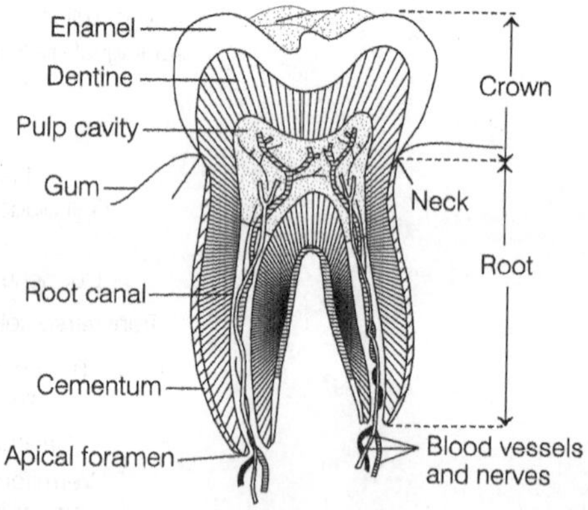

Section of a tooth

Dental Formula

- The number and the kinds of teeth in mammals are represented by an equation called dental formula. These are constant for every species.
- For **vertebrates**, this formula looks like $\frac{\text{I C Pm M}}{\text{I C Pm M}}$
- Here, **I** = Incisors, **C** = Canines, **Pm** = Premolars, **M** = Molars.
- The total number of teeth in each jaw = number of teeth in dental formula × 2.
- The dental formula in human being is given below

(i) **Human** (Adult) $= \frac{2123}{2123} \times 2 = 32$ (Permanent teeth)

(ii) **Human** (Child) $= \frac{2102}{2102} \times 2 = 20$ (Milk teeth)

Salivary Glands

- These glands secrete saliva which contain an enzyme called **salivary amylase** (ptyalin).
- It is due to these salivary glands that our mouth waters when we eat or smell something we like.
- Three pairs of salivary glands that secrete saliva are **parotid** (present below the pinna, i.e. portion of outer ear), **sub-maxillary** (present on inner side of lower jaw) and **sublingual** (present below the tongue).
- **Saliva** performs the following functions
  - Moisten and lubricates food which helps in swallowing.
  - Helps food particles to stick together to form bolus, so that they are easily swallowed.
  - Cleans the mouth and helps to destroy germs, thus preventing tooth decay.

Digestion in Buccal or Oral Cavity

- Digestion starts in oral cavity by the chemical hydrolytic action of the carbohydrates splitting enzyme, salivary amylase (ptyalin).
- About 30% of the starch gets hydrolysed in the oral cavity by the action of salivary amylase (at optimum pH 6.8) into a disaccharide, i.e. maltose.

$$\text{Starch} \xrightarrow[\text{pH 6.8}]{\text{Salivary amylase}} \text{Maltose}$$

- The food mixed with saliva in buccal cavity is known as **bolus.**

Pharynx

- It is a small funnel-shaped chamber located behind the oral cavity. It serves as a common passage for both food and air, i.e. it communicates with both **oesophagus** (food pipe) and **trachea** (windpipe).
- The opening of trachea or windpipe is called **glottis**, which is guarded by a cartilaginous flap or lid called **epiglottis**.
- The glottis normally remains open, but during swallowing of food it gets covered by epiglottis to prevent the entry of food in trachea.

Oesophagus

- It is a thin, long muscular tube that extends and leads into a J-shaped bag-like structure called **stomach**.
- It uses rhythmic muscle contraction called **peristalsis** to push the food downward.
- A muscular **gastro-oesophageal sphincter** regulates the opening of oesophagus into the stomach.

Stomach

- It is the most dilated J-shaped part of the alimentary canal, which is situated between the oesophagus and the small intestine, below the diaphragm.
- It serves as a storehouse of food where partial digestion takes place through the secretions of gastric glands.
- The muscular walls of the stomach help in mixing the food properly.

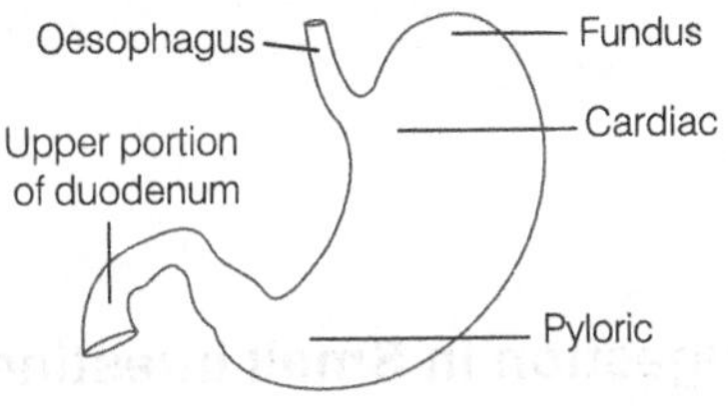

Anatomical regions of human stomach

- Stomach has three major parts as given below
  - **Cardiac stomach**, the upper portion into which the oesophagus opens.
  - **Fundic stomach**, the middle portion.
  - **Pyloric stomach**, the lower portion, which opens into the first part of small intestine, i.e. **duodenum**. It contains ring-like muscles called **sphincter** which regulates its opening.

Gastric Glands

- These are found in the wall of the stomach. The gastric glands release digestive juice containing HCl, pepsin, mucus, etc.
- **Hydrochloric acid** (HCl) kills the bacteria ingested with food. It creates an acidic medium of pH about 2, facilitating the action of **pepsin** enzyme, which acts on proteins present in food.
- The **mucus** protects the lining of the stomach from the action of the hydrochloric acid produced under normal conditions.

REVISION NOTES

Digestion in Stomach

- Food is stored for 4-5 hours in the stomach and get mixed with gastric juices secreted by gastric glands.
- This process turns food into chyme, a semi-digested, acidic, pulpy mass. Two key enzymes involved in this process are as follows
  - **Pepsin** (Activated from pepsinogen by the help of HCl) It breaks down proteins into **proteases** and **peptones**.

    (a) Pepsinogen (inactive) + HCl $\rightarrow$ Pepsin (active)

    (b) Proteins $\rightarrow$ Proteases + Peptones
  - **Rennin** It is found in infants, rennin helps to digest milk proteins by converting casein into paracasein.

    (a) Prorennin + HCl $\rightarrow$ Rennin

    (b) Casein (soluble) $\rightarrow$ Paracasein (insoluble)

Small Intestine

It is a coiled, 7 metre long tube, about 2.5 cm wide, It has three parts which are as follows

- **Duodenum** The short upper part next to the stomach, where the common bile duct opens.
- **Jejunum** The middle portion of small intestine.
- **Ileum** The longest part (4 metres) of small intestine.
- The inner lining of the ileum has tiny finger-like projections called **villi**, which increase the surface area for food absorption.
- **Lacteals** are **lymphatic capillaries** in the **villi** that absorb and transport fats and lipids.

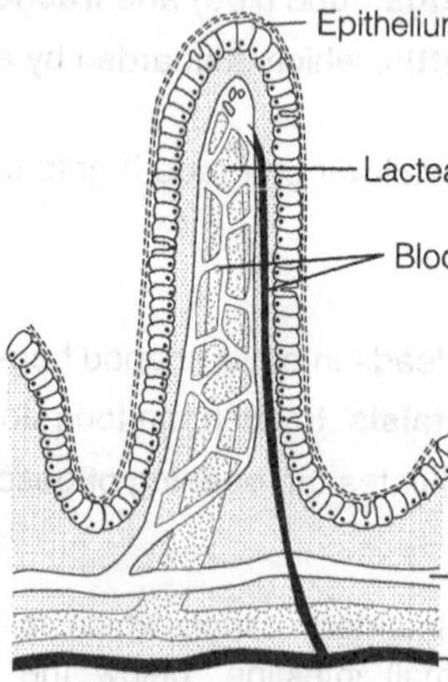

Villi of small intestine

Digestion in Small Intestine

- To facilitate the digestion, muscularis layer of small intestine shows various movements which allow thorough mixing of food with various secretions from liver and pancreas in the intestine.
- The respective digestive juices from the pancreas (pancreatic juice), the liver (bile juice) and small intestine (intestinal juices) bring out the further chemical simplification of food.

Liver and it's Secretions

- It is the largest gland of the body. It is a reddish-brown organ located in the upper right side of the abdomen just below the diaphragm.
- It secretes bile into the duodenum to breakdown large fat molecules into smaller globules. The gall bladder stores bile for later use. Bile contains bile pigments (bilirubin and biliverdin), bile salts, cholesterol and phospholipids. It makes food alkaline.

* Bile emulsifies fats, breaking them down into diglycerides and monoglycerides. Bile does not contain enzymes like gastric juice, but assists in emulsification through bile salts.

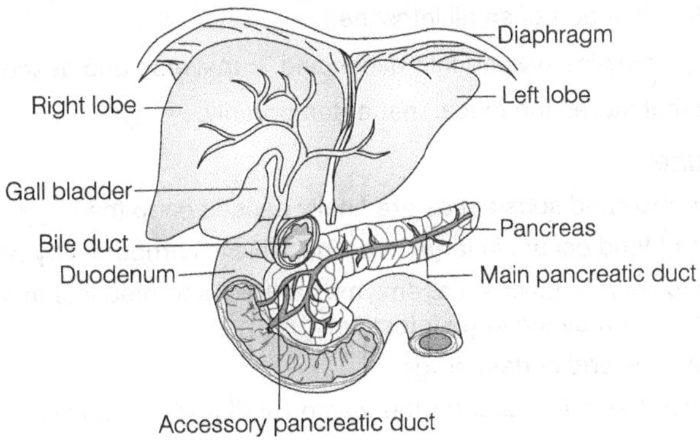

Liver and pancreas with associated structures

Pancreas and its Secretions

* It is located behind the stomach. The pancreatic duct opens into duodenum by an aperture common to that of the bile duct. The pancreatic juice is alkaline in nature.
* Pancreatic juice contains three enzymes
  * **Amylopsin** Breaks down starch into maltose.
  * **Trypsin** Breaks down proteins into peptides and amino acids.
  * **Steapsin** Breaks down fats into fatty acids and glycerol.
* The roles of pancreatic enzymes are as follows

(i) $\underset{\text{(Inactive)}}{\text{Trypsinogen}} \xrightarrow{\text{Enterokinase}} \underset{\text{(Active)}}{\text{Trypsin}}$

(ii) Proteins and Polypeptides $\xrightarrow{\text{Trypsin}}$ Smaller peptides + Amino acids

(iii) Leftover starch $\xrightarrow[\text{(Pancreatic amylase)}]{\text{Amylopsin}}$ Maltose

(iv) Emulsified fat $\xrightarrow{\text{Steapsin}}$ Fatty acids + Glycerol

Enzymes from Intestine

* Walls of small intestine contain numerous glands that secrete intestinal juice also known as **succus entericus.**
* The succus entericus contains various enzymes. All enzymes act on the end products of below mentioned reactions in order to form their respective simpler forms.
  * Dipeptides $\xrightarrow{\text{Dipeptidases}}$ Amino acids
  * Maltose $\xrightarrow{\text{Maltase}}$ Glucose + Glucose
  * Lactose $\xrightarrow{\text{Lactase}}$ Glucose + Galactose
  * Sucrose $\xrightarrow{\text{Sucrase}}$ Glucose + Fructose
  * Nucleotides $\xrightarrow{\text{Nucleotidases}}$ Nucleosides $\xrightarrow{\text{Nucleosidases}}$ Sugars + Bases
  * Emulsified fat $\xrightarrow[\text{Lipolytic enzyme}]{\text{Lipases}}$ Fatty acids + Glycerol
* All the biomacromolecules mentioned above are broken down in the duodenum region of small intestine, while the simpler forms are absorbed in the other two regions of small intestine, i.e. jejunum and ileum.
* The contraction of the muscles in the small intestine allows the further churning and kneading of the chyme and finally pushing it into the large intestine.

Large Intestine

- It is about 1.5 metre long. It is distinguishable into three main parts, i.e. **caecum, colon** and **rectum**.
  - **Caecum** is present at terminal part of small intestine.
  - **Colon** is the part of large intestine divided into ascending, transverse and descending colon.
  - **Rectum** is the last part that stores the faecal matter temporarily.

Digestion in Large Intestine

- The undigested and the unabsorbed substances are finally passed on to the large intestine.
- The last stage of digestion of food occurs in large intestine. This is carried out by bacterial action.
- Glands of this region tend to secrete mucus, i.e. enzymes are not secreted into this part of the digestive system. Following functions are performed by the large intestine
  - Absorption of water, minerals and certain drugs.
  - Secretion of mucus which helps in adhering the waste (undigested) particles together and lubricates it for an easy passage.

Anus

- It is the end point of alimentary canal, which helps in the exit of waste materials. The exit of waste materials is regulated by **anal sphincter**.
- Expulsion of undigested remains of food from the alimentary canal is called **defaecation**.

Absorption of Food

- It is the process by which digested nutrients, such as glucose, amino acids, fatty acids, vitamins and minerals, pass through the intestinal walls into the bloodstream or lymph.
- The food is absorbed in the small intestine. Amino acids, simple sugars (like glucose, fructose), minerals, vitamins are absorbed through the villi, reach the blood capillaries and finally enter into the blood circulation and are distributed to the whole body.
- Fatty acids and glycerol are absorbed into the lacteal or lymph vessel in order to enter the lymphatic system. Water is absorbed in large intestine.

Assimilation

- It is the distribution of digested food products to various cells of the body.
- The villi in small intestine are richly supplied with blood vessels, which take the absorbed food to each and every cell of the body, where it is utilised for obtaining energy, building up new tissues and repairing the older ones.

Egestion

- The remaining material after reabsorption of water and ions is stored in the rectum for some time and is ultimately removed from the body through anus.
- The elimination of undigested food formed in the colon of the large intestine through anus is called **egestion**.

EXAM ORIENTED QUESTIONS

TYPE - 1 01 Mark

Multiple Choice Questions

Q.1 What is the approximate length of the alimentary canal in the human digestive system?
(a) 7-8 metres (b) 4-6 metres
(c) 8-9 metres (d) 2-3 metres

Ans. (a)

Q.2 Where does the process of digestion begin in humans?
(a) Stomach (b) Mouth
(c) Intestine (d) Pharynx

Ans. (b)

Q.3 Which part of tooth is embedded in the bony socket of the jaw?
(a) Dentine (b) Crown
(c) Root (d) Neck

Ans. (c)

Q.4 Radha tried to match the glands with their location. She tabulated the pairs as follows.

Glands	Location
P	Below the ear.
Q	Beneath the tongue.

(a) *P*- Sublingual gland, *Q*- Sub-maxillary gland
(b) *P*-Parotid gland, *Q*- Sublingual gland
(c) *P*-Sub-maxillary gland, *Q*-Salivary gland
(d) *P*-Salivary gland, *Q*- Maxillary gland

Ans. (b)

Q.5 The diagram shows a large food molecule changing into smaller molecules. What is process *X*?

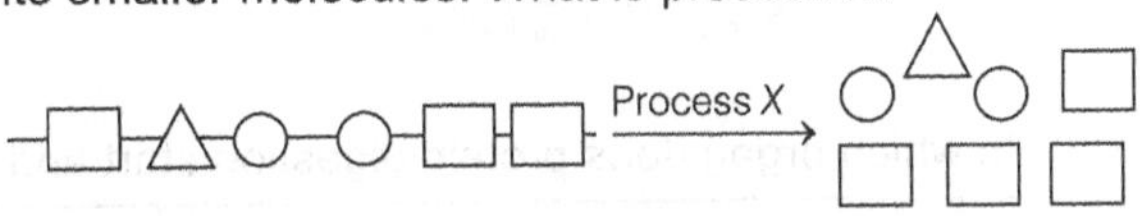

(a) Absorption (b) Chewing
(c) Digestion (d) Secretion

Ans. (c)

Q.6 Which of the following enzyme in the human body starts the digestion of proteins?
(a) Trypsin (b) Lactose
(c) Pepsin (d) None of these

Ans. (c)

Q.7 The table shows the nutrients present in four foods.

Foods	Carbohydrates	Fats	Proteins
P	✔	✗	✔
Q	✗	✗	✔
R	✗	✔	✗
S	✔	✔	✗

Which foods would both be partly digested in the stomach?
(a) P and Q (b) P and R
(c) Q and S (d) R and S

Ans. (d) Food in the mouth undergoes mechanical digestion as well as a form of chemical digestion. Salivary enzymes reduces starch to maltose, while mechanical digestion physically breaks the food down to increase its surface area for enzyme action.

Q.8 The oesophagus leads into a bag-like structure called the stomach, which contains enzymes that aid in protein digestion. The stomach is also equipped with a muscular sphincter that prevents the backflow of food.

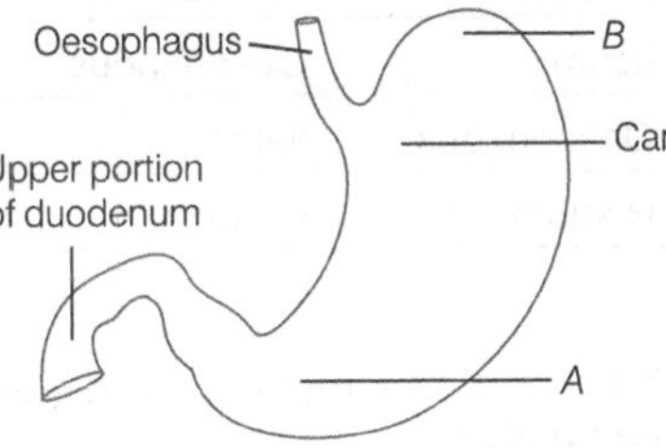

Identify the correct name of the structures labelled as *A* and *B* in the given diagram.
(a) *A*-Pyloric, *B*-Fundus
(b) *A*-Cardiac, *B*-Duodenum
(c) *A*-Cardiac, *B*-Pyloric
(d) *A*-Fundus, *B*-Oesophagus

Ans. (a)

Q.9 Gastric glands are found in the wall of the ......*P*....... Gastric juices turn food into ......*Q*..... .
(a) *P*-small intestine, *Q*-basic
(b) *P*-duodenum, *Q*-alkaline
(c) *P*-stomach, *Q*-chyme
(d) *P*-ileum, *Q*-bolus

Ans. (c)

Q.10 In which region of the alimentary canal is maltose digested?

(a) Colon (b) Rectum

(c) Small intestine (d) Stomach

Ans. (c)

Q.11 Observe the table below and identify the correct functions of the colon.

	Water Absorption	Enzyme Secretion
(a)	No	No
(b)	Yes	No
(c)	No	Yes
(d)	Yes	Yes

Ans. (b) Colon of large intestine helps in the absorption of water, but no digestion occurs inside it.

Q.12 The diagram shows a fat globule (*P*) in one part of the alimentary canal and the same globule (*Q*) as it appears in another part of the alimentary canal.

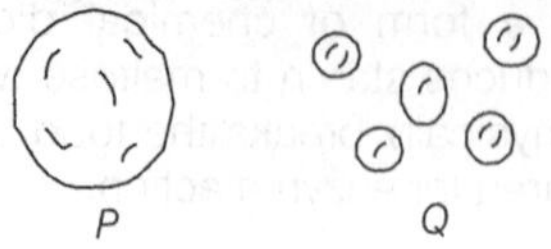

In which parts of the alimentary canal are *P* and *Q* found?

	P	*Q*
(a)	Duodenum	Stomach
(b)	Ileum	Oesophagus
(c)	Oesophagus	Ileum
(d)	Rectum	Ileum

Ans. (c)

Q.13 Which is the longest segment of the digestive system in the human body?

(a) Pancreatic duct (b) Small intestine

(c) Large intestine (d) Oesophagus

Ans. (b)

Q.14 The diagram below shows a villus.

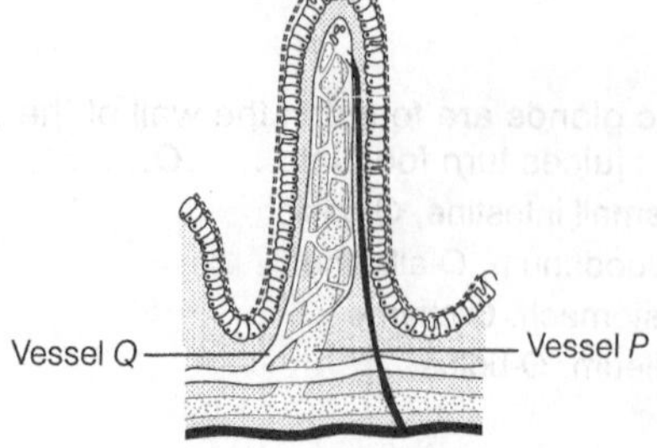

After a meal containing starch and oil, which substance(s) is/are absorbed mainly into vessel *P* and vessel *Q*, respectively.

	Vessel *P*	Vessel *Q*
(a)	Amino acids	Water
(b)	Fats	Glucose
(c)	Glucose	Amino acids
(d)	Water	Fats

Ans. (b)

Q.15 Mr. Raghav asked his students to give the name of the pigments present in the bile juice.

Monika said: Bilirubin and chlorophyll

Hema said: Bilirubin and biliverdin

Pooja said: Only biliverdin

Who gave the right answer, choose the correct option?

(a) Hema and Pooja (b) Pooja

(c) Hema (d) Monika

Ans. (c)

Q.16 The majority of the water from the indigestible food is absorbed in the ....

(a) stomach (b) food pipe

(c) pancreas (d) large intestine

Ans. (d)

Q.17 The diagram below shows a section of the human digestive system.

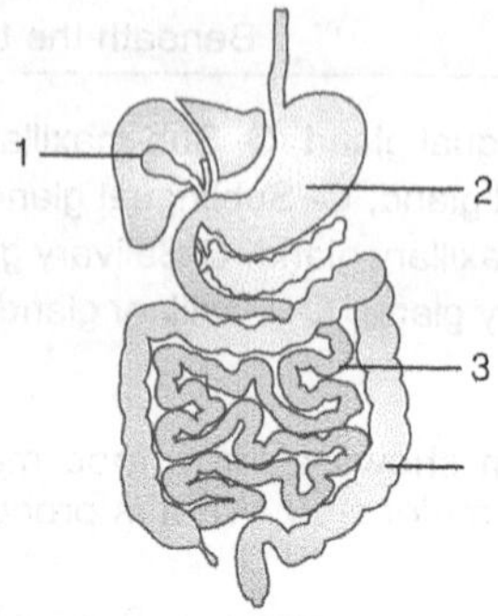

In which organ does protein digestion start and end?

	Organ Where Protein Digestion Start	Organ Where Protein Digestion End
(a)	1	3
(b)	1	4
(c)	2	3
(d)	2	4

Ans. (d)

TYPE - 2 — 01 Mark

Matching Type Questions

Q.1 Match the following structures with their respective functions.

Mouth Parts	Functions
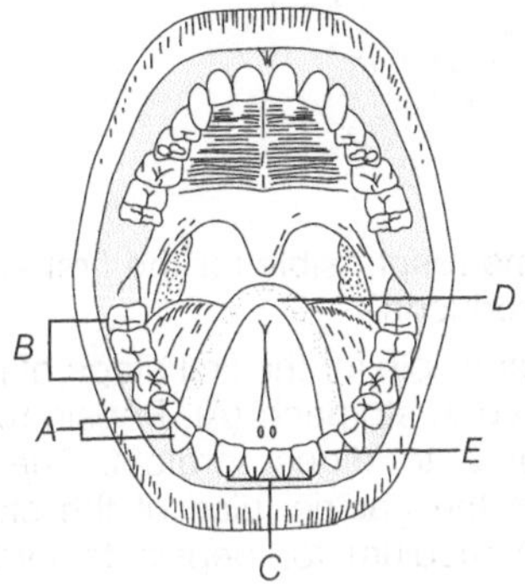	I. Muscular structure which helps to speak.
	II. Used for cutting or clipping food.
	III. Used for holding or tearing food.
	IV. These structures are used for crushing and grinding food.
	V. Found at the back of the mouth, also used for grinding food.

Ans. A- IV, B-V, C-II, D-I, E-III

Q.2 Observe the diagram of human digestive system.

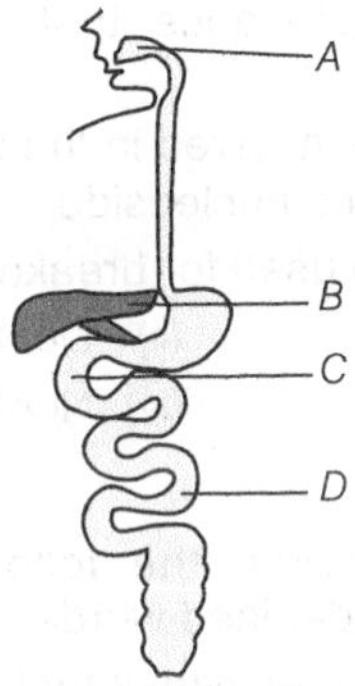

Match the labelling referred in Column I and correlate with the functions in Column II.

Column I		Column II
A	I.	The length of this depends on food the organism eats.
B	II.	Initial phase of starch digestion.
C	III.	Increases the efficiency of lipase enzyme action.
D	IV.	This is the site of the complete digestion of carbohydrates, proteins and fats.

Ans. A-II, B-III, C-IV, D-I

TYPE - 3 — 01 Mark

Assertion-Reason Type Questions

Direction (Q. Nos. 1-5) In the following questions statements are given as Assertion (A) and Reason (R).

(a) A is true, but R is false.
(b) A is false, but R is true.
(c) Both A and R are true.
(d) Both A and R are false.

Q.1 Assertion (A) Digestion is a catabolic process that breaks down large food molecules into simpler forms with the help of digestive enzymes.

Reason (R) These simpler molecules are absorbed by different parts of the body and used for energy, growth and repair.

Ans. (c)

Q.2 Assertion (A) Oesophagus pierces the diaphragm and enters the abdominal cavity.

Reason (R) Peristaltic movement starts from oesophagus.

Ans. (c)

Q.3 Assertion (A) Absorption of digested food mainly occurs in the stomach.

Reason (R) Gastric juice helps in the absorption of food in stomach.

Ans. (d) Both A and R are false. These can be corrected as Absorption of food mainly occurs in small intestine and gastric juices helps in the digestion of food in stomach.

Q.4 Assertion (A) Lipases of bile help in the emulsification of fats.

Reason (R) Lipases can break large fat droplets into smaller ones.

Ans. (b) A is false, but R is true. A can be corrected as Bile juice contains bile salts, which helps in the emulsification of fats.

Q.5 Assertion (A) Pancreatic juice is secreted by pancreatic duct.

Reason (R) Pancreatic juice is alkaline in nature.

Ans. (c)

TYPE - 4 — 01 Mark

Very Short Answer Type Questions

Q.1 Name the process in which large and complex food molecules are broken down into simpler forms.

Ans. Digestion

Q.2 *X* is the muscular organ which forms the floor of the buccal cavity. Identify the *X*.

Ans. Tongue

Q.3 State the function of molar teeth.

Ans. The function of molar teeth is to grind and crush food into smaller particles, aiding in the mechanical digestion of food.

Q.4 An organ connects the food pipe and windpipe, creating a common passage for both food and air. Identify the organ.

Ans. Pharynx

Q.5 *P* is a cartilaginous flap present at the opening of trachea which covers the glottis during swallowing the food. Identify *P*.

Ans. Epiglottis

Q.6 Which part of stomach is open into the duodenum of small intestine?

Ans. Pyloric part

Q.7 Name the enzyme which is secreted by gastric glands.

Ans. Pepsin

Q.8 Which is the largest gland of the body?

Ans. Liver is the largest gland of the body.

Q.9 Name any two enzymes of succus entericus or intestinal juice.

Ans. Maltase and invertase.

Q.10 Identify the process in which the absorbed nutrients are mixed in the blood stream and distributed to every cell of the body.

Ans. Assimilation

Q.11 In which region are most amino acids absorbed into the blood stream?

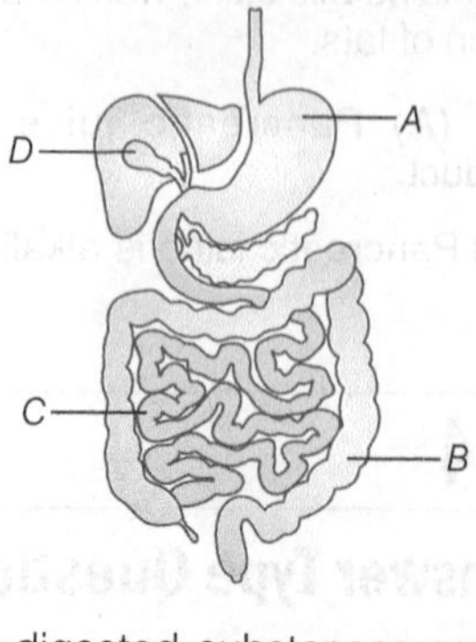

Ans. Most of the digested substances are absorbed in the small intestine (*C*). Peptones are broken down to amino acids in the small intestine.

Q.12 The diagram shows the alimentary canal.

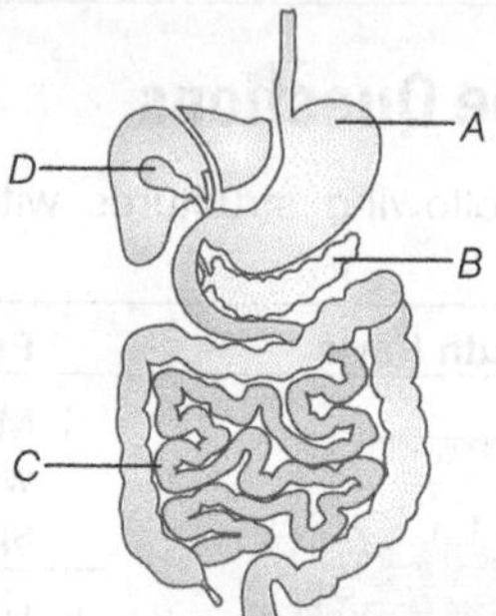

Where is the enzyme responsible for the first stage of protein digestion produced?

Ans. Enzyme pepsin responsible for the first stage of protein digestion is produced in stomach (A). Pepsin requires an optimum pH of 2 to digest protein. The dilute hydrochloric acid in the gastric juice of the stomach provides the acidic medium for pepsin to hydrolyse protein.

Q.13 Name the following. **(1 Mark each)**

(i) Phenomenon of wave-like contractions in the wall of alimentary canal.

(ii) The arrangement of teeth in the jaw.

(iii) Chemical substance that changes pepsinogen into pepsin.

(iv) The enzyme involved in the breakdown of nucleotide into nucleoside.

(v) The enzyme used for breakdown of fats.

Ans. (i) Peristalsis (ii) Dentition

(iii) HCl (iv) Nucleotidase

(v) Lipase

Q.14 Correct and rewrite the following statements by changing the underlined words. **(1 Mark each)**

(i) Saliva contain enzymes that digest <u>protein</u>.

(ii) Gastric glands of stomach mucosa have <u>chief cells</u> which secrete HCl.

(iii) Fats are broken down into simpler forms with the help of <u>amylase</u>.

(iv) Rennin converts casein into <u>peptidase</u>.

(v) <u>Amylase</u> activates trypsinogen.

Ans. (i) Saliva contain enzymes that digest starch.

(ii) Gastric glands of stomach mucosa have oxyntic cells which secrete HCl.

(iii) Fats are broken down into simpler forms with the help of lipases.

(iv) Rennin converts casein into paracasein.

(v) Enterokinase activates trypsinogen.

Q.15 Rearrange the following terms in a logical sequence, starting with the term that is underlined. **(1 Mark each)**

(i) Small intestine, <u>Buccal cavity</u>, Glottis, Stomach

(ii) <u>Food</u>, Chyme, Bolus, Faeces.

Ans. (i) Buccal cavity, Glottis, Stomach, Small intestine

(ii) Food, Bolus, Chyme, Faeces

Q.16 Choose the odd one out from the following terms given below and name the category to which other three belong. **(1 Mark each)**

(i) Teeth, Tongue, Sub-maxillary, Glottis.

(ii) Rectum, Ileum, Colon, Caecum

(iii) Dentine, Crown, Pulp cavity, Parotid gland

(iv) Buccal cavity, Oesophagus, Nerves, Anus

(v) Pepsin, HCl, Lipase, Mucus

Ans. (i) The odd term is glottis as it is part of the trachea. The other three teeth, tongue, sub-maxillary are parts of the buccal cavity.

(ii) The odd term is ileum as it is part of the small intestine. The other three rectum, colon, caecum are parts of the large intestine.

(iii) The odd term is parotid gland as it is a salivary gland. The other three dentine, crown, pulp cavity are parts of the tooth structure.

(iv) The odd term nerves as it is part of the nervous system. The other three buccal cavity, oesophagus, anus are parts of the digestive system.

(v) The odd term is mucus as it is involved in the protection of stomach lining while the rest three are involved in the chemical digestion of food.

Q.17 State the exact location of the following. **(1 Mark each)**

(i) Liver (ii) Stomach

(iii) Jejunum (iv) Caecum

(v) Anus

Ans. (i) Liver is found in the upper abdomen, under the diaphragm and mostly to the right side.

(ii) Stomach is located under the diaphragm on the left side of the abdominal cavity.

(iii) Jejunum is located in the abdominal cavity after the duodenum.

(iv) Caecum is located at the junction of the small intestine and large intestine.

(v) Anus is located in pelvic cavity connected to rectum.

Q.18 The digestion of food starts in the ......(i)....... . Enzymes present in saliva, such as amylase, breakdown carbohydrates, while the ......(ii)...... grind the food into smaller pieces, making it easier to digest. The food enter the stomach through oesophagus and is further broken down by ......(iii)......, which contain acids and enzymes, preparing it for absorption in the small intestine. Nutrients are ......(iv)...... in the small intestine and the remaining waste moves to the large intestine for ......(v)...... absorption before being excreted. **(1 Mark each)**

Ans. (i) buccal cavity (ii) teeth (iii) gastric juice

(iv) absorbed (v) water

Q.19 Mention one difference in each of the following pairs on the basis of what is given in the bracket. **(1 Mark each)**

(i) Milk teeth and Permanent teeth (number)

(ii) Homodont and Heterodont (definition)

(iii) Pepsin and Trypsin (mode of action)

Ans. (i)

Milk Teeth	Permanent Teeth
They are 20 in numbers.	They are 32 in numbers.

(ii)

Homodont	Heterodont
All the teeth are same, e.g. snake.	All the teeth vary in size, shape and function, e.g. human.

(iii)

Pepsin	Trypsin
It acts in acidic medium.	It acts in alkaline medium.

TYPE - 5 02 Marks

Short Answer Type Questions

Q.1 Which organ forms the boundaries of buccal cavity? State its functions.

Ans Lower and upper lip forms the boundaries of buccal cavity.

The functions of lips are as follows

(i) They help to close the mouth.

(ii) Lips help in sucking and sipping liquids.

Q.2 Name the different types of teeth present in humans, mention their functions also.

Ans. Four types of teeth present in humans are as follows

(i) **Incisors** are located at the front of the mouth, used for cutting or clipping food.

(ii) **Canines** are next to the incisors, used for puncturing, holding or tearing food.

(iii) **Premolars** are located behind the canines, used for crushing and grinding food.

(iv) **Molars** are found at the back of the mouth, also used for grinding food.

Q.3 **Which teeth is shown in the diagram below? Mention the dental formula of human.**

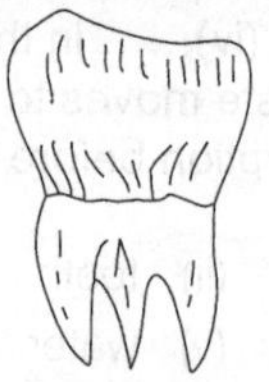

Ans. Molar is represented in the given diagram.

Dental formula of human is as follows

$$DF = \frac{\text{Incisors, Canines, Premolars, Molars}}{\text{Incisors, Canines, Premolars, Molars}}$$

$$= \frac{2.\,1.\,2.\,3}{2.\,1.\,2.\,3} \times 2$$

Q.4 **Observe the diagram below and answer the questions that follows.**

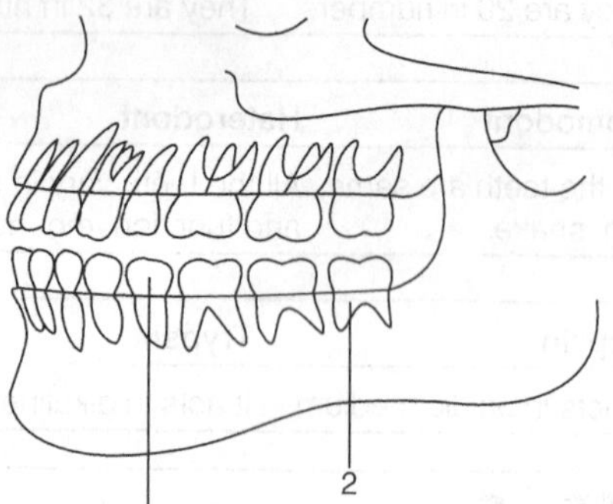

(i) Label the parts marked as 1 and 2.

(ii) For what purpose the parts 1 and 2 are used?

Ans. (i) Premolars and Molars

(ii) Both parts 1 and 2 are used for the chewing and grinding of food.

Q.5 **Which enzyme is present in saliva? Mention its function.**

Ans. Salivary amylase is present in saliva. It breaks down starch into simpler sugars and initiating the process of carbohydrate digestion in the mouth.

Q.6 **What will be the effect of lacking the enzyme salivary amylase in the saliva?**

Ans. Human saliva contains an enzyme called salivary amylase that helps to breakdown of the starch (carbohydrates) that present in the food into sugar. In case, saliva is lacking the enzyme salivary amylase, the breakdown of starch into sugar will be affected.

Q.7 **Which process is shown in the diagram? Name the organ in which this process occurs.**

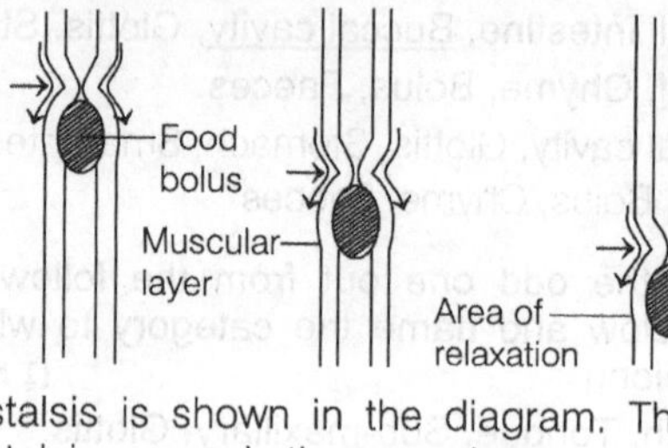

Ans. Peristalsis is shown in the diagram. The process of peristalsis occurs in the oesophagus.

Q.8 **The figure below shows some parts of the human alimentary canal.**

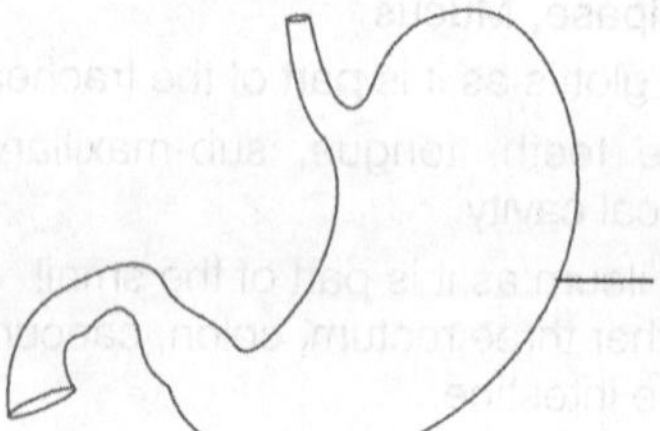

The pain from the stomach ulcer may be relieved by taking a drug that reduces the amount of acid produced by the cells in the stomach wall. Identify this acid and its function in the stomach.

Ans. Name of the acid that is produced in the stomach is hydrochloric acid.

This acid present in the stomach helps in providing acidic environment to the stomach enzymes.

Q.9 **Name the part of small intestine in which the pyloric part is open, also mention the longest part of small intestine.**

Ans. Pyloric part is open in the duodenum. Ileum is the largest part of small intestine.

Q.10 **How the liver helps in the process of digestion?**

Ans. The liver aids in digestion by producing bile, which is stored in the gall bladder and released into the small intestine. Bile helps to emulsify fats, breaking them down into smaller droplets, making it easier for digestive enzymes to further process and absorb them.

Q.11 **Why amylase is not able to function in the stomach?**

Ans. Amylase as an enzyme is not able to function in the stomach due to the pH of the stomach which is acidic in nature which denatures the structure of the amylase enzyme.

Q.12 Name the parts of large intestine and mention the function of large intestine.

Ans. The parts of the large intestine are the caecum, colon, and rectum. The function of the large intestine is to absorb water and salts from undigested food, form solid waste (faeces) and store it until it is excreted.

Q.13 How is food assimilated in the body for growth, energy and repair?

Ans. Food is assimilated in the body when the absorbed nutrients from digested food are transported to cells, where they are used for energy production, growth and repair of tissues. This process involves the cells utilising the nutrients like glucose, amino acids and fatty acids for various metabolic activities.

Q.14 Explain the process of egestion of food.

Ans. The process of the elimination of undigested food through the anus is known as egestion. Undigested food reached from the small intestine to the large intestine through peristalsis, where water and ions are reabsorbed. The remaining material is stored in the rectum and eventually expelled through the anus.

TYPE - 6

03 Marks

Short Answer Type Questions

Q.1 Explain the following terms.

(i) Ingestion
(ii) Enamel
(iii) Deciduous

Ans. (i) **Ingestion** The process of taking in food and liquids through the mouth.

(ii) **Enamel** It is the hard, outermost layer of a tooth, providing protection against decay.

(iii) **Deciduous** These are temporary teeth, also known as baby teeth, which are eventually replaced by permanent teeth as a child grows.

Q.2 Draw a labelled structure of teeth.

Ans.

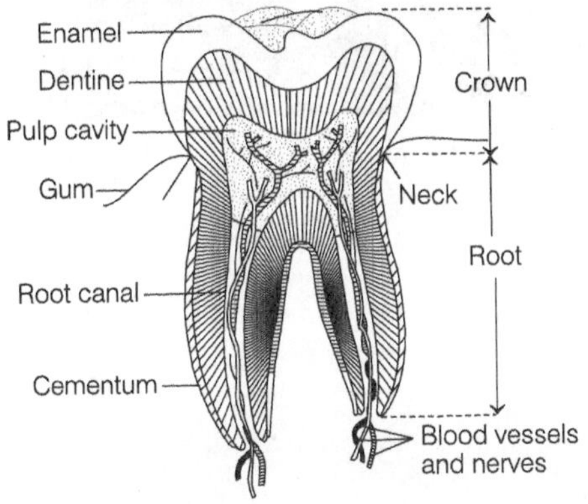

Q.3 Given below are the different types of teeth. Observe them carefully and accordingly answer the questions that follows.

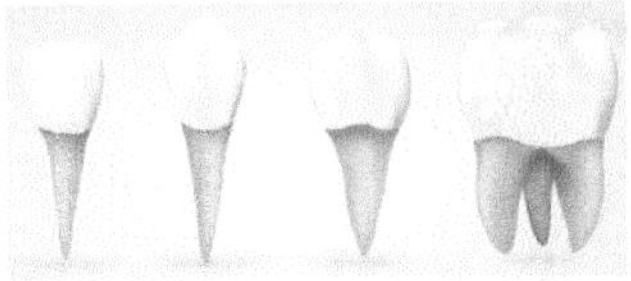

A *B* *C* *D*

(i) Identify the types of teeth labelled as *A-D*.
(ii) What are the different parts of teeth?
(iii) State the function of incisors and canines.

Ans. (i) *A*-Incisors
B-Canines
C-Premolars
D-Molars

(ii) A teeth has different parts as crown, neck and root

(iii) **Incisors** For cutting and biting of food.
Canines For tearing and piercing of food.

Q.4 What is epiglottis? Mention its main function.

Ans. The epiglottis is a flap of cartilage located at the opening of trachea. Its main function is to prevent food and liquids from entering the trachea (windpipe) during swallowing by covering the glottis, ensuring that food passes into the oesophagus instead.

Q.5 Explain the process of digestion of milk protein in infants, also mention the organ in which this process occurs.

Ans. In infants the process of digestion of milk protein occurs by the help of rennin enzyme. It helps to curdle the milk protein casein into paracasein. This process occurs in the stomach.

Q.6 State the name and function of enzymes found in pancreatic juice.

Ans. There are three types of enzymes found in pancreatic juice which are as follows

(i) **Amylopsin** Breaks down starch into maltose.
(ii) **Trypsin** Breaks down proteins into peptides.
(iii) **Steapsin** Breaks down fats into fatty acids and glycerol.

Q.7 Explain the function of following enzymes.

(i) Erepsin
(ii) Maltase
(iii) Lipase

Ans. (i) **Erepsin** breaks down peptides into amino acids.
(ii) **Maltase** converts maltose into glucose.
(iii) **Lipase** breaks down fats into fatty acids and glycerol.

Q.8 **The diagram shows the human alimentary canal with the labels *A*, *B* and *C*, mention the functions of each part.**

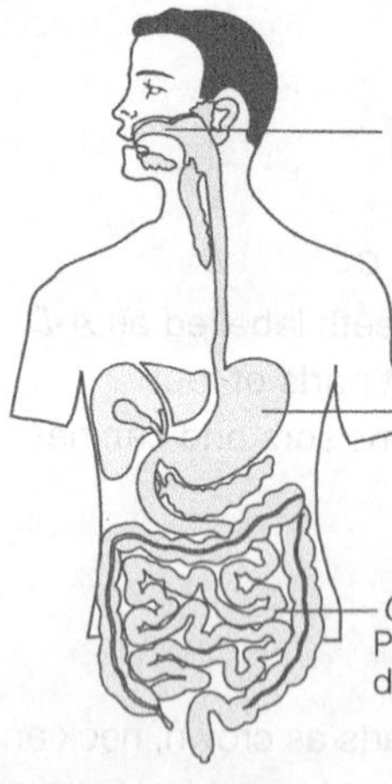

Ans. **Label *A*** Mouth

Ingestion and carbohydrate digestion.

Label *B* Stomach

Protein digestion only. The gastric juice in the stomach contains pepsin that digest protein and rennin that converts caseinogen into insoluble casein. Food normally remains in the stomach for about three to four hours before passing into the duodenum.

Label *C* Ileum

Protein, carbohydrates and fats digestion.

Q.9 **Discuss the main steps in the digestion of proteins as the food passes through different parts of the alimentary canal.**

Ans. The digestion of proteins involves these main steps

(i) **Stomach** Proteins are broken down into peptides by pepsin, which is activated in the acidic environment of the stomach.

(ii) **Small Intestine** Enzymes like trypsin and chymotrypsin from pancreatic juice further breakdown peptides into smaller peptides and amino acids.

(iii) **Intestinal Enzymes** Erepsin break peptides into individual amino acids, which are then absorbed into the blood stream.

Q.10 **A woman's digestive system is pictured below.**

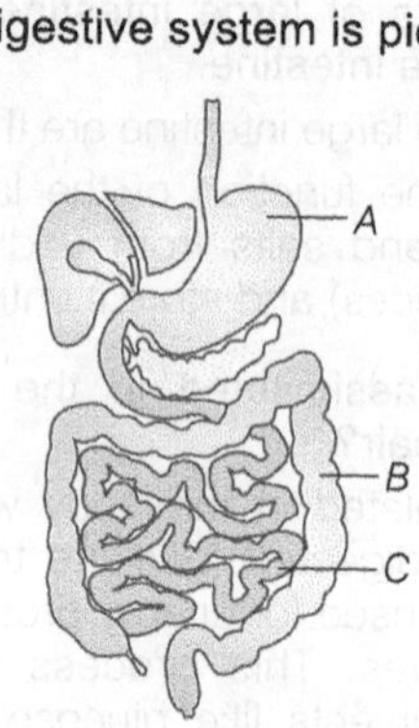

(i) **Name the organ marked as 'A'.**

(ii) **What enzyme is secreted by this organ that helps in digestion of protein in food?**

(iii) **Suggest what effect this would have on her digestion if this organ is removed from her body.**

Ans. (i) The stomach

(ii) Pepsin

(iii) If this organ will be removed from the body then, there will be no churning of food and also chemical digestion will be slower or less food will be digested chemically.

TYPE - 7 — 03 Marks

Structured Based Questions

Q.1 **A lion is a carnivorous animal that preys upon other animals to fulfil its food requirements. In the given diagram, a lion is eating meat. Observe the diagram carefully and answer the following questions.**

(i) Which type of teeth helps the lion to eat meat?

(ii) Are these teeth present in humans? If yes, mention the number of these teeth in humans.

(iii) Which type of teeth helps in churning the food?

Ans. (i) The canines help the lion to eat meat by tearing and holding it.

(ii) Yes, canines are present in humans. Humans have 4 canines (2 in the upper jaw and 2 in the lower jaw).

(iii) Molars and premolars help in churning the food.

Q.2 Raman suffered from stomach pain and vomited in the morning. He visited his doctor, who carefully examined his symptoms and diagnosed him with food poisoning, a condition caused by consuming contaminated food or water. Observe the diagram carefully and answer the following questions.

(i) Which sphincter opens when the given condition occurs?

(ii) Where is this sphincter located?

(iii) State the function of this sphincter.

Ans. (i) The gastro-oesophageal sphincter (cardiac sphincter) opens when vomiting occurs.

(ii) This sphincter is located between the oesophagus and the stomach.

(iii) The function of this sphincter is to regulate the passage of food from the oesophagus into the stomach and prevent the backflow of food from the stomach.

Q.3 Figure *A* shows the human alimentary canal.

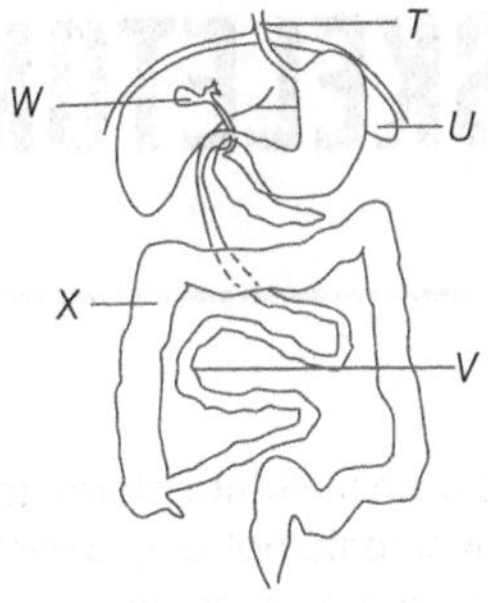

A

(i) In figure *A*, label structures *T*, *U* and *V*.

(ii) Name the secretion, which passes down from tube *W* and explain how it helps in fat digestion?

(iii) In case of diarrhoea, name the major process which is no longer occurring normally in region

Ans. (i) *T* – Oesophagus, *U* – Liver, *V* – Small intestine

(ii) The secretion which passes down from tube *W* is bile. Role of bile in fat digestion are as follows

(a) It makes the acidic food alkaline to facilitate the action of enzyme lipase on it.

(b) Bile salts breakdown fats present in food into small globules for enzymes to act.

(iii) In case of diarrhoea the process of absorption of water will not occur normally in region *X* (large intestine).

SKELETON : MOVEMENT AND LOCOMOTION

- Most animals are characterised by a definite shape and their ability to move different parts of their body. These movements not only assist in performing essential functions, but also enable locomotion, i.e. allowing movement from one place to another.
- The skeletal system, along with the muscular system, plays a crucial role in structural support and protecting vital organs.

Skeletal System

The hard structures in the body that provide a supportive framework are collectively known as the **skeletal system.** It is classified into two types

- **Endoskeleton** It is located inside the body. It consists of bones and cartilage which are **mesodermal** in origin. Humans, horses, dogs and sharks have endoskeleton.
- **Exoskeleton** It is situated on the outer surface of the bodies. It is always dead and **ectodermal** in origin. Insects, crabs, clams, spiders and shell fish have exoskeleton.

Functions of Skeletal System

- The skeleton provides a rigid framework that supports the body and determines its shape.
- It safeguards vital organs, such as the skull protecting the brain and the rib cage shielding the heart and lungs.
- Bones act as levers and form joints, allow muscles to create movement.
- Bones store essential minerals like calcium and phosphorus, maintaining mineral balance in the body.
- The production of blood corpuscles is known as **haemopoiesis**. Bone marrow present in long bones produces blood cells, including red blood cells, white blood cells and platelets.
- The skeleton works with muscles to generate force for precise and powerful movements.

The Human Skeletal System

- The human skeletal system is a vital structure that forms the supportive and protective framework of the body.
- In adults, it consists of 206 bones, while a newborn baby has 270 bones. This system composed of **bones, cartilage** and **ligaments**.
- In humans, endoskeleton system is divided into two main parts; the **axial skeleton** and the **appendicular skeleton**.

Axial Skeleton

This system forms the central framework of the body and includes **80 bones**. It consists of the **skull**, **vertebral column**, **rib cage** and **sternum**.

1. Skull

It is the bony framework of the head. It is composed of **29 bones** (22 skull bones and 7 associated skull bones).

Bones of skull are as follows

- **Cranium** (8) includes frontal (1), parietal (2), temporal (2), occipital (1), sphenoid (1) and ethmoid (1). They form the hard protective outer covering (cranium) for the brain, thus also called as **brain box**. These 8 flattened bones form immovable joints called **sutures**.

- **Facial bones** (14) include maxillae (2), palatine (2), mandible (1), vomer (1), nasal (2), zygomatic (2), lacrimal (2) and inferior turbinate (2). They form the front part of the skull.
- **Ear ossicles** (6) include 2 malleus, 2 incus and 2 stapes. These three tiny bones belong to the middle ear.
- **Hyoid** A U-shaped bone present at the base of buccal cavity. It is the only bone which is not in contact with any other bone. This is also called **tongue bone**.

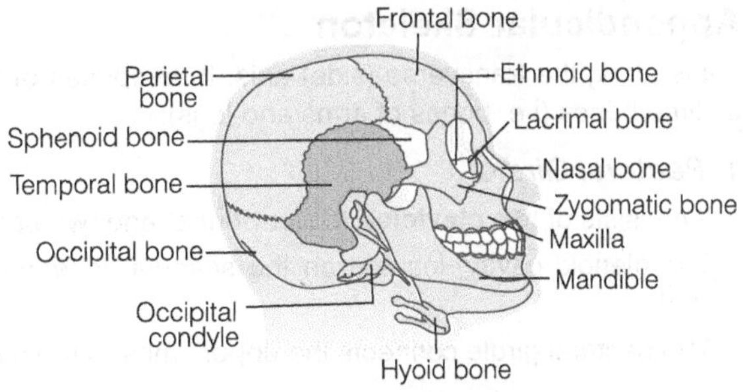

Diagrammatic view of human skull

2. Vertebral Column

- The vertebral or spinal column is popularly known as the **backbone**. It is made up of **33 ring-like bones** called **vertebrae**.
- The vertebral column is curved to maintain the balance in the body when is in an erect position. This curve also absorbs pressure and shock, while walking or running, protecting the column from breaking.
- The vertebral column is divided into five regions based on the areas they occupy. These regions are as follows
  - **Cervical Vertebrae** (7) They are found in the neck region and are 7 in number. The first cervical vertebra called the **atlas** and the second vertebra is the **axis**.
  - **Thoracic Vertebrae** (12) They are found in the chest region. These 12 vertebrae form the dorsal side of rib cage to protect the heart and lungs.
  - **Lumbar Vertebrae** (5) They are found in the waist region. These are the strongest vertebrae of human body.
  - **Sacral Vertebrae** (5) They are fused together to form the sacrum in the pelvis region. In humans, the female sacrum is wider than male sacrum.
  - **Coccygeal Vertebrae** (4) These are fused to form the **coccyx** in adults and found in the region of lower pelvis. In humans, it is considered as a vestigial tail.

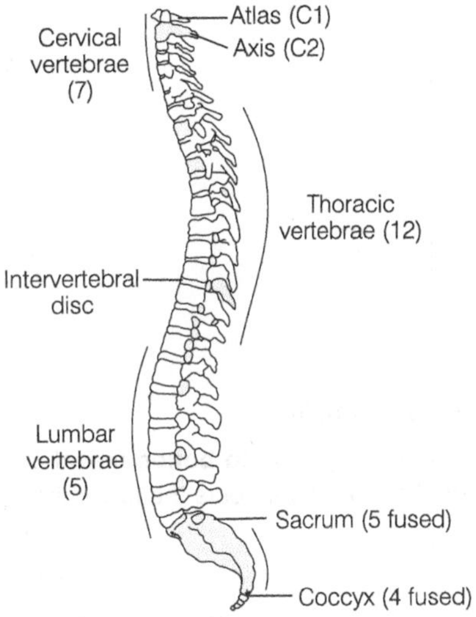

Vertebral column

Thus, vertebral formula for human is $C_{(7)}\ T_{(12)}\ L_{(5)}\ S_{(5)}\ C_{(4)} = 33$

3. The Sternum or Breast Bone

It is a flat, elongated bone located in the centre of the chest. It connects to the rib cage *via* cartilage. The sternum protects vital organs like the heart and lungs and provides point of attachment for ribs and chest muscles.

4. Ribs

- These are curved bones that forms the rib cage which protects the heart and lungs. There are **12 pairs** of ribs connected to the thoracic vertebrae.
- The first **7 pairs** are **true ribs**, which directly attached to the sternum *via* **hyaline cartilage**.
- The next 3 pairs are **false ribs**, indirectly attached to the sternum, while the last 2 pairs are **floating ribs**, not connected to the sternum at all.
- Hyaline cartilage provides **flexibility** and helps in **breathing movements**.

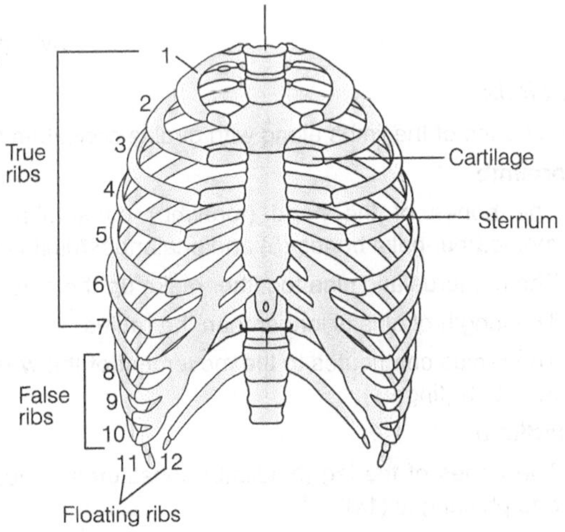

Sternum and ribs

REVISION NOTES

Appendicular Skeleton

It lies along the transverse (side) axis. It comprises of **126 bones,** which include pectoral and pelvic girdles as well as limb bones (i.e. bones of arms and legs).

1. Pectoral Girdle

- It consists of two **clavicles** (collar bones) and two **scapulae** (shoulder blades).
- The glenoid cavity, located on the scapula, is where the head of the humerus articulates, forming the shoulder joint.
- The pectoral girdle connects the upper limbs to the axial skeleton, allowing for a wide range of arm movement.

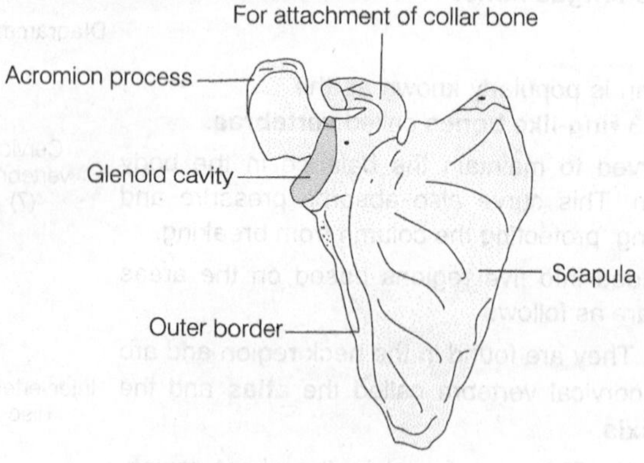

Pectoral (shoulder) girdle (left)

2. Pelvic Girdle

It is formed by two **hip bones** (coxal bones), each made up of the **ilium, ischium** and **pubis**. It supports the weight of the body and connects the lower limbs to the axial skeleton. It also protects the organs of the lower abdomen.

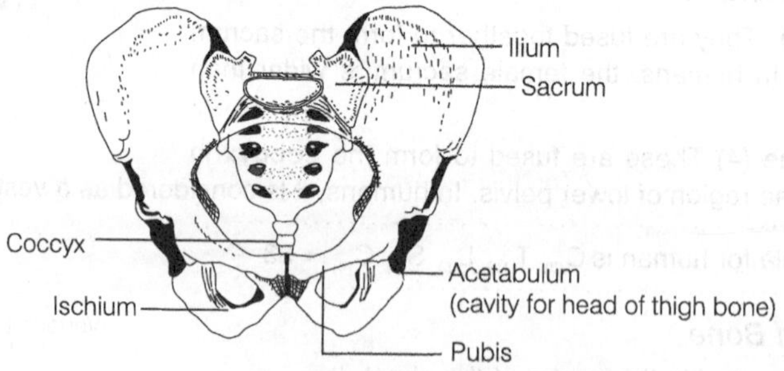

Pelvic girdle (seen from the front)

3. Limbs

The bones of the limbs along with girdles constitute the appendicular skeleton. Each limb is made up of **30 bones.**

Forelimb

- The bones of the hand (forelimb) constitutes humerus (1), radius (1), ulna (1), carpals/wrist bones (8), metacarpal-palm bones (5) and phalanges/digits (14).
- The humerus and ulna together make up the elbow.
- The length of ulna is longer than the radius.
- The radius contributes to the movement of the wrist. The phalangeal formula for human hand is 2 (thumb), 3, 3, 3, 3 (fingers).

Hindlimb

- The bones of the leg (hindlimb) constitutes femur (1), tibia (1), fibula (1), patella (1), tarsals (7), metatarsals (5) and phalanges (14).
- A cup-shaped bone called **patella** covers knee ventrally.

- Femur, tibia and fibula bones together support the **shank** of leg. Tarsals form the ankle, metatarsals form the sole and phalanges form the digits of the foot.
- The phalangeal formula for human foot is 2 (thumb), 3, 3, 3, 3 (fingers).

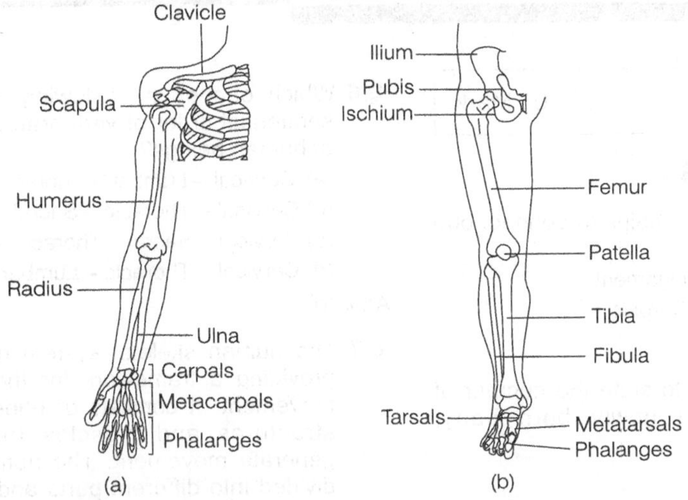

(a) Right pectoral girdle and forelimb (frontal view) and (b) Right pelvic girdle and lower limb (frontal view)

Joints

These are the points where two or more bones meet, allowing movement and flexibility in the body. They are classified into three types; **immovable, partially movable** and **freely movable.**

Joints

- **Immovable Joints**
  Joints are of fixed type, bones are joined by fibrous connective tissues very tightly, e.g. skull bone.
- **Slightly Movable Joints**
  Joints allow little movement, bones are joined with the help of cartilage, e.g. joint between sternum and ribs, joints between vertebrae.
- **Freely Movable Joints**
  There is synovial sac present between two ends of bone, filled with synovial fluid, joints are capable of free movement, e.g. elbow joint, hip joint.
  - **Gliding Joint**
    Bones glide over other to some extent, e.g. wrist bones, ankle bones.
  - **Pivot Joint**
    Joints allow rotation about an axis (the pivot), e.g. joint between atlas and axis vertebrae.
  - **Hinge Joint**
    Joint allows restricted movement in one plane only. They are capable of bearing heavy load, e.g. elbow, knee, finger.
  - **Ball and Socket Joint**
    Most movable joint, ball-like end of one bone, articulates into cup-shaped depression of another bone, so that structure could move in all planes, e.g. shoulder and hip joints.

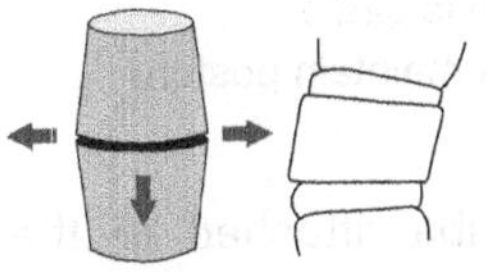

Gliding joint, e.g. in between tarsal bones.

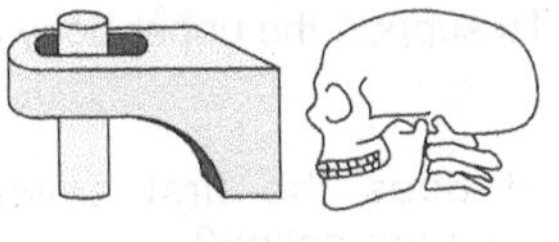

Pivot joint, e.g. atlas and axis of spine

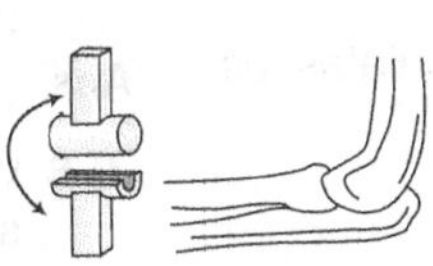

Hinge joint, e.g. elbow

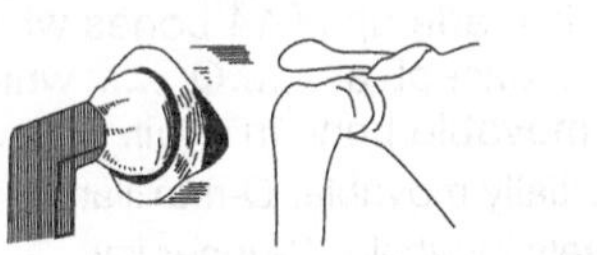

Ball and socket joint, e.g. hip joint

Muscles

- The movements in the body are facilitated by muscles only.
- The muscles provides shape to the body and help in maintaining the body posture during sitting, walking or standing.
- Muscles can contract and relax. On contraction the muscles shorten and they return to their normal on relaxation.
- Muscles which contract on folding the forelimb are **flexor muscles**, e.g. biceps
- Muscles which contract on extending the forelimbs are **extensor muscles**, e.g. triceps.
- Muscles which cause opposing movements are called **antagonistic muscles**, e.g. biceps and triceps.

EXAM ORIENTED QUESTIONS

TYPE - 1 01 Mark

Multiple Choice Questions

Q.1 Which of the following structure helps to connect one bone to another?

(a) Cartilage (b) Ligament
(c) Red bone marrow (d) Carpals

Ans. (b)

Q.2 Mrs. Riya asked her students to state the number of bones in adults and in a newly born baby, respectively.

Raj said: 206 and 217

Atul said: 208 and 218

Shikha said: 206 and 270

Anokhi said: 251 and 260

Who gave the right answer?

(a) Shikha (b) Atul (c) Raj (d) Anokhi

Ans. (a)

Q.3 Choose the incorrect pair from the following.

(a) Facial bones	Made up of 14 skeletal elements.
(b) Sacral vertebrae	2 fused
(c) Vertebrochondral ribs	False ribs (8th, 9th and 10th)
(d) Pivot joint	Between atlas and axis

Ans. (b) Sacral vertebrae (5 fused) are fused together to form the sacrum in the pelvis region.

Q.4 The face is made up of 14 bones which are ....*P*...... except a ....*Q*....... which articulates as the only movable bone in skull.

(a) *P* - partially movable, *Q*-maxillary
(b) *P* - freely movable, *Q*-upper jaw
(c) *P* - immovable, *Q*- mandible
(d) *P* - immovable, *Q*-hyoid

Ans. (c)

Q.5 Our vertebral column is formed by the

(a) 26 serially arranged units called vertebrae
(b) 27 serially arranged units called vertebrae
(c) 33 serially arranged units called vertebrae
(d) 35 serially arranged units called vertebrae

Ans. (c)

Q.6 Which one of the following is showing the correct sequential order of vertebrae in the vertebral column of human beings?

(a) Cervical – Lumbar – Thoracic – Sacral – Coccygeal
(b) Cervical – Thoracic – Sacral – Lumbar – Coccygeal
(c) Cervical – Sacral – Thoracic – Lumbar – Coccygeal
(d) Cervical – Thoracic – Lumbar – Sacral – Coccygeal

Ans. (d)

Q.7 The human skeletal system helps in locomotion by providing a framework for the body and facilitating movement. It consists of bones that act as support structures and muscles that work together to generate movement. The human skeletal system is divided into different parts and each part performs a specific function.

Observe the diagram and answer the following question.

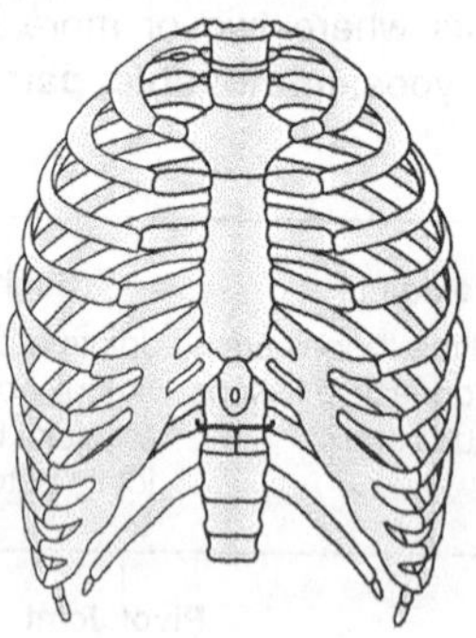

What is the incorrect function of the given structure?

(a) To provide attachment points for chest muscles
(b) To protect vital organs and assist in breathing
(c) To connect the spine to the pelvic girdle
(d) To support the upper body and maintain posture

Ans. (c)

Q.8 What does the first seven ribs attached to the sternum are called?

(a) False ribs (b) True ribs
(c) Incomplete ribs (d) Floating ribs

Ans. (b)

Q.9 Which pairs of ribs are known as false ribs?

(a) 1st and 2nd
(b) 11th and 12th
(c) 8th, 9th and 10th
(d) 6th and 7th

Ans. (c)

Q.10 Which of the following is a part of pectoral girdle?
(a) Ilium (b) Ischium
(c) Acetabulum (d) Glenoid cavity

Ans. (d)

Q.11 Number of tarsals, metatarsals and phalanges in human skeleton is
(a) 7, 5, 14 (b) 8, 5, 14
(c) 9, 5, 14 (d) 5, 6, 7

Ans. (a)

Q.12 Anshika tried to match the following structures with their functions. She tabulated a pair as follows.

Structures	Functions
P	Formation of white blood cells.
Q	Formation of red blood cells.

Choose the correct pair.
(a) *P* - Villi, *Q*- Meninges
(b) *P* - Yellow bone marrow, *Q*- Red bone marrow
(c) *P* -Yellow fibre, *Q*- Red bone marrow
(d) *P* - White fibres, *Q*- Collagen fibres

Ans. (b)

Q.13 Synovial joints in humans are characterised by
(a) joining of two bones
(b) presence of fluid-filled synovial cavity
(c) rare movement
(d) no movement at all

Ans. (b)

Q.14 Knee joint and elbow joint are examples of
(a) saddle joint (b) ball and socket joint
(c) pivot joint (d) hinge joint

Ans. (d)

Q.15 Identify the type of joint that is similar to the joint found at shoulder.
(a) Knee (b) Hip
(c) Elbow (d) Ankle

Ans. (b)The shoulder joint is a type of a ball and a socket joint. This type of joint is also present in the hip region.

Q.16 The diagram shows three bones from the forelimb of a mammal.

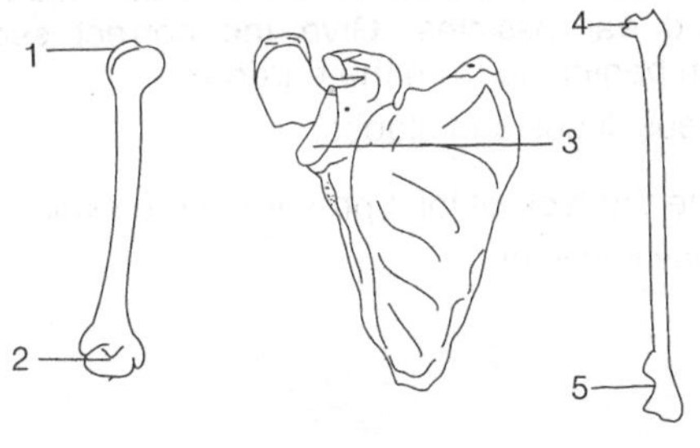

Between which parts is a ball and socket joint formed?
(a) 1 and 3 (b) 1 and 5
(c) 2 and 5 (d) 2 and 4

Ans. (a)

TYPE - 2

01 Mark

Matching Type Questions

Q.1 Match the structures *A* to *E* with their respective functions.

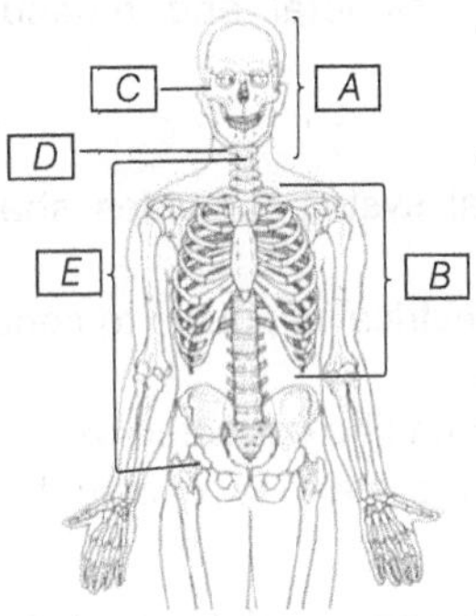

Structures	Functions
	I. Only movable point of skull.
	II. Forms pivot joint with axis vertebrae
	III. It protects vital organs like the heart and lungs, while allowing for breathing movements.
	IV. Supports the body, protects the spinal cord and enables flexibility and movement.
	V. It protects the brain and houses sensory organs like the eyes, ears and nose.

Ans. A- V, B-III, C-I, D-II, E-IV

Q.2 Match the following columns.

Column I	Column II
A. Cranium	I. 22
B. Skull (facial and cranial)	II. 8
C. Face	III. 14
D. Hindlimb	IV. 12
E. Ribs	V. 30

Ans. A-II, B-I, C-III, D-V, E-IV

Q.3 Match the following columns.

Column I	Column II
A. Ball and socket joint	I. Between humerus and pectoral girdle
B. Hinge joint	II. Knee joint
C. Pivot joint	III. Between atlas and axis
D. Gliding joint	IV. Between the carpals

Ans. A-I, B-II, C-III, D-IV

TYPE - 3 01 Mark

Assertion-Reason Type Questions

Direction (Q. Nos. 1-6) In the following questions, statements are given as Assertion (A) and Reason (R).

(a) A is true, but R is false.
(b) A is false, but R is true.
(c) Both A and R are true.
(d) Both A and R are false.

Q.1 Assertion (A) Most animals have a definite shape and can move different parts of their body to perform various functions, including locomotion.

Reason (R) This ability is made possible by the coordination between the skeletal and muscular systems.

Ans. (c)

Q.2 Assertion (A) The skeletal system provides shape and support to the body.

Reason (R) It generates electrical impulses to control body movements.

Ans. (a) A is true, but R is false. R can be corrected as It works with the muscular system to enable body movements.

Q.3 Assertion (A) The adult human skeletal system is made up of 206 bones.

Reason (R) During infancy, the human body has many bones that later fuse together to form 206 bones in adulthood.

Ans. (c)

Q.4 Assertion (A) The sternum is a flat, elongated bone located at the centre of the chest.

Reason (R) It connects to the rib cage and protects vital organs like the heart and lungs.

Ans. (c)

Q.5 Assertion (A) The pectoral girdle does not allow arm movement.

Reason (R) It connects the upper limbs to the axial skeleton.

Ans. (b) A is false, but R is true. A can be corrected as Pectoral girdle connects the upper limbs to the axial skeleton and allows for a wide range of arm movement.

Q.6 Assertion (A) Muscles have the ability to contract and relax.

Reason (R) Biceps and triceps are the antagonistic muscles.

Ans. (c)

TYPE - 4 01 Mark

Very Short Answer Type Questions

Q.1 Name the type of skeletal system found inside the human body.

Ans. Endoskeleton

Q.2 Which type of bone marrow contributes to the production of red blood cells?

Ans. Red bone marrow

Q.3 Name the three main components, which together formed the skull.

Ans. The three main components of the skull are the cranium, facial bones and mandible.

Q.4 The axial skeleton comprises of ...*A*.... It includes ...*B*..., ...*C*... ribs and ...*D*... .

Ans. *A*- 80 bones, *B*- skull, *C*- vertebral column, *D*- sternum.

Q.5 *X* is the structure which is found at the base of buccal cavity. Identify the *X*.

Ans. Hyoid bone

Q.6 Name the region of vertebrae found in the pelvic region that connects to the hip bones.

Ans. The sacral vertebrae are found in the pelvic region and connect to the hip bones.

Q.7 State the function of the sternum.

Ans. It provides attachment points for the ribs and chest muscles, which are involved in breathing and upper body movements.

Q.8 *X* are the pairs of ribs which are not attached to the sternum. Identify the *X*.

Ans. Floating ribs

Q.9 Name the skeleton that includes the bones of the limbs and the girdles attaching them to the axial skeleton.

Ans. Appendicular skeleton

Q.10 *B* is the longest bone found in the thigh region. Identify the *B*.

Ans. Femur.

Q.11 The three tiny bones present in the middle ear are called ear ossicles. Give the correct sequence of them beginning from the eardrum.

Ans. Malleus, incus and stapes.

Q.12 Name the type of joint present in the skull.

Ans. Immovable joint

Q.13 Name the muscles which are opposite in their action during the movements.

Ans. Antagonistic muscles.

Q.14 Name the following. **(1 Mark each)**

(i) The smallest bone of the body.

(ii) Large hollow box-like part of the skull that houses brain.

(iii) The only bone in our body which does not form any joint.

(iv) The first vertebra of the vertebral column.

(v) The bone of the pelvic girdle.

Ans. (i) Stapes (ii) Cranium

(iii) Hyoid (iv) Atlas

(v) Ilium/Ischium/Pubis

Q.15 Observe the diagram carefully and fill the blank spaces with correct words.

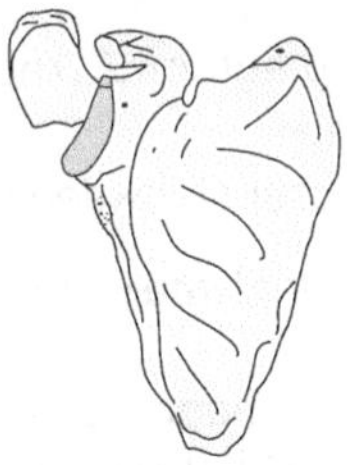

The appendicular skeleton includes the bones of the limbs and the girdles that attach them to the axial skeleton. Bones of the forelimbs and the hindlimbs largely correspond to each other. **(1 Mark each)**

Pectoral girdle consists of two ......(i)...... and two ......(ii)...... The glenoid cavity, located on the scapula, is where the head of the ......(iii)...... articulates, forming the ......(iv)....... The pectoral girdle connects the upper limbs to the axial skeleton, allowing for a wide range of ......(v)...... movement.

Ans. (i) clavicle, (ii) scapula, (iii) humerus, (iv) shoulder joint, (v) arm

Q.16 Correct and rewrite the following statements by changing the underlined words. **(1 Mark each)**

(i) The first seven ribs are called floating ribs.

(ii) The axial skeleton comprises of 126 bones.

(iii) Pectoral girdle consists of two bones, i.e. scapula and ilium.

(iv) The place of articulation between two or more bones is called muscle.

(v) The joint present between atlas and axis is hinge joint.

Ans. (i) The first seven ribs are called true ribs.

(ii) The appendicular skeleton comprises of 126 bones.

(iii) Pectoral girdle consists of two bones, i.e. scapula and clavicle.

(iv) The place of articulation between two or more bones is called joint.

(v) The joint present between atlas and axis is pivot joint.

Q.17 Rearrange the following terms in a logical sequence, starting with the term that is underlined. **(1 Mark each)**

(i) Hip, Thigh, Knee, Ankle, Leg, Foot.

(ii) Pelvis, Patella, Femur, Tarsals, Tibia.

Ans. (i) Hip, Thigh, Knee, Leg, Ankle, Foot.

(ii) Pelvis, Femur, Patella, Tibia, Tarsals.

Q.18 Choose the odd one out from the following terms given below and name the category to which the other three belong. **(1 Mark each)**

(i) Cranium, Facial bones, Backbone, Ear ossicles

(ii) Clavicle, Ilium, Scapula, Sternum

(iii) Humerus, Radius, Patella, Ulna

(iv) Cervical, Sacrum, Lumbar, Hyaline

(v) Femur, Tibia, Fibula, Carpals

Ans. (i) The odd term is backbone because it is related to vertebral column, while rest three belong to the bones of skull.

(ii) The odd term is sternum because it is a part of axial skeleton, while rest three are belong to the bones of the appendicular skeleton.

(iii) The odd term is patella because it is a part of hindlimb, while rest three are belong to the bones of forelimbs.

(iv) The odd term is hyaline because it is cartilage, while rest three are bones.

(v) The odd term is carpals because they are the part of forelimb, while rest three belong to the lower limbs.

TYPE - 5 02 Marks

Short Answer Type Questions

Q.1 State any two functions of skeletal system.

Ans. Functions of skeletal system are as follows

(i) **Support and Shape** The skeleton provides a rigid framework that supports the body and determines its shape.

(ii) **Protection** It safeguards vital organs, such as the skull protecting the brain and the rib cage shielding the heart and lungs.

Q.2 State the differences between cartilage and ligament.

Ans. Differences between cartilage and ligament are as follows

Cartilage	Ligament
Provides support, flexibility and cushioning.	Connects bones to other bones, stabilising joints.
Found in joints, ears, nose and respiratory tract.	Found connecting bones at joints.

Q.3 Write the name of the bones present in ear ossicle also state the main function of ear ossicle.

Ans. The bones present in the ear ossicles are as follows

(i) Malleus (ii) Incus (iii) Stapes

The primary function of the ear ossicles is to transmit sound vibrations from the ear drum to the inner ear, amplifying the sound in the process.

Q.4 Explain the following structures.

(i) Coccyx

(ii) Hyaline cartilage

Ans. (i) **Coccyx** The coccyx or tail bone, is a small bone at the bottom of the spine, made up of four fused bones. It provides support when sitting and is a remnant of a tail in humans.

(ii) **Hyaline Cartilage** It is a smooth cartilage found in joints, ribs, nose and the respiratory tract. It provides cushioning, reduces friction and supports structural integrity.

Q.5 The diagram of a pectoral girdle human is shown below. Observe the diagram and fill in the blanks in the description of the structure of a pectoral girdle of humans.

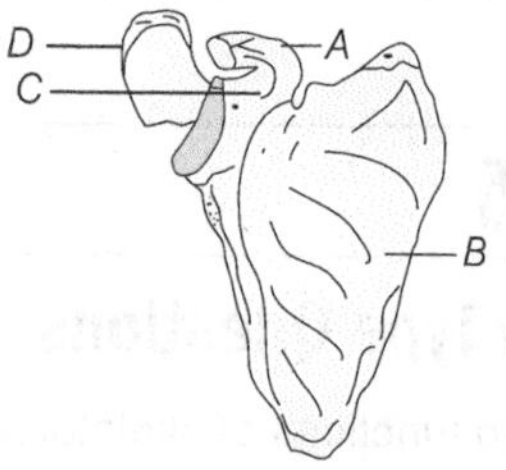

Each pectoral girdle is formed of two bones ...*A*... and ...*B*... shown in the diagram. The bone *B* has an elevated ridge, called ...*C*... which projects as a flat expanded process, called ...*D*..., where the *A* articulated.

Ans. *A*- Clavicle

B- Scapula

C- Spine

D- Acromion

Q.6 The diagram below shows the part of the skeletal system. Please observe it carefully and answer the following questions.

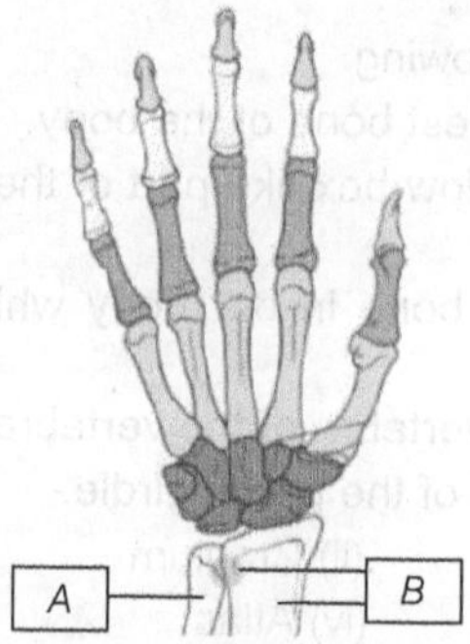

(i) Based on the diagram, name the structures represented by *A* and *B*.

(ii) Which type of joint is present between these two structures?

Ans. (i) In the given diagram *A* represents ulna and *B* represents radius.

(ii) Pivot joint is present between radius and ulna.

Q.7 Name the bones that make up the pelvic girdle and state its function.

Ans. The pelvic girdle is made up of two hip bones (coxal bones). Its main function is to support the weight of the body, connect the lower limbs to the axial skeleton, and protect the organs of the lower abdomen.

TYPE - 6

03 Marks

Short Answer Type Questions

Q.1 Explain the structure of the vertebral column and describe any three regions of it.

Ans. The vertebral column, also known as the back bone, consists of 33 ring-like bones called vertebrae. It is curved to maintain balance and absorb shock, protecting the spine from injury during activities like walking or running.

Three regions of the vertebral column are as follows

(i) **Cervical Vertebrae** (Neck Region) The first cervical vertebra is called the atlas and the second is the axis. The remaining cervical vertebrae are numbered sequentially.

(ii) **Thoracic Vertebrae** (Upper Back Region) These vertebrae have long neural spines and facets on their transverse processes for rib attachment.

(iii) **Lumbar Vertebrae** (Lower Back Region) These vertebrae have well-developed neural spines and transverse processes that serve as attachment point for strong back muscles.

Q.2 Appendicular skeleton comprises 126 bones, including the pectoral and pelvic girdles, along with the limb bones.

(i) What is the glenoid cavity?

(ii) Name three bones that make up the hip bone.

(iii) How many bones are present in each limb?

Ans. (i) The glenoid cavity is a small socket located below the acromion, where the head of the humerus fits to form the shoulder joint.

(ii) The ischium, ilium and pubis make up the hip bone.

(iii) Each limb consists of 30 bones.

Q.3 Given below are the structures of skeletal system of living being. Observe them carefully and answer the questions that follows.

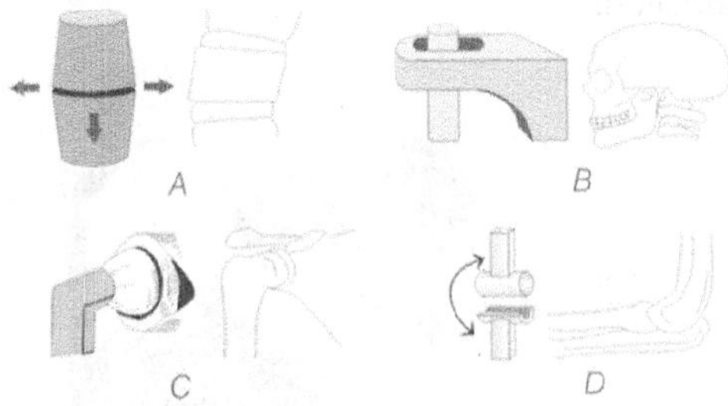

(i) Name the structure labelled as *A-D*.

(ii) In which organ does the structure *B* is found?

(iii) Which fluid acts as a lubricant and is responsible for reducing the friction?

Ans. (i) *A*–Gliding joint *B*–Pivot joint

C–Ball and socket joint *D*–Hinge joint

(ii) Joint between radius and ulna.

(iii) Synovial joint

Q.4 A diagram of the pelvic girdle is shown below. Observe the diagram and answer the questions that follows.

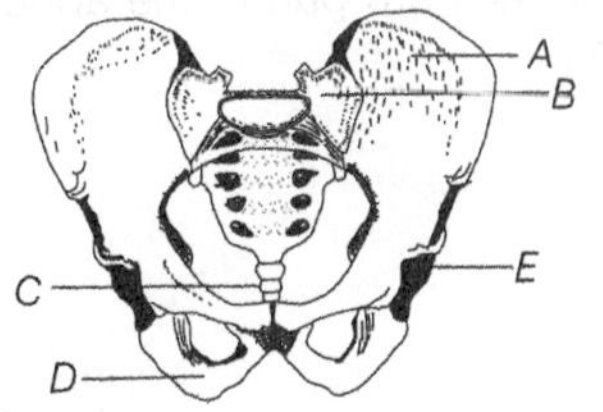

(i) Label the components marked as *A-E*.

(ii) Name the joint that is found by the two halves of pelvic girdle.

(iii) To which skeleton does the above given part of the skeleton belong?

Ans. (i) *A*- Ilium *B*- Sacrum

C- Coccyx *D*- Ischium

E- Acetabulum

(ii) Pubic symphysis

(iii) Appendicular skeleton

Q.5 Draw a well labelled diagram of a pectoral girdle with arm.

Ans.

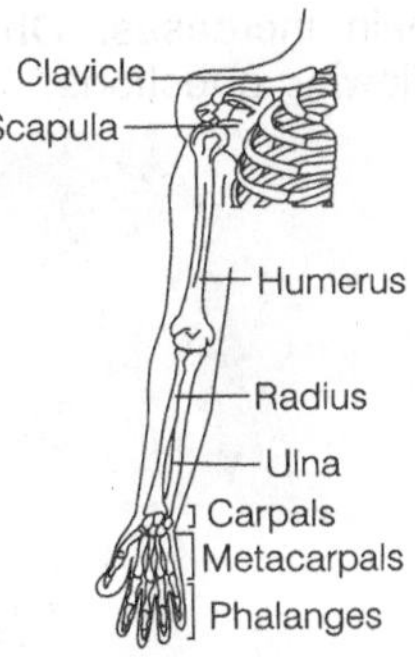

Pectoral girdle and forelimb (frontal view)

Q.6 State the difference between immovable and freely movable joint. Give the examples of synovial joint.

Ans. Difference between immovable and freely movable joints is as follows

Immovable Joints	Freely Movable Joints
These joints do not allow any movement.	These joints allow a wide range of movements.

Synovial joint is a type of freely movable joint, e.g. knee joint, shoulder joint.

TYPE - 7 03 Marks

Structured Based Questions

Q.1 Observe the diagram and answer the questions that follows.

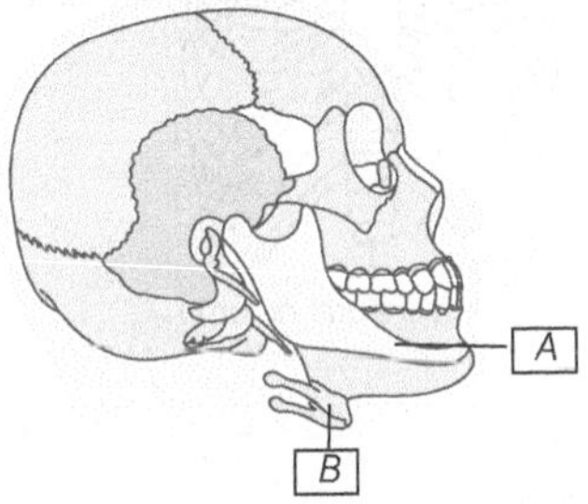

(i) Identify *A* and *B* in the given diagram of human skull.

(ii) Name the opening of skull through which spinal cord passes.

(iii) What is the name given to the hard covering of brain?

Ans. (i) The parts *A* and *B* in given diagram of human skull are

A– Mandible, *B*– Hyoid bone.

(ii) Foramen magnum is the large opening in the posterior portion of skull through which spinal cord passes.

(iii) The brain box or cranium.

Q.2 Vikram feels severe neck pain after working on his laptop for an extended period. After sometime, he notices the pain increases. Observe the figure and answer the following questions.

(i) Does this condition relate to the back bone?
(ii) Which region of the vertebral column is affected?
(iii) Name the first and last bones of the vertebral column.

Ans. (i) Yes, this condition is related to the back bone.
(ii) The cervical region of the vertebral column is affected, as this is where the neck is located.
(iii) The first bone is the atlas (C1) and the last bone is the coccyx (tail bone) present at the bottom of the vertebral column.

Q.3 Below given is the diagram of the rib cage. Observe the diagram carefully and answer the following questions.

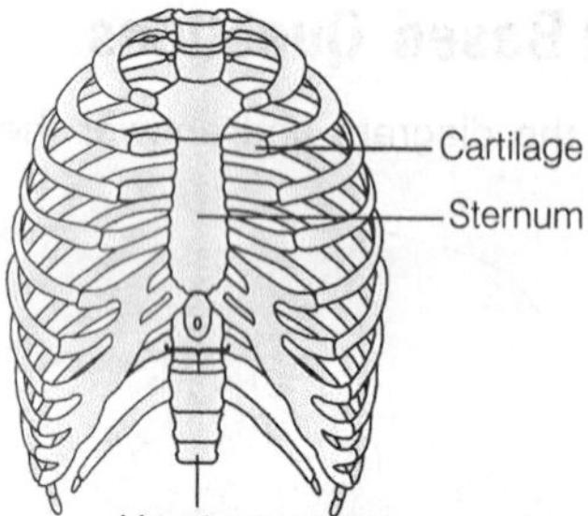

(i) What are true ribs?
(ii) How many true ribs are there?
(iii) What are vertebrochondral ribs?

Ans. (i) The ribs that are attached dorsally to the thoracic vertebrae and ventrally connected to the sternum are called true ribs.
(ii) The first seven pairs of ribs are true ribs.
(iii) Vertebrochondral ribs are the 8th, 9th, 10th pair of ribs, which are attached dorsally to the thoracic vertebrae and ventrally to the 7th rib by hyaline cartilage.

Q.4 Anisha had a crack in her leg. Her doctor told her that the joint between the bones had broken. Observe the figure and answer the following questions.

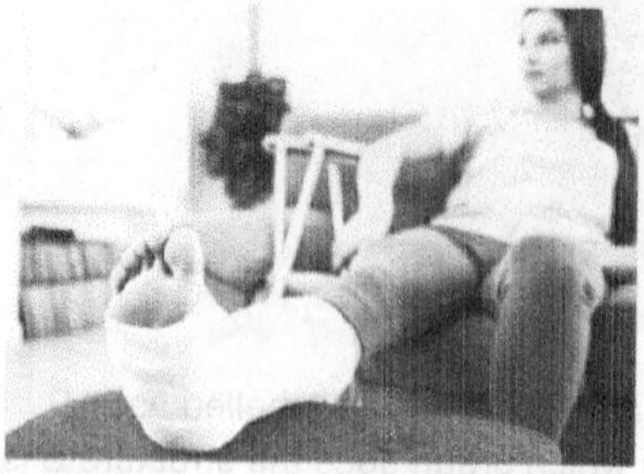

(i) Which bones are present in this region (ankle)?
(ii) What type of joint has broken?
(iii) Write the name of the skeletal system in which these bones are present.

Ans. (i) The bones present in the ankle region are the tibia, fibula and tarsals.
(ii) The synovial joint (specifically the hinge joint) between the bones has broken.
(iii) These bones are part of the appendicular skeletal system.

12

THE SKIN

Skin

- It is the outermost protective layer which covers the whole body and plays a key role in protection. This layer makes up about 15% of an adult's total body weight and is the **largest organ** by surface area.
- Although it is thin and delicate, it acts as the first line of defence against external threats.
- The skin, along with its structures like hair, nails and glands, forms the **integumentary system**, which helps to protect and maintain the body's overall health.
- Various parts of integumentary system in mammals are shown in the flowchart below

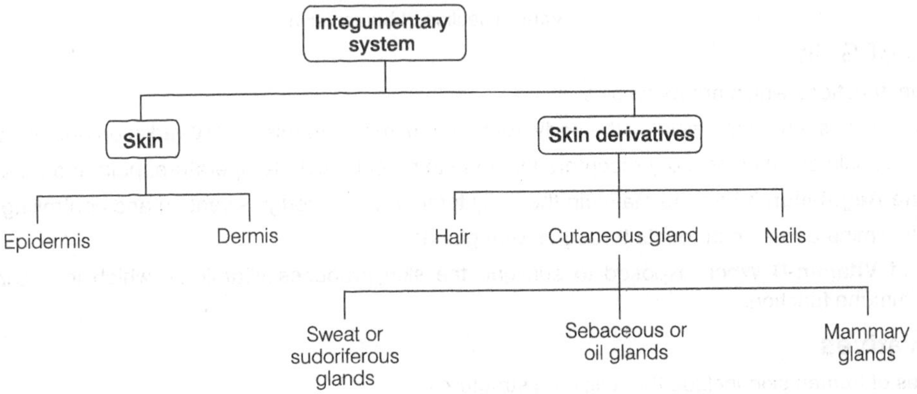

Structure of Skin

It is composed of two types of layers which are as follows

Layers	Description
1. Epidermis	The outermost layer of skin made up of stratified epithelium. It has three main sub-layers.
• **Stratum corneum** (Cornified layer)	Contains dead skin cells made up of keratin, providing a tough outer barrier that protect against pathogens, mechanical damage and water loss. Cells are continuously replaced by new cells from deeper layers.
• **Stratum granulosum** (Granular layer)	Made up of two to three layers of flattened cells.
• **Stratum Malpighi** (Malpighian or Germinative layer)	The innermost layer composed of column-shaped living cells that divide constantly to form new cells. Contains melanin, which gives skin colour and protects from UV light.

Layers	Description
2. Dermis	The layer beneath the epidermis, made up of connective tissue. It is thicker and contains blood vessels, nerves, hair follicles and glands.The outer region of the dermis which lies next to the epidermis is raised into numerous small processes called **papillae**, which contain blood and nerve endings and sense organs here concerned with sensations of touch and pain.

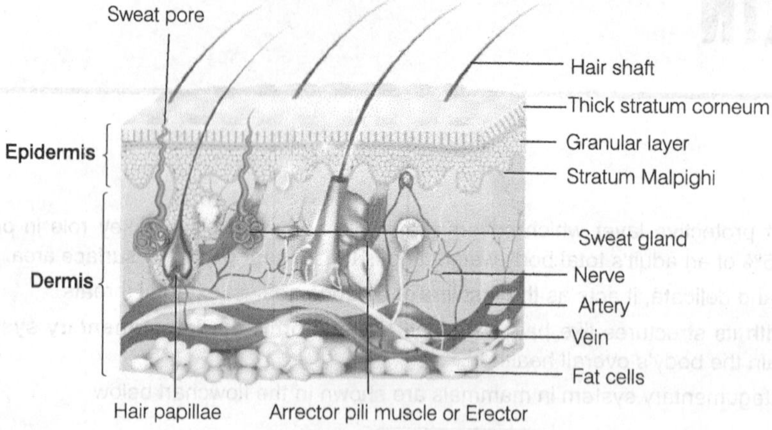

Vertical section of human skin

Functions of Skin

It performs vital functions which are as follows

- **Protection** It acts as a barrier, shielding the body from harmful microorganisms, UV radiation and physical injuries.
- **Sensation** The skin contains sensory receptors that help to detect touch, temperature, pain and pressure.
- **Temperature Regulation** It helps to maintain the body temperature through sweating and controlling blood flow.
- **Excretion** It eliminates waste products through sweat glands.
- **Synthesis of Vitamin-D** When exposed to sunlight, the skin produces vitamin-D, which is essential for bone health and immune function.

Skin Derivatives

The derivatives of human skin include the following structures

1. Hair

These are slender, thread-like outgrowth that originates from follicles in the skin. Each hair consists of three parts; the hair shaft, hair root and hair bulb.

- The **hair shaft** is the visible part of the hair that extends above the skin, usually lying obliquely. The **hair root** is embedded within the dermis, with its lowest part expanding into the **hair bulb**, which contains the **hair papilla**, a projection from the dermis with a blood supply.
- The **hair follicle**, composed of epithelial and connective tissue sheaths. It encloses the hair root. Together, the hair follicle and bulb are responsible for hair growth.
- Hair provides insulation to the body against external temperature of the environment in which the organisms live. During extreme cold or fright condition, the **arrector muscle** present in the dermis pull the hair into a verticle position. It is called **'goose flesh'**.
- Eyelashes protect the eyes by preventing debris and raindrops from entering, while nasal hairs filtre dust particles from the air.

2. Nails

- These are formed by the epidermal layer present at the tips of fingers and toes.
- Nails are very hard, slightly arched plates formed of **keratin** protein.
- Nails protect the fingertip and the surrounding soft tissues from injuries.
- A nail has three parts

- **Plate** The hard outer part of the nail, made up of dead, keratinised cells.
- **Bed** The tissue beneath the nail plate.
- **Matrix** Located just beneath the skin at the base of the nail. It produces new cells that push older cells toward the tip, causing nail growth. The matrix is visible as the whitish half-moon at the nail base.

3. Sebaceous Glands

- These branched glands typically opens into hair follicles, but can also open directly to the skin's surface.
- They secrete **sebum**, an oily substance that keeps hair and skin supple, waterproof and prevents water loss.
- They reduces the sebum secretion in cold and dry weather, making the skin rough and powdery, while their secretion is increased in hot, humid weather leading to oilier skin.
- Three common sebaceous gland problems are **pimples** (bacterial infection due to sebum buildup), **acne** (inflammation caused by hormonal changes) and **blackheads** (oxidised sebum accumulation in open pores).

4. Sweat Glands

- These are highly coiled glands present in dermis. These open on the skin through ducts as small sweat pores which in turn are surrounded by network of small capillaries.
- Sweat glands absorb fluid from surrounding cells and blood capillaries, which is then excreted through the sweat duct.
- **Sweating**, which occurs continuously in small amounts (incipient perspiration), can increase during exercise or hot weather. Sweating helps regulate body temperature through evaporation.
- Sweat is 99% water, 0.2-0.5% salts (mainly sodium chloride) and traces of urea (0.08%). The loss of urea *via* sweat is about 1% of the body's total excretion.

5. Mammary Glands

- These are modified sweat glands present in both males and females.
- In males, they remain rudimentary, while in females, they enlarge at puberty to form breasts.
- Each breast has a nipple with 15-20 milk ducts that branch into lobes of the mammary glands.
- Their activity is influenced by reproductive hormones (like prolactin) and pregnancy, producing milk that nourishes newborns.

Heat Regulation

- It is the process of maintaining body temperature, primarily performed by the skin through two mechanisms; **vasodilation** and **vasoconstriction** of blood vessels.
  - **In Hot Weather** (Vasodilation) When the external temperature increases, the hypothalamus signals blood vessels to dilate, allowing more blood to flow through them. This results in greater loss of heat by radiations.
  - Sweat glands also produce more sweat and its evaporation helps cool the body, restoring the normal temperature.
  - **In Cold Weather** (Vasoconstriction) When the external temperature decreases, blood vessels constrict, reducing blood flow to the skin. This minimises heat loss, helping the body retain warmth.

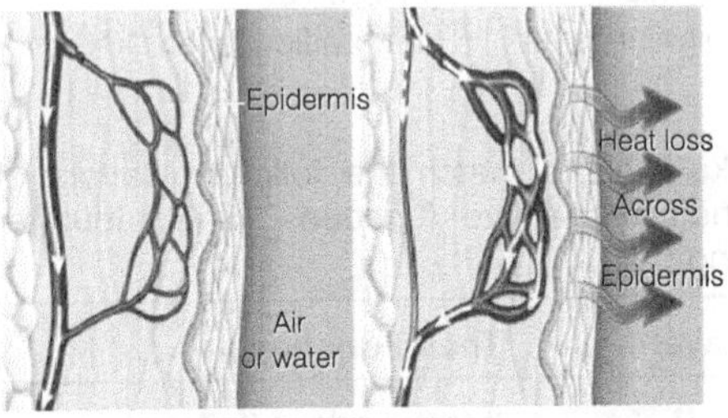

Vasoconstriction Vasodilation

- Classification of organisms based on thermoregulation are
  - **Cold-blooded Animals** (Ectotherms) These animals cannot maintain a constant body temperature and rely on external heat sources, e.g. reptiles.
  - **Warm-blooded Animals** (Endotherms) These animals maintain a constant body temperature regardless of external conditions, e.g. humans (37°C).

Heat Stroke

- A condition that occurs when sweat production cannot keep up with evaporation in extremely hot conditions, causing a dangerous rise in body temperature. This condition can be fatal.
- To prevent heat stroke, it is important to stay hydrated and consume extra salt during hot weather.

EXAM ORIENTED QUESTIONS

TYPE - 1 01 Mark

Multiple Choice Questions

Q.1 Which of the following functions in humans is not performed by skin?

(a) Absorption (b) Circulation
(c) Excretion (d) Protection

Ans. (b)

Q.2 When exposed to sunlight, the skin produces .....*P*..... which is essential for .....*Q*..... .

(a) *P*- vitamin-D, *Q*-bone health
(b) *P*- vitamin-E and D, *Q*- blood clotting
(c) *P*- vitamin-C, *Q*-digestion of food
(d) *P*- ascorbic acid, *Q*- transport of oxygen

Ans. (a)

Q.3 Mr. Rastogi asked his students the outer and the inner most layer of epidermis.

Vani said: Dermis and stratum granulosa

Anamika said: Stratum corneum and stratum Malpighi

Dhruv said: Stratum granulosa and Malpighi

Rishi said: Granulosa and corneum.

Who gave the right answer, choose the correct option given below?

(a) Dhruv (b) Vani and Dhruv both
(c) Anamika (d) Rishi

Ans. (c)

Q.4 The vascular region of skin is found in

(a) epidermis (b) dermis
(c) Malpighian layer (d) cornified layer

Ans. (b)

Q.5 Priyanka tried to match the following layers of skin with their respective functions. She tabulated the following pair.

Layers	Their Functions
P	It forms ridges that makes fingerprints.
Q	This provides strength to the skin and serves as a home for hair follicles and sebaceous glands.

(a) *P* - Granulosa layer, *Q* - Reticular layer
(b) *P* - Malpighi layer, *Q* - Substratum layer
(c) *P* - Cornified layer, *Q* - Germinative layer
(d) *P* - Papillary layer, *Q* - Reticular layer

Ans. (d)

Q.6 A transverse section of skin is shown in the given diagram. Observe the diagram carefully and answer the following question.

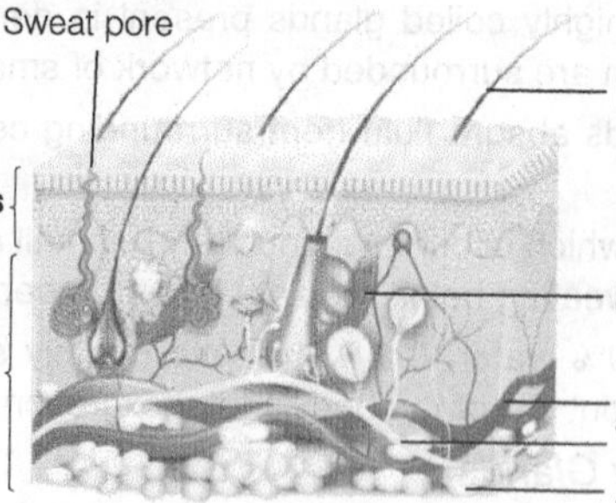

Name the structures represented by *A* and *B*.

(a) *A*- Fat cells, *B*- Affector muscles
(b) *A*- Papillae, *B*- Nerve cells
(c) *A*- Epidermis, *B*- Dermis
(d) *A*- Sweat glands, *B*- Sebaceous gland

Ans. (a)

Q.7 The structure that covers the hair root is

(a) follicle (b) bulb
(c) papilla (d) shaft

Ans. (a)

Q.8 If due to some reason the sebaceous glands fails to function

(a) the body will not be able to regulate the body temperature
(b) the skin will trun darker with more melanin
(c) the hair will fail to grow
(d) the skin will turn dry and rough.

Ans. (d) The sebaceous gland keeps the skin oily and conserves moisture in the body.

Q.9 The location of sweat glands within the layers of the skin can be identified as

(a) present specifically in the dermis, the deeper layer of the skin beneath the epidermis
(b) found exclusively within the epidermis, the outermost layer of the skin.

(c) distributed across both the dermis and the epidermis, covering multiple skin layers
(d) not located in either the dermis or the epidermis, but in other tissues or structures

Ans. (a)

Q.10 The average temperature maintained by the human body under normal conditions is
(a) 40°C (b) 25°C (c) 37°C (d) 28°C

Ans. (c)

Q.11 Sweating primarily serves the function of
(a) maintaining body temperature within normal limits
(b) controlling the balance of water content in the body
(c) eliminating excess water through the skin
(d) excretion

Ans. (a)

TYPE - 2 — 01 Mark

Matching Type Questions

Q.1 Match the following.

Column I	Column II
A. Mammary glands	I. Hair
B. Goose flesh	II. Sweat
C. Oily secretion	III. Rudimentary in male
D. Traces of urea	IV. Sebaceous gland

Ans. A-III, B-I, C-IV, D-II

Q.2 Match the following.

Column I	Column II
A. Decrease in melanin	I. Excretory material
B. Mammary glands	II. Sebaceous glands
C. Urea	III. Production of milk
D. Oily secretion	IV. Grey hair

Ans. A-IV, B-III, C-I, D-II

TYPE - 3 — 01 Mark

Assertion-Reason Type Questions

Direction (Q. Nos. 1-5) In the following questions, statements are given as Assertion (A) and Reason (R).
(a) A is true, but R is false.
(b) A is false, but R is true.
(c) Both A and R are true.
(d) Both A and R are false.

Q.1 Assertion (A) The skin is the largest organ of the human body and constitutes about 15% of an adult's total body weight.

Reason (R) The skin, along with its associated structures like hair, nails and glands, forms the integumentary system, which provides protection and supports overall health.

Ans. (c)

Q.2 Assertion (A) Hair is a derivative of the skin that provides protection and regulates body temperature.

Reason (R) Hair grows from follicles in the dermis and is composed of keratin a protein that strengthens and protects it.

Ans. (c)

Q.3 Assertion (A) Hair is a slender, thread-like outgrowth that originates from follicles in the skin and consists of the hair shaft, hair root and hair bulb.

Reason (R) The hair bulb is the visible part of the hair that extends above the skin and contains the hair papilla with a blood supply.

Ans. (a) A is true, but R is false. R can be corrected as
The hair bulb is not the visible part of the hair, but is located at the base of the hair root within the dermis and contains the hair papilla with a blood supply.

Q.4 Assertion (A) Nails are hardened keratinous structures that grow from the nail root beneath the skin.

Reason (R) The matrix, located at the base of the nail, produces new cells for nail growth.

Ans. (c)

Q.5 Assertion (A) In cold weather, blood vessels constrict, reducing blood flow under the skin, which helps the body to retain warmth.

Reason (R) The constriction of blood vessels increases the amount of heat released from the body.

Ans. (a) A is true, but R is false. R can be corrected as
The constriction of blood vessels reduces the amount of heat released from the body, helping to retain warmth and prevent the body from getting too cold.

TYPE - 4 — 01 Mark

Very Short Answer Type Questions

Q.1 Name the organ that forms the first line of defence in the human body.

Ans. Skin

Q.2 What are the two main layers of skin proper?

Ans. Epidermis and dermis.

Q.3 **Which substance stored in the skin that serves as an energy reserve?**

Ans. Fat

Q.4 ***X*** **is the layer present in the skin, it is filled with keratin and acts as an outer protective barrier. Identify** ***X*****.**

Ans. Stratum corneum.

Q.5 **Where does hair originate in the skin?**

Ans. Hair originates from hair follicles present in the dermis.

Q.6 **Name the structure of hair which is made up of epithelial and connective tissue sheaths.**

Ans. Hair follicle.

Q.7 **Which condition occurs when the arrector pili muscle, which runs between the hair follicle and dermis, contracts?**

Ans. Goosebumps occur when the arrector pili muscle contracts.

Q.8 **Name the gland that secretes an oily substance which make the hair and skin supple and waterproof.**

Ans. Sebaceous gland.

Q.9 **Which condition is formed when sebum oxidises and turns black in enlarged pores on skin?**

Ans. Blackheads

Q.10 **In which conditions do cold sweat occur?**

Ans. Fear, nervousness, nausea or pain.

Q.11 **Name the hormone which influenced the activity of mammary glands.**

Ans. Prolactin.

Q.12 **How do blood vessels respond to cold temperatures?**

Ans. They constrict (vasoconstriction) to reduce heat loss.

Q.13 **Name the following.** **(1 Mark each)**

(i) **Enlargement of sebaceous glands because of the accumulation of sebum.**

(ii) **The hard and outer part of nail.**

(iii) **Rise in body temperature in summer during which heat loss is reduced and sweating decreases.**

Ans. (i) Pimples (ii) Plate

(iii) Heat stroke

Q.14 **Choose the odd one out from the following terms given below and name the category to which other three belong.** **(1 Mark each)**

(i) **Sweat glands, Sebaceous glands, Nails, Mammary glands**

(ii) **Malpighian layer, Cornified layer, Dermal layer, Granular layer**

(iii) **Dermis, Epidermis, Hair shaft, Stratum granulosum**

(iv) **Arrector pili, Hair follicle, Hair papillae, Nail bed**

Ans. (i) The odd term is nails, while the rest three sweat glands, sebaceous glands and mammary glands are types of glands.

(ii) The odd term is dermal layer, while the rest three Malpighian layer, cornified layer and granular layer are layers of the epidermis.

(iii) The odd term is hair shaft, while the rest three dermis, epidermis and stratum granulosum are layers of the skin.

(iv) The odd term is nail bed, while the rest three arrector pili, hair follicle and hair papillae are parts of the hair structure.

Q.15 **Correct and rewrite the following sequence by changing the underlined words.** **(1 Mark each)**

(i) **Cornified layer, Papillary layer, Germinative layer, Dermis**

(ii) **Nail plate, Nail bulb, Nail matrix**

(iii) **Hair dermis, Hair shaft, Hair bulb, Hair follicle**

Ans. (i) Cornified layer, Granulosa layer, Germinative layer, Dermis.

(ii) Nail plate, Nail bed, Nail matrix

(iii) Hair shaft, Hair root, Hair follicle, Hair bulb

Q.16 **Mention one difference between each of the following pairs on the basis of what is given in the bracket.** **(1 Mark each)**

(i) **Vasodilation and Vasoconstriction (blood flow)**

(ii) **Ectothermal and Endothermal (behaviour)**

Ans. (i)

Vasodilation	Vasoconstriction
Dilated blood vessels have wider lumen which allows more flow of blood.	Constricted blood vessels have narrower lumen, so less blood flows.

(ii)

Endothermal	Ectothermal
They maintain the constant body temperature irrespective of change in the environment.	They cannot maintain constant temperature.

Q.17 **Give biological reasons for the following.** **(1 Mark each)**

(i) **We shiver and our teeth chatter when it is very cold in winter.**

(ii) **An otherwise normal healthy young man started perspiring, while it was intensely cold outside.**

Ans. (i) To maintain constant body temperature in very cold winter, the heat production is increased by speeding up metabolic rate and increasing muscular activity, like shivering.

(ii) Fever and sickness or any kind of vigorous activity can lead to perspiration even in cold outside.

Q.18 Observe the diagram carefully and fill in the blank spaces.

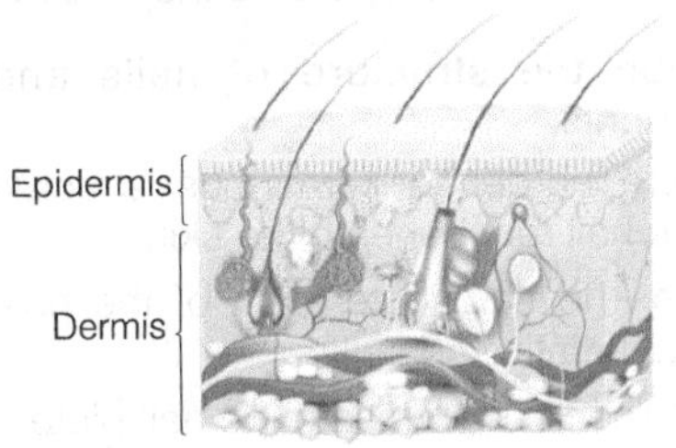

The human body is covered by an outer layer that plays a key role in protection. This layer makes up about 15% of an adult's total body weight and is the largest organ by surface area. Although it is thin and delicate, it acts as the first line of defence against external threats.

The ......(i)...... is the largest organ of the body, serving as a protective barrier against environmental damage, regulating body temperature and preventing water loss. It is composed of two main layers; the epidermis, dermis. The epidermis is the outermost layer, consisting of ......(ii)...... and keratinised cells. Beneath it, the dermis contains connective tissue, ...(iii)......, nerves and structures like sweat glands, sebaceous glands and hair follicles. Skin derivatives include hair, nails and ......(iv)...... which perform various functions like protection, temperature regulation and secretion. Together, these components maintain the skin's ......(v)...... and functional roles. **(1 Mark each)**

Ans. (i) skin (ii) dead (iii) blood vessels (iv) glands (v) protective

TYPE - 5   02 Marks

Short Answer Type Questions

Q.1 State any two functions of skin.

Ans. Skin performs different functions which are as follows

(i) **Protection** It acts as a barrier, shielding the body from harmful microorganisms, UV radiation and physical injuries.

(ii) **Sensation** The skin contains sensory receptors that help detect touch, temperature, pain and pressure.

Q.2 Which vitamin is produced by the skin? Mention two advantages of this vitamin.

Ans. The vitamin produced by the skin is vitamin-D.

Two advantages of vitamin-D are as follows

(i) It helps in the absorption of calcium and phosphorus, promoting healthy bones and teeth.

(ii) It boosts the immune system, aiding in the body's defence against infections.

Q.3 Name the layer present beneath the epidermis and explain it briefly.

Ans. Dermis is made up of connective tissue and contains blood vessels, nerves, hair follicles, sebaceous (oil) gland, sweat glands and lymphatic vessels. The dermis provides strength, elasticity and support to the skin, while also playing a role in temperature regulation, sensation and protection.

It has two layers, i.e. papillary layer and reticular layer. The dermis is essential for maintaining skin structure, sensing touch and temperature and supporting overall skin function.

Q.4 Why nails are considered as skin derivatives?

Ans. Nails are considered skin derivatives because they originate from the epidermis and are composed of keratin the same protein found in the skin and hair. They develop from the nail matrix, a specialised region of the epidermis and serve protective function, such as safeguarding fingertips and enhancing grip. Since they arise from the skin's outer layer and share its structural components, they are classified as skin derivatives.

Q.5 What causes goosebumps (piloerection) and how does it occur?

Ans. Goosebumps or piloerection, occur when the arrector pili muscle, which runs between the hair follicle and dermis, contracts. This contraction pulls the hair upright and causes the skin to appear wrinkled and contracted.

Q.6 What is the function of sebaceous glands and how does their secretion vary with weather conditions?

Ans. Sebaceous glands secrete sebum, an oily substance that helps keep the skin and hair supple, waterproof and prevents water loss. In cold, dry weather sebum secretion is reduced, which can make the skin rough and powdery, while in hot, humid weather, increased sebum secretion leads to oily skin.

Q.7 Why are mammary glands classified as modified sweat glands?

Ans. Mammary glands are modified sweat glands that produce milk for nourishing offspring. They originate from the same tissue as sweat glands but are specialised to respond to hormones like prolactin and oxytocin regulating milk production and release. Their development and function are influenced by reproductive hormones, especially during pregnancy and lactation.

Q.8 Explain sweat gland.

Ans. Sweat glands are specialised structures in the skin that produce and secrete sweat, a watery fluid. Sweat helps regulate body temperature by cooling the skin as it evaporates.

Q.9 What is heat stroke?

Ans. A condition that occurs when sweat production cannot keep up with evaporation in extremely hot conditions, causing a dangerous rise in body temperature.
This condition can be fatal. To prevent heat stroke, it is important to stay hydrated and consume extra salt during hot weather.

Q.10 List any two advantages of constant body temperature.

Ans. (i) Warm blooded animals can remain active throughout the days and years, irrespective of the environment temperature.
(ii) Enzymes works best at a constant temperature.

TYPE - 6 — 03 Marks

Short Answer Type Questions

Q.1 Explain the functions and parts of epidermis.

Ans. The epidermis is the outermost layer of the skin and serves as a protective barrier against environmental damage, infection and dehydration. It is made up of following layers

(i) **Cornified Layer** (Stratum Corneum) This outermost layer consists of dead, keratin-filled skin cells that form a tough, protective barrier against pathogens, mechanical damage and water loss. These cells are continuously replaced by new ones from the germinal layer.

(ii) **Granular Layer** (Stratum Granulosum) Made up of two or three layers of flattened cells. This layer plays a role in the process of keratinisation, where cells become more rigid and begin to lose their nuclei.

(iii) **Malpighian Layer** (Stratum Malpighi or Germinative Layer) The innermost layer of the epidermis, composed of column-shaped living cells that constantly divide to produce new cells. These cells contain the pigment melanin, which gives skin its colour and protects against ultraviolet light.

Q.2 Explain the structure of hair.

Ans. Hair is a slender, thread-like outgrowth that originates from follicles in the skin. It consists of three main parts; the hair shaft, hair root and hair bulb.

- The hair shaft is the visible part that extends above the skin and usually lies obliquely.
- The hair root is embedded within the dermis and its lowest part expands into the hair bulb, which contains the hair papilla, a projection from the dermis that provides a blood supply.
- The hair follicle consists of epithelial and connective tissue sheaths that enclose the hair root. The hair follicle and bulb work together to support hair growth, with new cells being added at the base of the bulb, where they die as they move upward.

Q.3 Describe the structure of nails and explain its components.

Ans. Nails are hardened keratinous structures that grow from the nail root beneath the skin.

(i) **Plate** The hard outer part of the nail, made up of dead, keratinised cells.

(ii) **Bed** The tissue beneath the nail plate.

(iii) **Matrix** Located just beneath the skin at the base of the nail, it produces new cells that push older cells toward the tip, causing nail growth. The matrix is visible as the whitish half-moon at the nail base.

Q.4 Explain three common problems of sebaceous glands.

Ans. Three common problems of sebaceous glands are as follows.

(i) **Pimples** Sebum, an oily substance produced by sebaceous glands, builds up in hair follicles. This buildup creates an environment for bacteria to grow, leading to infection and the formation of pimples or boils.

(ii) **Acne** Inflammation of sebaceous glands due to hormonal changes, commonly affecting adolescents.

(iii) **Blackheads** Enlarged open pores on the skin accumulate sebum, which oxidises and turns black, forming blackheads.

Q.5 Explain the following terms.
(i) Mammary gland
(ii) Thermoregulation
(iii) Cold-blooded animals

Ans. (i) **Mammary glands** are modified sweat glands found in both males and females. In males, they remain small and underdeveloped, while in females, they enlarge during puberty to form breasts. Each breast contains **15-20 milk ducts** that are connected to into lobes of the mammary glands. The function of these glands is influenced by reproductive hormones like **prolactin** and pregnancy, enabling them to produce milk to nourish newborns.

(ii) **Thermoregulation** is the process by which an organism maintains its internal body temperature within a certain range, despite external temperature variations. It helps ensure optimal functioning of enzymes and metabolic processes.

(iii) **Cold-blooded animals** or ectotherms, are organisms that cannot regulate their body temperature internally. Their body temperature fluctuates with the environment, such as reptiles, amphibians and fish.

TYPE - 7   03 Marks

Structured Based Questions

Q.1 Medhavi, a young woman, has noticed the appearance of a pimple on her face and is quite concerned about it. She decides to visit a doctor for advice. After thoroughly examining her condition, the doctor explains that the pimple is a result of excess sebum buildup, which provides an environment for bacterial growth in the hair follicles, leading to infection. Observe the image provided below and answer the following questions.

(i) Based on the doctor's explanation and the image, which specific gland in the skin is responsible for the formation of pimples?

(ii) What is some other common skin-related issues or problems that are associated with this particular gland?

(iii) What is the major function of this gland in maintaining overall skin health and function?

Ans. (i) The gland responsible for the formation of pimples is the sebaceous gland.

(ii) Other common problems associated with the sebaceous gland include

- **Blackheads** Enlarged open pores on the face accumulate sebum, which oxidises and turns black, forming blackheads.
- **Acne** Inflammation of sebaceous glands due to hormonal changes, commonly affecting adolescents.

(iii). The major function of the sebaceous gland is to produce **sebum**, an oily substance that

- Keeps the skin and hair moisturised.
- Forms a protective barrier to prevent water loss.
- Protects the skin from bacterial and fungal infections.

Q.2 Observe the diagram carefully and answer the questions that follows.

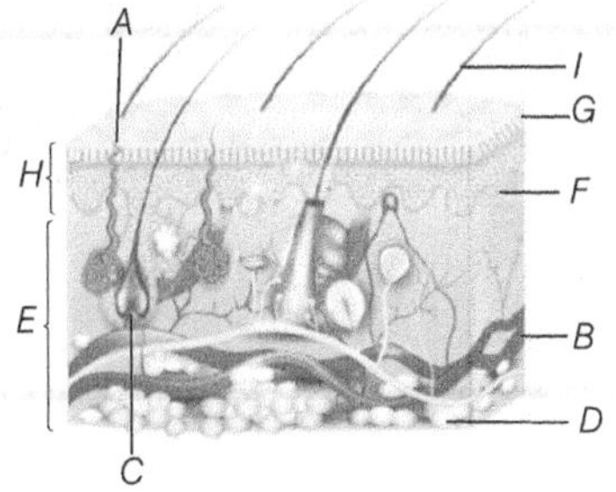

(i) Label the parts *A* to *I*.

(ii) How does skin helps in maintaining body temperature?

(iii) State the functions of parts, *D* and *I*.

Ans. (i) The parts *A*-*I* are labelled as
A-Sweat pore; *B*-Artery; *C*-Hair papillae; *D*-Fat cells; *E*-Dermis; *F*-Stratum Malpighi; *G*-Stratum corneum; *H*-Epidermis; *I*-Hair shaft.

(ii) When temperature rises, the skin helps to lose extra heat by sweating and dilation of blood vessels. When temperature falls down, sweating is reduced and the blood vessels constrict.

(iii) The functions of parts *D* and *I* are as

Part *D* (Fat cells) store fat to insulate the body heat.

Part *I* (Hair shaft) keeps the body warm.

Q.3 Study the diagram carefully and answer the questions that follows.

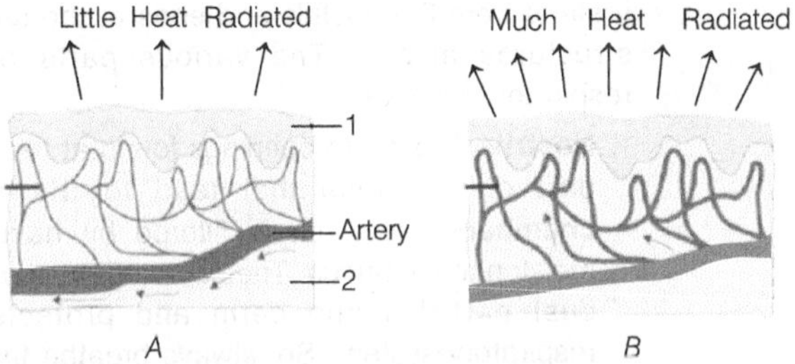

(i) Identify the mechanism in *A* and *B*.

(ii) Identify the labels numbered as 1 and 2.

(iii) What are warm-blooded animals?

Ans. (i) The mechanism in *A* and *B* is
A-Vasoconstriction
B-Vasodilation

(ii) The labels numbered as 1 and 2 are
1-Epidermis and 2-Dermis

(iii) The animals whose body temperature does not fluctuate according to the atmospheric temperature.

THE RESPIRATORY SYSTEM

- Every living cell requires energy to perform physical activities, carry out essential chemical reactions and maintain vital functions. This energy is obtained through **respiration**, a process in which oxygen is taken in to breakdown glucose, releasing energy in the form of ATP (Adenosine Triphosphate).
- Respiration can be of two types, **aerobic respiration**, which requires oxygen and produces a high amount of energy and **anaerobic respiration**, which occurs in the absence of oxygen and produces less energy. Both types of respiration play crucial roles in maintaining cellular functions and energy production.
- The process of respiration is facilitated by the **respiratory system**, which ensures the exchange of gases by delivering oxygen to the cells and removing carbon dioxide, as a waste product of metabolism.

Human Respiratory System

All organs in an organism that carries oxygen and helps in the removal of carbon dioxide from the body are called **respiratory organs**. These organs collectively constitute the **respiratory system**.

The human respiratory system can be divided into two major components, i.e. the **respiratory tract** and the **lungs**.

Respiratory Tract

- It serves as the passage for air, transporting oxygen to the lungs and removing carbon dioxide from the lungs to the exterior.
- It starts from the nostrils and ends at the sac like structures alveoli. The various parts of the respiratory tract are

1. **Nostrils** These are openings found at the lower part of the nose that lead to the **nasal chambers**. Here, air is filtered by hairs and moistened by mucus. The secreted mucus traps dust particles and germ and protects the respiratory system. So, always breathe through nose and not mouth.
2. **Pharynx** A common passage at the back of the mouth for both air and food.
3. **Larynx** (Voice Box) Located at the upper part of the trachea, it allows air to pass into the lungs and helps to produce sound. The larynx is more prominent in men and is often referred as the **Adam's apple.**

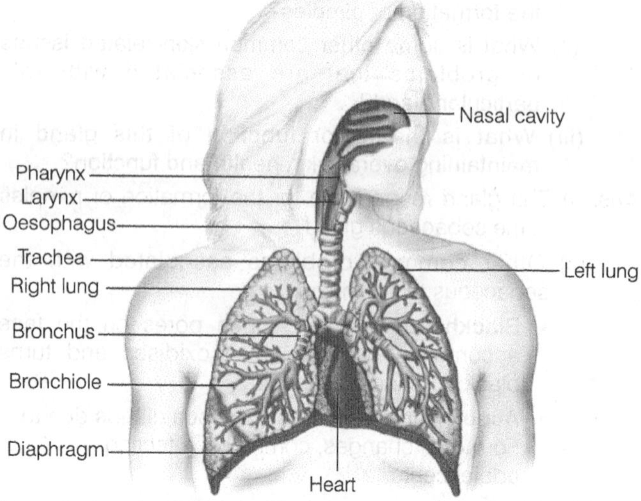

Respiratory system of human beings

4. **Trachea** (Windpipe) A thin-walled tube about 11 cm long and 2.5 cm wide that extends into the thoracic cavity and passes air to the bronchi. It is supported by **C-shaped cartilaginous rings** that provide structural support and prevent it from collapsing during breathing. These rings keep the trachea open and flexible, allowing air to pass through easily.
5. **Bronchi** The trachea divides into the right and left bronchi, which enter into the lungs. Once inside the lungs, the bronchi further divide into secondary and tertiary bronchi, forming a network of smaller branches that lead to the bronchioles.

6. **Bronchioles** These are the smaller branches of the bronchi. These tubes continue to divide into even finer branches, eventually leading to the alveolar ducts and alveolar sacs. Bronchioles do not have cartilage, but are lined with smooth muscle to regulate airflow. The inner lining of the, trachea, bronchi and bronchioles has tiny **cilia** that constantly move to push mucus and dust particles towards the mouth for the removal.
7. **Alveoli** These are tiny, sac-like structures at the end of the bronchioles. These microscopic air sacs are surrounded by capillaries and are the primary sites for gas exchange in the lungs, enabling oxygen to enter the blood stream and carbon dioxide to be expelled.

Lungs

- These are the site of gaseous exchange between the blood and atmospheric air.
- They are thin-walled, spongy, elastic, pinkish and paired organs that make up the respiratory system.
- Located in the thoracic cavity, the lungs are enclosed by the thoracic cage, which includes the ribs, sternum and diaphragm.
- The left lung consists of two lobes and has a cardiac notch where the heart is situated, while the right lung is slightly larger with three lobes.
- Each lung is covered by two protective membranes called the **pleura**. Between these membranes is a narrow **pleural cavity**, which contains **pleural fluid** that reduces friction during lung movement.

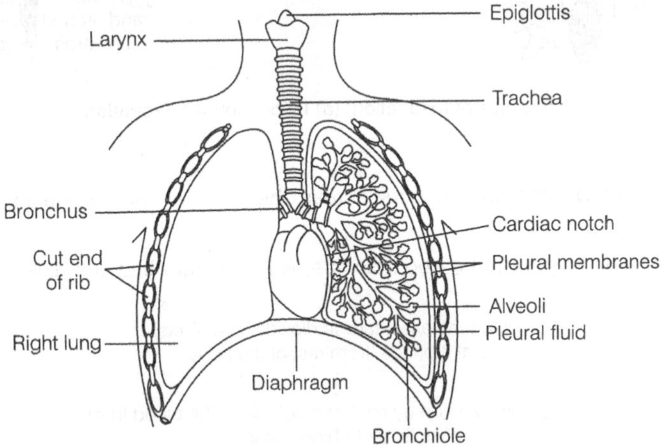

Diagrammatic view of human respiratory system (sectional view)

Mechanism of Respiration

The main mechanism of respiration is categorised into following three steps, which are discussed below

1. Breathing

- It is an energy-consuming, physical process that facilitates the inflow of oxygen (O_2) and the outflow of carbon dioxide (CO_2), with a normal breathing rate of an adult being 12–16 breaths per minute.
- Breathing is controlled by the respiratory centre in the medulla oblongata, which responds to carbon dioxide levels in the blood. Higher CO_2 levels make breathing faster.
- It involves the movement of the thoracic cage, lung expansion and deflation and the flow of air into and out of the lungs, creating a pressure gradient.
- The process of air moving in and out of the lungs is called **ventilation**. Breathing has two primary phases which are as follows

(a) Inspiration (Inhalation)

- It is an **active process** (i.e. it requires energy) where fresh air enters into the lungs.
- The diaphragm contracts and flattens, while the **external intercostal muscles pull** the ribs upward and outward, increasing the thoracic cavity's volume.
- This reduces the air **pressure** in the lungs, causing air to flow in, filling the alveoli where oxygen is exchanged with the blood.

(b) Expiration (Exhalation)

- This is a **passive process**, i.e. it takes place without the use of energy and where air is expelled from the lungs.
- The diaphragm relaxes and becomes convex, while the **external intercostal muscles relax**, allowing the ribs to move downward and inward.
- This reduces the thoracic cavity's volume, increasing lung pressure and forcing the air out of the lungs.
- During forced expiration internal intercostal muscles activity contract to further decrease lung volume.

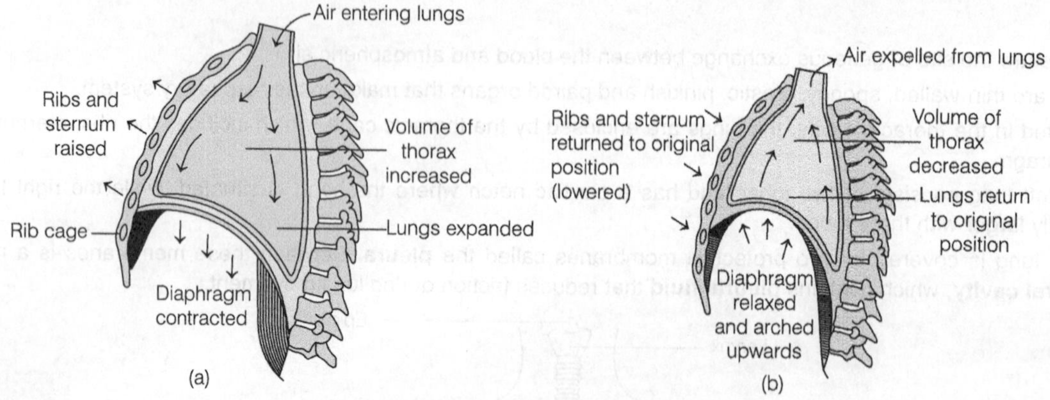

Process of respiration; (a) Inspiration (b) Expiration

2. *Exchange of Gases*

- The process of exchange of O_2 and CO_2 occurs across the alveolar membrane in the lungs and in tissues throughout the body.
- The sequence of exchange of oxygen and carbon dioxide, which occurs between blood vessels and alveoli is as follows

Blood releases carbon dioxide into alveoli that it brings from rest of the body.

↓

Oxygen is taken up by the haemoglobin in the blood from alveolar air to blood vessels.

↓

Oxygen in blood is then transported to all cells in the body by respiratory pigment (haemoglobin) and due to diffusion pressure.

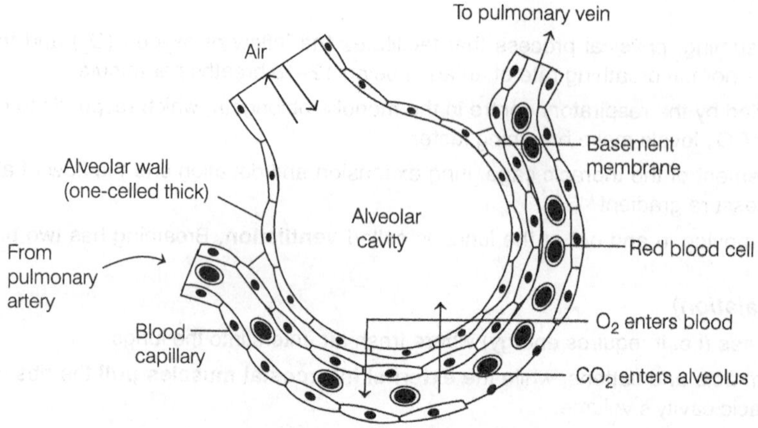

A diagram of a section of an alveolus with a pulmonary capillary

REVISION NOTES

3. Transport of Gases

Blood carries oxygen from the lungs to tissues and carbon dioxide from tissues to the lungs for elimination. The exchange of gases between the blood and tissues is called **tissue respiration**.

Transport of Oxygen

- About 3% of oxygen is carried in a dissolved form in plasma.
- About 97% of oxygen binds to haemoglobin as **oxyhaemoglobin**.

Transport of Carbon Dioxide

- About 7% of CO_2 is carried in dissolved form in plasma.
- About 70% is carried as bicarbonate ions (HCO_3^-).
- Nearly 20-25% binds to haemoglobin and carried as **carbaminohaemoglobin**.

Differences between Breathing and Respiration

Breathing	Respiration
It is a physical process in which only inhalation and exhalation is involved. Basically an external process.	It is a biochemical process. Respiration is an internal process, occurs in mitochondria and cytoplasm of the cell.
No enzymes are required.	Enzymes are required.
Energy formation does not occur.	Energy is released in the form of ATP.

Respiratory Volumes and Capacities

The amount of air lungs can receive, hold or expel under different conditions is known as **respiratory volumes**. A healthy person can inhale or exhale about 6000-8000 mL of air per minute. The different volumes and capacities are as follows

Respiratory Volume/Capacity	Definition	Average Value
Tidal Volume (TV)	The amount of air inhaled or exhaled during normal breathing.	500 mL
Inspiratory Reserve Volume (IRV)	The maximum amount of air that can be inhaled forcefully	3000 mL
Expiratory Reserve Volume (ERV)	The maximum amount of air that can be exhaled forcefully	1100 mL
Residual Volume (RV)	The amount of air remaining in the lungs after a maximal exhalation.	1200 mL
Inspiratory Capacity (IC)	The maximum amount of air that can be inhaled after a normal exhalation (TV + IRV).	3500 mL
Vital Capacity (VC)	The maximum amount of air that can be exhaled after a maximum inhalation (TV + IRV + ERV).	4600 mL
Total Lung Capacity (TLC)	The total volume of air in the lungs after a maximum inhalation (TV + IRV + ERV + RV)	5800 mL

Effect of Altitude on Breathing

At higher altitudes, atmospheric pressure and oxygen levels **decrease**. This can cause **mountain sickness** or **altitude sickness**, above 4500 metres. Symptoms include fatigue, dizziness, nausea, loss of hearing and even complete backouts.

Hypoxia It is a condition in which O_2 supply to the tissues get reduced. It may be due to high altitudes or sitting for long hours in a crowded room with poor ventilation.

- **Anaemic Hypoxia** It occurs when the blood's oxygen-carrying capacity is reduced due to decrease in RBCs or presence of non-functional haemoglobin.

- **Asphyxia** (suffocation) It happens when oxygen in the blood drops and carbon dioxide increases, leading to paralysis of the respiratory centre and potentially death.
- **Emphysema** It is a respiratory disease that occurs commonly in smokers. The surface area for gaseous exchange gets reduced as the wall separating alveoli get broken.

Respiration in Plants and Animals

It is a characteristic feature of all living organisms, including plants and animals. Both during aerobic respiration shares the following similarities

- Free O_2 is required.
- CO_2 and H_2O are produced.
- Energy is stored as ATP molecules.
- Aerobic respiration occurs in mitochondria.
- Glucose is the respiratory substrate.

However, there are a few differences as well.

Differences between respiration in plants and animals

Respiration in Plants	Respiration in Animals
Breathing does not take place in plants.	Breathing occurs in animals, except in some lower animals.
There is no transporting system for gases in plants; gases diffuse between cells.	Animals have a blood vascular system for the transportation of O_2 and CO_2.
Only a very small amount of detectable heat is produced during respiration in plants.	A considerable amount of detectable heat is produced during respiration in animals.
Plants have an additional source of oxygen from photosynthesis.	Animals rely only on air as the source of oxygen.
The rate of respiration in plants is low.	The rate of respiration in animals is high.
CO_2 produced in plant respiration is utilised in photosynthesis.	CO_2 produced in animal respiration is released into the atmosphere.

Differences between anaerobic respiration in plants and animals

Anaerobic Respiration in Plants	Anaerobic Respiration in Animals
Anaerobic respiration in plants produces ethyl alcohol.	Anaerobic respiration in animals produces lactic acid.
CO_2 is produced during anaerobic respiration in plants.	No CO_2 is produced during anaerobic respiration in animals.
More heat energy is released during anaerobic respiration in plants.	Less heat energy is released during anaerobic respiration in animals.

EXAM ORIENTED QUESTIONS

TYPE - 1 — 01 Mark

Multiple Choice Questions

Q.1 The table given below compares the aerobic and anaerobic respiration in muscle cells.

Which comparison is correct?

	Level of Energy Released		Level of Fatigue Produced	
	Aerobic	Anaerobic	Aerobic	Anaerobic
(a)	+	–	+	–
(b)	+	–	–	+
(c)	–	+	+	–
(d)	–	+	–	+

Ans. (b)

Q.2 The human respiratory system can be divided into two main components ......*P*...... and .....*Q*...... .

(a) *P* - respiratory tract, *Q* - lungs
(b) *P* - alveoli sacs, *Q* - lungs
(c) *P* - nasal cavity, *Q* - alveoli
(d) *P* - diaphragm, *Q* - bronchi

Ans. (a)

Q.3 Which portion of the human respiratory system is called sound box?

(a) Larynx (b) Trachea (c) Nasopharynx (d) Glottis

Ans. (a)

Q.4 The trachea eventually branches into which of the following structures?

(a) Bronchi (b) Bronchioles
(c) Alveoli (d) Pharynx

Ans. (a)

Q.5 The diagram shows some structures in the human neck and thorax.

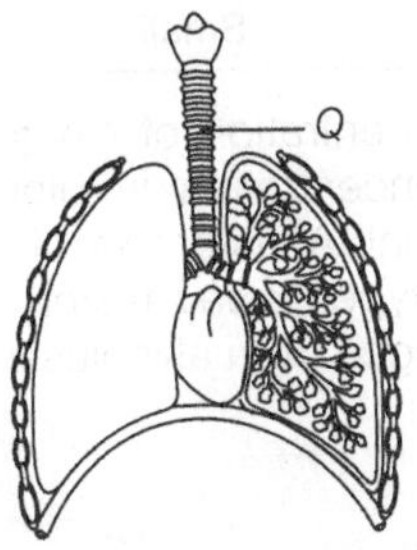

The lining of tube *Q* has cilia.

What is an important function of the cilia?

(a) To help in the exchange of gases
(b) To increase the internal surface area of tube *Q*
(c) To moisten the air entering and leaving the lung
(d) To move mucus towards the throat

Ans. (d)

Q.6 What is the path of carbon dioxide as it leaves the lungs?

(a) Alveolus → Bronchiole → Bronchus → Trachea
(b) Alveolus → Bronchus → Bronchiole → Trachea
(c) Trachea → Bronchiole → Bronchus → Alveolus
(d) Trachea → Bronchus → Bronchiole → Alveolus

Ans. (a)

Q.7 The three structures below are the parts of the gaseous exchange system.

1. Bronchiole 2. Bronchus 3. Trachea

What is the order of the structures according to size, with the largest diameter air passage first?

Largest ⟶ Smallest

(a) 2, 1, 3 (b) 2, 3, 1 (c) 3, 1, 2 (d) 3, 2, 1

Ans. (d)

Q.8 Which of the following does not occur during breathing?

(a) Brings the air to body temperature
(b) Warms up the air
(c) Diffusion of gases
(d) Clean up the air

Ans. (c)

Q.9 Inspiration begins when the diaphragm undergoes which of the following actions?

(a) Extension of the diaphragm
(b) Contraction of the diaphragm
(c) Extension of the lungs
(d) Contraction of the lungs

Ans. (b)

Q.10 When a mammal breaths in, what happens to the diaphragm and to the rib cage?

	Diaphragm	Rib Cage
(a)	Become flatter	Downwards and inwards
(b)	Become flatter	Outwards and upwards
(c)	Becomes more domed	Downwards and inwards
(d)	Becomes more domed	Outwards and upwards

Ans. (b) During inhalation, the contraction of the external intercoastal muscles lifts the rib cage upwards and outwards. The diaphragm flattens to increase the volume of the chest cavity.

Q.11 In humans, the process of gas exchange takes place
(a) through passive transport
(b) between blood and tissue
(c) between the alveoli and pulmonary blood capillaries
(d) in all of the above ways

Ans. (d)

Q.12 What describes the actions of the intercostal muscles and the diaphragm when we breathe out?

	External Intercostal Muscles	Internal Intercostal Muscles	Diaphragm
(a)	Contract	Relax	Falls
(b)	Contract	Relax	Rises
(c)	Relax	Contract	Falls
(d)	Relax	Contract	Rises

Ans. (d)

Q.13 When the external intercostal muscles contract, how do the pressure and the volume inside the lungs change?

	Pressure	Volume
(a)	Decreases	Falls
(b)	Decreases	Rises
(c)	Increases	Falls
(d)	Increases	Rises

Ans. (b)

Q.14 Observe the given diagram and answer the following question.

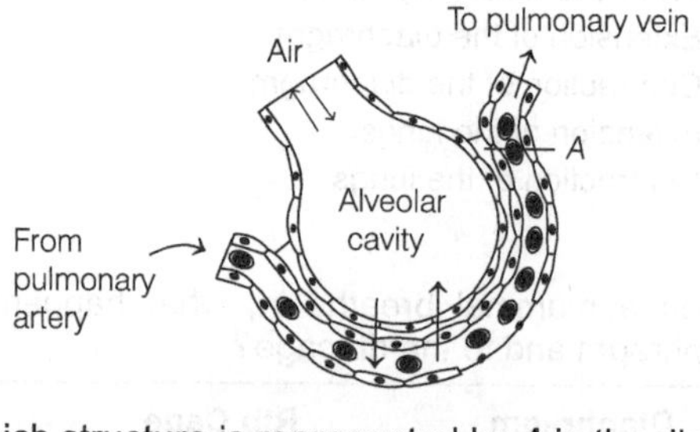

Which structure is represented by *A* in the diagram?
(a) Red blood cells (b) Pleural membrane
(c) Basement membrane (d) Epithelium

Ans. (c)

Q.15 The diagram shows a section through an alveolus and a blood capillary. In which region is the concentration of carbon dioxide is highest.

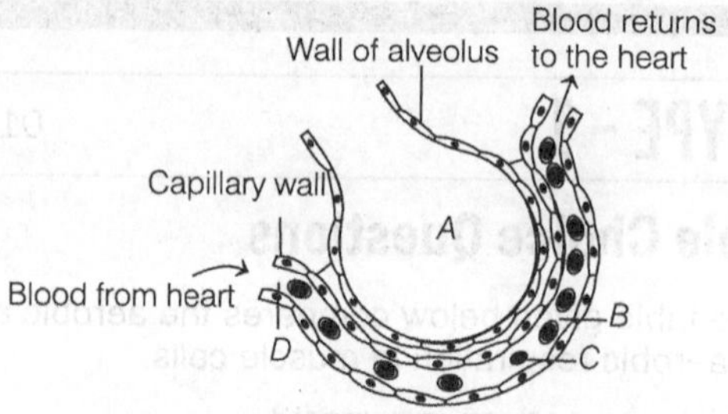

(a) *A* (b) *B*
(c) *C* (d) *D*

Ans. (d) Blood entering the capillaries (*D*) near the arteriole end has the highest concentration of carbon dioxide compared to that in the alveolar air, creating a greater diffusion gradient. This ensures a maximum rate of diffusion of carbon dioxide from the blood capillary to the alveolus.

Q.16 The diagram shows a section of an alveolus in a human being.

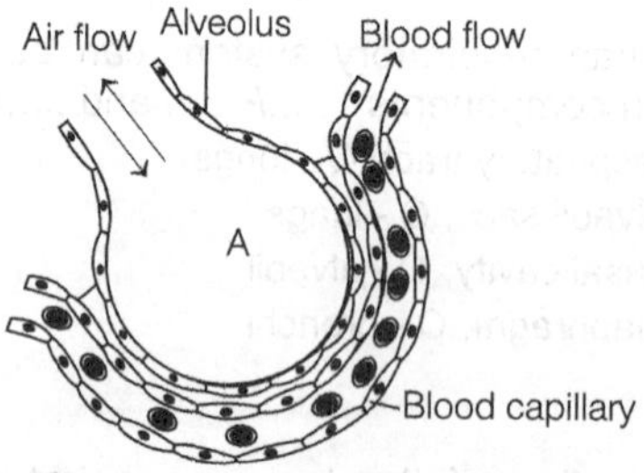

Which conditions would result in the maximum rate of diffusion of oxygen from the alveolus into the blood capillary?

	Amount of Oxygen in Alveolar Air	Amount of Oxygen in Blood	Rate of Blood Flow
(a)	Small	Large	Fast
(b)	Small	Large	Slow
(c)	Large	Small	Fast
(d)	Large	Small	Slow

Ans. (c) A high concentration of oxygen in the alveolar air and a low concentration in blood creates a higher diffusion gradient. A faster rate of blood flow also helps to carry the oxygen away faster, thus maximising the diffusion of oxygen from alveolus into blood capillary.

Q.17 The graph shows changes in the volume of air in the lungs a person at rest over a period of 30 seconds.

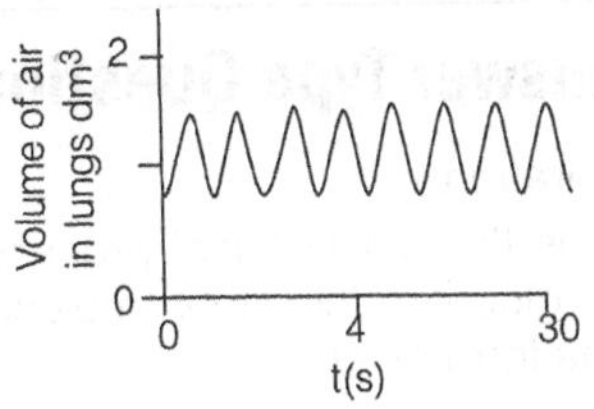

Which graph shows changes in the volume of air in the lungs of the same person immediately after they have done five minutes of vigorous exercise?

(a)
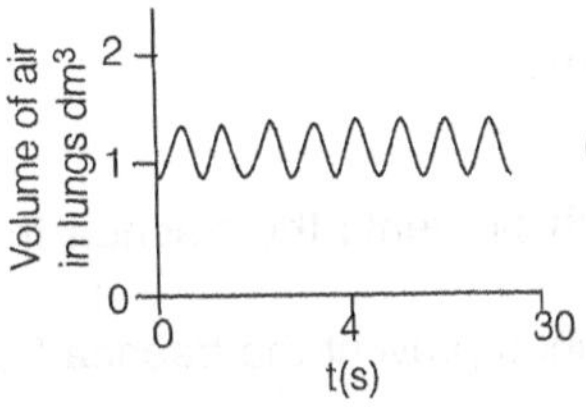

(b)
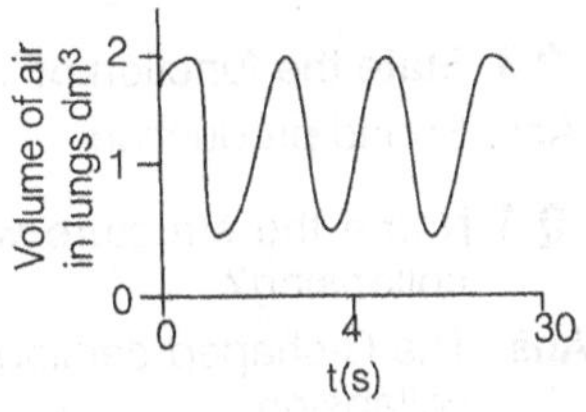

(c)
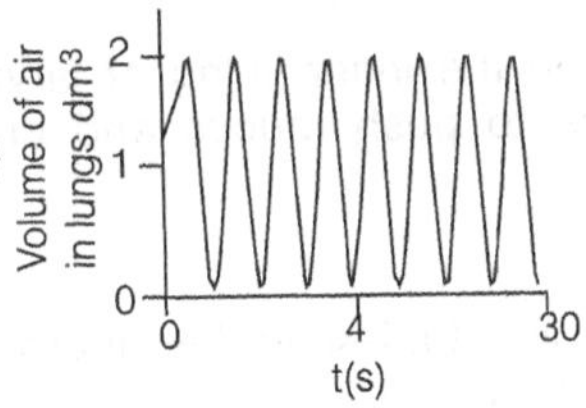

(d)
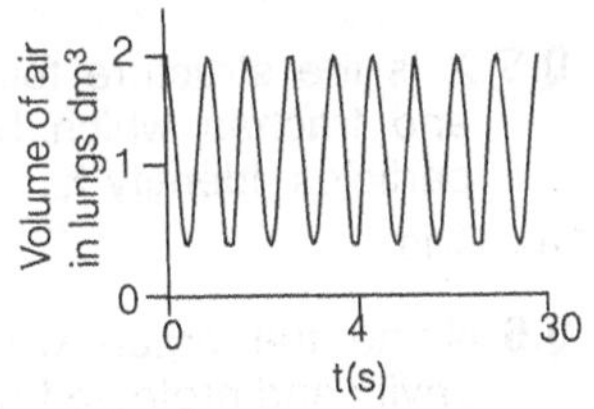

Ans. (c) After exercise, breathing rate changes in two ways, i.e. the rate of breathing increases (shown on a graph by more complete breaths in a given time period) and the depth of breathing increases (shown on a graph by higher peaks and lower troughs).

Q.18 Deepali tried to match the following structures with their functions. She tabulated a pair as follows.

Structures	Functions
P	Transport of oxygen.
Q	Exchange of gases.

Choose the correct pair.
(a) *P* - Alveoli, *Q* - Bronchi
(b) *P* - Red blood cells, *Q* - Alveoli
(c) *P* - Trachea, *Q* - Lungs
(d) *P* - Diaphragm, *Q* - Nasal cavity

Ans. (b)

Q.19 Ms. Riya asked her students to state the average tidal volume and residual volume in adults, respectively.
Manohar said: 500 mL and 1200 mL
Rama said: 400 mL and 1500 mL
Shaily said: 600 mL and 1000 mL
Anokhi said: 250 mL and 1400 mL
Who gave the right answer?
(a) Shaily (b) Rama (c) Manohar (d) Anokhi

Ans. (c)

Q.20 In the blood, carbon dioxide is transported by haemoglobin in the form of
(a) carboxyhaemoglobin (b) carbaminohaemoglobin
(c) carbamidohaemoglobin (d) deoxyhaemoglobin

Ans. (b)

Q.21 In what way is carbon monoxide in tobacco smoke harmful?
(a) It causes emphysema
(b) It causes lungs cancer
(c) It combines with haemoglobin
(d) It kills the cells lining of trachea

Ans. (c) Carbon monoxide is a toxic gas that combines permanently with haemoglobin to form carboxy haemoglobin. Thus, reducing the amount of red blood cells available to absorb oxygen.

TYPE - 2 — 01 Mark

Matching Type Questions

Q.1 Choose the correct match of structures *A* to *E* with their respective functions.

Respiratory Structure	Functions
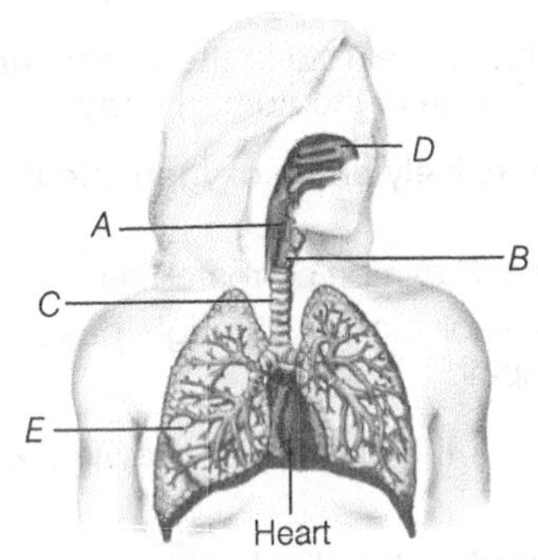	I. Transports air from the larynx to the bronchi.
	II. Common passage for food and air
	III. Filtres, warms and moistens incoming air.
	IV. Site of gaseous exchange in lungs.
	V. Produces sound and protects the airway during swallowing.

Ans. A- II, B-V, C-I, D-III, E-IV

Q.2 Match the following columns.

Column I	Column II
A. Diaphragm	I. Exchange of gases
B. Epiglottis	II. C-shaped rings
C. Air sacs	III. Regulates lung volume
D. Lungs	IV. Drives mucus
E. Alveoli	V. Closes windpipe during swallowing
F. Trachea	VI. Network of capillaries
G. Cilia	VII. Spongy and elastic

Ans. A- III, B-V, C-VI, D-VII, E-I, F-II G-IV

TYPE - 3 — 01 Mark

Assertion-Reason Type Questions

Direction (Q. Nos. 1-5) In the following questions, statements are given as Assertion (A) and Reason (R).

(a) A is true, but R is false.
(b) A is false, but R is true.
(c) Both A and R are true.
(d) Both A and R are false.

Q.1 Assertion (A) Every living cell requires energy to carry out essential functions, which is obtained through the process of respiration.

Reason (R) During respiration, oxygen is used to breakdown glucose, releasing energy in the form of ATP (Adenosine Triphosphate).

Ans. (c)

Q.2 Assertion (A) The primary function of the respiratory system is to supply oxygen to the body and remove carbon dioxide.

Reason (R) The respiratory system transports oxygen to the tissues *via* the heart.

Ans. (a) A is true, but R is false. R can be corrected as The respiratory system transports oxygen to the tissues *via* blood.

Q.3 Assertion (A) Lungs play a vital role in the exchange of oxygen and carbon dioxide in the human body.

Reason (R) The alveoli actively pump oxygen into the blood.

Ans. (a) A is true, but R is false. R can be corrected as Gas exchange in the alveoli occurs through passive diffusion, not active pumping.

Q.4 Assertion (A) Inhalation is the process of drawing air into the lungs.

Reason (R) During inhalation, the diaphragm contracts and moves downward.

Ans. (c)

Q.5 Assertion (A) Vital capacity is the maximum amount of air a person can exhale after a forceful expiration.

Reason (R) Vital capacity is the sum of tidal volume, inspiratory reserve volume and expiratory reserve volume.

Ans. (c)

TYPE - 4 — 01 Mark

Very Short Answer Type Questions

Q.1 Define respiration.

Ans. Respiration is the biochemical process by which cells breakdown glucose (or other molecules) to release energy in the form of ATP.

Q.2 Name the substance which is oxidised in body during respiration.

Ans. Glucose

Q.3 State the function of larynx.

Ans. Sound production

Q.4 Name the structure which prevents the trachea from collapsing?

Ans. The C-shaped cartilage rings prevent the trachea from collapsing.

Q.5 *X* is the structure found in the inner lining of larynx and trachea which helps to push mucus and dust particles. Identify *X*.

Ans. Cilia

Q.6 Name the organ which is situated in the thoracic cavity and protected by rib cage.

Ans. Lungs

Q.7 On which side of the lung is the cardiac notch located?

Ans. Left side

Q.8 Name the fluid which reduces the friction during lung movement.

Ans. Pleural fluid.

Q.9 Name the different phases of respiration.

Ans. Different phases of respiration are as follows

(i) Breathing
(ii) Gaseous exchange
(iii) Tissue respiration

Q.10 Name the process in which air is moving in and out from the lungs.

Ans. Ventilation

Q.11 What is the normal breathing rate of an adult person?

Ans. 12-16 breathes per minute.

Q.12 Y is a passive process in which air is expelled out from lungs. Identify the process.

Ans. Exhalation or expiration.

Q.13 Name the process in which the exchange of oxygen (O_2) and carbon dioxide (CO_2) occurs, between the lung alveoli and pulmonary capillaries.

Ans. External respiration

Q.14 Oxygen is taken up from the lungs to the tissues. Name the component by which oxygen is carried to the tissues.

Ans. Haemoglobin

Q.15 What is inspiratory capacity?

Ans. Inspiratory capacity is the maximum amount of air a person can inhale after a normal exhalation.

Q.16 Name the following.

(i) A hollow cartilaginous structure located at the start of windpipe.

(ii) The fluid present between the two membranes of the lungs.

(iii) Name the respiratory tubes formed by division of windpipe before they enter the lungs.

(iv) A physical process in which atmospheric air is taken in and forced out of the lungs.

(v) The complex chemical changes which occur inside the cell to release energy from glucose. **(1 Mark each)**

Ans. (i) Larynx (ii) Pleural fluid

(iii) Bronchi (iv) Breathing

(v) Cellular respiration

Q.17 Choose the odd one out from the following terms given below and name the category to which other three belong. **(1 Mark each)**

(i) Bronchioles, Bronchus, Alveolus, Diaphragm

(ii) Ethyl alcohol, Carbon dioxide, Starch, Oxygen absence

(iii) Hairy, Nasal septum, Mucus, Vocal cord

Ans. (i) The odd term is diaphragm as rest three are the parts of lungs.

(ii) The odd term is starch as rest three are related to anaerobic respiration.

(iii) The odd term is vocal cord, as rest three are present in the nostrils.

Q.18 Given below are sets of four terms each. Rewrite the term in correct order of a logical sequence beginning with the term that is underlined. **(1 Mark each)**

(i) Larynx, Pharynx, Bronchioles, <u>Nostrils</u>, Alveoli

(ii) Trachea, Bronchus, Bronchiole, Epiglottis, <u>Pharynx</u>

Ans. (i) Nostrils, Pharynx, Larynx, Bronchioles, Alveoli

(ii) Pharynx, Epiglottis, Trachea, Bronchus, Bronchioles

Q.19 Expand the following biological abbreviations. **(1 Mark each)**

(i) TLC (ii) RV

(iii) FRC (iv) ADP

(v) TV

Ans. (i) Total Lung Capacity

(ii) Residual Volume

(iii) Functional Residual Capacity

(iv) Adenosine Diphosphate

(v) Tidal Volume

Q.20 State the exact location of the following. **(1 Mark each)**

(i) Nostrils (ii) Epiglottis

(iii) Alveoli (iv) Lungs

Ans. (i) Nostrils are pair of slits present at the lower end of the nose.

(ii) Epiglottis is a cartilaginous leaf-like structure present at the top of trachea.

(iii) Alveoli are balloon-shaped structures present at the end of bronchioles.

(iv) Lungs lie in the thoracic cavity and are enclosed dorsally by thoracic cage.

Q.21 Give reason for the following. **(1 Mark each)**

(i) Why one should always breathe through nose and not mouth?

(ii) Our elders always advise us that we should not speak while eating food. Why?

(iii) Why does a person feels breathlessness at higher altitudes?

(iv) In the absence of air the trachea does not collapse. Why?

Ans. (i) The inner lining of the nostrils have small hairs and secretes mucus which traps the dust particles and germs present in inhaled air. Thus preventing the dust particles and germs to enter our system.

(ii) The trachea and the oesophagus lie close to each other and the entrance to the trachea is guarded by a flap called epiglottis that closes when we swallow food, but when we speak while eating the incomplete closure of epiglottis during swallowing leads to cough and choking.

(iii) At higher altitudes, atmospheric pressure and oxygen levels decrease. Thus, one may suffer air sickness due to lack in oxygen.

(iv) Because it is made up of incomplete C-shaped rings of hyaline cartilage which provide flexibility and keep the trachea distended permanently, thus preventing it from collapsing.

Q.22 Observe the figures and fill in the blanks spaces.

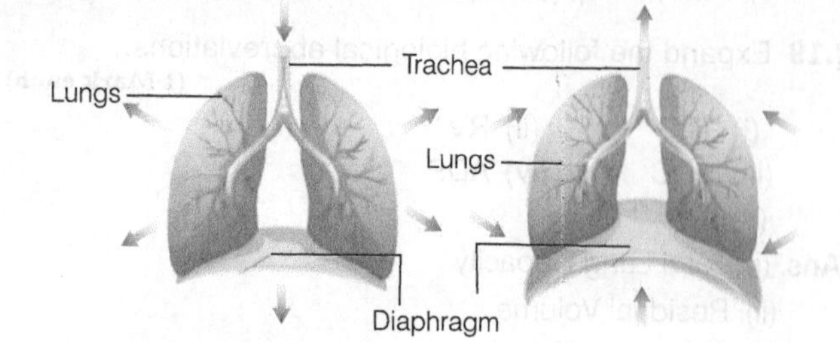

Breathing is the process of taking in oxygen (inhalation) and expelling carbon dioxide (exhalation) from the lungs. It involves the coordinated movement of the diaphragm and intercostal muscles to allow the exchange of gases necessary for cellular respiration.

(1 Mark each)

During inspiration, which is an (i) .... process, the diaphragm contracts and flattens, while the external intercostal muscles lift the ribs (ii)......... , expanding the thoracic cavity. This decrease in lung pressure causes air to flow into the lungs, filling the alveoli where (iii) .... is exchanged with the blood. In contrast, expiration is a passive process, where the diaphragm relaxes and becomes (iv) ...., and the external intercostal muscles relax, pulling the ribs downward and inward. This reduces the thoracic cavity's volume, increasing (v) .... and expelling air from the lungs.

Ans. (i) active, (ii) upward and outward, (iii) oxygen, (v) convex, (v) lung pressure

TYPE - 5 02 Marks

Short Answer Type Questions

Q.1 The trachea divides into the right and left bronchi, which further divide into smaller branches. What is the structure that forms as a result of this division and what is its role in airflow regulation?

Ans. The bronchioles are formed as a result of this division, and they regulate airflow through contraction and relaxation of smooth muscle.

Q.2 Name the tiny sac-like structure present inside the lungs. State their main function.

Ans. The tiny sac-like structures present inside the lungs are alveoli and their main function is the exchange of gases (oxygen and carbon dioxide) between the air and blood.

Q.3 State the condition of the following muscles during expiration.

(i) Diaphragm muscles

(ii) Internal intercostal muscles

Ans. (i) The diaphragm muscles are relaxed, making the diaphragm convex.

(ii) The internal intercostal muscles contract, pulling the ribs downward and inward during force expiration.

Q.4 In normal breathing, which process is active: inspiration or expiration? Explain.

Ans. In normal breathing, inspiration is an active process as it is brought about by the contraction of the diaphragm and external intercostal muscles. Expiration is a passive process, as it simply involves the relaxation of the inspiratory muscles.

Q.5 State the role played by cilia in the gaseous exchange.

Ans. The cilia in the air passages moves in a sweeping motion to keep the air passages clean.

The constant action of these cilia carry mucus and debris upward into the pharynx, where they are swollwed.

Q.6 Study the diagram below and answer the questions that follows.

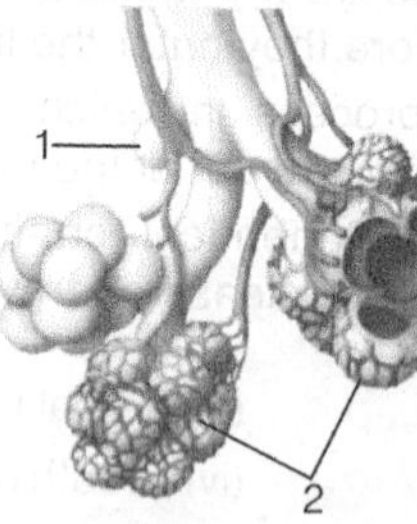

(i) Identify the structure and where it is found.

(ii) Label the parts marked as 1 and 2.

Ans. (i) The structure given is of a bronchiole with a alveolar sac. It is found in the lungs.

(ii) Part 1- Respiratory bronchioles

Part 2- Alveoli

Q.7 Observe the given diagram carefully and answer the following questions.

Name the process shown in the given diagram and identify the organs where this process occurs.

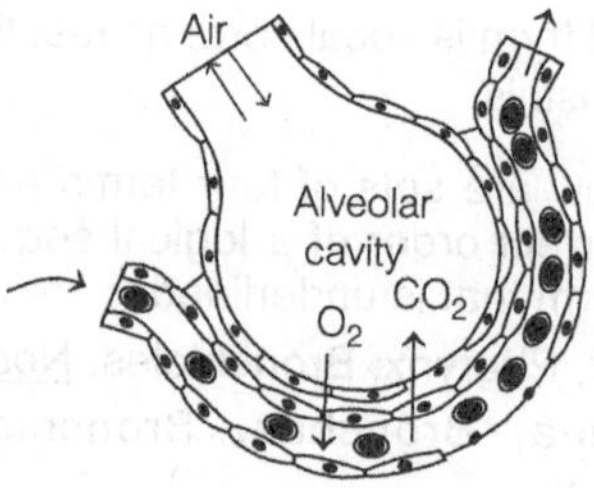

Ans. The process is gas exchange, which occurs in the alveoli of the lungs. Oxygen is transferred from the alveoli to the blood, while carbon dioxide is transferred from the blood to the alveoli to be exhaled.

Q.8 The blood carries gases to and from tissues. How is oxygen and carbon dioxide transported in the blood?

Ans. Oxygen is transported by 3% being dissolved in plasma and 97% binding to haemoglobin as oxyhaemoglobin.

Carbon dioxide is transported by 7% dissolved in plasma, 70% carried as bicarbonate ions (HCO_3^-) and 20-25% binding to haemoglobin as carbaminohaemoglobin.

Q.9 At higher altitudes, what causes mountain sickness and what are its common symptoms?

Ans. Mountain sickness occurs due to decreased atmospheric pressure and oxygen levels at higher altitudes, especially above 4500 metres. Common symptoms include fatigue, dizziness, nausea, loss of hearing and even complete blackouts.

TYPE - 6 — 03 Marks

Short Answer Type Questions

Q.1 How are the lungs designed in human beings to maximise the area for the exchange of gases?

Ans. The lungs contain balloon-like structures called alveoli, which provide a large surface area for gas exchange. The alveoli have very thin walls and are surrounded by an extensive network of blood vessels, facilitating efficient gas exchange.

Q.2 Write the role of the diaphragm and intercostal muscles in the inspiratory process.

Ans. The diaphragm and intercostal muscles (both external and internal) between the ribs help to generate a pressure gradient between the lungs and the atmosphere.

During inspiration, the diaphragm contracts and moves downward, becoming flat. The external intercostal muscles contract, pulling the ribs and sternum upward and outward.

This increases the volume of the thoracic cavity and decreases intrapulmonary pressure. The higher atmospheric pressure outside the body causes air to flow into the nasal passages, eventually reaching the alveoli, resulting in inspiration.

Q.3 For completion of respiration process, write the given steps in sequential manner.

(i) Diffusion of gases (O_2 and CO_2) across alveolar membrane.

(ii) Transport of gases by blood.

(iii) Utilisation of O_2 by the cells for catabolic reactions and resultant release of CO_2.

(iv) Pulmonary ventilation, by which atmospheric air is drawn in and CO_2 rich alveolar air is released out.

(v) Diffusion of O_2 and CO_2 between blood and tissues.

Ans. The steps in the process of respiration are as follows

(i) Pulmonary ventilation, by which atmospheric air is drawn in and CO_2 rich alveolar air is released out.

(ii) Diffusion of gases (O_2 and CO_2) across the alveolar membrane.

(iii) Transport of gases by blood.

(iv) Diffusion of O_2 and CO_2 between blood and tissues.

(v) Utilisation of O_2 by the cells for catabolic reactions and the resultant release of CO_2.

Q.4 State the differences between respiration in plants and respiration in animals.

Ans. The differences between respiration in plants and respiration in animals are as follows

Respiration in Plants	Respiration in Animals
Breathing does not take place in plants.	Breathing occurs in animals, except in some lower animals.
There is no transporting system for gases in plants; gases diffuses between cells.	Animals have a blood vascular system for the transportation of O_2 and CO_2.
Only a very small amount of detectable heat is produced during respiration in plants.	A considerable amount of detectable heat is produced during respiration in animals.
Plants have an additional source of oxygen from photosynthesis.	Animals rely on air as the source of oxygen.
The rate of respiration in plants is low.	The rate of respiration in animals is high.
CO_2 produced in plant respiration is utilised in photosynthesis.	CO_2 produced in animal respiration is released into atmosphere.

Q.5 Explain the following terms.

(i) Residual volume **(ii) Exhalation**

(iii) Asphyxia (suffocation)

Ans. (i) **Residual Volume** The amount of air remaining in the lungs after a forceful exhalation.

(ii) **Exhalation** The process of expelling air from the lungs, typically following inspiration.

(iii) **Asphyxia** (suffocation) A condition where the body is deprived of oxygen, leading to unconsciousness or death if not resolved.

TYPE - 7

03 Marks

Structured Based Questions

Q.1 The diagram shows human respiratory system front view.

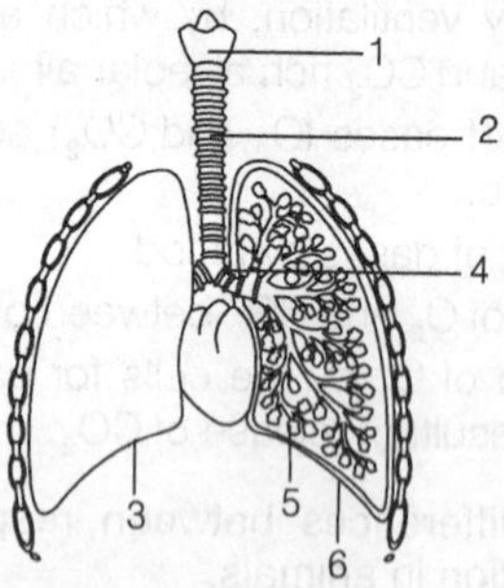

(i) Label the parts numbered 1 to 6.

(ii) Why are C-shaped cartilaginous rings present in the part labelled?

(iii) How many times does a man breathe per minute at rest?

Ans. (i) The parts numbered 1 to 6 are labelled as

1. Larynx 2. Trachea 3. Right lung 4. Bronchus
5. Alveoli 6. Left lung

(ii) Rings provide flexibility and keep the trachea distended permanently.

(iii) 12-14 times per minute at rest.

Q.2 Raman goes for mountain climbing with his friends. As they reach higher altitudes, he begins to feel dizziness. Observe the diagram and answer the following questions.

(i) What is the problem Raman is experiencing?

(ii) What are the other symptoms of this problem?

(iii) How can this problem be treated?

Ans. (i) Raman is experiencing altitude sickness or mountain sickness.

(ii) Other symptoms of altitude sickness include fatigue, nausea, loss of hear and even complete blackout.

(iii) This problem can be treated by descending to a lower altitude, resting, staying hydrated and in some cases, using oxygen supplementation or medication.

14

HEALTH AND HYGIENE

Health

It is a state of complete physical, mental and social well-being and not merely the absence of disease or infirmity. Thus, a healthy person is physically, mentally and socially sound.

Good health can be achieved and maintained through

- following a balanced diet, maintaining personal hygiene and engaging in regular exercise.
- practicing yoga for better physical and mental well-being.
- raising awareness about diseases and their impact on body functions.
- getting vaccinated to protect against infectious diseases.
- ensuring proper waste disposal, controlling disease-spreading vectors and keeping food and water resources clean and hygienic.

Hygiene

It is the science of maintaining and promoting good health to prevent diseases. This can be achieved at both personal and public levels by practicing personal hygiene and ensuring public hygiene.

Personal Hygiene

It is the practice of keeping oneself clean and maintaining healthy habits to prevent diseases. The major aspects of personal hygiene are as follows

- Eating food rich in all essential nutrients to support overall health.
- Keeping the body clean to prevent infections and diseases.
- Ensuring adequate sleep to rejuvenate the body and mind.
- Staying active to maintain fitness and improve bodily functions.
- Avoiding harmful practices like smoking or overeating and adopting a disciplined lifestyle.

Public Hygiene and Sanitation

- Personal health focuses on an individual's well-being, while public or community health involves maintaining and improving the well-being of the entire community. Since, humans live in communities, community health, including sanitation, directly impacts individual health. Factors affecting health are as follows
- Social environment
- Public cleanliness
- Personal hygiene
- Social equality and harmony
- Economic conditions

Measures for Maintaining Community Health

- Maintenance of proper sanitation, management of waste disposal and control of pollution.
- Prevention of diseases through vaccination, pest control and effective infection management.
- Educating people about diseases, addictions and healthy lifestyle practices.
- Providing healthcare services such as hospitals, community health centres and maternity care facilities.

Diseases

It is a condition that affects the normal function of the body or mind, often caused by infections or other factors.

Categories of Diseases

Diseases can be categorised in several ways, which are as follows

- **On the Basis of Mode of Transmission**
  - **Communicable/Infectious Diseases** The diseases that are easily transmitted from one person to another, e.g. influenza, tuberculosis, cholera, smallpox, malaria, etc.
  - **Non-communicable/Non-infectious Diseases** The diseases that cannot be transmitted from one person to another, e.g. cancer, colour blindness, heartattack, beri-beri, etc.
- **On the Basis of Extent of the Occurrence**
  - **Epidemic** When a disease affects large segment of a population in a specific time period at one place, it is said to be epidemic outbreak of a disease, e.g. plague spread in 1994 in India.
  - **Endemic** When a disease gets confined to a specific place and reoccurs again and again there only, it is endemic disease, e.g. goitre in hilly areas.
  - **Pandemic** When a disease affects the population on a global scale, e.g. COVID-19.
  - **Sporadic** When there is scattered individual cases of a disease, e.g. malaria and cholera.

Modes of Transmission of Communicable Diseases

Infectious diseases can spread through various means such as food, air, water and vectors.

- **Air-borne Diseases** These diseases are transmitted through the air when an infected person sneezes or coughs, releasing droplets containing microbes. Therefore, close proximity to an infected person or poor ventilation in crowded spaces increases the risk of infection. Some of the common examples of air-borne diseases are common cold, pneumonia and tuberculosis.
- **Water-borne Diseases** These diseases spread through contaminated water due to sewage, animal waste or improper sanitation. Industrial pollutants and excessive fluoride in water can also cause health issues. Cholera, typhoid and dysentery are examples of water-borne diseases.
- **Vector-borne Diseases** Vector is any agent that acts as an intermediate carrier of a pathogen. There are a number of organisms which spread diseases from diseased individuals to healthy ones.
  Few of them are as follows
  - **Houseflies** They spread a large number of diseases like **cholera**, **dysentery**, etc. Flies deposit germs of these diseases on the food materials and contaminate them.
  - **Cockroaches** These are serious pests as they are omnipresent and are omnivorous. They are suspected to be carriers of many diseases such as, cholera, amoebic dysentery and typhoid germs as they contaminate food materials.
  - **Mosquitoes** These are also serious vectors of many diseases such as malaria (*Anopheles*), dengue and yellow fever (*Aedes*), etc.

Control of Vectors

Methods for controlling vectors are as follows

- Food and drinking material should be covered properly.
- Garbage and refuse should be properly disposed off.
- Insect vectors can be killed and controlled by insecticides and pesticides.
- Rats can be killed by using rat killer, chemicals or can be trapped and disposed off.

Common Diseases in Humans

Some common diseases in humans are listed in the table below

Types of Diseases	Diseases	Symptoms	Measures to Control
Bacterial Diseases	Cholera	Watery stools, vomiting, abdominal pain, severe dehydration (lethal, especially in children).	Improve sanitation, clean drinking water, proper sewage disposal.
	Typhoid	Severe headache, fever rising in the afternoon and increasing over 7-8 days, slow pulse.	Vaccination, proper hygiene, clean water, sanitation.
	Tuberculosis (TB)	Loss of weight and appetite, weakness, lung infection (coughing with blood, chest pain), typical fever patterns, night sweats, swelling and pain in lymph glands.	Early detection, proper ventilation, treatment, immunisation by BCG.
Viral Diseases	AIDS	Periods of fever, diarrhoea, weight loss, decreased immunity, increased susceptibility to infections.	Safe sex practices, avoid sharing of needles.
	Chickenpox	Fever, aching muscles, loss of appetite, rashes/sports on the entire body.	Vaccination, avoid contact with infected individuals.
	Hepatitis	Jaundice (yellowing of skin/eyes), dark urine, nausea, diarrhoea, abnormal discomfort, fever, chills.	Vaccination, safe sex, avoid sharing needles, proper hygiene.
Protozoan Diseases	Malaria	Fever, chills, sweating headache, fatigue	Use bed nets and insect repellents, mosquito control, antimalarial drugs.
	Amoebic dysentery	Diarrhoea (often bloody), abdominal cramps, fever.	Safe drinking water, good sanitation, proper hygiene.
	Sleeping sickness	Fever, headache, joint pain, sleep disturbances.	Use of insecticides, control of tse-tse fly, early diagnosis.
Helminthic Diseases	Ascariasis	Abdominal pain, coughing malnutrition, worms in stool.	Proper sanitation hand, washing.
	Taeniasis	Abdominal pain, weight loss, visible worms in stool.	Cook meat thoroughly, proper sanitation.
	Filariasis	Swelling of limbs (elephantiasis), fever, pain.	Mosquito control, use of insecticide-treated nets, medication.

EXAM ORIENTED QUESTIONS

TYPE - 1 — 01 Mark

Multiple Choice Questions

Q.1 Human health can be maintained by

(a) balanced diet (b) personal hygiene
(c) regular exercise (d) All of these

Ans. (d)

Q.2 Among the following, which could be considered a unhealthy habit?

(a) Washing hands before eating food
(b) Keeping the mouth closed while breathing
(c) Sleeping for only 6-7 hours
(d) Sharing towels with others

Ans. (d)

Q.3 Which one of these is the aim of community health?

(a) Care of infants and the old
(b) Care of women
(c) Healthcare for all
(d) Care of pregnant women

Ans. (c)

Q.4 Among the following, a non-communicable disease is

(a) measles (b) rabies (c) diphtheria (d) diabetes

Ans. (d)

Q.5 Anvita tried to match the following diseases with their mode of transmission. She tabulated a pair as follows

Diseases	Modes of Transmission
P	Air borne
Q	Water borne

Choose the correct pair.

(a) *P* - Tuberculosis, *Q*- Cholera
(b) *P* - Influenza, *Q*- AIDS
(c) *P* - Malaria, *Q*- Dysentery
(d) *P* - Chickenpox, *Q*- Malaria

Ans. (a)

Q.6 Neha asked her students to give examples of vector-borne diseases.

Zoya said: Malaria and influenza
Akshay said: Malaria and beri-beri
Riva said: Malaria and dengue
Shreyas said: Malaria and cholera

Who gave the correct answer?

(a) Riva (b) Akshay (c) Zoya (d) Shreyas

Ans. (a)

Q.7 The control of vector-borne diseases involves various methods, such as .....*P*..... and .....*Q*..... which help to reduce the spread of diseases.

(a) *P* - use of insecticides, *Q*- proper waste disposal
(b) *P* - vector elimination, *Q*- vaccination programs
(c) *P* - spraying, *Q*- prevention of breeding sites
(d) *P* - education campaigns, *Q*- wearing protective clothing

Ans. (c)

Q.8 Which disease is caused by bacteria?

(a) AIDS (b) Cholera (c) Obesity (d) Scurvy

Ans. (b)

Q.9 What can be passed from one person to another during blood transfusion?

(a) Cholera
(b) Chronic Obstructive Pulmonary Disease (COPD)
(c) HIV
(d) Scurvy

Ans. (c)

Q.10 Amoebic dysentery can be spread by which of these?

(a) Rats (b) Cockroaches
(c) Mosquitoes (d) Houseflies

Ans. (d)

Q.11 Which of the following is a helminthic disease caused by parasitic worms?

(a) Malaria (b) Ascariasis
(c) Tuberculosis (d) Chickenpox

Ans. (b)

TYPE - 2 — 01 Mark

Matching Type Questions

Q.1 Match the following columns.

	Column I	Column II
A.	Sporadic disease	I. Plague
B.	Pandemic disease	II. Goitre
C.	Endemic disease	III. Malaria
D.	Epidemic disease	IV. COVID-19

Ans. A-III, B-IV, C-II, D-I

Q.2 Match the following diseases with their correct symptoms.

	Diseases		Symptoms
A.	Tuberculosis (TB)	I.	Severe diarrhoea, dehydration, vomiting
B.	AIDS	II.	Weak immune system, recurrent infections, weight loss
C.	Cholera	III.	Persistent cough, weight loss, night sweats, fever
D.	Typhoid	IV.	High fever, weakness, abdominal pain, constipation or diarrhoea

Ans. A-III, B-II, C-I, D-IV

TYPE - 3 01 Mark

Assertion-Reason Type Questions

Direction (Q. Nos. 1-5) In the following questions statements are given as Assertion (A) and Reason (R).

(a) A is true, but R is false.
(b) A is false, but R is true.
(c) Both A and R are true.
(d) Both A and R are false.

Q.1 Assertion (A) Practicing both personal and public hygiene is essential for preventing diseases.

Reason (R) Good health can be maintained by following personal hygiene practices and ensuring a clean and safe environment at the public level.

Ans. (c)

Q.2 Assertion (A) Personal cleanliness is a key aspect of hygiene.

Reason (R) Eating junk food daily can help the body stay strong and healthy.

Ans. (a) A is true, but R is false. R can be corrected as A balanced diet can help the body stay strong and healthy.

Q.3 Assertion (A) Sporadic diseases affect a small group of people over an entire country.

Reason (R) These diseases are always caused by viruses.

Ans. (d) Both A and R are false. These can be corrected as Sporadic diseases affect isolated or scattered cases, not large groups over an entire country. Sporadic diseases can be caused by various factors, including bacteria, fungi and other pathogens, not just viruses.

Q.4 Assertion (A) Non-communicable diseases can be transmitted from one person to another.

Reason (R) These diseases are mainly caused by lifestyle factors like diet, exercise and smoking.

Ans. (b) A is false, but R is true. A can be corrected as Non-communicable diseases cannot be transmitted from one person to another.

Q.5 Assertion (A) Tuberculosis (TB) can be spread through the air when an infected person coughs or sneezes.

Reason (R) Tuberculosis is caused by a virus that weakens the immune system.

Ans. (a) A is true, but R is false. R can be corrected as Tuberculosis is caused by a bacterium (*Mycobacterium tuberculosis*).

TYPE - 4 01 Mark

Very Short Answer Type Questions

Q.1 State any one method of maintaining good health.

Ans. Methods of maintaining good health are as follows

(i) Practicing yoga for better physical and mental well-being.
(ii) Raising awareness about diseases and their impact on body functions. (Any one)

Q.2 Name the process that involves the practice of maintaining clean environments and proper waste disposal to prevent the spread of diseases.

Ans. Sanitation

Q.3 Give any one unhealthy habit.

Ans. Sharing towels with others.

Q.4 What are the key methods for disease prevention?

Ans. Vaccination, pest control and managing infections.

Q.5 Name the type of disease which spread across the globe.

Ans. Pandemic disease

Q.6 Give any two examples of sporadic diseases.

Ans. Malaria and cholera are sporadic diseases.

Q.7 Name the type of disease which can easily spread from one person to another.

Ans. Infectious diseases.

Q.8 Give two examples of water borne diseases.

Ans. Cholera and dysentery.

Q.9 Name the mode of transmission of malaria.

Ans. Malaria is a vector borne disease.

Q.10 What are the symptoms of typhoid disease?

Ans. High fever, headache, weakness, abdominal pain and loss of appetite.

Q.11 *X* is a viral disease that weakens the immune system, causes weight loss and persistent fever. Name the disease.

Ans. AIDS

Q.12 Give two examples of helminthic diseases.

Ans. Ascariasis, filariasis.

Q.13 Filariasis is caused by mosquitoes. True or False.

Ans. False. This disease caused by parasitic worms that are spread by mosquitoes.

Q.14 Name the following. **(1 Mark each)**

(i) A state of complete physical, mental and social well-being and not merely absence of diseases.

(ii) The disease group which spreads from place to place affecting many people.

(iii) The disease which affects the population on a global scale.

(iv) Organisms that transmit microbes that cause disease.

(v) A disease that weakens body's defence system against infections.

Ans. (i) Health (ii) Epidemic diseases

(iii) Pandemic (iv) Vector

(v) AIDS

Q.15 Choose the odd one out from the following terms given below and name the category to which the other three belong. **(1 Mark each)**

(i) Typhoid, AIDS, Cholera, Tuberculosis

(ii) AIDS, Chickenpox, Malaria, Hepatitis

(iii) Malaria, Sleeping sickness, Amoebic dysentery, Ascariasis

Ans. (i) The odd term is AIDS, as it is caused by a virus, whereas the rest are diseases caused by bacteria.

(ii) The odd term is malaria, as it is caused by a protozoan, whereas the rest are diseases caused by viruses.

(iii) The odd term is ascariasis, as it is caused by a helminth (worm), whereas the rest are diseases caused by protozoans.

Q.16 Expand the following biological abbreviations. **(1 Mark each)**

(i) BCG (ii) AIDS

Ans. (i) Bacillus Calmette Guerin

(ii) Acquired Immuno Deficiency Syndrome

Q.17 Arrange and rewrite the terms in each group in the correct order so as to be in a logical sequence beginning with the term that is underlined. **(1 Mark each)**

(i) Sneeze, Droplets, Inhalation, Disease

(ii) Bacteria, Contaminated food, Ingestion, Food poisoning

Ans. (i) Sneeze, Droplets, Inhalation, Disease

(ii) Bacteria, Contaminated food, Ingestion, Food poisoning

Q.18 Give biological reasons for the following. **(1 Mark each)**

(i) One should breathe by nose and never by mouth.

(ii) Eating places must be kept free of flies.

Ans. (i) One should breathe by nose and never by mouth because nose contains hair and mucus to trap dust and microorganisms, so that the inhaled air becomes clean and the respiratory passage remains free of dust and microorganisms.

(ii) Flies are the carrier of many disease-causing germs and bacteria. Therefore, eating places must be kept free of flies to avoid possible contamination of food.

Q.19 Mention the year in which plaque become epidemic in India?

Ans. 1994

Q.20 Mention one difference in each of the following pairs on the basis of what is given in the bracket. **(1 Mark each)**

(i) Personal health and Community health (definition).

(ii) Infectious and Non-infectious diseases (definition).

Ans. (i)

Personal Health	Community Health
Personal health refers to the well being of an individual.	Community health refers to maintaining and improving the health of an entire community.

(ii)

Infectious Diseases	Non-infectious Diseases
Infectious diseases refers to those that spread from one person to another through pathogens.	Non-infectious diseases refers to those that do not spread and are caused by genetic, nutritional or environmental factors.

21. Fill the blank spaces with correct words.

Food should never be left uncovered as exposure can lead to contamination from pests such as houseflies, rats and cockroaches, which can carry harmful pathogens. **(1 Mark each)**

When food is .....(i)..... by harmful organisms, it can lead to various health issues such as food poisoning, stomach infections and diseases such as cholera, typhoid. Cholera causes severe vomiting, abdominal cramps and dehydration. Typhoid is characterised by .....(ii)....., weakness, stomach pain, headache and loss of appetite. Dysentery results in diarrhoea with .....(iii)..... or mucus, along with abdominal pain and fever. These diseases spread through poor .....(iv)..... and contaminated food, making it crucial to keep food .....(v)..... and maintain proper sanitation to prevent contamination.

Ans. (i) contaminated (ii) high fever (iii) blood (iv) hygiene (v) covered

TYPE - 5

02 Marks

Short Answer Type Questions

Q.1 What are the significances of good health?

Ans. The significances of good health are as follows

(i) It makes our life joyful.

(ii) It increases our working efficiency and helps us to do various activities at our best.

(iii) It helps us to cope with social and mental pressure without much difficulty.

Q.2 What are the key measures for maintaining community health?

Ans. Key measures for maintaining community health are as follows

(i) **Cleanliness** Maintain proper sanitation, manage waste disposal, ensure safe drinking water and control pollution.

(ii) **Disease Prevention** Prevent diseases through vaccination, pest control and effective infection management.

(iii) **Health Education** Educate people about diseases, addictions and healthy lifestyle practices.

(iv) **Healthcare Services** Provide healthcare services such as hospitals, community health centres and maternity care facilities.

Q.3 Classify the following diseases into communicable or non-communicable.

Cholera, Plaque, Malaria, Colour blindness, Cancer, Heart attack, Hepatitis, Beri-beri.

Ans.

Communicable Diseases	Non-communicable Diseases
Cholera	Colour blindness
Plaque	Cancer
Malaria	Heart attack
Hepatitis	Beri-beri

Q.4 What is a disease and how are diseases classified based on their extent of occurrence?

Ans. A disease is a condition that disrupts normal body functions, leading to discomfort or impaired health. Based on the extent of occurrence, diseases are classified into four types

(i) Epidemic (ii) Endemic (iii) Pandemic (iv) Sporadic

Q.5 What are communicable diseases, give two examples of it?

Ans. These diseases spread from one person to another through direct contact, air, water or vectors, e.g. tuberculosis, influenza.

Q.6 Explain air-borne diseases in brief and give examples of it.

Ans. Air-borne diseases are transmitted through the air when an infected person sneezes or coughs, releasing droplets containing microbes. Diseases like the common cold, pneumonia and tuberculosis are air borne in nature.

Q.7 What are the measures to prevent the water-borne diseases?

Ans. To prevent water-borne diseases, water bodies, ponds, water tanks reservoirs in the city or village should be cleaned periodically.

The proper disposal of house wastes, excreta, sewage should be done. At personal level, boiling of water, using aquaguard, washing hands before meals should be practiced.

Q.8 What are the methods for controlling vectors to prevent the spread of diseases?

Ans. The methods for controlling vectors to prevent the spread of diseases are as follows.

(i) Properly cover food and drinking water.

(ii) Dispose of garbage and refuse properly.

(iii) Use insecticides and pesticides to control insects.

(iv) Eliminate rats using chemicals or traps.

Q.9 Write two symptoms of tuberculosis.

Ans. The two symptoms of tuberculosis are as follows

(i) Persistent cough with sputum, sometimes containing blood.

(ii) Loss of appetite and weight.

Q.10 State the action mechanism of HIV virus.

Ans. The HIV virus attacks the cell of the immune system and causes a marked reduction in the T-cell of the thymus.

Q.11 Give one example of the following.

(i) A helminthic disease (ii) A viral disease

Ans. (i) Filariasis (ii) Hepatitis

Q.12 Explain the following terms.

(i) Hygiene (ii) Disease carrier

Ans. (i) Hygiene is defined as living conditions or practices performed by an individual or public for maintaining health and thus prevents the appearance of disease.

(ii) An organism which harbours the germs of the diseases is called disease carrier.

TYPE - 6 03 Marks

Short Answer Type Questions

Q.1 List any three methods of maintaining personal hygiene.

Ans. Common methods of maintaining personal hygiene are as follows

(i) **Taking a Nutritious Balanced Diet** Eating food rich in all essential nutrients to support overall health.

(ii) **Personal Cleanliness** Keeping the body clean to prevent infections and diseases.

(iii) **Moderate Physical Exercise** Staying active to maintain fitness and improve bodily functions.

Q.2 Write three measures for public hygiene.

Ans. Measures for public hygiene are as follows

(i) Proper disposal of wastes and excreta.

(ii) Cleaning and disinfection of pools, water tanks and other water reservoirs.

(iii) Hygienic practices should be adopted at restaurants and hotels.

Q.3 What are the immediate and the contributory causes of diseases?

Ans. (i) Immediate causes of diseases are various microorganisms like viruses, bacteria, fungi, etc.

(ii) Contributory causes of diseases are as follows

(a) poor health due to inadequate diet.

(b) genetic disorders.

(c) improper functioning of body organ.

Q.4 Write preventive measures for vector-borne diseases.

Ans. Preventive measures for vector-borne diseases are

(i) Breeding places of vector should be eliminated.

(ii) Stagnation of water should be avoided to control the breeding of mosquitoes.

(iii) Use of mosquito repellents, nets and wire mesh on doors and windows.

Q.5 Answer the following questions briefly.

(i) What are the dimensions of health according to World Health Organisation (WHO)?

(ii) Write two methods to maintain community health.

(iii) Give the methods of transmission of AIDS.

Ans. (i) According to WHO, a healthy person should be physically, mentally and socially healthy.

(ii) Two methods to maintain community health are as follows

(a) Public cleanliness (b) Health education

(iii) AIDS can be transmitted by following methods

(a) Sexual intercourse with infected person.

(b) Contaminated blood transfusion.

(c) Sharing of infected needles.

(d) From infected mother to her child through placenta. (Any two)

Q.6 Answer the following questions.

(i) State any condition essential for good health.

(ii) What are the different ways by which disease can be spread?

(iii) How can good health be achieved?

Ans. (i) Better sanitation and clean environment are essential for good health.

(ii) Diseases can be spread by different ways such as through air, water and vectors.

(iii) Good health can be achieved by balanced diet, personal hygiene and regular exercise.

TYPE - 7 03 Marks

Structured Based Questions

Q.1 Observe the figure given below and answer the following questions.

(i) What is the common cause of the disease shown in the figure?

(ii) Give two preventive measures for this disease.

(iii) How does this disease spreads?

Ans. (i) The common cause of the disease shown in the figure is the rhinovirus, which causes the common cold.

(ii) Two preventive measures for the common cold are

(a) Washing hands regularly.

(b) Avoiding close contact with infected individuals.

(iii) This disease spreads through air borne droplets or direct contact.

Q.2 The given figure shows the legs of a patient. Study the figure and answer the questions that follows.

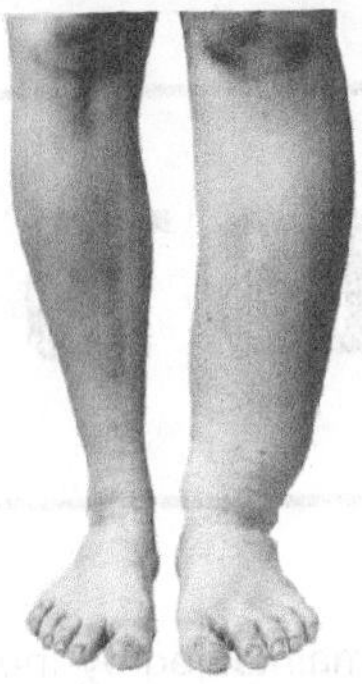

(i) What disease is the patient suffering from?

(ii) How can this disease be prevented?

(iii) What are the symptoms of this disease?

Ans. (i) The patient is suffering from filariasis/elephantiasis.

(ii) Prevention involves protection from mosquito bites.

(iii) Symptoms of the disease include

(a) Blockage of lymph nodes in the limbs.

(b) Swelling of scrotal sacs and other body parts.

Q.3 Given below is the figure of a vector. Study this and answer the questions that follows.

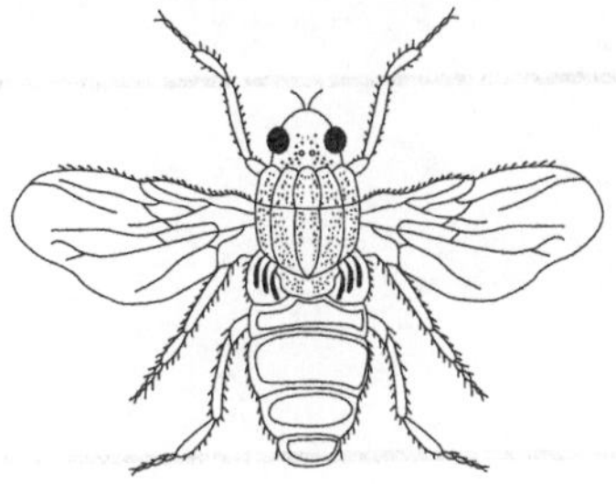

(i) Name the organism.

(ii) Give one example of the disease spread by this.

(iii) How does it spread disease?

Ans. (i) The organism is housefly.

(ii) The diseases spread by this are cholera.

(iii) Housefly sits on the garbage, faecal wastes, sewage, etc., and the disease causing germs stick to their legs. After that when it sits on eatables, germs are transmitted to food items which then enter into the body of man and cause diseases.

AIDS TO HEALTH

Health is a state of complete physical, mental and social well-being. It is maintained by the efficient working of the immune or defence system of the body.

Defence System

It refers to the various mechanism and structures that protect the body from harmful pathogens, toxins and foreign substances. Defence system in our body works in two ways as given below; local defence and immune defence.

Local Defence System

It acts as a type of barrier system to fight with germs/ pathogens at their entry points. This system includes

- **Physical Barriers** These barriers are first line of defence for our body. These are as follows
  - **Skin** It prevents the entry of pathogens into the body (which can enter either through cuts or injury on the skin) by its outer tough layer.
  - **Hair** It interferes with the entry of germ's into the skin, such as the hair inside the nostrils which helps to trap dust.
  - **Mucus** It is the slimy secretion of epithelial lining of various organs that prevents the entry of germs inside the body, e.g. mucus secreted in nasal passage, windpipe, etc.
- **Germ-killing Secretions** Different body parts secrete several secretions in order to prevent the entry of germs/pathogens, e.g. **saliva** (in mouth), **sweat** (on skin), **tears** (in eyes) and **nasal secretions** (in nostrils).
- **Hydrochloric acid** (HCl) secreted by stomach kills germs that gain entry along with the food.
- **Coughing, Sneezing and Vomiting** These are the intense body responses to directly throw out the pathogen or foreign substances entering the body and interfering with the normal respiratory and digestive system.
- **Germ-fighting White Blood Cells** (WBCs) They have the ability to fight with the germs/foreign substances by engulfing them through the process of **phagocytosis**.

Merits of Local Defence System

Local defence system possesses the following merits

- It starts working instantaneously.
- It is not dependent on the previous exposure of infections.
- It is effective against almost all types of infectious agents.

Immune System

- The ability of a person to resist or defend itself from the development of disease due to the entry of foreign organism is called **immunity**.
- It develops when the local defence system fails or is ineffective due to the poisonous secretions (toxins) of certain microbes entering the deeper tissues and various organ systems.
- In response, the body fluids such as blood starts fighting against the germs and **antigens**. Blood secretes **antibodies** and **antitoxins** to destroy harmful germs.

> - **Antigens** These are foreign substances that have the ability to elicit immune responses.
> - **Antibodies** These are special chemicals or serum proteins found in blood which are produced in response to specific antigens or their secretions.

Types of Immunity

Immunity is classified into two main types as follows

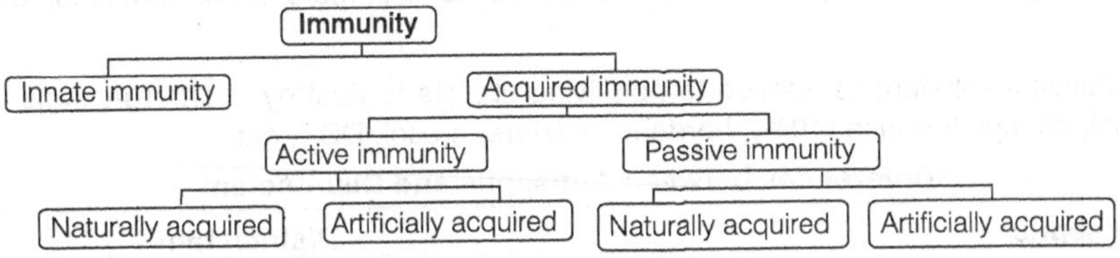

(i) Innate Immunity

- The immunity inherited by organisms from parents since birth, also known as **natural** or **inborn immunity**.
- It is also called **non-specific immunity** because it does not differentiate between different type of pathogens. It consists of various types of barriers (skin, mucous membrane, etc.) that prevent the entry of foreign agents.

(ii) Acquired Immunity

- The immunity acquired by an individual after birth, i.e. during its lifetime when he/she gets exposed to certain microorganisms.
- Acquired immunity can be of two main types
- **Active Acquired Immunity** The immunity developed within an individual due to encounter with previous infection or antigen. It is further divided into two types
  - **Naturally Acquired Active Immunity** Natural infection by a pathogen generates antibodies and specialised lymphocytes.
  - **Artificially Acquired Active Immunity** Vaccines are administered to the body which generates antibodies and specialised lymphocytes.
- **Passive Acquired Immunity** The immunity provided to an individual from an outside source in the form of readymade antibodies, e.g. antibodies provided in case of rabies and snake bite, antibodies received by foetus from mother through placenta and antibodies received by infant through milk.
  Passively acquired immunity is also of two types
  - **Naturally Acquired Passive Immunity** Antibodies that passively pass from mother to foetus *via* placenta and mother to infant *via* milk.
  - **Artificially Acquired Passive Immunity** Antibodies formed within other organisms, are introduced into the patient's body through injection for defensive purpose against the pathogen.

Other Methods of Defence Against Microorganisms

Immunisation

- It is the process that makes an individual immune to a specific disease.
- It can occur naturally, when the body gains immunity after exposure to a pathogen, or artificially, through vaccines that stimulate the immune system to fight future infections without causing the disease.

Vaccination

- It is the practise of injecting dead or weakened pathogens into the living body in order to develop resistance (immunity) against a particular disease without infection.
- The substance (antibody provoking agent) which is introduced into the body is called **vaccine**. It induces the formation of certain specific antibodies.
- Vaccine can either be given **orally** (e.g. polio vaccine) or in the form of **injections**, e.g. TAB vaccine (for typhoid), Salk's vaccine (for poliomyelitis).

Antibiotics

- These are chemical substances secreted by microorganisms and used against other pathogens in order to kill or prevent their growth inside the body, e.g. penicillin (first antibiotic that was discovered by **Alexander Fleming in 1929** from a fungi *Penicillium notatum*), streptomycin, chloromycin, ampicillin, etc.
- Now-a-days, they can be produced synthetically. These are primarily used as a medicine.
- Certain antibiotics also act as food preservatives, used in treating animal infections and to control plant diseases.

Antiseptics

These are mild chemical substances used to kill germs. These are applied to the living tissue/skin to reduce the possibility of infection, e.g. carbolic acid, iodine, boric acid, benzoic acid, mercurochrome, lysol, etc.

Disinfectants

These are strong chemical substances applied to non-living objects to destroy microorganisms which are living on them., e.g. lime, lysol, phenol, formalin (40%), bordeaux mixture, cresol, DDT, etc.

Differences between Antiseptic and Disinfectant

Antiseptic	Disinfectant
It is applied on the body to kill germs.	It is applied on non-living objects and places where germs can grow and multiply.
It is a mild treatment.	It is a strong treatment.
It does not cause any harm to the body, e.g. iodine.	It causes harm to the body, e.g. bordeaux mixture.

Antitoxins

These are the chemical substances produced inside the body in response to the entry of foreign poisonous substance or toxins to neutralise its effect, e.g. antivenoms for snake bite is produced inside host.

Serum

- It is an antitoxin rich blood preparation (blood plasma) used against a specific disease. Serum can be injected into the body of a patient against a specific disease for which it is prepared.
- The antibodies present in the serum neutralise the antigens and the patient begins to recover. Serum helps in providing passive immunity.

Health Organisations

- Organisations that make programmes for the maintenance of public health are known as **health organisations**.
- These are divided into three main categories, i.e. **local bodies**, **national organisations** and **international organisation.**

1. World Health Organisation (WHO)

It is a special agency of **United Nations Organisation** (UNO) which was established in 1948.
Its headquarter is situated in **Geneva**. **194 member** states, are a part of this organisation.

WHO : Emblem

The main activities of WHO are as follows

- To promote and support projects for research on diseases such as cancer.
- To collect and supply information about diseases of epidemic nature, such as plague, ebola, etc.
- To supply information about the latest developments related to the use of vaccines.
- To organise campaigns for controlling the spread of various **epidemic** (widespread) and **endemic** (local) **diseases**.
- To suggest quarantine measures (isolation of patients) to prevent the spread of disease to others.
- To lay pharmaceutical standards for important drugs to ensure purity and size of the doses.

2. Red Cross

It is an organisation that was formed with the original purpose of providing medical help to wounded soldiers. It is a national as well as an international agency. It was later extended to include the alleviation and prevention of human suffering in both peace and war. Red Cross Day is celebrated on **8th May**.

The activities of the Red Cross are as follows

- Care and treatment of soldiers wounded in war.
- Providing relief to victims of natural calamities like earthquakes, famine, floods, etc., through procurement and supply of food, medicines, etc., to needy people.
- Providing ambulance services, arranging blood through voluntary donations, etc., for people and supplying the same to hospitals.
- Looking after maternity and child welfare centres.
- Training of midwives, etc.
- Educating people in road safety.

Red Cross : Emblem

EXAM ORIENTED QUESTIONS

TYPE - 1
01 Mark

Multiple Choice Questions

Q.1 Which of the following statement is true for health?
(a) A state of complete physical well-being
(b) A state of complete mental well-being
(c) A state of complete social well-being
(d) All of the above

Ans. (d)

Q.2 Foreign invaders which affect our health badly, include
(a) bacteria (b) fungi
(c) viruses (d) All of these

Ans. (d)

Q.3 .....*P*..... and .....*Q*..... acts as germ killing secretions in the body, to prevent the entry of germs.
(a) *P*-Mucus, *Q*-saliva (b) *P*-Tears, *Q*-sweat
(c) *P*-WBCs, *Q*-HCl (d) *P*-HCl, *Q*-WBCs

Ans. (b)

Q.4 Which part of a pathogen is recognised by the immune system? **(CIE IGCSE Biology)**
(a) Active site (b) Antibiotic
(c) Antibody (d) Antigen

Ans. (d)

Q.5 Which of the following cells show phagocytosis?
(a) White blood cells (b) Red blood cells
(c) Hormones (d) None of these

Ans. (a)

Q.6 Which of the following is correct for passive immunity?
(a) It is received from outside
(b) Provides effective protection
(c) It has no side effects
(d) It is induced by immunogens or by infection

Ans. (a)

Q.7 Priya tried to match the type of immunity with its example. She tabulated the pairs as follows

Types of Immunity	Examples
P	Skin acting as a physical barrier.
Q	Recovering from chickenpox.

Identify the correct pair.
(a) *P*- Innate, *Q*- Acquired (b) *P*- Innate, *Q*- Innate
(c) *P*- Acquired, *Q*- Innate (d) *P*- Acquired, *Q*- Acquired

Ans. (a)

Q.8 The antibiotic penicillin is obtained from
(a) protozoan (b) bacteria
(c) virus (d) fungus

Ans. (d)

Q.9 Introduction of dead or weak pathogens into the body is called
(a) antitoxin (b) vaccination
(c) sterilisation (d) immunisation

Ans. (b)

Q.10 What happens when a child is vaccinated against tuberculosis? **(CIE IGCSE Biology)**

	Types of Immunity	Production of Memory Cells
(a)	Active	No
(b)	Active	Yes
(c)	Passive	No
(d)	Passive	Yes

Ans. (b) Active immunity occurs when a person produces their own antibodies and memory cells, providing long-lasting protection. It develops through vaccination with weakened pathogens.

Q.11 The antibodies that give immunity to a disease can be acquired in the following different ways. **(CIE IGCSE Biology)**
I. Feeding on breast milk
II. Infection by disease
III. Vaccination

Which give active immunity?
(a) I and II (b) I and III
(c) II and III (d) I, II and III

Ans. (c) Active immunity develops when a person produces their own antibodies and memory cells, lasting for years. It occurs through infection or vaccination with weakened pathogens. Passive immunity is acquired from another organism's antibodies, such as through breastfeeding or antibody injections. It is short-lived as no memory cells are formed.

Q.12 Which row describes the features of passive immunity? **(CIE IGCSE Biology)**

	Antibodies Made	Involves Memory Cells	Effective Period
(a)	No	No	Short term
(b)	No	Yes	Short term
(c)	Yes	No	Long term
(d)	Yes	Yes	Long term

Ans. (a)

Q.13 A biology teacher asked her students to give two examples of the disinfectants.

Sunny said: Lime and lysol

Aabha said: Cresol and DDT

Zoya said : Benzoic acid and mercurochrome

Uma said : Carbolic acid and boric acid

Who were correct ?

(a) Sunny and Aabha (b) Aabha and Zoya

(c) Zoya and Uma (d) Sunny and Uma

Ans. (a)

Q.14 During a biology lecture, the teacher displayed the emblem of WHO and asked one main activity of this organisation.

(a) Educating people in road safety

(b) Looking after maternity and child welfare centers

(c) Care and treatment of soldiers wounded in war

(d) Promote and support projects for research on disease

Ans. (d)

TYPE - 2 01 Mark

Matching Type Questions

Q.1 Match the following columns.

Column I	Column II
A. Penicillin	I. Bordeaux
B. Antiseptic	II. Alexander Fleming
C. Disinfectant	III. BCG
D. Vaccine	IV. Boric acid

Ans. A-II, B-IV, C-I, D-III

Q.2 Match the following columns.

Column I	Column II
A. Toxin	I. Phagocytosis
B. Slimy secretion	II. Passive immunity
C. WBCs	III. Snake venom
D. Serum	IV. Mucus

Ans. A-III, B-IV, C-I, D-II

Q.3 Match the following columns.

Column I	Column II
A. BCG	I. Ensure purity of doses
B. Chloromycin	II. Colourless fluid
C. Iodine	III. Antiseptic
D. WHO	IV. Tuberculosis
E. Serum	V. Antibiotics
	VI. Antigen

Ans. A-IV, B-V, C-III, D-I, E-II

TYPE - 3 01 Mark

Assertion-Reason Type Questions

Direction (Q. Nos. 1-4) In the following questions statements are given as Assertion (A) and Reason (R).

(a) A is true, but R is false.

(b) A is false, but R is true.

(c) Both A and R are true.

(d) Both A and R are false.

Q.1 Assertion (A) Mucus in the respiratory tract prevents the entry of germs into the body.

Reason (R) Mucus traps dust particles and pathogens, preventing them from reaching the lungs.

Ans. (c)

Q.2 Assertion (A) Vaccines provide passive immunity to the body.

Reason (R) Vaccines introduce weakened or dead pathogens that stimulate the body to produce antibodies.

Ans. (b) A is false, but R is true. A can be corrected as Vaccines provide active immunity to the body.

Q.3 Assertion (A) Antitoxins are effective in treating snake bites.

Reason (R) Antitoxins stimulate the production of antibodies in the body to neutralise the venom.

Ans. (a) A is true, but R is false. R can be corrected as Antitoxins are effective in treating snake bites because they are pre-formed antibodies that directly neutralise the venom.

Q.4 Assertion (A) The Red Cross organisation provides relief during natural calamities.

Reason (R) The primary function of the Red Cross is to establish international standards for pharmaceuticals.

Ans. (a) A is true, but R is false. R can be corrected as The Red Cross organisation provides relief during natural calamities by offering food, medicines and other aid.

TYPE - 4 — 01 Mark

Very Short Answer Type Questions

Q.1 Name any two physical barriers.

Ans. Skin and hair.

Q.2 Name the process by which a cell engulf the foreign particels.

Ans. Phagocytosis

Q.3 What role do antibodies play in immunity?

Ans. Antibodies are proteins produced by the immune system in response to antigens. They recognise and neutralise foreign substances, such as bacteria or viruses, to protect the body from infection.

Q.4 What is the difference between vaccination and immunisation?

Ans. Vaccination is the process of introducing a vaccine into the body, while immunisation is the overall process by which the body gains immunity, which can result from vaccination or natural exposure.

Q.5 What is the role of antibiotics in medicine?

Ans. Antibiotics are used to treat bacterial infections by either killing the bacteria or inhibiting their growth.

Q.6 Which type of immunity does serum provide to the body?

Ans. Serum provides **passive immunity** to the body, as it contains antibodies that are directly introduced into the bloodstream to help fight infections.

Q.7 Which health organisation coordinates international health efforts and sets global health standards?

Ans. The World Health Organisation (WHO) coordinates international health efforts and sets global health standards.

Q.8 Name the following. **(1 Mark each)**

(i) Barrier that prevents entry of pathogens into the body by its outer tough layer.

(ii) Immunity acquired after the first attack of the disease.

(iii) Immunity received from outside that is short-lived and provides less protection.

(iv) Immunity effective only after a certain time gap.

(v) Immunity provided by the mother to a growing foetus.

(vi) Organisation that directs and coordinates authority on international health work and promotes technical cooperation.

(vii) Organisation that looks after maternal and child welfare centres.

Ans. (i) Skin

(ii) Natural immunity

(iii) Passive immunity

(iv) Active immunity

(v) Naturally acquired passive immunity

(vi) WHO (World Health Organisation)

(vii) Red Cross

Q.9 Choose the odd one out from the following terms given below and name the category to which the other three belong. **(1 Mark each)**

(i) Skin, Saliva, Hair, Mucus

(ii) Iodine, Boric acid, Phenol, Benzoic acid

(iii) Lysol, Mercurochrome, Lime, Bordeaux mixture

Ans. (i) The odd term is saliva because it is a germ killing secretion, while the rest skin, hair and mucus act as physical barriers to defend the body against diseases and infections.

(ii) The odd term is phenol because it is a disinfectant, while the rest iodine, boric acid and benzoic acid are antiseptics used to kill germs.

(iii) The odd term is mercurochrome because it is a antiseptic, while the rest lysol, lime and bordeaux mixture are disinfectants.

Q.10 Arrange and rewrite the terms in each group in the correct order, so as to be in a logical sequences beginning with the term that is underlined. **(1 Mark each)**

(i) <u>Bacteria</u>, WBCs attack, Phagocytosis, Skin

(ii) Phagocytosis, <u>Pathogen</u>, WBCs, Blood

(iii) <u>Antigen</u>, Immunity, Vaccine, Antibodies production

Ans. (i) Bacteria, Skin, WBCs attack, Phagocytosis.

(ii) Pathogens, Blood, WBCs, Phagocytosis

(iii) Antigen, Vaccine, Antibodies production, Immunity

Q.11 Mention one difference in each of the following pairs on the basis of what is given in the bracket. **(1 Mark each)**

(i) Active and Passive immunity (effect)

(ii) Antibiotic and Antibody (source)

Ans. (i)

Active Immunity	Passive Immunity
It is effective and long lasting.	It is less effective and short-lived.

(ii)

Antibiotic	Antibody
It is secreted by microorganism.	It is found in blood of organism.

12. Read the information below the diagram and fill in the blank spaces.

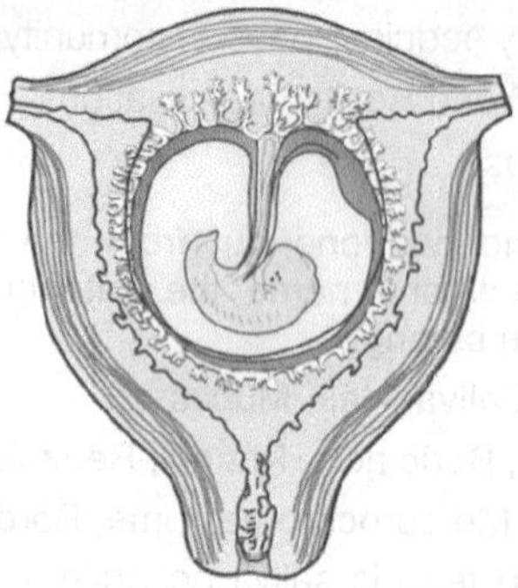

Passive immunity provided through the maternal placenta occurs when antibodies from the mother are transferred to the foetus during pregnancy. These antibodies help to protect the newborn from infections during the early months of life before their immune system matures. **(1 Mark each)**

Passive immunity is a type of immunity where the body receives .....(i)..... antibodies from an external source, rather than producing them itself. It provides .....(ii) ..... protection against diseases. Since, the body does not actively produce these antibodies, the immunity lasts for a .....(iii)..... period. Passive immunity can be further classified into two types, i.e. .....(iv)....., which occurs naturally and .....(v)..... which is acquired through medical treatments.

Ans. (i) pre-formed

(ii) temporary

(iii) limited

(iv) natural passive immunity

(v) artificial passive immunity

TYPE - 5   02 Marks

Short Answer Type Questions

Q.1 Write any two merits of the local defence system.

Ans. Two merits of the local defence system are as follows

(i) It starts working instantaneously.

(ii) It is not dependent on previous exposure to infections.

Q.2 Give biological reasons for the following.

(i) We sneeze whenever we inhale any kind of dust particle along with the air that we breathe.

(ii) WBCs defend the body against various infections and diseases.

Ans. (i) Sneezing is the intense body response to directly throw out the dust particle or any foreign substance inhaled that interferes with normal respiration.

(ii) WBCs have the ability to fight with the germs or foreign substances by engulfing them through the process of phagocytosis. Thus, providing defence against infections and diseases.

Q.3 How is immunity classified?

Ans. Immunity is classified into two main types

(i) **Innate Immunity** It is present since birth.

(ii) **Acquired Immunity** It is acquired by an individual during their lifetime.

Q.4 State the main function of the following.

(i) Mucus

(ii) Antigens

Ans. (i) Mucus is the slimy secretion of epithelial lining of various organs that prevents the entry of germs inside the body.

(ii) Antigens are foreign substances which are capable of eliciting immune response.

Q.5 Write the names of any four defence methods against microorganisms.

Ans. The four methods of defence are as follows

(i) Vaccination

(ii) Antibiotics

(iii) Antitoxins

(iv) Antiseptics

Q.6 Briefly explain the following terms

(i) Antiseptics   (ii) Disinfectants

Ans. (i) **Antiseptics** are the chemical substances that are applied to living tissues or skin to reduce or prevent the growth of harmful microorganisms, thereby preventing infections, e.g. Boric acid, iodine.

(ii) **Disinfectants** are the chemical substances that are used on non-living surfaces, like floors or equipment, to kill or inhibit the growth of harmful microorganisms. They are generally more concentrated and stronger than antiseptics, e.g. bleach, formaldehyde.

Q.7 Answer the following questions briefly.

(i) How are vaccines supplied to an individual's body?

(ii) When was World Health Organisation (WHO) established?

Ans. (i) Vaccines can either be given orally (e.g. polio vaccine) or in the form of injections, e.g. TAB vaccine.

(ii) WHO is special agency of **United Nations Organisation** (UNO) which was established in 1948.

Q.8 Identify the given figure of the organisation below and write one main activity of this organisation.

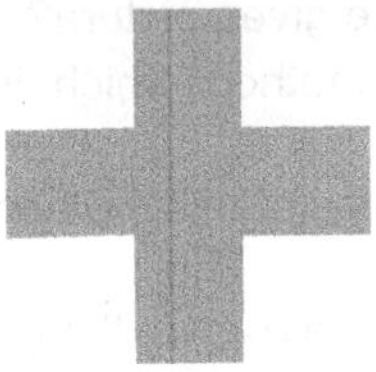

Ans. The figure is the emblem of the Red Cross. One main activity of the Red Cross is providing relief to victims of natural calamities such as floods, earthquakes and famines.

TYPE - 6 — 03 Marks

Short Answer Type Questions

Q.1 What are the various parts and secretions of the body that constitute the first line of defence?

Ans. The following parts and secretions of the body constitute the first line of defence

(i) **Skin** It secretes sweat to prevent the entry of germs/pathogens.

(ii) **Nasal Secretions** These prevent the entry of foreign substances in the nasal passage.

(iii) **Earwax** It has the ability to kill germs.

Q.2 Our body is invaded by various harmful pathogens, but most of the time we remain healthy due to the presence of the body's own defence system.

(i) Name any two secretions which prevent the entry of germs into the body.

(ii) Name the two secretions from blood that destroy harmful germs.

(iii) Which type of immunity does not show any side effects?

Ans. (i) Tears (in eyes) and nasal secretion (nostrils) prevent the entry of germs into the body.

(ii) Antibody and antitoxin secretions from blood can destroy harmful germs.

(iii) Active immunity does not show any side effects.

Q.3 Give one example of the following.

(i) Passive acquired immunity

(ii) Oral vaccine

(iii) A disinfectant

Ans. (i) Antibodies provided in case of snake bite.

(ii) Oral polio vaccine (for polio)

(iii) Formalin (40%)

Q.4 Mention three uses of antibiotics.

Ans. The three uses of antibiotics are as follows

(i) They are used to fight infections.

(ii) Certain antibiotics are used as food preservatives, especially fresh meat and fish.

(iii) Some are used to control plant pathogens.

Q.5 Write three major functions of WHO.

Ans. Three major functions of WHO are

(i) It assists countries in improving health and sanitation services.

(ii) It promotes medical education and training.

(iii) It regulates quarantine measures to prevent the spread of disease to unaffected areas.

TYPE - 7 — 03 Marks

Structured Based Questions

Q.1 Study the given diagram and answer the questions that follows

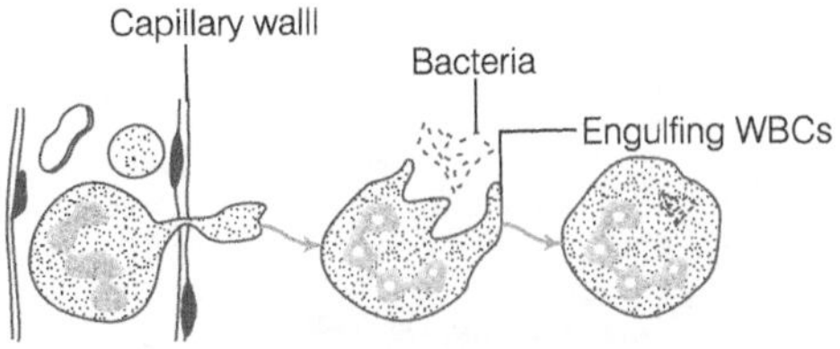

(i) Identify the process shows.

(ii) State the role played by leucocytes.

(iii) Give any one merit of local defence system.

Ans. (i) Phagocytosis

(ii) Leucocytes or WBC's takes part in the body defence system. This is because they have the ability to fight with the germ foreign substances by engulfing them through the process of **phagocytosis**.

(iii) The local defence system is advantageous as it is effective against almost all types of infectious agents.

Q.2 Observe the picture and answer the questions given below.

(i) Which type of immunity is provided in such cases?

(ii) Mention two characteristics of this type of immunity.

(iii) Give two more examples of this type of immunity.

Ans. (i) Passive immunity will be provided in this case.

(ii) Two characteristics of passive immunity are as follows

- It is temporary, as the immunity is provided through an external source, such as antibodies from another organism.
- The body does not produce its own antibodies; they are transferred from another individual or organism.

(iii) Two more examples of passive immunity are as follows

- Antibodies passed from mother to foetus through the placenta.
- Antibodies administered *via* serum to treat diseases like rabies or snake bites.

Q.3 Maintaining a sterile environment in labs is essential to prevent microbial contamination, which can interfere with experiments, alter results and pose health risks. Sterilisation ensures controlled, pathogen-free conditions.

(i) Which method of defence against microorganism is used in the given picture?

(ii) Define the method which is used in the given picture.

(iii) Give examples of this method of defence against microscopes.

Ans. (i) Disinfectants are used in the given picture.

(ii) These are strong chemical substances applied to non-living objects to destroy microorganisms living on them.

(iii) Examples. lime, lysol, phenol, formalin (40%), bordeaux mixture, cresol, DDT, etc.

16

WASTE GENERATION AND MANAGEMENT

Ever since human society has been evolving with significant population growth, an ever-increasing demand for primary needs such as food, shelter and clothing has been observed, along with rapidly growing industrialisation and urbanisation. Consequently, the amount of waste being generated is also increasing.

Wastes and their Sources

The useless, leftover or discarded substances are called **waste substances**. There are five major categories of waste, i.e. domestic waste, industrial waste, agricultural waste, municipal waste and electronic waste. These are explained in the detail below

Domestic Wastes

The wastes generated from daily household activities in our surroundings are classified as domestic wastes. An average home produces the following types of waste

- **Kitchen waste** includes waste from the kitchen, such as peels of vegetables and fruits, stale or rotten food items, etc.
- **Plastic waste** includes plastic used in packaging and wrapping objects, as well as discarded or broken plastic items like bottles, toys, etc.
- **Glass waste** includes broken glass utensils, mirrors, containers, window panes, etc.
- **Rags** include various waste pieces of cloth, torn towels, handkerchiefs, old bed sheets, blankets, etc.
- **Paper** includes daily newspapers and magazines.

Industrial Wastes

It typically includes toxic chemicals, metals, plastics, paints, oils, inorganic chlorinated solvents and ashes. Some industries that release significant amounts of toxic waste are as follows

- **Mining Operations** India alone has hundreds of mines extracting copper, silver, gold, zinc, iron, coal, etc. During processing, large quantities of waste are produced known as **mine tailings**. These can be used for making tiles, masonry, cement, etc., when mixed with other materials.
- **Cement Factories** Cement manufacturing generates solid, liquid and gaseous wastes. **Solid wastes** are used in construction or dumped in landfills. **Liquid wastes** including wash-offs, are treated to remove harmful substances before being released into rivers or ponds. **Gaseous wastes** like fly ash, which contain solid particles, are emitted into the environment.
- **Oil Refineries and Petrochemical Units** Release a mixture of hydrocarbons, including Volatile Organic Compounds (VOCs), sulfur dioxide (SO_2), soot and other chemical byproducts.
- **Construction Units** Produce wastes such as broken bricks, waste stones, pebbles, wood waste, concrete, plaster and metal.

Agricultural Wastes

It is a waste produced as a result of agricultural operations. Agricultural waste mainly includes

- **Animal waste** includes waste from fields, dairy farming and animal excreta.
- **Plant wastes** from harvesting, threshing, winnowing, etc. It includes organic matter like carbohydrates, fats, crop residues, etc.

- **Bagasse** is the plant residue left after extracting the sugarcane juice. These are used as fire wood or in paper industry.
- **Pesticides** and **fertilisers** collect into the soil and are washed off with the irrigation and rainwater, leading to water pollution.

Municipal Wastes

- It includes the household discharge of excreta (faecal matter from toilets) and kitchen washings and the discharge from public toilets, hospitals, hotels, restaurants, offices, etc.
- All this waste is carried away through sewers and is called the **sewage**. This sewage is separated into the degradable part and the non-degradable part. The septic tanks are used to breakdown the degradable part, while the non-degradable part is dumped or buried in safe places.
- Contaminants/Constituents of the sewage can be studied as follows

Organic Impurities	Human excreta, animal wastes, oil, fruits, vegetables, etc.
Inorganic Impurities	Nitrates, phosphates, metals, pesticides and fertilisers.
Microbes	Bacteria, fungi and viruses.

E-Waste

- It is a common, informal term for electronic waste. E-waste refers to discarded electronic devices and equipment, such as old computers, televisions, mobile phones, printers and batteries.
- These items contain hazardous materials like lead, mercury and cadmium, making improper disposal harmful to both the environment and human health.
- As technology advances, E-waste has become one of the fastest-growing waste streams worldwide. Recycling and proper disposal are essential to recover valuable materials and minimise pollution from toxic components.

Biodegradable and Non-biodegradable Wastes

Waste materials can be in the form of solid, liquid or gas. Based on their decomposition by environmental factors, they can be classified as

1. Biodegradable Wastes

These are waste materials that can be broken down in the soil by the action of soil microbes and other decomposers like fungi. Examples include fruit, vegetable peels, leaves, grasses, wood, clothes, papers, etc.

2. Non-biodegradable Wastes

- These are waste materials that cannot be decomposed in the soil. There is no natural process available for their decomposition, e.g. plastic bags, synthetic clothes, metal containers, radioactive and electronic wastes, etc.
- Some non-biodegradable wastes, however can be recycled, such as plastic goods, metals and glass. Recycling is the only non-polluting and feasible solution for controlling non-biodegradable wastes.

Methods of Safe Disposal of Wastes

There are various types of wastes, each requiring specific disposal methods. These methods include segregation, dumping, composting, drainage, effluent treatment, incineration, scrubbers, electrostatic precipitators, etc.

Segregation

- This refers to the separation of waste materials into different categories on the basis of reusable, biodegradable, and non-biodegradable wastes.
- The waste materials can also be segregated according to their features like
  - Sharp-edged wastes like blades and knives.
  - Inflammable wastes like batteries and spray cans.
  - Recyclable wastes like plastic and glass.
  - Infectious wastes like hospital wastes.

Dumping

The process of depositing the collected wastes in an area is called **dumping**. Several sites are designated as waste disposal sites, known as **landfills**.

Composting

- It is a method of solid waste disposal where organic waste matter is allowed to decompose by microbes and soil organisms. So, it can be used for fertilising the agricultural land.
- Following are the steps of composting
  - A pit of about 5 m long, approximately 1.5 m wide and 1.5 m deep is dugged in the soil.
  - The organic or biodegradable waste is piled up and layered in a loose manner for air passage.
  - The layer is fully wetted or moistened with a mixture of cow dung and mud.
  - After a few days, another layer of mixed refuse is added to accelerate decomposition.
  - Within 50-60 days, the compost or manure is ready for use in agricultural fields, gardens and other areas to promote plant growth.
  - Composting with the help of earthworms is called **vermicomposting**.

Incineration

- It is the disposal of waste materials by burning. The waste is subjected to controlled combustion, releasing incombustible residues along with gaseous emissions.
- The end products are ashes and clinkers. Ashes are dumped in low land areas, while clinkers are used as aggregate in low grade concrete.

Drainage

- It refers to the natural or artificial removal of excess water from an area to prevent waterlogging.
- The drainage system provides an open, adequate and readily accessible channel for the uninterrupted flow of surface water.

Effluent Treatment Before Discharge

- Industrial and municipal wastewater is treated in **Effluent Treatment Plants** (ETPs) before being released into water bodies.
- The sewage treatment process occurs in three stages
  - **Primary Treatment** Large debris is removed through sedimentation in tanks.
  - **Secondary Treatment** The wastewater is transferred to oxidation ponds, where microorganisms (such as bacteria and algae) breakdown organic matter, producing CO_2 and solid sludge, which can be used as **manure**.
  - **Tertiary Treatment** This stage removes dissolved chemicals, metals and pathogens before the treated wastewater is either discharged into natural bodies of water or used for irrigation.

Scrubbers

- These are the devices designed to remove gaseous and particulate air pollutants. In these systems, air is passed through either a dry or a wet packing material.
- They are also used to remove gases from the industrial exhausts, e.g. sulphur dioxide (SO_2).
- The exhaust is passed through a spray of lime or water. Water dissolves the gases, while lime reacts with SO_2 to form a precipitate of calcium sulphate and sulphide. It washes out undesirable gases from the exhaust.

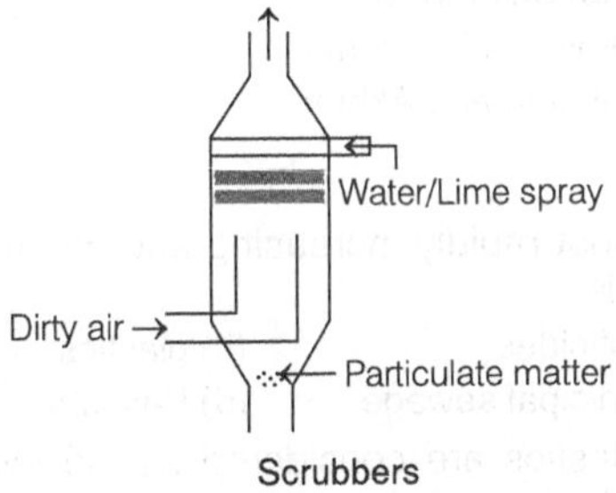

Scrubbers

Electrostatic Precipitators

- It is the most widely used method and can approximately remove 99% of particulate matter from exhaust of thermal power plant.
- It has electrode wires of high voltage maintained at several thousands volts, which produces a corona that releases electrons.
- These electrons get attached to the dust particles and give them negative charge. A collecting plate is there, which is grounded and positively charged and attracts the negatively charged dust particles.
- When the air passes through the collecting plate, it gets cleaned.

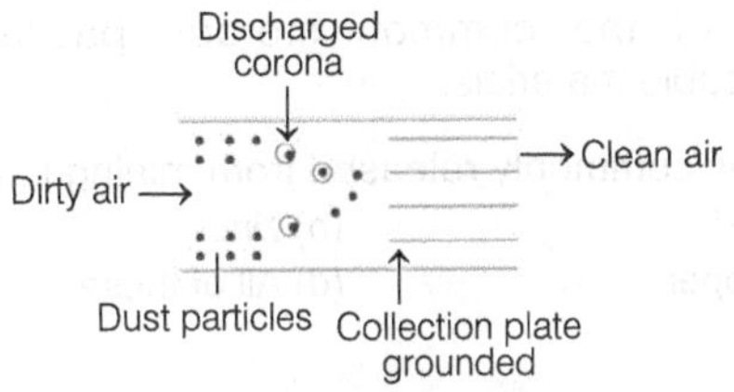

Electrostatic precipitator

EXAM ORIENTED QUESTIONS

TYPE - 1 01 Mark

Multiple Choice Questions

Q.1 Varun tried to match the categories of the waste with its examples. He tabulated the pairs below.

Categories of the Waste	Examples
P	Volatile organic compound.
Q	Residue like husks, seeds.

(a) *P*-Domestic waste, *Q*-Industrial waste
(b) *P*-Agricultural waste, *Q*-Municipal waste
(c) *P*-Industrial waste, *Q*-Agricultural waste
(d) *P*-Municipal waste, *Q*-Domestic waste

Ans. (c)

Q.2 A biology teacher asked her students to give two examples of industrial waste.

Karishma said: Sulphur dioxide and soot
Manvi said: Broken brick and pebbles
Tarun said: Window panes and utensils
Akhtar said: Television and old computers

Who were correct?
(a) Akhtar and Tarun
(b) Tarun and Manvi
(c) Manvi and Karishma
(d) Karishma and Akhtar

Ans. (c)

Q.3 The most rapidly increasing and much harmful waste today is
(a) pesticides (b) plastics
(c) municipal sewage (d) E-waste

Ans. (b) Plastics are considered as the most rapidly and much harmful waste of today because it is used in most of the common storage packaging and disposable materials.

Q.4 Wastes commonly released from mining industry are
(a) coal (b) zinc
(c) copper (d) All of these

Ans. (d)

Q.5 During the effluent treatment, ...*P*.... is removed through sedimentation and ....Q.... are removed through tertiary treatment.
(a) *P*-organic matter, *Q* - large debris
(b) *P*-dissolved chemical, *Q*-solid sludge
(c) *P*-pathogens, *Q* - dissolved chemicals
(d) *P*-large debris, *Q* -metals

Ans. (d)

Q.6 What is reduced when untreated sewage is released into rivers?
(a) The amount of nitrate
(b) The concentration of carbon dioxide
(c) The concentration of oxygen
(d) The number of bacteria

Ans. (c) When untreated sewage is released into rivers, organic matter decompses through microbial activity, consuming dissolved oxygen in the water. This leads to oxygen depletion, which can harm aquatic life.

Q.7 Why does the oxygen concentration in the water decrease when sewage is discharged into a river?
(a) Decrease in the number of plants
(b) Increase in the number of fish
(c) Less oxygen absorbed from the air
(d) Rapid growth of bacteria

Ans. (d) Sewage when discharged into a river, is decomposed by aerobic bacteria into nitrate. These bacteria will use up oxygen in the river and will flow rapidly.

Q.8 Which microbes are used in the treatment of sewage?
(a) Aerobic bacteria and anaerobic bacteria only
(b) Aerobic bacteria, anaerobic bacteria and fungi
(c) Anaerobic bacteria and viruses
(d) Anaerobic bacteria, fungi and viruses

Ans. (a) Only aerobic bacteria and anaerobic bacteria are used in the treatment of sewage.

Q.9 Air scrubbers are used to remove
(a) liquid
(b) particulate matter
(c) solid wastes
(d) Both (b) and (c)

Ans. (b)

Q.10 During the practical exam, the teacher showed a spot and instructed the students to observe it. Identify it, and specify the type of pollutant it cleans.

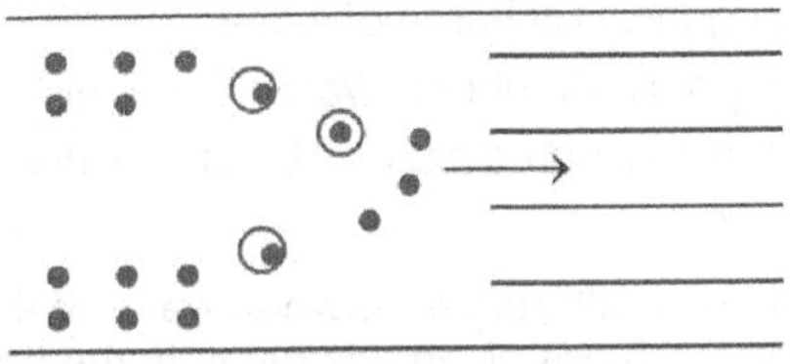

(a) Electrostatic precipitator and gaseous pollutants
(b) Scrubber and airborne dust
(c) Electrostatic precipitator and water droplets
(d) Air filtre and chemical fumes

Ans. (a)

TYPE - 2 — 01 Mark

Matching Type Question

Q.1 Match the following columns.

Column I	Column II
A. Magazines and newspaper	I. Paper and pulp industry
B. Wood chips	II. Inorganic chlorinated solvents
C. Industrial waste	III. Toxin released from e-waste
D. Cadmium	IV. Vegetable peels
	V. Paper waste

Ans. A-V, B-I, C-II, D-III

TYPE - 3 — 01 Mark

Assertion-Reason Type Questions

Direction (Q. Nos. 1-3) In the following questions statements are given as Assertion (A) and Reason (R).

(a) A is true, but R is false.
(b) A is false, but R is true.
(c) Both A and R are true.
(d) Both A and R are false.

Q.1 Assertion (A) Kitchen waste including vegetable peels and leftovers, is a common form of domestic waste.

Reason (R) Kitchen waste is biodegradable and can be composted to create natural fertilisers.

Ans. (c)

Q.2 Assertion (A) E-waste includes discarded electronic devices such as mobile phones, televisions and computers.

Reason (R) E-waste does not contain any hazardous substances and is safe for disposal in landfills.

Ans. (a) A is true, but R is false. R can be corrected as E-waste contains hazardous substances such as lead, mercury and cadmium and is not safe for disposal in landfills.

Q.3 Assertion (A) Scrubbers are used to remove solid waste and liquids from industrial emissions.

Reason (R) Scrubbers work by passing polluted air through a chamber where pollutants are absorbed or removed by a wet or dry packing material.

Ans. (b) A is false, but R is true. A can be corrected as Scrubbers are used to remove particulate matter and gaseous pollutants from industrial emissions.

TYPE - 4 — 01 Mark

Very Short Answer Type Questions

Q.1 What are mine tailings?

Ans. Waste materials left after extracting minerals in mining operations.

Q.2 Give an example of agricultural waste.

Ans. Bagasse, the residue from sugarcane after juice extraction.

Q.3 Why does the improper disposal of non-biodegradable waste pose a long-term environmental hazard?

Ans. Non-biodegradable waste accumulates in the environment, leads to soil, water and air pollution over time.

Q.4 Why is controlled combustion important in the process of incineration?

Ans. Controlled combustion ensures that harmful emissions are minimised and the waste is thoroughly destroyed.

Q.5 What are the main stages involved in effluent treatment?

Ans. The three stages involved in effluent treatment are **primary treatment** (physical removal of debris), **secondary treatment** (biological degradation of organic matter) and **tertiary treatment** (chemical and advanced purification).

Q.6 Name the following. **(1 Mark each)**

(i) Any substance that is discarded after primary use or is useless.
(ii) Waste that is generated as pieces of torn towels, old bed sheets, etc.

(iii) Wastes that are typically constituted by toxic chemicals and are the most threatening.
(iv) Waste generated from agricultural activities.
(v) Solid and liquid wastes produced due to activities in homes, offices, or any other public places.
(vi) Wastes which can be decomposed *via* microbial activity.
(vii) The wastewater from different sources which runs off into the drains.

Ans. (i) Waste
(ii) Rags
(iii) Industrial waste
(iv) Crop residue/Plant remains/Agricultural waste
(v) Municipal waste
(vi) Biodegradable waste
(vii) Sewage

Q.7 Choose the odd one out from the following terms given below and name the category to which other three belong. **(1 Mark each)**
(i) Stale bread, Rotten apple, Tissue paper, Vegetable peel
(ii) Soot, Bricks, Waste stones, Concrete
(iii) Organic acids, Styrofoam, Coal, Soot
(iv) Old refrigerators, DVD, Lead-acid batteries, Gold
(v) Segregation, Primary treatment, Dumping, Composting

Ans. (i) The odd term is tissue paper because it is a type of paper waste, while the stale bread, rotten apple and vegetable peel are categorised under kitchen waste.
(ii) The odd term is soot because it is a particulate pollutant, while the bricks, waste stones and concrete are wastes obtained from construction units.
(iii) The odd term is coal because it is a natural resource used as a fuel, while the organic acids, styrofoam and soot are wastes generated from oil refineries and petrochemical units.
(iv) The odd term is gold because it is a valuable metal, while the old refrigerators, DVD players and lead-acid batteries are categorised under E-waste.
(v) The odd term is primary treatment because it is a step in the wastewater treatment process, while the segregation, dumping and composting are methods of solid waste disposal.

Q.8 Arrange and rewrite the terms in each group in the correct order so as to be in a logical sequence beginning with the term that is underlined. **(1 Mark each)**
(i) Removal of pathogens, <u>Large debris</u>, Oxidation ponds, Discharge of water
(ii) Scrubber, <u>Polluted air</u>, Clean air, Water
(iii) Electrical charge, Particles, Plates, <u>Electrostatic precipitator</u>

Ans. (i) Large debris, Oxidation ponds, Removal of pathogens, Discharge of water
(ii) Polluted air, Scrubber, Water, Clean air
(iii) Electrostatic precipitator, Electrical charge, Plates, Particles

Q.9 Mention one difference between each of the following pairs on the basis of what is given in the brackets. **(1 Mark each)**
(i) Composting and Dumping (definition)
(ii) Segregation and Incineration (definition)

Ans. (i)

Composting	Dumping
It is a method of waste disposal where organic matter is allowed to decay.	It is the process of depositing the collected wastes in an area.

(ii)

Segregation	Incineration
It is the separation of waste materials into biodegradable and non-biodegradable wastes.	It is the disposal of waste materials by burning.

Q.10 Read the information below the diagram and fill in the blank spaces.

The E-waste problem posses a significant challenge to modern society due to the rapid pace of technological advancements, leading to the disposal of large amounts of obsolete electronics. Improper handling and disposal of E-waste can lead to release of hazardous materials causing serious health risks and environmental damage.
E-waste is a common, informal term for .....(i)..... waste. It refers to discarded equipment, such as old computers, televisions, mobile phones, printers and batteries. These items contain hazardous materials like .....(ii)..... , ...(iii)....., and .....(iv)....., making

improper disposal harmful to both the environment and human health. Therefore, ...(v)..... and proper disposal are essential to recover valuable materials and minimise pollution from toxic components.

(1 Mark each)

Ans. (i) electronic (ii) lead
(iii) mercury (iv) cadmium
(v) recycling

TYPE - 5 — 02 Marks

Short Answer Type Questions

Q.1 State the major action that can be taken in regard of the effective garbage management in and around your locality.

Ans.

Objectives	Suggested Major Actions
Prevention of plastic wastage	By avoiding the use of polythene bags for carrying lunch boxes.
Recycling and reuse	Reuse of old clothes as dusters for cleaning black boards.

Q.2 What are the two major categories of waste seen in everyday life?

Ans. Two major categories of waste seen in everyday life are

(i) Domestic waste

(ii) Industrial waste

Q.3 Answer the following questions briefly.

(i) Open landfill sites are potential centres to harm the environment. How?

(ii) State the purpose behind the study of waste management.

Ans. (i) Open landfill sites are potential centres to harm environment as leaching of chemicals and toxins may contaminate the environment.

(ii) To reduce the generation of waste by living beings.

Q.4 Briefly explain the following terms.

(i) E-waste (ii) Vermicompost

Ans. (i) **E-waste** refers to discarded electronic devices such as computers, smartphones, televisions and other electrical equipment, e.g. contains harmful metals such as lead, mercury, etc.

(ii) **Vermicompost** is organic compost produced by earthworms when they breakdown organic waste materials, e.g. earthworm converts organic material into nutrient-rich humus that can be used to improve soil fertility.

Q.5 List any two disadvantages of incineration.

Ans. Following are the disadvantages of incineration

(i) The incinerators are the expensive process.

(ii) It produces many harmful gases that may pollute an environment.

TYPE - 6 — 03 Marks

Short Answer Type Questions

Q.1 It is considered necessary to separate the constituents of municipal sewage before treatment and disposal. Give a reason.

Ans. It is necessary to separate the constituents of municipal sewage before treatment and disposal to ensure the effective removal of harmful pollutants.

Different components of sewage, such as solid waste, organic matter and dissolved chemicals, require different treatment methods by separating these constituents. The treatment process becomes more efficient, as each type of waste can be treated appropriately.

For example, solid waste can be removed through sedimentation, while dissolved chemicals may require advanced filtration or chemical treatment. Proper separation helps to reduce the burden on treatment plants, improves water quality and prevents environmental contamination.

Q.2 Briefly explain the treatment of liquid wastes.

Ans. Treatment of liquid wastes is carried out in three stages which are as follows

Primary Treatment This stage involves the removal of large objects and sedimentation of finer particles, which is achieved through physical processes like screening, grit removal and flocculation. This helps in the removal of suspended solids.

Secondary Treatment Here, biological processes using aerobic bacteria breakdown organic matter in the wastewater. **Aeration** helps in promoting the growth of these bacteria. **Chlorination** is used to disinfect the water and kill harmful pathogens.

Tertiary Treatment This advanced stage targets the removal of specific pollutants such as nitrogen compounds, phosphorus and other dissolved substances.

Q.3 How does an electrostatic precipitator work to remove particulate pollutants released from the thermal power plants?

Ans. Electrostatic precipitator removes the particulate matter with 99% efficiency. It has electrode wires maintained at high voltage, which produce a corona that releases electrons.

These electrons get attached to the dust particles and give them a negative charge. A positively charged collecting plate is also there, which attracts the negatively charged dust particles.

Thus, separating them from the air and collecting them on itself. Afterwards, the air passes through the collecting plate and gets cleaned.

TYPE - 7 03 Marks

Structured Based Questions

Q.1 Study the diagram given below and answer the questions that follows.

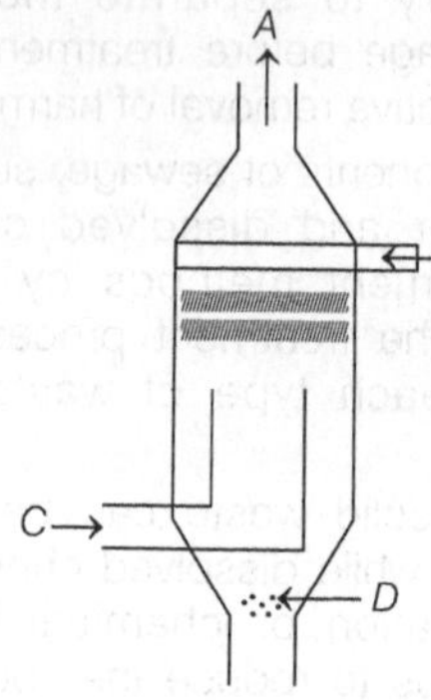

(i) Identify the above device.

(ii) Identify the parts labelled as *A*, *B*, *C* and *D*.

(iii) How many types of such devices ae available in the market?

Ans. (i) The above device is scrubber.

(ii) The part labelled as *A*, *B*, *C* and *D* are

A-Clean air

B-Water/Lime spray

C-Dirty air

D-Particulate matter

(iii) Scrubbers are of two types

(a) Wet scrubber

(b) dry scrubber

Q.2 Study the diagram and answer the questions that follows

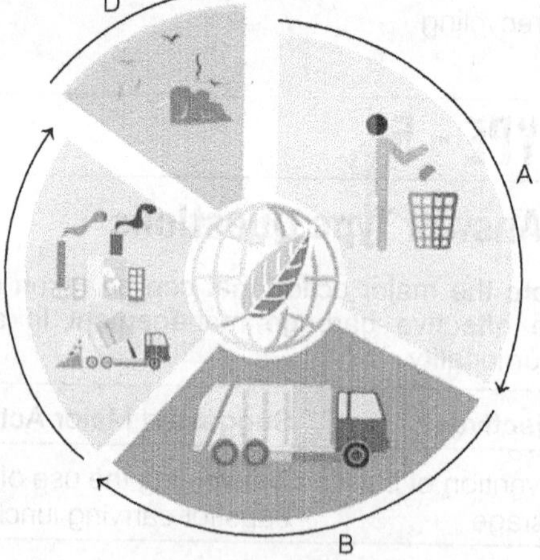

(i) Identify the steps marked as *A-D*.

(ii) What does the process of depositing the collected waste in an area?

(iii) How are waste materials can be segregated.

Ans. (i) *A*-Waste

B-Waste collection

C-Waste process

D-Clean land filling

(ii) Dumping

(iii) The waste materials can also be segregated according to their features like

(a) Sharp-edged wastes like blades and knives.

(b) Inflammable wastes like batteries and spray cans

SAMPLE QUESTION PAPER (BIOLOGY)

General Instructions

Maximum Marks : 80

Time allowed : Two hours

Answers to this paper must be written on the paper provided separately.

You will **not** be allowed to write during the first **15** minutes.

This time is to be spent in reading the question paper.

The time given at the head of this paper is the time allowed for writing the answers.

Attempt **all five** questions.

The intended marks for questions or parts of questions are given brackets ().

You are advised to spend not more than 30 minutes in answering **Question 1** and 20 minutes in answering **Question 2**.

Question 1

Choose the correct answer to the questions from the given options.

(i) In *Vallisneria*, pollination takes place by the agency of

(a) water
(b) wind
(c) birds
(d) insects

(ii) A well defined nucleus is absent in

(a) plant cell
(b) animal cell
(c) prokaryotic cell
(d) eukaryotic cell

(iii) **Assertion** (A) The permanent tissue loses the ability to divide.

Reason (R) The permanent tissues may be dead or living and have a definite shape, size and thickness.

(a) A is true but R is false
(b) A is false but R is true
(c) Both A and R are true
(d) Both A and R are false

(iv) Male flowers that have only ......*P*...... are called staminate flowers and female flowers that have only ......*Q*...... are called pistillate flowers.

(a) *P*-stamen, *Q*-pistill
(b) *P*-pistill, *Q*-stamen
(c) *P*-staminate, *Q*-neuter
(d) *P*-neuter, *Q*-perianth

(v) When the male organs (anther) mature first, followed by the female reproductive organs (stigmas) is called

(a) protogyny
(b) protandry
(c) self-sterility
(d) herkogamy

(vi) In hypogeal germination which out of these is not likely to take place?

(a) Hypocotyl elongates at a faster rate
(b) Cotyledons remains under the ground.
(c) Cotyledons plays a role in photosynthesis
(d) Usually found in dicot seeds

(vii) **Assertion** (A) Liver is the largest gland in the human body.

Reason (R) Liver secretes bile in the duodenum to breakdown fat molecules into small globules.

(a) A is true but R is false
(b) A is false but R is true
(c) Both A and R are true
(d) Both A and R are false

(viii) Arjun learnt about the functions of various glands and their location in the human body and tabulated the pairs in the following manner.

Glands	Location
P	In the walls of stomach.
Q	Upper side of the abdomen.

(a) *P*- Salivary gland *Q*- Parotid gland
(b) *P*- Gastric gland *Q*- Liver
(c) *P*- Sublingual gland *Q*- Sub-maxillary gland
(d) *P*- Parotid gland *Q*- Liver

(ix) The joint between the ribs and sternum is a type of

(a) cartilaginous joint
(b) gliding joint
(c) pivot joint
(d) ball and socket joint

(x) Ropes, mats and certain textiles are made from plant fibres. These fibres are the

(a) parenchyma cells
(b) collenchyma cells
(c) sclerenchyma cells
(d) aerenchyma cells

(xi) **Assertion** (A) *Euglena* is an example of a prokaryotic cell.

Reason (R) Prokaryotes have a well-defined nucleus.

(a) A is true but R is false
(b) A is false but R is true
(c) Both A and R are true
(d) Both A and R are false

(xii) Radha experiences painful breathing. This condition is referred to as

(a) eupnea
(b) dyspnea
(c) apnea
(d) claustrophobia

(xiii) **Assertion** (A) The immunity provided to an individual from an outside source in the form of readymade antibodies is called passive acquired immunity.

Reason (R) The antibodies provided in the case of snake bite and rabies are the examples of passive acquired immunity.

(a) A is true but R is false
(b) A is false but R is true
(c) Both A and R are true
(d) Both A and R are false

(xiv) A teacher in the class told the students to tell the function of skin.

Rahul said : It acts as a barrier.

Anu said : It protect the fingertips surrounding soft tissues from injuries.

Radha said : It contains sensory receptors.

Neelam said : It produces vitamin-D when exposed to sunlight.

Who were correct?

(a) Rahul and Anu
(b) Anu and Radha
(c) Rahul, Radha and Neelam
(d) Anu and Neelam

(xv) During an experiment related to respiration, the germinating seeds were put by the students in the thermoflask *A* and *B* and then put the thermometer in both flasks and plugged the mouth of both of them with the help of a cotton. After keeping the setup undisturbed for sometime, what will you conclude?

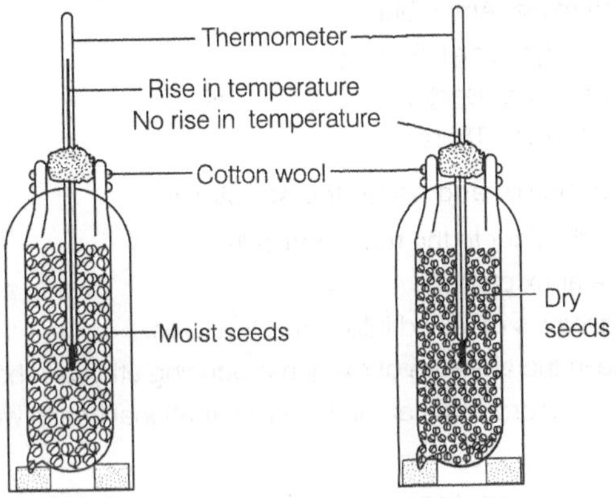

(a) The flask *A* will have rise in temperature
(b) The flask *B* will have a rise in temperature
(c) Both flasks *A* and *B* will have rise in temperature
(d) No change in temperature will be observed in both flasks *A* and *B*

Question 2

(i) Name the following.

(a) A chain of chemical reactions that enable all living organisms to synthesise energy.
(b) Common axis of the plant that bears flowers.
(c) The substances that are required for proper growth and maintenance of a living body.
(d) Movement of body parts that leads to the change of a place.
(e) The chemical substances that are produced inside the body in response to the entry of toxins to neutralise its effect.

(ii) **Given below is the structure of a villus of a small intestine. Read the information below the diagram and fill in the blanks**

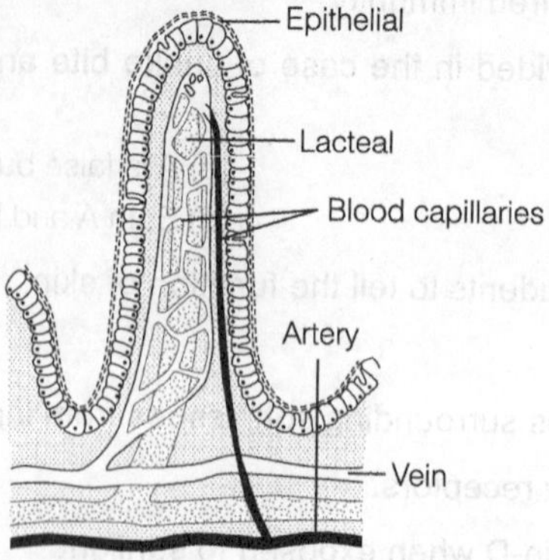

Small intestine is the site of complete (a) .... of food into different (b) .... The (c) .... lining of the small intestine has numerous finger like projections called (d) ...., which (e) .... the surface area for absorption.

(iii) **Arrange and rewrite the terms in each group in the correct order so as to be in a logical sequence beginning with the term that is underlined.**

(a) Duodenum, Colon, Caecum, Jejunum, Ileum

(b) Reptilia , Aves, Pisces, Mammalia, Amphibia

(c) Radicle, Cotyledon, Plumule, Hypocotyl, Epicotyl

(d) Active immunity, Antigen, Antibody, Bacteria, Lymphocytes

(e) Lumbar, Cervical, Coccyx, Sacrum, Thoracic

(iv) **Read the explanations given below and name the structures.**

(a) The pigment that imparts red colour to the red blood cells.

(b) Tissue that is present at the apex of roots.

(c) A specialised shoot having leaves modified into floral structures.

(d) Partial oxidation of glucose in the absence of oxygen producing ethyl alcohol or lactic acid.

(e) Organisation that directs and coordinates authority on international health work and promote technical cooperation.

(v) **Given below is a structure of a alimentary canal. Match the structures marked as (*A*- *E*) with their correct functions.**

Endocrine glands		**Functions**
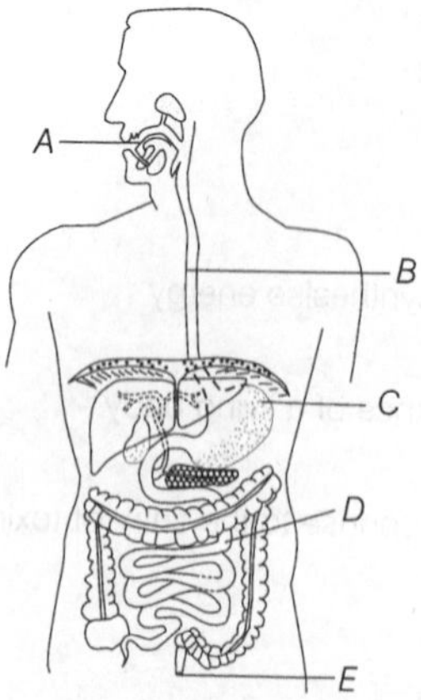	1.	**A storehouse where partial digestion takes place**
	2.	**Site of egestion**
	3.	**Part from where the food enters into the alimentary canal**
	4.	**Complete digestion occurs in this region**
	5.	**Transport food from mouth to stomach**

Question 3

(i) Explain the term nitrogen fixation.

(ii) Name the type of immunity that is provided by the mother to the foetus.

(iii) What happens to the following muscles during inhalation or inspiration?

(a) Diaphragm (b) External intercostal muscles.

(iv) Write the overall chemical reaction for respiration.

(v) Teacher has placed an experimental setup during the biology practical class for the students. Observe it carefully and answer the following questions.

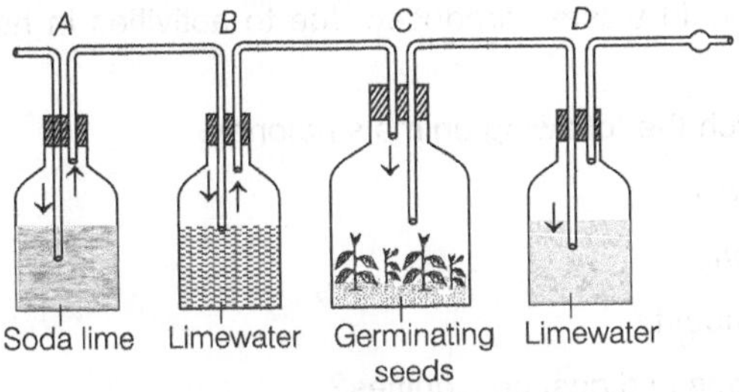

(a) Name the physiological process being studied.

(b) What is the purpose of using soda lime in the bottle *A* and why is limewater placed in bottle *B* ?

(c) Would there be any change taking place in bottle *D* ?

Question 4

(i) Why the walls of trachea and bronchi is supported by the C- shaped cartilaginous rings?

(ii) Expand the term BOD. What happens to the effluent after secondary treatment?

(iii) Mention the significance of the following

(a) Scrubbers (b) Electrostatic precipitators

(iv) State any two characteristic features of human skin.

(v) Draw a neat labelled diagram of mitochondria.

Question 5

(i) Mention what is incineration in solid waste disposal. Why it is carried out ?

(ii) What is pollination? Give its types with one example of each.

(iii) How is locomotion different from movement?

(iv) Write any two functions of androecium.

(v) Observe the diagram given below and answer the questions that follows.

(a) Identify the organism.

(b) State the mode of nutrition followed by the organism.

(c) State one point that makes it different from kingdom–Plantae.

Question 6

(i) State the term vaccination.

(ii) What are vector borne diseases? Give examples.

(iii) Differentiate between antiseptics and disinfectants.

(iv) Maize grain is a one seeded fruit. Comment.

(v) Draw a neat labelled diagram of flower.

Question 7

(i) What does the solid and liquid wastes produced due to activities in home, offices or any other public places is known as ?

(ii) Mention the phylum to which the following animals belongs.

(a) True crab, spider and *Julius*

(b) *Pila*, *Octopus* and *Chiton*

(iii) Give any two uses of a compost.

(iv) What does the following steps in digestion signifies?

(a) Assimilation

(b) Egestion

(v) The diagram shows human respiratory system front view.

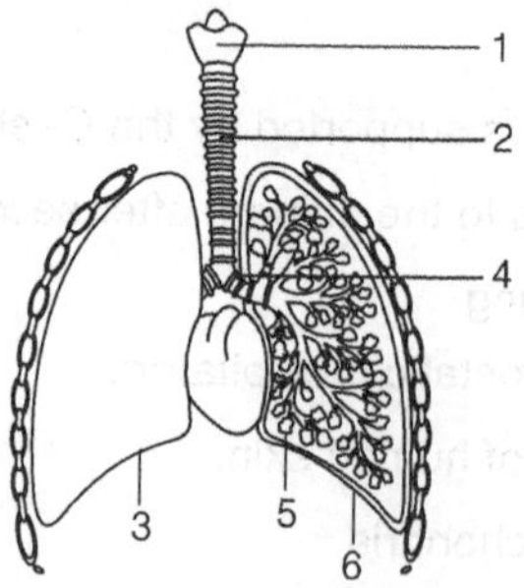

(a) Label the parts numbered 1 to 6.

(b) Why do lungs contract during exhalation?

(c) How many times a man breathes per minute at rest?

Question 8

(i) How is immunity classified?

(ii) Given below are the two statements that are incorrect. Rewrite the correct statement.

(a) Kwashiorkor is a form of malnutrition that is caused by the lack of carbohydrates in the diet.

(b) Vitamins are the building blocks of the body.

(iii) What are the exact location of the following?

(a) Sebaceous glands

(b) Hair follicle

(iv) Name the steps involved in the cycling of nitrogen in air.

(v) Draw a neat labelled diagram of nitrogen cycle.

Answers

1. (i) (a) (ii) (c) (iii) (c) (iv) (a) (v) (b)
(vi) (c) (vii) (c) (viii) (b) (ix) (a) (x) (c)
(xi) (d) (xii) (b) (xiii) (c) (xiv) (c) (xv) (a)

2. (i) (a) Respiration (b) Peduncle
(c) Nutrients (d) Locomotion
(e) Antibodies

(ii) (a) digestion
(b) components
(c) inner
(d) villi
(e) increases

(iii) (a) Duodenum, Jejunum, Ileum, Caecum, Colon
(b) Pisces, Amphibia, Reptilia, Aves, Mammalia
(c) Radicle, Hypocotyl, Cotyledon, Epicotyl, Plumule
(d) Bacteria, Antigen, Lymphocytes, Antibody, Active immunity
(e) Cervical, Thoracic, Lumbar, Sacrum, Coccyx

(iv) (a) Haemoglobin
(b) Apical meristem
(c) Flower
(d) Fermentation
(e) WHO or World Health Organisation

(v) A- 3, B- 5, C- 1, D- 4, E- 2

3. (i) Nitrogen fixation is the process in which free atmospheric nitrogen is converted into more soluble form like nitrates.

(ii) Naturally acquired passive immunity

(iii) During inspiration following changes takes place

(a) **Diaphragm** It is lowered by the contraction of its muscle fibres and becomes flat. This causes an increase in the volume of the thoracic chamber.

(b) **External intercostal muscles** They occur between the ribs. The external intercostal muscles contract and pull the ribs and the sternum upward and outward, thus increasing the volume of the thoracic chamber.

(iv) The overall reaction for respiration is

$$C_6H_{12}O_6 + 6O_2 \rightarrow 6CO_2 + 6H_2O + ATP$$

(v) (a) The physiological process being studied is aerobic respiration.

(b) Soda lime in bottle A is used to remove the carbon dioxide from the incoming air.
Limewater is placed in bottle B to ensure that all the CO_2 present in the air has been absorbed/air entering the bottle C is free from CO_2.

(c) Limewater turns milky.

4. (i) The walls of trachea and bronchi is supported by the C- shaped cartilaginous rings in order to keep the trachea and bronchi distended and prevent their collapsing when pressure inside them falls during inspiration.

(ii) BOD referred as Biochemical Oxygen Demand. The effluent from the secondary treatment plant is generally released into the natural water bodies such as streams and rivers.

(iii) (a) **Scrubbers** These are a simple and effective devices that are used to remove the particulates and effluents from the polluted air.

(b) **Electrostatic precipitators** These are most widely used method that removes approximately 99% of the particulate matter from the exhaust of the thermal power plant.

(iv) Two major characteristics of human skin are

(a) Skin is composed of epidermis and dermis both layers are separated by a thin basement membranes.

(b) The epidermis consists of flattened cells having keratin. This layer is called stratum corneum.

(v)

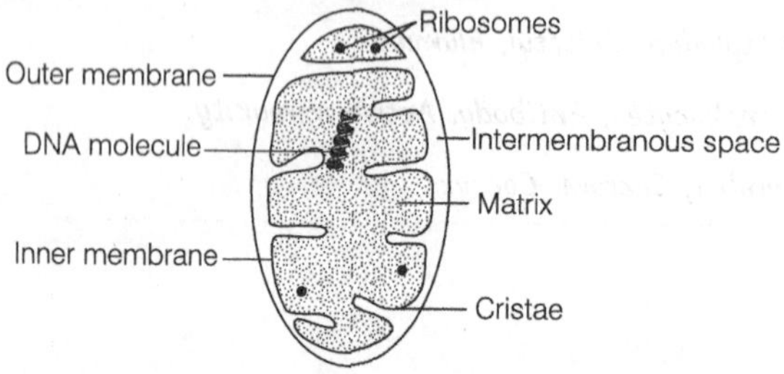

Internal structure of mitochondria

5. (i) **Incineration** is the disposal of waste materials by burning. It is carried out to reduce the volume of waste materials, to reduce the requirement of landfill sites and to allow the hygienic disposal of wastes.

(ii) **Pollination** is the method of transfer of pollen grains from anther to the stigma of either same or different flowers. It is of two main types

(a) **Self-pollination** It is also of two types, i.e autogamy (e.g. wheat) and geitonogamy (e.g. Cucurbita).

(b) **Cross-pollination** e.g. papaya.

(iii) **Locomotion** is the movement of body from one place to another. On the other hand, **movement** is the change in position or posture of any body part.

(iv) Important functions of androecium are

(a) The anthers produces pollen grains containing male gametes.

(b) The filaments attached to the anthers helps in making it more accessible for pollination.

(v) (a) The given organism is Agaricus.

(b) The organism follows heterotrophic mode of nutrition.

(c) The organism lacks chlorophyll. This makes it different from kingdom-Plantae.

6. (i) Vaccination is the practice of injecting dead or weakened pathogens into the living body in order to develop resistance (immunity) against a particular disease without infection.

(ii) Vector is known as any agent that acts as an intermediate carrier of a pathogen. The diseases caused by such vectors are called vector borne diseases. For example, dengue and amoebic dysentery.

(iii) **Antiseptics** are the chemical substances that are used to kill germs. these are applied to the living tissue/ skin to reduce the possibility of infection or putrefaction. While **disinfectants** are the strong chemical substances applied to non-living objects to destroy microorganisms living on them.

(iv) Fruit is a ripened ovary wherein the ovary wall develops to form a fruit wall. Maize grains is referred to as one seeded fruit because it has only one cotyledon or a seed leaf which stores food for the embryo.

(v)

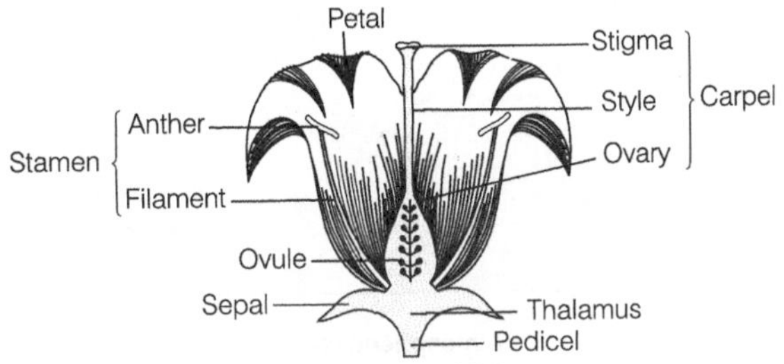

Structure of flower

7. (i) Biodegradable waste.

(ii) (a) Phylum- Arthrpoda

(b) Phylum- Mollusca

(iii) Compost are used in the following

(a) In nurseries, landscape sites, greenhouses, etc.

(b) By the farmers and gardeners.

(iv) (a) **Assimilation** It is the distribution of digested food products to various cells of the body. The villi of the small intestine which is richly supplied with the blood vessels takes the absorbed food to each and every cells of the body where it is utilised for obtaining energy, building up new tissues and repairing the older ones.

(b) **Egestion** It is the assimilation of undigested food formed in the colon of the large intestine through the anus. Peristalsis gradually pushes the undigested food from small intestine to the large intestine.

(v) (a) The parts numbered 1 to 6 are labelled as

1. Larynx 2. Trachea

3. Right lung 4. Bronchus

5. Alveoli 6. Left lung

(b) During exhalation the diaphragm relaxes, and the volume of thoracic cavity decreases and the pressure within it increases. As a result, lungs contract and air is forced out.

(c) 12 -14 times per minute at rest.

8. (i) Immunity is classifies into two main types as

(a) **Innate immunity** It is present since birth.

(b) **Acquired immunity** It is acquired by an individual during lifetime.

(ii) (a) Kwashiorkor is a form of malnutrition that is caused by the lack of proteins in the diet.

(b) Proteins are the building blocks of the body.

(iii) (a) Throughout the skin.

(b) Within the dermis enclosing the hair root.

(iv) The steps are

(a) Nitrogen-fixation

(b) Ammonification

(c) Nitrificatio

(d) Denitrification

(v)

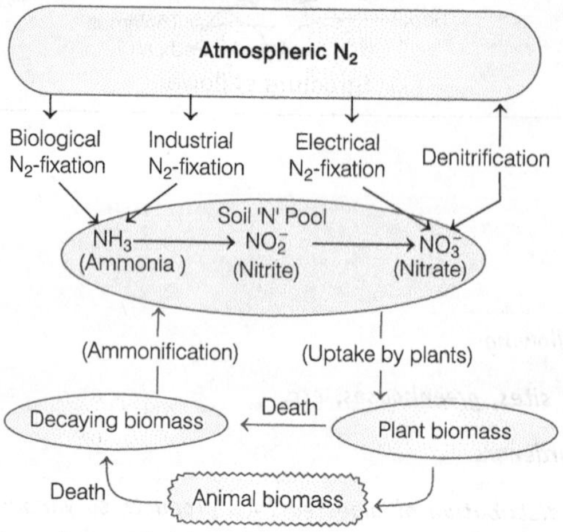

The nitrogen cycle showing relationship between the three main nitrogen polls, i.e. atmospheric, soil and biomass